Inside Ami Pro™ 2.0
Professional Tips and Techniques

Maria A. Hoath

Windcrest®/McGraw-Hill

FIRST EDITION
FIRST PRINTING

© 1992 by **Maria A. Hoath**.
Published by Windcrest Books, an imprint of TAB Books.
TAB Books is a division of McGraw-Hill, Inc.
The name "Windcrest" is a registered trademark of TAB Books.

Library of Congress Cataloging-in-Publication Data

Hoath, Maria A.
   Inside Ami Pro 2.0 : professional tips & techniques / by Maria A.
  Hoath.
    p. cm.
   Includes index.
   ISBN 0-8306-3606-4 (p)
   1. Desktop publishing—Computer programs. 2. Ami professional
(Computer program) I. Title.
Z286.D47H634 1991
686.2'2544536—dc20   91-36701
                                            CIP

TAB Books offers software for sale. For information and a catalog, please contact
TAB Software Department, Blue Ridge Summit, PA 17294-0850.

Acquisitions Editor: Brad Schepp
Book Editor: Melanie D. Brewer
Series Design: Jaclyn J. Boone
Cover: Sandra Blair Design and Brent Blair Photography, Harrisburg, PA   WT1

Dedicated to David Franklin Peagler.

Contents

PART 2. Using Ami Pro

Chapter 3.   Managing files   37

Chapter 4.   Creating and editing text   55

Chapter 5.   Style sheets   109

PART 4. Special topics

Chapter 20. Printing Tips 431

Chapter 21. Speed tips 443

Chapter 22. Safety tips 457

Acknowledgments

No project of this magnitude is a solitary effort. Many people contributed their time and care to this book to make it as detailed, thorough, and complete as possible. I would like to thank the following people for their help in creating and publishing this book: Matt Wagner of Waterside Productions; Brad Schepp of TAB Books; the entire Lotus Development Corporation Word Processing staff, including Doug Benson for his assistance and for never tiring of hearing my messages on his voice mail; John Briggs for his assistance in promoting Inside Ami Pro; Cheryl Ladd for sending me all the necessary information "yesterday"; Charlie Pappas for his help on macros; Robert Pernett for his help on DDE and OLE; Bill Jones; and the Ami Pro Technical Support staff for answering my questions, however complicated and "out there" they may have been, including Toby Banks, Todd Fuder, Ildiko Nagy, and Michael Wentz. I would also like to acknowledge the people at Alexander Communications for their help in locating contacts and in promoting this book.

Last, but never least, I owe my sanity and my success to David, who encourages me through all of my projects.

Introduction

The first time I saw Ami Pro was in the spring of 1990, when I was writing a series of articles on desktop publishing tips and tricks for *Computer Currents* magazine in Atlanta. The publisher of the magazine was particularly interested in my review of Ami Pro because SAMNA was located in Atlanta, and the product had won so many awards in the past year. After testing the product and writing my review, I had to admit that I never expected to like the product as much as I did. It was intelligently designed and contained features that made so much sense you wondered why the giants, like Word and WordPerfect, didn't have them. My two personal favorites are the ability to save a style sheet with its contents and to search for and replace styles. After writing that review, I became an avid Ami Pro user after years of being one of the biggest WordPerfect experts around.

I managed a department of technical writers that produced courseware materials around 100 to 200 pages long. We used WordPerfect and Ventura and were pleased with the results, but the writers were continually frustrated by the complicated process of writing and laying out documents. At the time, no better way existed to achieve those results. Since the introduction of Ami Pro, however, thousands of people discovered that creating professional-looking documents doesn't have to leave you frazzled and frustrated.

In December of 1990, Lotus Development Corporation acquired SAMNA, and started to work on the newest version of Ami Pro-2.0. When I first looked at 2.0, I couldn't believe what I saw: this inventive little word processor was beefing up its features to go head to head with the big guys. Ami Pro contained an improved SmartIcons Palette, power fields, master documents, outlining, an equation editor, revision marking, document compare, and Adobe Type Manager fonts. I used Ami Pro to write this book and was amazed by the new features I continually found. I now have personal favorites, without which I cannot fathom creating a document: Outline mode and the Icon Palette.

The whole idea behind Ami Pro is to give users all the powerful features contained in other word processors, but to make them easier to use and more accessible. This book explains those powerful features in detail, letting you get the most out of Ami Pro for your documents. Whether you create letters, memos, legal documents, contracts, advertisements, invoices, newsletters, or books, this reference will show you how to create those documents more efficiently, more safely, and how to make them look like you took them to a print shop.

Throughout the book you will find tips and techniques for results you previously thought were not possible using Ami Pro. You will see many sample documents that you can use a basis for your own and advice on designing your documents. Most chapters contain a troubleshooting section including commonly asked questions and answers from Lotus' technical support staff. Previous experience with Ami Pro is not needed to use this book; however, you should be familiar with basic Windows operations, such as opening and closing files, naming files, directory maintenance, and cut and paste.

Part 1, "Introduction to Ami Pro," discusses the new features in Ami Pro 2.0 and how the program works.

Chapter 1, "What's new in version two," describes all the new and improved features you'll find in Ami Pro 2.0, including brand new functions, menu changes, and enhancements to old features. Chapter 1 also contains a table listing all the new features and in which chapter you'll find them in this book.

Chapter 2, "How does Ami Pro 2.0 work?" discusses how Ami Pro organizes its features into menus and an icon palette. The chapter covers each menu in Ami Pro's menu bar and the features you'll find in the menu, lists all the icons available to you to use on the icon palette, and discusses each facet of the Ami Pro 2.0 program, including word processing, page layout, importing and exporting files, formatting text, drawing, charting, and worksheet and forms generation.

Part 2, "Using Ami Pro," discusses how to use Ami Pro to piece together the elements of your documents, including text, style sheets, fonts, tables, equations, and power fields. Also included are explanations of tools such as spell check, grammar checkers, merging and sorting text, and using macros.

Chapter 3, "Managing files," explains how Ami Pro creates a document as an assortment of files: the document file, the style sheet file, and graphics files. This chapter also discusses file management strategies such as protecting original style sheets, copying, moving, and backing up files, and how to effectively store your Ami Pro documents.

Chapter 4, "Creating and editing text," covers Ami's three editing modes and five display views that let you display and edit varying elements in your document. You learn the six different methods for creating text in your document, how to move around in the document, how to add special characters, and how to add notes. The chapter explains how to format text using the Text menu and how to find and replace text, text attributes, and styles. You also learn how to use Revision Marking to identify changes to your document and how to edit your document using Outline mode.

Chapter 5, "Style sheets," defines what a style sheet is and how it controls a document. The chapter covers how to choose a style sheet, how to assign styles to paragraphs using either the mouse or the keyboard, how to create a new style, and how to delete an old style. You also learn about the two styles available in Ami Pro's style sheets: document styles and global styles.

Chapter 6, "Using fonts," covers font terminology, font types, and font sources. You learn how to install fonts, including the ATM fonts bundled with Ami Pro. The chapter also explains the three methods you can use to select fonts for your documents.

Chapter 7, "Formatting text and pages," explains how to modify paragraph styles and page layouts to design your own look for your documents. The chapter covers how to change your paragraph style attributes, including alignment, spacing, page and column breaks, special effects, lines, and hyphenation. The chapter also includes how to change your page layout attributes, including margins and columns, page size and orientation, and lines.

Chapter 8, "Tables," explains how to create a table, how to move around and select text in a table, and how to modify a table's layout. The chapter covers how to create text tables for resumes, side-by-side text, and forms. You also learn how to create numeric tables and formulas, and how to modify the numeric formatting the table style uses. You learn how to create forms and print them on regular paper or on preprinted forms.

Chapter 9, "Publishing details," covers those elements that tie a document together and give it an identity of a book, newsletter, or other document type. The chapter covers how to create headers, footers, and footnotes. You learn how to automatically number lines and paragraphs, how to anchor frames, how to automatically insert text before paragraphs, and how to number pages. The chapter also covers multidocument features such as combining multiple files into a master document, generating a table of contents and an index, and creating cross references.

Chapter 10, "Putting a document together," covers the three methods for laying out a document. The chapter also provides guidelines for designing press releases, advertisements, flyers, newsletters and magazines, brochures, letterhead, business cards, forms, and books and manuals.

Chapter 11, "Checking your spelling and grammar," discusses spell checking, editing the user dictionary, and using Grammatik within Ami Pro.

Chapter 12, "Merging and sorting text," covers creating a standard and a data document to use in merging files. You learn how to merge only selected records in a data document by using conditions, how to use merge power fields to control the merge process, and how to use an external application file for the data document. You also learn how to create labels using the merge process. Chapter 12 also covers sorting text in documents.

Chapter 13, "Using macros," explains how to create, play, and edit macros. You also learn about the more than 40 macros supplied with Ami Pro that provide features and functions not available without playing back the macro.

Chapter 14, "Creating equations," covers building an equation using the equation editor. The chapter lists the equation icons in the equation icon bar and how you use them to build an equation. You learn that you can use the TeX language to build an equation, and you can save and import equations using the TeX language. You also learn how to change the equation's display by changing its defaults.

Chapter 15, "Power fields," covers how to use power fields to generate your documents' contents. The chapter defines power fields, explains power field syntax, how to insert a power field, and save a custom power field you create. You learn how to view power field's results, instructions, or both at the same time. You learn how to control when and how power fields update in your document. Lastly, you learn how delete power fields from your document. The chapter explains each power field, its syntax, and contains examples of the most useful power fields.

Chapter 16, "Importing and exporting files," explains how to import text, spreadsheet, and database files to create a document's content. You learn the file types Ami recognizes and the import options available for those files. The chapter also explains how to export Ami Pro files to external file formats.

Part 3, "Graphics," explains how to import graphics files and create drawings and charts in Ami Pro.

Chapter 17, "Importing graphics files," explains how to create a frame to hold a graphic and modify the frame's layout attributes, including the frame type, size and position, and lines and shadows. The chapter covers the three methods for loading a graphic into Ami Pro and the file types you can import into Ami. The chapter also explains how to crop, move, rotate, and size imported graphics.

Chapter 18, "Ami Pro's drawing tools," explains how to use the Drawing icon bar and menu to create drawings in your document. The chapter covers how to use the Draw Object icons, the Draw Command icons, and the Draw menu. The chapter also explains how to save a drawing you create and how to use the clip art supplied with Ami Pro.

Chapter 19, "Ami Pro's charting tools," covers how to create a chart within Ami Pro. The chapter explains how to create the chart using data in the clipboard or by entering data in the Chart Data dialog box. The chapter discusses the 12 chart types you can create and how to choose the chart type and its options. You learn how to create a chart using DDE or OLE links and how to modify a chart using Ami Pro Drawing feature.

Part 4, "Special topics," covers a miscellaneous assortment of topics that let you push Ami Pro to perform to new heights. You learn how to speed up Ami Pro, overcome memory problems, improve printer performance, print envelopes, and even more.

Chapter 20, "Printing tips," discusses how to speed up printing, how to print nonconsecutive pages, printing more than one document, printing crop marks and double-sided pages, and how to troubleshoot when your document isn't printing correctly.

Chapter 21, "Speed tips," explains how to increase Ami Pro's performance, no matter what type of PC you use. The chapter covers basic steps you can use to speed up Ami Pro, methods you can use with styles, moving around the document, displaying documents, and editing tools. The chapter discusses file management strategies for speeding up Ami's performance and steps you can take with your hardware. The chapter includes a special section for 286 PC users for steps they can take to increase Ami Pro's speed.

Chapter 22, "Safety tips," includes methods that safeguard your documents from data loss, unwanted changes, and data corruption. The chapter covers how to prevent changes to a document or a style sheet and how to devise a backup schedule. The chapter discusses strategies for saving documents often, undoing all changes to a document since you last saved, limiting file size, and reviewing the changes other have made to a file.

Chapter 23, "Customizing Ami Pro," explains how to change Ami Pro's display, user interface, and operations to suit your needs. The chapter covers changing the icon palette, the number of files listed on the File menu, undo levels, default paths, notes' display, and unit of measurement on the tab ruler, just to name a few features. The chapter covers a rich assortment of changes you can make to tailor Ami Pro to your and your document's changing needs.

Chapter 24, "Building a document," takes you through the process of creating a document step by step from preliminary directory maintenance and entering text to using styles, inserting tables, creating graphics, and adding a footer.

Finally, this book contains appendices that list the marks you view in your document, list names and addresses of companies whose products are listed in the book, explain how to use Ami Pro without a mouse, display samples of the style sheets included with Ami Pro, list all the icons available, and define the terms used throughout the book. The book also includes an index that helps you find a specific topic you need.

Part 1
Introduction to Ami Pro

1
CHAPTER

What's new
in version two?

Ami Pro has undergone over 50 changes in version 2.0, including its name—
Ami Professional, now Ami Pro 2.0. This chapter highlights the changes and new
features in 2.0, so you don't have to rummage through the entire book searching
for new features. Table 1-1 contains a list of the major new features of Ami Pro
and the chapter of this that book covers them.

Installation

Ami still uses the standard Window's installation user interface and process. Ami
has three new installation features that let you control where it places your files,
however, and it creates its own .INI file.

Customized installation

Ami lets you decide what portion of the program you need to install: the entire
program, the program and its options, or options only. Ami also displays the
amount of disk space your choice requires vs. the amount of disk space available
on your hard disk. If you don't have enough disk space, Ami still gives you the
option of installing the program, in case you are installing over an old version of
Ami Pro and don't need additional disk space.

Permission to overwrite style sheets, sample documents, macros

During the installation process, Ami asks whether you need to install its style
sheets, sample documents, macros, and graphics in the same place you stored

Table 1-1. Ami Pro 2.0's New and Enhanced Features

New or Enhanced Feature	Chapter Covering Feature
Adobe Type Manager fonts	Chapter 6
Ami Pro print spooler	Chapter 20
AMIPRO.INI	Chapter 23
Attaching a macro to a file	Chapters 13 and 23
Attaching a macro to a frame	Chapters 13 and 17
Attaching a macro to a style sheet	Chapters 5 and 13
Changing note marker's and note background color	Chapters 4 and 23
Changing unit of measurement on tab ruler	Chapter 23
Column breaks	Chapter 7
Creating an outline	Chapter 4
Cross references	Chapter 15
Custom colors	Chapter 18
Custom icons	Chapter 13
Customizable icon palette	Chapter 23
Disable warning messages and title bar help	Chapter 23
Dividing a table row between pages	Chapter 8
Document compare	Chapter 3
Draft mode	Chapter 4
Dynamic Data Exchange	Chapters 4, 18, and 19
Equations	Chapter 14
File menu lists last documents you opened	Chapter 3
Hyphenation override	Chapter 7
Import your own pictures for symbol charts	Chapter 19
Importing and exporting files	Chapter 16
Importing graphics	Chapter 17
Improved tab ruler at top of the window	Chapter 7
Inserted tab rulers	Chapter 7
Lock for annotation	Chapter 22
Macro Command Language	Chapter 13
Master document	Chapter 9
Multiple Document Interface	Chapter 3
New style sheets	Appendix D
Object Linking and Embedding	Chapters 4, 18, and 19
Outline mode	Chapter 4
Power fields	Chapter 15
Quick macro shortcut keys	Chapter 13
Revision marking	Chapter 4

Table 1-1. Continued

New or Enhanced Feature	Chapter Covering Feature
Running Grammatik within Ami	Chapter 12
Running a macro at program start or end	Chapters 13 and 23
Select Drawing or Charting without adding a frame	Chapters 18 and 19
Stamping notes with your initials	Chapters 4 and 23
Status bar	Chapter 4
Style by example	Chapter 5
Style tabs	Chapter 7

those files in version 1.2, or if you need to install them elsewhere on your hard disk.

AMIPRO.INI

Ami creates its own AMIPRO.INI during installation that controls features such as import/export filters, user setup options, default paths, and the last five documents you opened. In version 1.2, Ami saved these specifications in the Window's WIN.INI file.

Screen

Ami Pro's user interface changed dramatically, affecting everything from the icon palette and the menus to the Status Bar. None of these changes require you to modify the way you use Ami Pro; rather, the program simply contains more features that, along with the existing features, are more easily accessible from the document.

Menus

Ami moved many commands to different menus, added menus, changed command names, and removed some commands altogether. The following section lists each menu and the changes it has undergone.

File menu   The Append and Import/Export commands are gone, because you now can do these tasks using the File Open, File Save As, and Import Picture commands. You'll find Links under the Edit menu as Link Options. At the bottom of the File menu, Ami lists the last three files you used. To open one of these files, simply click on the filename.

Edit menu   Defaults is now under the Tools menu as User Setup. The Icons option under the old Edit Defaults command is now a command under Tools, only now it's called SmartIcons. Footnotes moved to the Tools menu. Conversely, Go To and Find & Replace moved from the Tools menu to the Edit menu. Insert Variable was shortened to Insert, from which you can insert notes, the date and the time, merge and description fields, glossary records, and new objects.

View menu   Display Preferences changed its name to View Preferences, which is more appropriate because it's under the View menu. Show/Hide Tab Ruler is now called Show/Hide Ruler. Hide Icon Palette moved to the Tools menu under the SmartIcons command. Show/Hide Styles Box moved to the View menu from the Style menu.

Text menu   You can now indent text from the Text menu using the Indention command.

Style menu   Save As a New Style Sheet lost the *New* part, and now is called Save As a Style Sheet, because it was confusing to change styles and to save the current style sheet using that command. Show Styles Box moved to the View menu.

Page menu   Insert/Remove Layout changed its name to Insert Page Layout. Modify Layout & Margins changed its name to Modify Page Layout. Both commands are now more consistent with the page layout theme. Page Breaks changed its name to simply Breaks.

Frame menu   Add a Frame changed its name to Create a Frame. Frame Layout changed its name to Modify Frame Layout. Image Processing moved to the Tools menu, and Group Frames changed its name to Group.

Tools menu   The Tools menu underwent the most changes, because many tools, such as Find & Replace and Go To, moved to more appropriate locations under their task names. Image Processing moved to the Tools menu from the Frame menu, while SmartIcons moved from its old location under the Edit Defaults command. Footnotes moved from the Edit menu. User Setup moved from the Edit menu, where it was called Defaults. Glossary moved to the Insert command under the Edit menu. Find & Replace and Go To also moved to the Edit menu.

Window menu   Ami added this new menu to control its use of MDI—Multiple Document Interface.

Help

The Help menu hasn't changed much; however, now you can press Shift-F1 for help on any feature of Ami Pro. After you press those keys, Ami displays a question mark. Move the mark to the feature you need help with and click.

Status Bar and Style Status

Ami combined the Status Bar and the Style Status indicator into one bar at the bottom of the screen. The Status Bar includes the Style Status, the current font and point size, the document path, whether you are using insert or typeover mode, a toggle to display or hide the icon palette, and the page number. You can turn on Revision Marking as well as change styles, fonts, and point size by clicking on the option in the Status Bar. A pop-up menu appears from which you can make your selection.

Icon Palette

The old Icon Bar is now called the Icon Palette displaying over 120 icons you can choose from. Virtually every Ami feature has its own icon now. The macro icons are gone, but an incredible feature took their place—you can create your own icons by importing a .BMP file and attaching a macro to them. Use Ami's drawing feature or import a file from another graphics package to create the icon graphic you want. You can move the icon palette to the top, bottom, left, or right edge of the screen, or tear it off as a floating palette.

Styles Box

The Styles Box is now hidden when you start the program.

Multiple Document Interface

Ami uses MDI (Multiple Document Interface), which lets you display multiple documents simultaneously. Each document has its own window, and you can minimize and restore them inside Ami's application window. When you start Ami, it automatically opens a new untitled file, which remains open until you close it.

Managing files

Before 2.0, Ami never had a direct way of closing a file. Now it does with the File Close command. The File Management and Document Description features have been expanded, so you can import more graphic file types than you could in 1.2.

Opening the same file twice

If you open the same file twice, Ami tells you that the second file is display-only and it displays "Read-Only" in the document's title bar.

Closing a file

A new command, File Close, lets you close the current file without opening an existing file or creating a new file. Previously, you had to use File New, File Open, or Exit command to close a file.

File management displays

The File Management dialog box automatically displays file descriptions of Ami documents, whereas before you had to select the Show Description check box.

Increased document descriptions

The Document Description is a good feature made even better, because it increased its number of fields from four to eight, and displays the document's page, word, character, and byte counts.

Importing graphics and graphics file types

Previously you used the Import/Export command to import a graphic; now you do so using the Import Picture command. Ami also expanded the graphic file formats it imports to .CGM, DrawPerfect, .EPS, Freelance, HPGL, .PIC, .PCX, .BMP, and .WMF files.

Creating and editing text

Ami generously improved its text creation and editing features to include an outlining feature, power fields, equations, a better draft view, and it even goes a step beyond DDE.

Outlining

Ami has a new Outline mode that you can use two ways. You can create a traditional outline, generating numbered levels and indenting outline text. The numbered levels are a permanent part of the outline that always display and print. Your other alternative is to display a regular document in Outline mode, using indents and buttons rather than numbered levels. The buttons and indentions indicate your text's hierarchy in the document, and are displayed only while you are in Outline mode, but they don't print. So you can return to Draft or Layout mode without affecting your document's format. You can hide and redisplay levels, which is a great feature when viewing a long document's hierarchy to maintain consistency, or when comparing sections of the same document. You can move entire blocks of text under one level to a new level, which is a much easier method of cut and paste for long documents.

Revision Marking and Document Compare

Ami provides two ways to compare different versions of a document. Use Revision Marking while you are editing a document on-line, and use Document Compare after a document has been edited and saved. Revision Marking indicates text deletions and insertions as you do them, while Document Compare marks the deletions and insertions in the current document when you compare it with a document on disk. You also can customize the method of marking for deletions and insertions.

An almost WYSIWYG Draft mode

Draft mode includes a few enhancements that make your on-screen document appear closer to its printed version. Ami displays fonts (which you can turn off), marks, and tables in Draft mode. You also can create and edit drawings, charts, and equations from Draft mode.

Preventing hyphenation

In Ami Pro 1.2, you could not override a word from being hyphenated, unless you turned hyphenation off. Now you can block the text and turn off hyphenation for that block.

Inserting the current time

Ami now lets you insert the current time as a variable, like you could with the date in version 1.2.

Object Linking and Embedding

Object Linking and Embedding lets you link information in the same way DDE does, but OLE gives you more options for pasting the information into your document. OLE also automatically starts the application from which the data was created when you double-click on the data, whereas DDE asks for your permission to do so.

Power fields

Ami provides an entire library of automated instructions, called power fields, that let you perform actions at a specific location in a document. You can use power fields to consecutively number figures, insert cross-references, insert document statistics into your document (number of pages, date created, etc.), along with many other uses. Ami has four types of power fields:

- Ami Pro function—Power fields that automate Ami Pro features at a specific location in your document. These functions can be considered location-specific macros.
- Document Description function—Power fields that insert document statistics into a specific location in your document.
- Field functions—Power fields that automate features normally not available as an Ami Pro feature, such as sequentially numbering frames in your document.

- Macro functions—Power fields that use Ami's macro command language to perform an action at a specific location in your document.

Equations

Ami lets you create complex mathematical, financial, and statistical equations easily. Point to the symbol or operator you need and Ami creates it at your cursor's location in the document. There's no need to learn a complex equation language, like most word processors/desktop publishers require.

Styles

Ami has a few new style features, but nothing dramatic. One new feature makes creating styles easier, and gives you more control over the tabs your styles use.

Defining a style from existing attributes

How about style-by-example? If you format a paragraph using the Text menu, and then realize you need a style using those same attributes, simply highlight the paragraph and tell Ami to create the style. That's all there is to it.

Style tabs

Each style has its own ruler, so you can create tab settings for each. The tabs affect every paragraph using that style. Style tabs override page layout tabs, but not inserted tab rulers.

Additional style sheets

Ami provides 55 style sheets you can use with your documents. Many of these style sheets were not available in 1.2 and are much more polished and professional than those in the last release. You can use the style sheets "off-the-shelf" or modify them to suit your needs.

Fonts

Only one new font feature was added, but it's a big one: Ami comes bundled with 13 scalable Adobe Type Manager soft fonts.

Page layout

Ami made the most commonly-used page layout features accessible from the document, without requiring you to access the Modify Page Layout command.

Inserted tab rulers

This feature is still available, however, an easier way to modify tabs was added. Each paragraph now has its own tab ruler, which produces the same result as inserting a new tab ruler. You no longer need to use the Tab Ruler/Insert command from the Page menu; simply change the tabs in the ruler at the top of the document.

Specify columns and spacing using the tab ruler

Changing margins, alignment, indention, and tabs using the tab ruler was always possible. Now you can change columns and spacing also.

Column breaks

Previously, Ami did not have a column breaks feature. When you need to begin entering text in the next column, simply choose Insert column break from the Insert command under the Page menu.

Tables

You now can divide a row between pages. Previously, if the row at the bottom of page contained too much text to fit on the page, Ami moved the entire row to the next page. Now, Ami divides the row the same way it divides paragraphs at the end of a page.

Publishing details

Ami has a new feature called a Master Document that lets you combine multiple chapters into one large publication. You can create an index, a table of contents, and number pages across chapters using the Master Document.

Speller/Thesaurus

You can now run Grammatik from within Ami. Grammatik includes a macro that adds a Grammatik command to the Tools menu. To run the grammar checker, click on Grammatik and the program begins without leaving Ami.

Graphics

Ami's graphics features have always made the word processor stand out from the crowd, and Lotus has made several excellent features even better. The drawing program is still easy, but Ami now has even more drawing tools and options than before. You can manipulate your drawings with even more precision than was available in 1.2.

No frames required for importing graphics

In 1.2 you had to create a frame and select it before you could import a graphic; now Ami automatically draws a frame and places the graphic inside it. Ami draws the frame the same size as the last frame you created.

Over 100 predrawn symbols available

Ami comes with over 100 of its own .SDW graphic drawings that you can use in your documents.

Import your own pictures for symbol charts

If the symbol you need isn't in Ami, simply import the graphic you need and Ami uses it in your symbol chart.

Create custom colors for fill patterns, text, and lines

Previously, your color options in Ami were somewhat limited. Ami now has over 120 colors to choose from for your text, fill patterns, and lines. If the color you need isn't there, however, double-click on the color closest to the one you need and then create it using Ami's own palette.

Printing

Ami now has its own spooler that returns control of the document to you much faster than when it used the Windows' spooler alone.

Setup

Ami lets you stamp notes with your initials, protect documents from changes, and eliminate help messages.

Stamping notes with your initials

You can display your initials next to notes for quick identification. You also can specify what color to display inside the Note dialog box.

Protecting documents from changes

When you turn on the lock for annotation feature, no one can edit that document. To turn on protection, however, you must enter your name in the User Setup dialog box, then only you can turn off protection.

Disabling warning messages and title bar help

You can turn off two levels of help: warning messages that display before you complete a destructive action (such as deleting a table, note, or inserted tab ruler), and descriptions displayed in the title bar of commands and icons.

Macros

Ami hasn't changed the process of creating or running macros. Ami now lets you run macros when you use a style sheet, click on a frame, open or close a file, or begin and end the program. Ami comes with over 40 ready-to-use macros, and includes a file that describes each macro.

Automatically activating macros

You can specify a macro to run each time you load a style sheet, open or close a file, or begin or end the program.

Frame macros

You can attach a macro to a frame, then click on that frame to activate the macro.

Macros supplied with Ami

Ami has over 40 macros that are ready for you to use with your own documents.

Summary

This chapter was designed to familiarize you with Ami Pro 2.0's new features, so you can identify the ones that will help you create documents. Now that you have reviewed this chapter, you probably have a good idea of the items you want to discover immediately, the features you want to test, but not necessarily learn in-depth, and the features you know you don't need to use. You don't have to learn all of the new features at once. Many of Ami Pro's new features are quite powerful, and require you to experiment with them before you feel totally comfortable trusting them to your documents.

2
CHAPTER

How does Ami Pro 2.0 work?

Ami Pro is a unique blend of the precise control of a page layout program, the text editing and manipulation of a word processor, the drawing and charting features of a graphics package, the form creation features of a forms generation program, and the scientific and mathematical formatting of an equation editor all in one. You might think using a program with all these features would be complicated, but you'll find exactly the opposite to be true. Ami Pro is quite intuitive with a smartly designed screen and menus.

What can Ami Professional do?

Before we discover the tips and tricks you can use with Ami Professional, let's take an overall look at what you can accomplish using the program:

- Write and edit text using Spell Check, Thesaurus, and Find and Replace.
- Create text and graphics files using other programs, then import the files into your document.
- Format your paragraphs and documents using predefined or customized style sheets. Format individual characters and words using text attributes.
- Make outlines or view a regular document in Outline mode.
- Construct tables that offer worksheet capabilities such as formulas and calculations.
- Design original drawings or enhance those graphics you import using the draw feature.

- Create complex equations by pointing to the symbol or operator you need.
- Draw charts from values you entered into Ami Professional or imported from a spreadsheet—no need to use a separate charting program.

Before you can use all these features, you need to understand how the program is organized and the concepts behind many of the features.

Viewing the Ami Professional screen

The first step towards getting the most out of Ami Professional is to become thoroughly familiar with its screen. Because Ami Pro is a Windows' application, it uses the standard Windows' user interface. However, Ami Professional also has features on its screen not found in Windows or in any other Windows' application. Figure 2-1 shows the Ami Professional screen and its elements.

The following paragraphs describe each of the screen elements:

Control box   Click on the Control box to display the Windows' Control menu. Use the menu to change or close the Ami Professional Window, or display the Windows' Task List, Control Panel, or Spooler. Double-click on the Control box to close the Ami Professional Window.

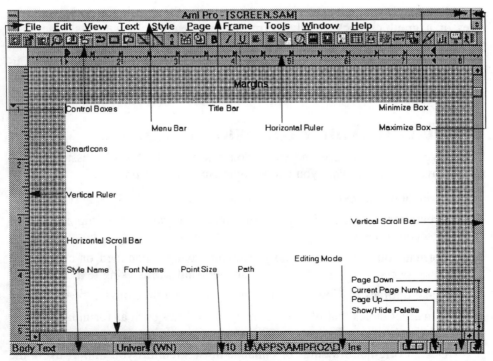

2-1   Elements of the Ami Pro screen. You optionally display rulers, the icon palette, margins, and the Styles Box.

Horizontal ruler   The horizontal ruler appears at the top of the Ami Professional Window. The ruler is useful for placing and measuring text elements and graphics.

Horizontal scroll bar   The scroll bar displays a scroll box that represents the cursor's horizontal position on the page. Drag the scroll box to move across the page, or click to the right or left of the scroll box to move in that direction. To move in smaller units, click on one of the arrows at either end of the scroll bar.

Margins   The area using a fill-pattern or shading that surrounds the document represents its margins.

Maximize button   Click on this button to increase the window to fill the entire screen.

Menu bar   The menu bar displays the available Ami Professional menus.

Minimize Button   Click on this button to reduce the window to an icon.

Page status   The page status displays the current page number. Click on the Page Status to display the Go To dialog box.

Page up/page down arrows   Click on the page up arrow to move to the previous page. Click on the page down arrow to move to the next page.

Icon palette   The icon palette represents Ami Professional tasks that you can choose by clicking on the icon rather than choosing a command from the menu or using a keyboard shortcut. You can customize the palette to display the icons for the tasks you use most often, and you can create your own icons.

Status bar   The Status Bar displays the current style, font, point size, document path, and whether you are using Insert or Typeover mode.

Styles box   The Styles box displays the filename of the current style sheet and the paragraph styles it contains. You can move the Styles box to a new location in the window, or close it altogether.

Tab ruler   The tab ruler displays the tab locations and tab types for the current paragraph. The tab ruler also displays the current paragraph's margins and indention. The tab ruler displayed at the top of the screen can be a page layout tab ruler, a style tab ruler, or an inserted tab ruler, depending upon which type the paragraph uses.

Title bar   The Title bar displays the filename of the current document, along with descriptions of the menu commands you select with your mouse.

Vertical scroll bar   The scroll bar displays a scroll box that represents the cursor's vertical position on the page. Drag the scroll box to move vertically on the page, or click above or below the scroll box to move in that direction. Click on one of the arrows at either end of the scroll bar to move in smaller units.

Vertical ruler The vertical ruler appears at the left of the Ami Professional window. The ruler is useful for placing and measuring text elements and graphics.

An example

Ellen, for example, is a freelance technical writer who writes manuals, brochures, and other user materials for computer software companies. Because Ellen creates materials for several different firms, she has a style sheet for each that adheres to that companies' publication standards. To begin creating a document, Ellen needs to enter the text. Usually she writes most of the text herself. When she works on a team, however, she uses the File Open command to import files from other writers, and the company's text files that are imported for copyright and disclaimer purposes.

Once Ellen has the text that makes up the document, she uses the Styles box to assign styles to format the text. Styles have names like Body Text, Bullet, and Bold & Center, which appear in the Styles box on the right side of the window. Each style contains formatting information that suits a particular paragraph type. She highlights a paragraph and then clicks on the appropriate style in the style box. Ellen doesn't need to assign styles to every paragraph, because all paragraphs entered in or imported into Ami Professional start out using the Body Text style.

Once Ellen assigns styles to the text, she adds frames to the document that will hold graphics files. Ellen could use the Frame menu to add a frame, but she prefers to click on the icon in the icon palette. Again, Ellen creates most graphics using Ami, but she also receives graphics files from other writers, the companies, or their vendors. Ellen imports the graphics files using the Import Picture command on the File menu, and controls the frame's layout and fine tunes the graphic image using the Graphics Scaling command on the Frame menu.

After Ellen has all the text and graphics correctly placed in the document, she checks its spelling. She then creates headers and footers for the document, and names and prints the document using the File menu.

The main menu and the Icon Palette

Ami Professional's menus and icons let you access its commands to create, layout, and format your documents. Once you become familiar with the commands available on each menu and in the icon palette, you can choose the method that best suits you. If you prefer using the icon palette over the menu, you can display and create icons for the commands you use often. You also can use keyboard shortcuts for many commands. Refer to chapter 23 for more information on customizing Ami Professional.

The Menu Bar

The Menu Bar contains ten menus; however, the Outline, Table, Equation, and Draw menus do not appear at the start of the program. Let's discuss what the menus control and how you can use them.

File menu   Think of the File menu as the Grand Central Station for all files. If a file needs to come in or out of Ami Professional, it does so here. Using the File menu, you can create new documents, open, save, revert to existing documents, and import or export text and graphics files. You also can perform file management operations usually done in Windows or DOS, such as copy, delete, change directory, and view files' contents. You can create and view a description of Ami Pro documents and identify the text and/or graphics files imported into the document. You can combine several chapter files into one large publication for page numbering, printing, and generating a table of contents or index. You can merge documents to create labels and form letters, and print your documents.

Edit menu   Use the Edit menu to add or remove text and other items from your document. The Edit menu also controls undo, links, and power fields. Using the Edit menu, you can undo the last task you performed (up to four levels of tasks); cut, copy, and paste text and graphics within and between documents; and paste DDE and OLE links into a document. You can insert variables, such as the current date, into a document; identify text that you need to include in a table of contents or index; and add nonprinting notes, similar to a post-it note, to a document. You also can add bookmarks, power fields, glossary entries, perform a find and replace, and go to specific page, frame, or mark using the Edit menu.

View menu   Use the View menu to change the way Ami displays your document on the screen, and add or remove items that help you place text and graphics on a page. Using the View menu, you can select from three different editing modes: Layout mode (WYSIWYG), Draft mode (minimal formatting), and Outline mode (document takes on an outline hierarchy). You can choose from five different document views while you are in Layout mode and select screen features, such as rulers, column guides, and margins that you need displayed for any mode. You also can display or hide the tab ruler, the Styles Box, and power fields from the View menu.

Tip 2-1: Adding a custom view to the View Menu   The CUSTVIEW macro lets you add another view to the View menu. This macro is useful if you use a custom page size, work frequently with landscape pages, or if you switch between Working View's level of 91% and another percentage.

Once you run CUSTVIEW, Ami displays the Custom View dialog box, as shown in Figure 2-2. You can specify another view level for both Working view and the new Custom view. After you enter the new view levels and select OK, Ami adds two new menu items to the View menu: Custom and Custom View. The

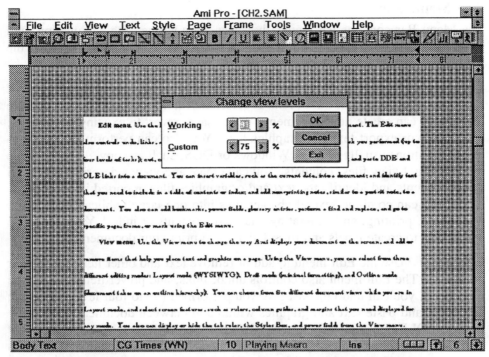

2-2 The Change View Levels dialog box, as displayed by the CUSTVIEW macro.

Custom menu item displays its view level percentage on the menu, and when you select it Ami changes to that view. The Custom View menu item displays the Custom View dialog box, letting you adjust the view levels for Working and Custom views.

The Custom view you add is active only for the current work session. The next time you load Ami, the Custom and Custom View menu items do not appear on the View menu. You can specify CUSTVIEW as an AutoRun macro, however, so that the Custom views are a permanent part of your menus.

Text menu Use the Text menu to format individual characters and words, but not the entire paragraph. Using the Text menu, you can format text by changing the fonts, alignment, indention, spacing, bold, italic, underline, capitalization, superscript, subscript, double underline, strikethrough, and overstrike.

Style menu The Style menu controls page and paragraph formatting, which enables you to select or create the style sheets and paragraph styles you need. With this menu you can select an existing style sheet or create a new style sheet based on an existing one. You also can create a new paragraph style, basing its attributes on an existing style or formatted paragraph in the document. The Style menu lets you create a hierarchy for your styles when you display a document in Outline mode. You can modify a paragraph style by changing its font, alignment, spacing, page breaks, special effects, lines, and table format. You can change from document-only styles to global, select a paragraph style for a current paragraph, and display the Styles Box.

Page menu   Even though this menu is called Page, most of its options affect the entire document. The Page menu lets you control the document layout, tab settings, headers and footers, and other options that appear throughout the entire document. The Page menu enables you to create a new page layout or modify an existing layout, change its margins, columns, page settings, lines, headers, and footers. You can create floating headers and footers and new tab rulers. You can control the page numbering style, starting numbers, and leading text; activate line numbering and control numbering style and frequency; and insert page or column breaks.

Frame menu   Use this menu to access Ami Professional's powerful graphics features. From the Frame menu, you can create a frame, change its appearance, or group multiple frames. The Frame menu enables you to change a frame's layout, including the way text flows around the frame, borders, lines, columns, and tabs, and change the size and rotation of graphics inside the frame. You can enhance the detail of TIFF images inside frames; group multiple frames; and move frames to the front or the back of other frames. The contents of these frames, however, is imported from text and graphics files using the File menu.

Tools menu   The Tools menu contains some of Ami's most powerful features, including charting, drawing, equations, and more. With the Tools menu you can check your document's spelling; use the thesaurus to find a selection of similar words; and sort text. You can generate a table of contents and an index, record and playback keystrokes using a macro, and create a new table. You can add a drawing, a chart, a footnote, or an equation to your document, and enhance a frame's TIFF image. You can compare two documents and display their differences; customize the icon palette and its position on the screen; and define Ami's default settings.

Window menu   The Window menu lets you access Ami's support of MDI. From the Window menu, you can display the same document in two windows, move among document windows, and tile or cascade document windows.

Help menu   The Help menu provides instructions on using Ami Pro's menu, features, and functions. The Help menu also includes documentation on Ami's Macro Command Language, which isn't included with the product (although you can order it from Lotus Word Processing).

Customizing Ami's menus

The AMIMENUS macro lets you customize Ami's menus by adding and removing menu items. The menu items can be existing Ami Pro functions that you want to place on another menu, or they can be selections inside a dialog box that you make easier to access by placing them directly on a menu. You also can add commands to menus that execute macros shipped with Ami or macros you create.

Once you play the AMIMENUS macro, Ami displays the Customize Menus dialog box, as shown in Figure 2-3. The dialog box lists the menus in a list box, displaying an ampersand (&) in their names. The ampersand precedes the letter that serves as the accelerator key for that menu.

Adding a menu item

To add a menu item to Ami's menus, follow these steps:

1. From the Customize Menus dialog box, highlight the menu that you want to add to and select Add. Ami displays the Add Menu Item dialog box, as shown in Figure 2-4.

2. Type the name of the new menu item in the Appear On Menu text box. If you plan to add an accelerator key to the menu item, place an ampersand before that letter in the menu item name. Ami will underline that letter when it appears on the menu.

3. Select where to place the new menu item from the Insert Before List box. Highlight the name of the item you want to appear after your new menu item.

4. If you want to add an accelerator key, type the letter or number of the keystroke in the Keystroke Text box, and select the key combinations to use with it. For example, if you want to use Ctrl—Shift—A as the accelerator key, type A in the Keystroke Text box and select the Ctrl and Shift check boxes.

5. Select the command button representing the action you want to include as a menu item. If you want to place an Ami Pro function on a menu, select Function. If you want to place a macro on a menu, select Macro.

6. Select the function or the macro you want to include on a menu and select OK. Ami displays the following message:
   "Do you want to make this permanent?"

7. If you want the menu item to appear every time you load Ami, select Yes. If you want the menu item only for this work session, select No. If you select Yes, Ami creates an AUTOEXEC.SMM macro that adds your new menu item to the menu you selected. Each time you start Ami Pro, it runs this macro, activating your new menu item.

8. Select OK and then Done from the Customize Menu dialog box.

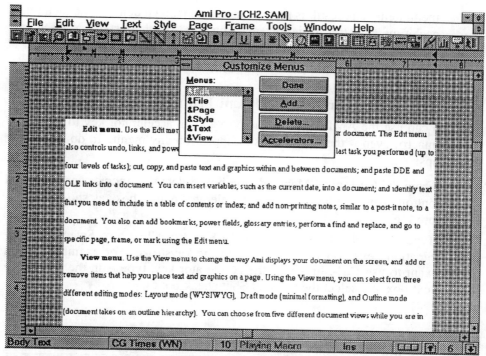

2-3 The Customize Menus dialog box, as displayed by the AMIMENUS macro.

Deleting a menu item

You can delete a regular menu item or one you added with the Customize Menus dialog box. It is never an irreparable step if you delete a menu item, because you can replace it later using the Customize Menus dialog box.

To delete a menu item from Ami's menus, follow these steps:

1. From the Customize Menus dialog box, highlight the menu from which you want to delete an item and select Delete. Ami displays the Delete Menu Item dialog box, as shown in Figure 2-5. Then Ami displays the menu items available on the menu you selected.

2. Highlight the menu item you want to delete and select OK. Ami displays the following message:

   "Do you want to make this permanent?"

3. If you want the menu item omitted every time you load Ami, select Yes. If you want the menu item omitted only for this work session, select No. If you select Yes, Ami updates the AUTOEXEC.SMM macro to remove the menu item. Instead of deleting the previous reference to the menu item, Ami adds an additional section to the macro removing the

menu item. The result is that the macro adds, then deletes, the menu item each time you start Ami; however, you don't see these steps. You see only the end result, which is omitting the menu item altogether.

4. Select Done from the Customize Menu dialog box.

Adding an accelerator key to an Ami Pro function or macro

You also can use the AMIMENUS macro to add an accelerator key to any menu item or macro, even if the macro doesn't appear on any menu. To do so, follow these steps:

1. From the Customize Menus dialog box, select the Accelerator command button. Ami displays the Add Accelerator dialog box, as shown in Figure 2-6.

2. Type the accelerator keystroke in the Keystroke Text box. Select the combination keys you want to use with the keystroke. For example, if you want to use Ctrl-Shift-A as the accelerator key, type A in the Keystroke text box and select the Ctrl and Shift check boxes.

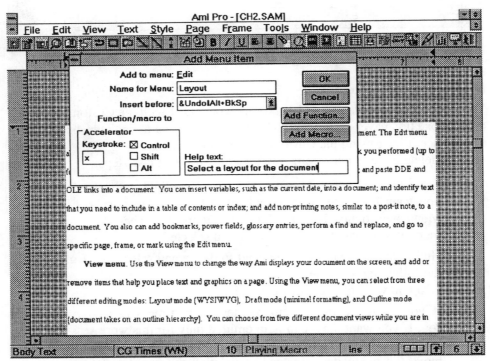

2-4 The Add Menu Item dialog box lets you add a macro or an Ami Pro function to any menu on the menu bar.

3. Select the Function or Macro command button, depending upon which you want to add an accelerator key.

4. Select the function or macro to which you want to add an accelerator key. Ami displays the following message:
"Do you want to make this permanent?"

5. If you want to use the accelerator key every time you load Ami, select Yes. If you want to use the accelerator key only for this work session, select No. If you select Yes, Ami updates the AUTOEXEC.SMM macro to include the new accelerator key.

6. Select Done from the Customize Menus dialog box.

Displaying Ami's short menus

If you don't need to use the advanced functions listed on Ami's menus, you can run the MENULITE macro to change to Ami's short menus. Ami displays a new menu item on the View menu called Short Menus. When you select Short Menus, Ami displays only basic document creation and editing tasks. The Short Menus command is a toggle; once you select it, Ami displays Long Menus. Thus,

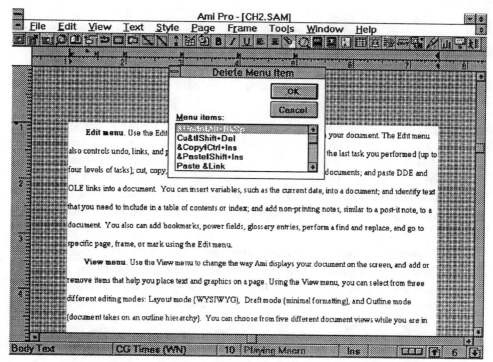

2-5 The Delete Menu Item dialog box lets you remove a macro or an Ami Pro function from any menu on the menu bar.

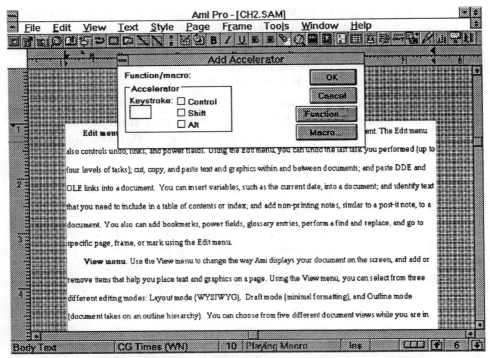

2-6 The Add Accelerator dialog box lets you assign a shortcut key to any command on a menu.

switching between short and long menus is as easy as selecting the command from the View menu.

Tip 2-2: Starting other applications from Ami Pro   Ami Pro provides macros you can use to start other Lotus applications from Ami. The macros are 123W.SMM to start 1-2-3 for Windows, CCMAIL.SMM to run cc:Mail, FLW.SMM to start Freelance for Windows, and NOTES.SMM to start Lotus Notes. Ami also provides custom icons to which you can assign these macros. You can create your own macros to start other applications using the Macro Command Language.

Tip 2-3: Adding a task list to the menu bar   The WINAPPS macro adds a menu of active applications, both Windows and nonWindows, to the menu bar. You can use the Active Apps menu in the same way you do the Windows Task List: to move among currently active Windows applications. You also can update the menu to add newly activated applications or remove closed ones by selecting Update Apps from the menu. Selecting Exit Apps removes the Active Apps menu from the menu bar.

Tip 2-4: Starting File Manager from Ami Pro   The WINFILE macro starts the Window File Manager and switches to it. This macro is useful for doing the preparatory work before creating a large document, such as creating a document and backup directory, and copying any necessary files to that directory.

The Icon Palette

Ami Professional has a total of 120 icons; it displays the first 12 of them in the icon palette. Each icon represents a commonly used command from one of Ami Professional's menus. You can remove and add icons as you become familiar with the commands you use most. Table 2-1 displays the icons available in Ami Professional.

Customizing the Icon Palette

When you load Ami for the first time, the icon palette appears at the top of the screen containing 12 icons. However, you can change the icon palette's position and the icons it contains. You can move the palette to the bottom, left, or right sides of the screen, or even display it as a floating palette that you can move around the screen. You can add, remove, and rearrange the icons Ami displays in the palette, and you can even create your own icons.

To move the icon palette, follow these steps:

1. Select SmartIcons from the Tools menu. Ami displays the SmartIcons dialog box as shown in Figure 2-7.

2. Select the position on the screen where you want to place the icon palette. Select Left to display the icon palette on the left side of the screen, before the vertical ruler. Select Right to display it on the right side of the screen, before the vertical scroll bar.
   Choosing Top will move it to the top of the screen, underneath the menu bar but above the horizontal ruler.
   Pressing Below will display the icon palette at the bottom of the screen, above the Status Bar but below the horizontal scroll bar; and entering Floating will place it anywhere on the screen. Ami initially displays four icons across and down the palette, but you can adjust the palette to any size.

3. If you want to hide the icon palette, turn off the Show SmartIcons check box.

4. Select OK to return to the document and view the newly positioned icon palette.

Customizing the icons in the palette

To select the icons you want to display in the palette, choose SmartIcons from the Tools menu and then Customize. Ami displays the Customize SmartIcons dialog box, as shown in Figure 2-8. The icons Ami displays in the icon palette are listed in the Current Palette box. Your monitor might not be able to display all the icons

Table 2-1. Ami Pro Icons

Icon	Macro	Icon	Macro	Icon	Macro	Icon	Macro
	123W.SMM		Delete Column in Table		GAME.SMM		Mark Index Entry
	Add a Frame		Delete Row in Table		Go To Next		Merge
	All Caps		Delete Table Columns or Rows		Go To Next Field		Modify Frame Layout
	AMIMENUS.SMM		Document Compare		Go To Previous Field		Modify Layout
	AUTORUN.SMM		DOS.SMM		Graphic Scaling		Modify Style
	Bold Text		Double Underline Text		Group/Ungroup Frames Toggle		Modify Table Layout
	Bookmark		Draft/Layout Mode Toggle		Import Picture		Modify Table Lines
	Bring Frame to Front		Drawing		Initial Caps		New
	Cascade Windows		Edit Table Formula		Insert Break		No Hyphenation
	CCMAIL.SMM		Equations		Insert Column in Table		Normal Text
	Center Text		Exit		Insert Date		NOTES.SMM
	Charting		FAX.SMM		Insert Footnote		Open
	Close		Field Instructions/Results Toggle		Insert Glossary Record		OPENBOOK.SMM
	CLOSEALL.SMM		File Management		Insert Note		OPENDOCS.SMM
	Column Guides On/Off Toggle		Find and Replace		Insert Page Number		Outline/Layout Mode Toggle
	Copy		FINDTXT.SMM		Insert Row in Table		Paste
	COPYRITE.SMM		Floating Header/Footer		Italic Text		PHONBOOK.SMM
	Customize Icons		Floating SmartIcons		Justify		Print
	CUSTVIEW.SMM		FLW.SMM		KEYWORD.SMM		Printer Setup
	Cut		FONTDN.SMM		Left Align Text		PRNBATCH.SM
	Define Style		FONTUP.SMM		Macro Play		PRNPAGES.SMM
	Delete		Full Page/Current View Toggle		Margins in Color Toggle		PRNSHADE.SMM

Table 2-1. Continued

Icon Macro	Icon Macro	Icon Macro	Icon Macro
Quick Play	Set Frame and Add	Spelling	TM.SMM
Quick Record/End Record Toggle	Show/Hide Marks Toggle	Start/End Macro Record	Underline Text
REGMARK.SMM	Show/Hide Notes Toggle	Subscript Text	Undo
Revision Marking	Show/Hide Pictures Toggle	Superscript Text	Update All Fields
Right Align Text	Show/Hide Tab Ruler Toggle	Table of Contents, Index	Update This Field
Save	Show/Hide Tabs and Returns	Tables	View Preferences
SAVEBOOK.SMM	Show/Hide Vertical Ruler Toggle	Tables Connect Cells	WINFILE.SMM
SAVEINFO.SMM	Size Table Columns or Rows	Thesaurus	Word Underline Text
SAVSHADE.SMM	SMARTYPE.SMM	Tile Windows	
Send Frame to Back	Sort	TILEHORZ.SMM	

listed, depending upon the graphics card you have installed and the resolution you selected in Windows Setup. Drag the icon you want to add from the Standard Icons box to the Current Palette box. Ami shifts the remaining icons over one position in the palette.

Creating custom icons

If Ami doesn't come with an icon for your favorite feature, you can create one. Custom icons are icons you can create to automate the tasks you perform frequently. Creating a custom icon requires two major steps: create a drawing to use as the icon, and create a macro to assign to the icon. The steps for creating a custom icon are as follows:

1. Record a macro containing the task to which you want to assign an icon. For example, if you want to create a custom icon to update the word count in the document and display it on the screen, record that process in a macro. For more information on macros, refer to chapter 13.

2. Create the graphic to use in the icon using Ami's drawing tools or an external graphics application. For more information on creating drawings

within Ami, refer to chapter 18. For more information on importing graphics files, refer to chapter 17.

3. If you have an EGA display, make the picture 24 × 24 pixels. If you have a VGA display, make the picture 32 × 32 pixels. If you do not scale the picture according to your display, the icon will be too small to see in Ami. (In Windows Write, select the Image Attributes command under the Options menu. Select pels as the unit of measurement, and make the width and height the appropriate measurements.)

4. Save the graphic to a .BMP file format in the \AMIPRO directory

5. Load Ami Pro.

6. Select SmartIcons from the Tools menu. Select Customize. Ami displays the Customize SmartIcons dialog box and the icon you created appears in the Custom icons box.

7. Select the icon to which you need to assign a macro from the Custom icons box. If too many icons are displayed in the Custom Icons box, skip this step.

8. Click on the Assign Macro button. Ami displays the Assign Macro dialog box.

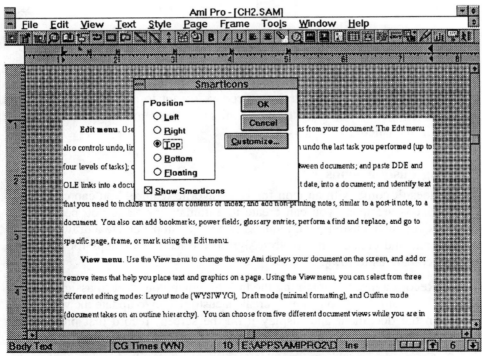

2-7 The SmartIcons dialog box lets you control the placement of the icon palette on the Ami Pro screen. You also decide whether to display or hide the palette from here.

9. Select the macro you need to assign to the icon from the Macros list box.

10. Select the Next Icon button until the icon you need appears.

11. Select Save to assign a macro to the icon.

12. Select OK to return to the Customize SmartIcons dialog box.

13. Drag your icon from the Custom icons box to the appropriate location in the Current Palette box. Continue dragging icons until all the customized icons you need appear in the Current Palette box.

14. Click OK to return to the document. Ami displays your customized icons in the icon palette.

Eight programs in one

Ami Professional offers a diverse array of features, so many that it actually can be considered eight different programs combined into one master program using a standard user interface. Each program lets you create a separate part of your document, and each program's commands are located on different menus—some programs have commands on several menus. Let's review these programs not in terms of what menu to use, but what they let you accomplish.

Ami Professional's eight different programs are: Word processing, Page lay-

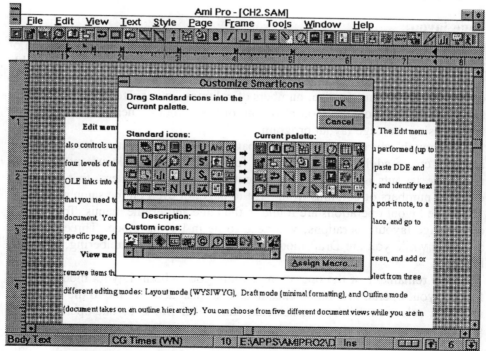

2-8 The Customize SmartIcons dialog box let you add, remove, or move icons to your palette and create custom icons for the tasks you perform frequently.

out, File management, Formatting, Drawing, Charting, Form/Worksheet generation, and Customizing the interface

Word processing

The heart of any document is its text, which you can create using Ami's word processor. You can use the word processor throughout the life of your document, from its beginning stages, through editing, and the final stages of spell checking and indexing.

Word processing commands reside in the Edit, Text, and Tools menus. The Edit menu contains the Cut/Copy/Paste operations, along with inserting text items such as notes, and identifying marks for tables of contents and indexes. Edit also has Find & Replace and Go To. The Text menu contains formatting operations for individual characters or words within a paragraph (to format an entire paragraph or page, use the Style menu). The Tools menu contains powerful word processing operations, including spell checking, a thesaurus, sorting, and macros. You'll find merge operations in the File menu.

Some word processing operations are mode specific (as are other operations outside the word processing area). You can use the following features only when you are in Layout mode: merge, generating a table of contents and index, modifying a page layout, and creating frames.

Page layout

Use the page layout program to change the overall dimensions and orientation of your printed page. The operations of this program will be the first tasks you tackle when you create your document. Before you write your first word, you need to decide page size, margin size, numbers of columns, gutter size, page orientation, tab settings, and borders. You also control the layout of headers, footers, and frames using the page layout program.

Although you create one master page layout for the entire document, you also can create additional page layouts for use in the same document. Inserting new page layouts is useful for documents, such as newsletters, that often use different numbers of columns from page to page, or even on the same page.

Page layout operations are found in the Page and Frame menus. To use most of the page layout operations, you need to be in Layout mode. Three tasks are available while you are Draft mode: page numbering, line numbering, and page breaks.

The remainder of the operations require you to be in Layout mode. Before frame layout operations can be executed, you must add a frame to the document and then select it. Without a selected frame, all frame layout operations are grayed.

File management

Before you can format your first paragraph, you need text and graphics in your document. You will probably create a lot of your document's content, however, most projects are a team effort and require you to use files that come from many different sources and were created from a variety of programs. Fortunately, Ami realizes this and lets you import and export a wide range of text and graphics files.

Use the File Management program's operations to create, save, and open Ami documents; to import and export text and graphics files; to add or view a document description; to perform various housekeeping tasks, such as copying and moving files; and to print documents.

All File Management operations are found in the File menu, except for managing style sheet files, which is in the Style menu. File management operations are not mode-specific.

Formatting

Formatting is the heart of any fullfeatured word processor or desktop publishing program. Ami lets you format your documents using style sheets. Style sheets contain collections of paragraph styles that let you control the appearance of paragraphs in your document. You will use the formatting program's operations after you have created a page layout and created or imported your text and graphics. Formatting operations reside in the Style menu and they are not mode-specific.

Formatting involves creating the styles you need for a particular document and then assigning a style to each paragraph in your document. Although this sounds simple, creating a style involves making choices from hundreds of options. Fortunately, Ami provides help by displaying examples of the effect your choices will have on a paragraph—sort of "instant WYSIWYG" without the ramifications. Once you create all the necessary styles, you usually end up fine-tuning them as you use the style sheet.

Charting

Use the charting program operation to create charts without leaving Ami to load a separate program. You can create charts from data in your document, data that you pasted in the clipboard from another application, or data in another application file that is linked to your chart. You can also enter your data using the charting program.

The charting program's operations that let you choose a chart type and display options are found in the Tools and Chart menus. Ami does not display the Chart menu until you activate the charting program. Charting is located in the Tools menu and is not mode-specific.

Drawing

Ami's drawing program is so powerful you will never need to use an outside drawing application. Use the drawing program to create original line drawings or to enhance bit-mapped or gray-scaled images imported into your document.

To use the drawing program, you can be in any mode. The drawing program's operations reside in the Tools and Draw menus (Ami does not display the Draw menu until you activate the drawing program).

Forms and worksheet generation

Ami's table feature lets you create data entry forms, worksheets, or a combination of the two. Uses of the table feature's are limited only by your imagination and creativity.

The table operations are found in the Tools and Table menus (the Table menu does not display until you create a table using the Tools menu). Initially, you decide how many rows and columns the table has, and then you can change features such as size, lines, shading, connecting and protecting cells, and calculations. You can be in any mode to create a table. To change a table's specifications, your cursor must be inside the table.

Customizing the interface

A user interface is not perfect for everyone unless you can change it. When you purchase a program and begin using it, you need helpful features such as menus, rulers, and other display features. After you become familiar with the program, however, you don't need those features, and you probably find them cumbersome. Fortunately, Ami lets you change just about everything in its user interface, including different views of your document; choosing an editing mode; displaying or hiding column guides, pictures, marks, notes, rulers, the Status Bar, table gridlines, rows/column headings; displaying or hiding tabs and returns, indentation, space between paragraphs, and colors in Draft mode; and choosing the icons you need to display in the sidebar.

Commands for these options are located in the View menu. All commands are available while you are working in Layout mode. Only these operations are not available while you are working in Draft or outline mode: Full page view Facing Pages view, and rulers.

Summary

This chapter was designed to be a road map of Ami Professional's features: what the features are and how you can use them to create your documents. Ami might seem complex at first, with endless choices, but hopefully this chapter has shown you how to wade through all the confusion to identify the features you really need. Maybe you recognized those features you need to use immediately, and you saw some that you would like to learn later. After all, the more choices you have, the more control you have over your documents.

Part 2
Using Ami Pro

3
CHAPTER

Managing files

An unwritten rule of personal computer software is that word processing programs are the easiest of all software types to use. After all, you have only one file to keep track of when you save a document, versus remembering several files for a database or spreadsheet program. That simplicity has disappeared, however, as word processing programs evolved into more than just text editors.

When you create a document in Ami Professional, that document is a combination of files—not just one. Some of these files are the text and graphics you created outside of Ami and now are merged with your document. Other files are created by Ami for its own use.

Why keep track of files?

Because Ami documents are the combined effort of several files, you must remember those filenames and paths. Why? Your hard disk space frequently becomes tight, requiring you to remove a document and its associated files; or what if you need to provide a disk copy of a document to a coworker? How do you know what files to include on the disk, other than the document file?

Once you become proficient using Ami, it's easy to continue creating documents without noticing all of the files that contribute to them and where you save them on your hard disk. When you need to remove or copy a document and its associated files, however, those details that didn't seem important become essential.

Every document is a group of files

Like many of its features, Ami's file management capabilities combine features of word processing and desktop publishing programs. Word processing programs save all of their document information in one file, and desktop publishing programs save one master file that points to its associated files. Ami Pro does both: it saves text, both originally created within Ami and imported text files, in the document file, but points to its style sheet and graphics files.

The document file

The document file, using an .SAM extension, contains text (either created originally in Ami or imported from a word processing, spreadsheet, or database program) and pointers to the following items: imported graphics files, drawings and charts created within Ami, and a style sheet file.

When you import a text, database, or spreadsheet file into Ami, the contents of that file are saved in the document file. Thus, you can change the text, spreadsheet, or database contents within the Ami document file without altering the original file you imported.

When you import a graphics file, Ami points to the file but does not save the graphic as part of the document. Ami remembers the filename and the path from which you imported it, so the graphic always appears as part of the file without requiring additional disk space. When you change the scaling of the graphic within Ami, the original graphics file remains unaltered.

Why does Ami point to only graphics files? Text, spreadsheet, and database files require much less disk space than most graphics files. If you have a graphic that you reuse frequently in several documents, you need only one copy of the file. If Ami saved the graphic as part of the document, you would have two copies of the graphic—the original file and the copy inside the document—and twice the space needed to store the graphics. Ami's uses chapter files so you can reuse outside text and graphics files in more than one document file. For example, if you have a company logo scanned into a TIFF file, you can import that file into all your company documents. You can reuse the file without proportionately increasing the disk space required. Another benefit is that your imported files do not need to be located in the same directory or the same drive.

Tip 3-1: Opening a document and moving to the cursor's last position If you save a document using the SAVEBOOK macro instead of File Save, Ami remembers the cursor's position in the document when you execute the macro. When you open a document using the OPENBOOK macro instead of File Open, Ami opens the document and places the cursor in its last position—the position it was in when you executed SAVEBOOK. These macros are handy for authors and writers of long documents. Even when you use bookmarks to move to a position in the document, you usually have to scroll or page through a bit to find your last place of editing. OPENBOOK and SAVEBOOK remember where you left off, so you can begin there without searching through the document.

To mark the cursor's position in the document, the SAVEBOOK macro creates two bookmarks—| and °—which you can see if you select the Bookmarks icon or the Edit Bookmarks command. If you see these bookmarks in your documents, do not delete them because the OPENBOOK and SAVEBOOK macros need them to locate the cursor's position in the document. Ami provides two custom icons to which you assign the OPENBOOK and SAVEBOOK icons. For more information on these icons, refer to chapter 13.

Displaying document statistics

Did you ever wish you could find out a document's file size or the date you created it without having to exit to DOS or the Windows File Manager? Have you longed to keep a document's authors, editors, style sheets, graphics, and other vital information easily in one place? Ami has a feature called Doc Info that keeps such vital statistics just a mouse click away. Using Doc Info, you can display the following characteristics of your current document:

- filename
- directory
- style sheet
- description
- imported graphics files
- page, word, character, and byte count
- date and time created
- date and time of last revision
- total number of revisions
- total editing time in minutes

Ami does not list any graphics files imported using the Copy Image option, because those files become part of the document just as imported text files do. Most of the information in the Doc Info dialog box is current, except for the page, word, character, and byte counts. To display the most current counts, select the Update button.

Tip 3-2: Updating Doc Info when you save a document   You know you should complete the Doc Info dialog box for all your documents, but you never get around to it, right? Now you can remind yourself to update the Doc Info before you save a document by using the SAVEINFO macro. It adds a new command to the File menu, called Save with Doc Info, which displays the Doc Info dialog, prompting you to enter the information. After you update the Doc Info and select OK, Ami saves the document. Ami Pro supplies a custom icon to which you can assign the SAVEINFO macro.

Tip 3-3: Using description vs keywords   The Doc Info dialog box has two fields that sound similar, but perform quite differently. The Description field lets you enter a description that Ami displays anytime you use the File Open or File Management commands. Keywords is a field that you can search using a macro. Keywords do not display anywhere but inside the Doc Info dialog box. Unless you plan to search for keywords using a macro, always use the Description field.

Tip 3-4: Searching for keywords among documents   If you ever wondered what the Keywords text box was for in the Doc Info dialog box, this is it. When you enter keywords for the document in that text box, you can use the KEYWORD macro to search the contents of the Keyword text box for multiple documents. Ami finds those documents using the keywords it lists in a dialog box.

Tip 3-5: Printing Doc Info with the document   You can print the statistics in the Doc Info dialog box as a title page when you print the document. When you display the Print dialog box, select the Options button. Select With doc description. Ami prints the title page to include the document information when it prints the document. Ami includes any user-defined document information, and prints the title page using the Courier font regardless of the font the document uses.

Defining your own Doc Info

Who wrote your employee benefits handbook? What print shop did the duplicating? Who was the contact? What type of paper and ink did the print shop use? Unfortunately, the names, places, and phone numbers of all the people involved in creating, duplicating, and shipping a publication are usually scattered throughout different file cabinets and are easily lost. Ami supplies standard document information that most people can use no matter what type of documents they create, but wouldn't it be handy if you could keep your own document information, specific to your letters and publications? Ami lets you define up to eight additional fields that you can display using the Doc Info command. These fields can hold any type of information about your document, but make sure the fields are meaningful to those who might update the document in the future.

To define your own Doc Info fields, follow these steps:

1. Select Doc Info from the File menu.

2. Select the Other Fields button.

3. Select the Rename button.

4. Enter a descriptive name, up to 31 characters, for each field you want to create. Select OK when you are done to return to the Doc Info Fields dialog box.

5. Enter the document information into each field you named. Select OK.

Ami saves the Doc Info fields and lets you reuse them for all of your documents. You must enter new document information for each document you want to track.

Inserting Doc Info into the document

Once you view a document's statistics in the Doc Info dialog box, it can be difficult to remember all of that information, but using the Doc Info command each time you need to find a phone number, service bureau, or contact name can be tedious. Ami lets you place any information you can view in the Doc Info dialog box into your document. You can do so using one of two methods: the Edit Insert Doc Info Field command, or power fields.

The Edit menu lets you insert any Doc Info field, including those you created, but updating that information requires you to use several different commands. Although most of the information is current, you must update the word, character, and byte counts, by selecting the Update button inside the Doc Info dialog box. It's not much of a timesaver though, because you're including the fields in the document to prevent using the Doc Info command. Also, to update the document description you must use the Edit Power Fields Update All command.

A better way to include doc into fields in your document is to use power fields. power fields cannot include any fields you created, but they can supply most of the information you see in the Doc Info dialog box. The advantage to using power fields is that you can update all the Doc Info fields with one command: Edit Power Fields Update All. The power fields that insert Doc Info fields are:

- Description
- EditDate
- FileSize
- NumChars
- NumEdits
- NumPages
- NumWords
- TotalEditingTime

To insert a Doc Info power field into your document, use these steps:

1. Select Power Fields from the Edit menu.
2. Select Insert.
3. Scroll through the Fields list box until you see the power field you want.
4. If you are inserting a date or time power field, select the formatting option from the Options list box.
5. Highlight the Power Field and select OK.

Ami inserts the Doc Info Power Field into your document. To update the fields with the latest statistics, select the Edit Power Fields Update All command.

Opening more than one document

Ami supports Windows' MDI (Multiple Document Interface), a technology that lets you open up to nine multiple documents. When you load several documents, Ami places each in its own window and cascades the windows on the screen. You can choose to tile, minimize, restore, or maximize the windows as you like using the same procedure you use in Windows. Each time you load Ami, an untitled document appears on the screen. Ami keeps the untitled document open until you close it.

To open more than one document, choose the File Open command, select the filename of the document you need, and select OK. Continue selecting File Open for each document you need. Use the Window menu to tile, cascade, and move among windows within Ami.

Tip 3-6: Use the filenames on the File menu to open a document   Ami lists the last three documents you opened at the bottom of the File menu. To open one of these documents, select the filename from the menu. Ami also lists any macros you edited on the File menu, so be sure to distinguish each file by its extension: .SAM for documents and .SMM for macros.

Tip 3-7: Increasing the filenames Ami displays on the File menu   Although Ami automatically displays the last three files you opened on the File menu, you can display up to five files, or none at all. To change the number of files Ami displays on the File menu, select User Setup from the Tools menu. In the Recent Files text box, type the number of files you want to display and select OK.

Tip 3-8: Opening a second document   Once you have one document displayed on the screen, you can display additional documents by selecting File Open and choosing the document you need. Ami reduces the size of the current window and places the second document in a window of the same size. Ami cascades the windows, placing the second in front of the first window. Ami places any additional documents you open into windows of the same size as the ones displayed on the screen.

Tip 3-9: Displaying the same document in two windows   You can display your document in two windows on the screen. Displaying the same document twice is useful for viewing two sections you cannot see at once. You only can edit one window though, because the other is display only indicated by "Read Only" displayed in that window's title bar. To display the same document in two windows, you can open the file twice using the File Open command, or you can select New Window from the Window menu.

Tip 3-10: Tiling documents horizontally   When you select the Tile command from the Window menu, Ami tiles all open documents vertically on the screen, so they are displayed next to each other. If you use Layout mode in each window, you cannot see an entire line of text extending from the left margin to the right margin. The TILEHORZ macro adds a Tile Horizontally command to the Window menu. When you select Tile Horizontally, Ami stacks the open documents on top of each other, making it easier to see an entire line of text in each document. Figure 3-1 shows documents after selecting Tile Horizontally from the Windows menu. Ami provides a custom icon to which you can assign the TILEHORZ macro. For more information on macros, refer to chapter 13.

Tip 3-11: Inserting one document into another You can use the File Open command to insert one document anywhere inside another document. To do so, open the first document using File Open. Place your cursor at the position in the document where you need to insert the second document. Select File Open again, select the filename, and select the Insert button. Do not select OK, because Ami will open the document in another window. After you select Insert, Ami places the second document inside the first at the cursor's position.

Tip 3-12: Opening multiple documents at once Normally you must choose File Open each time you need to open a document. However, Ami has a macro you can use to open up to nine documents at once. The macro name is MDI-OPEN, and when you select it, Ami displays a dialog box from which you select several documents to open. Refer to chapter 13 to learn more about macros.

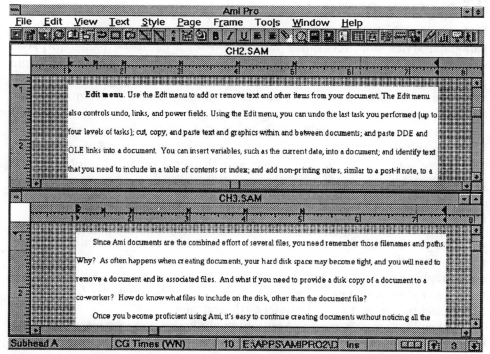

3-1 Two documents tiled horizontally by executing the TILEHORZ macro. Notice that Tile Horizontally is now a command on the Windows menu.

Tip 3-13: Closing all documents at once   If you have more than one document displayed on the screen, saving and closing each file becomes repetitive. You can automate that process by using a macro supplied with Ami that saves and closes all files at once. The macro name is CLOSEALL, and when you playback the macro, Ami saves all files and closes them without any prompts or messages. Be sure you want to save the changes in all the files before you use this macro.

Tip 3-14: Closing all documents and exiting Ami   The quickest way to close all your files and leave Ami at the same time is to minimize Ami and double-click on the Windows Control bar or to select Exit from the Program Manager's File menu. It closes all programs and exit Windows. If you have any files that haven't been saved, Ami prompts you to save them by selecting OK.

Tip 3-15: Creating workgroups from related files   Most word processing users work with the same files over and over again. They can be templates for new documents, or files that you simply cannot do without. The WORKGRUP macro lets you define a group of files you use together as a workgroup, or a group of files that you can open and edit simultaneously. You can build new workgroups and open workgroups using this macro. Once you playback the WORKGRUP macro, Ami adds a Workgroup command to the bottom of the View menu.

The style sheet file

Style sheets, which use an .STY extension, store formatting information. Just as paragraph styles store formatting information for a particular paragraph, style sheets contain a collection of paragraph styles. In addition, style sheets contain page settings, including margins and columns, tab settings, page size and orientation, lines around the page and between columns, header/footer margins and columns, and header/footer tab settings.

A document can use only one style sheet at a time. However, if you don't like the results of your original style sheet, you can use another. Refer to chapter 5 for more information on style sheets and chapter 7 for more information on paragraph styles.

Other files

Anytime you create a frame, chart, or drawing, Ami stores it in an internal graphics file using the same name as your document file, but a .G00 extension. With each graphic you create, Ami increases the extension number. So, if you had three internally-created graphics in a document called Newslet, the Ami graphics files would be Newslet.G00, Newslet.G01, and Newslet G02.

When you create a macro, Ami saves your keystrokes in a macro file using the filename you choose and a .SMM extension. You can edit macro files using Ami and write new macros using Ami's Macro Command Language (refer to the

Macro Command Language manual for more information on Ami's macro language).

Choosing the right directory

When you tell Ami to use a particular file, Ami automatically looks in a specific directory. How it knows where to look depends on the file you plan to use.

Selecting default paths

You can tell Ami to use a separate default path for documents, style sheets, macros, and backup files. Anytime you need to save, open, or otherwise use one of these files, Ami automatically looks in the directory you specified as the default path for that file type. To specify a default path, select User Setup from the Tools menu, and then press the Paths button. Enter a default path for each file type in the box provided. Once you have entered all the default paths you need, select OK until you return to the document. Ami saves your default path changes in the AMIPRO.INI file.

Tip 3-16: Put backup files and document files in separate directories   If you select the Auto Backup feature under Tools User Setup, Ami saves backup files of your documents. Ami saves the backup files under the same name as the document files, so be sure to specify a separate path for backup files. Otherwise, your backup files, which contain the previous version of your document file, overwrite your document files.

Tip 3-17: Temporarily exiting to DOS   If you ever needed to exit to DOS, you know that you had to minimize Ami Pro and then select DOS from the Windows Main program group. Now you can exit to DOS directly from Ami Pro using the DOS macro. Ami Pro exits to DOS; you can return to Ami Pro by typing "Exit." Your document remains in its original condition, so you can resume working on it as you did before you exited to DOS.

Default paths for imported text files

The first time you load an imported text file using the File Open command, you must tell Ami what directory in which to look for that file type. After you specify the directory for the file type, Ami continues to look there until you specify another directory. For more information on importing text files, refer to chapter 16.

Changing directories within Ami

Even though you can specify a default path for Ami to use, at times you will need to use a different one. If you need to import a text file from a floppy disk rather than using the application's default path, you need to tell Ami to look to the floppy drive. Whenever you need to save, load, or use a file, you can change the path that Ami searches by clicking on a series of directories and drives until Ami displays the correct path.

When you use Ami to view the contents of a directory, subdirectory names are enclosed in brackets, and the parent directory (the directory above the current directory) is displayed as two dots enclosed in brackets. Figure 3-2 displays the File Open dialog box viewing the contents of the E:\Apps\Amipro2\DOCS directory:

Let's say you need to import a text file a coworker created, but you're not sure where it is on the hard disk. You can select Open from the File menu, and then choose the drive to search from the Drives list box. Select the directory to search from the Directories list box. Continue to select directories or drives until the path you need is displayed.

The next time you open a file (or perform the same operation you did when you changed directories), Ami views the contents of the default path. Each time you need to view a path other than the default, you must repeat the process to change directories.

Protect the \STYLES directory

One of the directories Ami creates when you install the program is the \STYLES directory. This holds all the sample style sheets that come with Ami. You'll probably use Ami's style sheets quite frequently, because they provide a large number of templates for a variety of documents, and it is easier to modify an existing style sheet than to create a new one. However, be sure to save the existing style sheet under a new name and in a path other than \STYLES before you make any changes.

If you rename sample style sheets before you modify them, all the original style sheets are available to you under the \STYLES directory so you can reuse them. If, however, you accidentally change one of those style sheets, you can copy the original to the \STYLES directory from your Ami source disks.

Copying, moving, and backing up documents

Copying and moving documents is as much a part of the publishing process as creating documents. Coworkers need copies of your files, you might need to move a document and its associated files to another part of your hard disk, or you might need to remove some files to create space on your hard disk.

Previously, you probably used the DOS COPY command or the Windows' File Manager to copy and move your documents. When you need to move an Ami Professional document, however, these file transfer commands are not your best option, because they cannot tell you what associated files you need move in addition to your document file. If you copy or move a document file without the

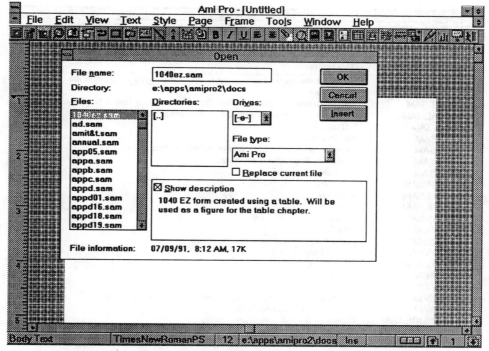

3-2 The File Open dialog box listing the Ami Pro document files in the E:\Apps\AmiPro2\DOCS subdirectory.

style sheet and imported files it uses, your document will be missing some vital pieces.

To copy, move, or backup documents to a floppy disk, use the File Management command on the File menu. From here you can copy, move, delete, and rename files, and change directories. Ami asks you whether you need to copy the associated style sheet and graphics along with the document file.

These are the steps you need to follow to copy a document and its associated files to a floppy disk:

1. Select File Management from the File menu. Ami displays the File Manager dialog box as displayed in Figure 3-3.

2. Use the scroll bars to display the document you need to copy. Click on that document.

3. Select Copy from the File menu. Ami displays the document you need to copy in the Copy box. Type the floppy drive you want to copy to in the To box, and select OK. Ami displays the File Options dialog box. Here you can choose to copy the graphics files and style sheet along with the document file.

```
┌──────────────────────────────────────────────────────────────────────────┐
│ ▓▓▓▓▓▓▓▓▓▓▓▓▓▓▓▓▓▓▓▓▓ Ami Pro File Manager ▓▓▓▓▓▓▓▓▓▓▓▓▓▓▓▓▓▓▓     │▼│▲│ │
├──────────────────────────────────────────────────────────────────────────┤
│  File   View   Help                                                        │
├──────────────────────────────────────────────────────────────────────────┤
│  Directory:   e:\apps\amipro2\docs                                         │
│                                                                            │
│  File/Directory:        Description:                                       │
│ ┌──────────────────────────────────────────────────────────────────────┐ │
│ │1040EZ.SAM     1040 EZ form created using a table.  Will be used as a figure for the table chapter│
│ │AD.SAM         Figure 10-3                                              │ │
│ │AMIT&T.SAM     Master Document for Inside Ami Pro: Professional Tips & Techniques.│
│ │ANNUAL.SAM     Annual report sample for building a document chapter.    │ │
│ │APP05.SAM      Default.sty                                              │ │
│ │APPA.SAM       Ami Pro marks                                            │ │
│ │APPB.SAM       Resources for products listed in Inside Ami Pro          │ │
│ │APPC.SAM       Using Ami Pro without a mouse.                           │ │
│ │APPD.SAM       Style sheet appendix                                     │ │
│ │APPD01.SAM     Basic.sty                                                │ │
│ │APPD16.SAM     Index.sty                                                │ │
│ │APPD18.SAM     label.sty                                                │ │
│ │APPD19.SAM     appd19                                                   │ │
│ │APPD21.SAM     letter3                                                  │ │
│ │APPD22.SAM     Letter4.sty                                              │ │
│ │APPD29.SAM     Newslt1.sty                                              │ │
│ │APPD32.SAM     Newslt4.sty                                              │ │
│ │APPD34.SAM     Outlin1.sty                                              │ │
│ │APPD37.SAM     Outline.sty                                              │ │
│ │APPE.SAM       List of all icons, including equations, drawing, and charting│
│ │APPF.SAM       Glossary for Inside Ami Pro                              │ │
│ │BROCHURE.SAM   Figure 10-5                                              │ │
│ │BULLETG.SAM    Graphic bullets                                          │ │
│ │BUSCARD.SAM    Figure 10-7                                              │ │
│ └──────────────────────────────────────────────────────────────────────┘ │
└──────────────────────────────────────────────────────────────────────────┘
```

3-3   The Ami Pro File Manager dialog box displays all Ami Pro documents and macros in the default document directory.

4. Select the Take Associated Graphics Files and Take Associated Style Sheet options and select OK. Ami will copy all the necessary files to make your document complete.

If you create backups of your documents by copying them to a floppy disk, be careful when you are ready to copy them back to a computer. The documents should be placed in a directory with the same name as the one in which they were created. Why? Ami points to imported graphics files, remembering their filenames and paths. If the files are no longer in that particular path, Ami will not be able to find those files. So if you created a brochure in a directory named C:\AMIPRO\BRO on your computer, your coworkers will need to create the same directory on their computers when they copy your backup files to their PC.

Comparing two versions of a document

Ami's new Document Compare feature lets you compare and contrast two documents. Ami reads both documents and displays any differences between them in the current document. Document Compare is useful when two or more people contribute to the same document, if someone else edits your document on-line, or if you have two versions of the same document but you can't remember how they differ.

Document Compare is similar to another new Ami feature called Revision Marking. They differ is that Revision Marking marks any changes in the current document as you make them. When you are ready to save the document, Ami lets you review, save, or cancel the changes you made. Revision Marking also marks any inserted or deleted pictures or tables, while Document Compare does not. Refer to chapter 4 for more information on Revision Marking.

Before you can tell Ami the documents to compare, you must specify how to display any text insertions and deletions. You need to distinguish these text changes so they stand out from the unchanged text. To do so, select Revision Marking from the Tools menu. Select the Options button and Ami will display the Revision Markings Options dialog box, as shown in Figure 3-4. The choices you make in this box affect both Document Compare and Revision Marking. The following paragraphs discuss tips for using the Revision Marking Options dialog box.

Mark Insertions As Select an appearance for text inserted into the document. Select from Bold, Italic, Underline, or Double Underline. Ami also provides No

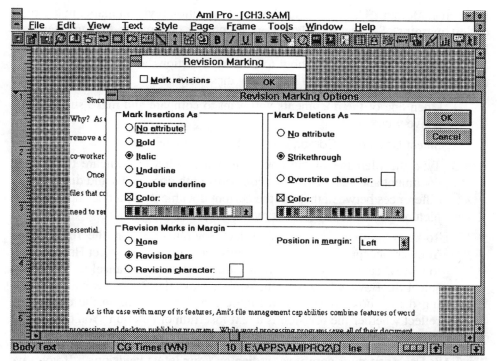

3-4 Choices you make in the Revision Marking Options dialog box affect both the Revision Marking and Document Compare.

Attribute as a choice, but if you select this option you cannot distinguish inserted text from unchanged text. You also can select from 120 colors to use for any text or pictures inserted into the document. If you do not see the color you need after selecting the down arrow, double-click on the closest color and create your own custom color.

Mark Deletions As   Select an appearance for text deleted from the document. Select from Strikethrough and Overstrike. If you select Overstrike, type the character in the text box that you wish to appear above the text. You can use any keyboard or ANSI character. Ami also provides No Attribute as a choice, but if you select this option you cannot distinguish deleted text from unchanged text. Again, you can choose from 120 colors for any text or pictures inserted into the document. If you do not see the color you need after selecting the down arrow, you can double-click on the closest color and then create a custom color.

Revision Marks in Margins   If other people frequently review your document, revision marks guide them to the places in the document that have changed. You can select None, Revision Bars (displaying a vertical line in the margin next to any lines that have changed), or specify a unique character to appear in the margin. To do so, type the character in the Revision Character text box. You can use any keyboard or ANSI character.

Position in Margin   Use Position in Margin to position revision marks in the right or left margins. Select Left, Right, or Rt/Left for documents that use separate layouts for right and left pages.

Once you have specified how to display insertions and deletions, you can compare two documents. To do so, follow these steps:

1. Open one of the documents you want to compare and make sure it is the active window.

2. Select Document Compare from the Tools menu.

3. Type the filename of the document with which to compare the current document and click OK. Ami compares both documents and displays any differences between them in the current document. Ami does not compare pictures or tables using Document Compare.

4. To keep the marked revisions, select Rev Marking from the Tools menu. You can accept or cancel all the revisions, or you can select Review Rev. to review each revision before deciding to accept or cancel it. When you select the Review Rev. button, Ami displays the Review Revision Marking dialog box, as shown in Figure 3-5. The options in the dialog box reflect whether the revision is a text insertion or deletion. You can choose to accept, cancel, or skip this revision and move to the next.

Tip 3-18: Use document compare to display your latest revisions   If you save your document frequently as you write, you can use Document Compare to dis-

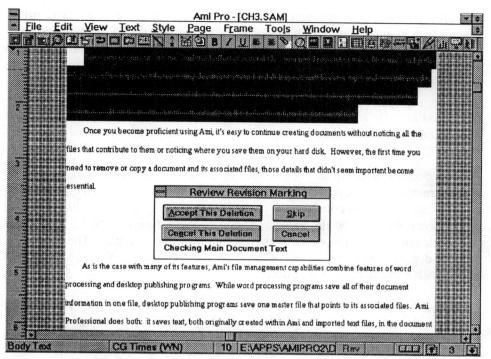

3-5 The Review Revision Marking dialog box lets you accept, cancel, or skip changes to a document individually.

play the editing changes you made since the last time you saved the document. Simply choose Document Compare from the Tools menu and specify the filename of the document in the active window. Ami marks any changes between the file on disk and the file on the screen. To return any new text to its normal appearance in the document, select Revision Marking from the Tools menu and choose Accept Revisions.

Questions and Answers

Q: I am using File Open to load my documents, but when I try to open more than one, Ami closes the current document before it opens the next. Why can't I open multiple documents?

A: Make sure you do not have the Replace Current File check box selected in the File Open dialog box. If you do, Ami will not open more than one file. It always closes the current file before opening another.

Q: I am using File Management to copy files to a floppy disk, but Ami gave me a message stating "Too many files selected." How many files can I select using File Management?

A: Ami can accept 160 characters, including spaces, in the text box you use to specify filenames. Because each filename and extension contain up to eleven characters (twelve characters including the period between the name and the extension), you can specify an average of thirteen files at a time. You can specify more or less, depending on the length of your filenames.

Q: I tried to copy some of my documents using the Copy *command in the File Management dialog box, but Ami gave me a "Too many files selected message." Is there a limit on how many files I can copy or move?*

A: Ami doesn't limit the number of files you can work with, but it can read only 160 characters in the Copy or Move text box inside the File Management dialog box. Because each file consists of a maximum of twelve characters, including the dot between the file and the extension, and because Ami counts the spaces between filenames, you can work with a minimum of twelve files. The maximum number depends upon the length of the filenames. Generally, you can work with about twelve to fifteen files at a time.

Q: I used Document Compare *to check two versions of the same file. Now that Ami has marked the changes, I want to remove the markings from my file.*

A: Once Ami identifies the changes in the active document, the only way to remove the markings is to select Revision Marking from the Tools menu. You then can review, accept, or cancel all the changes. Once you tell Ami what action to take on the changes, it removes the markings, and possibly the text, if you choose Cancel.

Q: My document directory has .G00 files that I don't remember creating. What are .G00 files and can I remove them from my hard disk?

A: Ami creates .G00 files to increase its display of imported graphics, drawings, and charts on the screen. Each time you display a page containing a graphic, Ami must redraw it on the screen. You can speed up your document's display by letting Ami store files containing the screen display of each graphic. The next time you move to a page with a graphic, Ami pulls the display from the file rather than recreating it in memory.

You should not delete the files from your hard disk. Instead, you can tell Ami to delete them by selecting User Setup from the Tools menu. Select the Options button and select Conserve Disk Space under Graphic display speed options. The other options available are Save for Fast Display, which creates the files and keeps them on your hard disk, and Save while Open, which creates the files and then deletes them when you close the document.

Q: I've noticed a large number of .TMP files in my root directory, but they usually have a size of zero. What are .TMP files and can I delete them?

A: Anytime your PC locks up or encounters an Unrecoverable Application Error, Ami creates .TMP files on the hard disk. Ami does not need these files the next time it loads, so you can delete them.

Q: I was editing my document and Ami displayed the "Out of memory for this document" message. I selected OK, but the message kept appearing and I was forced to restart my PC, losing my most recent changes. How much memory does Ami need for a document, and how can I get out of that message?

A: Ami does not have a limited amount of memory for each document. It uses the memory available on your PC. However, don't rely on the free memory message Ami displays when you select the About Ami Pro command from the Help menu. Ami includes available disk space in that figure, so you might not have any memory left even if Ami says you do.

When you receive the "Out of memory" message, continue clicking on the OK button, even if it takes twenty or thirty tries. Eventually, Ami will return to your document and you can save your changes. Try to free up some RAM by reducing your disk cache size and removing any TSR's from memory.

Q: I created a new document based on an original document that was saved with a password. I loaded the original document and selected Save As from the File menu. When I loaded the new document, however, it didn't ask me for a password. Why not?

A: Anytime you create a new document using Save As, you need to turn on the Password protect option. Even if the original document used a password, Ami does not carry over the password to the new document.

Q: When I open a file, Ami display "Read Only" in the title bar. I can't make changes to the document, but I can view it. What causes that message?

A: If you work on a netwok, someone else has opened the document and is using it. Ami does let two people open a document, but only one can make changes in it, thereby protecting the document's integrity. If you don't work on a network, you must have opened two copies of the file. Minimize the document and check the Ami window for another copy of the document.

Q: Can I select a default path for my style sheets?

A: Yes. Ami creates its own directory for style sheets during install, which is normally \AMIPRO\STYLES. You can change that default path by selecting User Setup from the Tools menu and selecting the Paths button. If you move a style sheet to a directory other than the default, Ami will not be able to find the style sheet.

Summary

Managing files in Ami Pro is not as difficult as you might imagine, because Ami provides many tools to make the job easier. Each document is a group of files, including the document file, the style sheet file, and any graphics files, and Ami helps you keep track of these files using the File Management command. You can display statistics about your document and create a document history using the Doc Info command on the File menu. You should always rename a style sheet before modifying it, and place all style sheets in the same directory. Otherwise, you won't be able to load the style sheet you need using the File New or Use Another Style Sheet commands. Ami also provides tools to let you mark changes to a document: Document Compare is for comparing two versions of the same document, while Revision Marking is for marking changes to the current document as you create them. All these tools help you manage your documents efficiently.

4
CHAPTER

Creating and editing text

Ami excels at handling both text and graphics, but creating text is usually the first step in creating any document. Before we look at graphics, let's look at how you can create your text with a minimum investment of time and effort.

Choosing from three display modes

Ami can display your document with varying degrees of detail, from true WYSIWYG to plain text and no pagination. Each mode is appropriate for various stages of editing. When you enter large amounts of text, you want a fast display that lets you work quickly. When you edit a long document, you need a display that lets you collapse and expand sections of your document to see section headings and move sections easily. When you import graphics or create charts or drawings, you need a true WYSIWYG display. Ami lets you choose the display that is appropriate for your needs. Ami three display modes are: Layout mode, Draft mode, and Outline mode.

Layout mode

Layout mode displays everything you will see on your printed page and more, including:

- columns and column guides
- margins displayed in color
- graphics

- marks for bookmarks, notes, tab rulers, headers/footers, and table of contents and index entries
- horizontal and vertical rulers
- a status bar
- tables
- page numbers
- separate pages

Use Layout mode to view the appearance of your final printed pages and to create and precisely place frames and graphics.

Tip 4-1: Displaying horizontal and vertical rulers in Layout mode   If you use Layout mode, you can display a horizontal and a vertical ruler on the screen. The vertical ruler appears at the left side of the screen and is useful for placing frames, graphics, drawings, and equations on the page. To display the vertical ruler, select View Preferences from the View menu. Select the Vertical ruler check box and select OK. Figure 4-1 displays the Ami Pro screen with horizontal and vertical rulers displayed.

The horizontal ruler appears at the top of the document window. You can modify the current page layout using the horizontal ruler by specifying tab settings, margins, and indentions. You also can define the number of columns for the page layout. To modify the page layout, display the ruler by selecting Show Ruler from the View menu. Click the mouse on the upper portion of the ruler and Ami displays the tab bar.

To modify tab settings, select the tab type you want to create from the tab icons at the bottom left of the ruler. Click on the position in the ruler at which you want to create a new tab setting. To remove a tab setting, drag it off of the ruler. The new tab settings affect the current paragraph only.

To redefine margins, move the margin markers to their new positions. The left margin marker is a vertical bar, and the right margin marker is a triangle. The margin change affects the current paragraph only.

To change alignment, move the alignment markers to the new alignment position. The ruler has two alignment markers: one triangle on top and another on the bottom. To create a first line indent, move only the top marker. To create a hanging indent, move only the bottom marker. To create an indent for the entire paragraph, move both of the markers. The alignment change affects the current paragraph only.

To modify the number of columns in the page layout, enter a new number of columns in the Cols text box.

To change the unit of measurement displayed on the ruler, select the Inches button. Ami cycles through inches, centimeters, picas, and points as the unit of measurement for the ruler.

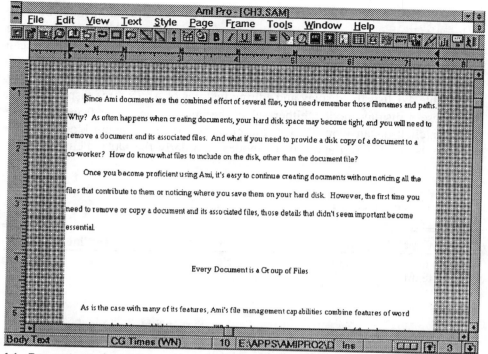

4-1 Turn on the Horizontal Ruler using the Show Ruler command on the View menu. Turn on the Vertical Ruler using the View Preferences dialog box.

Draft mode

Draft mode has evolved into a more accurate WYSIWYG (what you see is what you get) display in Ami Pro 2.0. Draft mode can display fonts, graphics, tables, marks, tab rulers, line spacing and indentions. Draft mode does not display columns, pagination, rulers, or page numbers. In Draft mode you see only one endless page. Ami works more quickly in Draft mode, because the screen does not need to create the details you see in a true WYSIWYG display. Use Draft mode to enter large amounts of text or when you don't need to see your document's final appearance.

Outline mode

Outline mode is a powerful long document management feature new to Ami Pro 2.0. Outline mode lets you display any document in an outline format that can expand and collapse entire sections underneath outline headings. Outline mode is excellent for viewing headings of the same hierarchy, for editing one section of a long document without being distracted by other text and graphics, and for moving and changing the hierarchy of large text sections. Outline mode is similar to

Draft mode in display, but you can see more of your text in Outline mode because it doesn't display line or paragraph spacing or indentions. All text uses single spacing and each level uses greater indentions than the previous level. You can create drawings and tables from Outline mode, but you cannot create frames by themselves.

Table 4-1 lists the display and editing features of Ami's three display modes. To choose a display mode, either select the appropriate mode from the View menu or click on an icon. When you click on the Draft/Layout Mode icon, it switches between Draft and Layout modes; similarly the Outline/Layout Mode

Table 4-1. Ami's Display Modes and Their Features

Display Capability	Layout Mode	Draft Mode	Outline Mode
Collapse and Expand Text Under Headings	No	No	Yes
Columns	Yes	No	No
Fonts	Yes	Yes. System font also available.	Yes. System font also available.
Frames	Yes. Fully editable. Can cut/copy/paste frames and contents.	No.	No.
Graphics/Charts	Yes. Full editable. Can cut/copy/paste frames and contents.	Yes.	Yes. Create by selecting command from Tools.
Horizontal and Vertical Rulers	Yes	No	No
Icons	Yes	Yes	Yes
Indentions	Yes	Yes	No
Line and Paragraph Spacing	Yes	Yes	No
Margins	Yes	No	No
Marks	Yes	Yes	Yes
Notes	Yes	Yes	Yes
Outline Buttons	No	No	Yes
Page Numbers	Yes	No	No
Pagination	Yes	No	No
Tables	Yes. Fully editable.	Yes. Fully editable.	Yes. Fully editable.
Tabs and Returns	Yes	Yes	Yes

icon switches between Outline and Layout modes. Ami does not have an icon to change from Draft to Outline mode. You can do so using the View menu or by creating a custom icon. Refer to chapter 13 for more information on creating custom icons.

Tip 4-2: Viewing an entire line of text in a smaller window If you work with multiple documents, you probably have several smaller windows open at the same time. If you use Layout mode in the windows, you can see only a portion of your text: an entire line from left to right margin isn't visible. However, you can use Draft or Outline mode to see your lines from left to right margin. Ami wraps the text according to the size of the window. The display isn't WYSIWYG, but it is readable.

Tip 4-3: Selecting a Default mode Ami automatically uses Layout mode each time you begin the program. If you create your documents using another mode and would like Ami to use it automatically, you can specify that mode as the default. Select User Setup from the Tools menu. Select the Load button. Select the mode you need from the Mode box. The next time you load Ami, it automatically uses the mode you chose.

What a view!

Not only does Ami let you choose what display mode to use, but you also can decide how much of your page you want to display on the screen. Ami has five views that display various portions of your page, from two facing pages to an enlarged section of one page. Ami's five views are: full page, working, standard, enlarged, and facing pages.

Full-page view

Full-page view displays an entire page on the screen. Whether or not you can read the text in a full-page view depends upon your monitor and graphics card. Full-page view is available only while you use Layout mode.

Working view

Working view displays a larger view of your page, showing an entire line of text across the screen. Working view probably is the one you will use the most, because you edit text and place frames and graphics on the page. You can enlarge or shrink the amount of the page you see in Working view by selecting View Preferences from the View menu. Specify the percentage of the page you need to see in the Working View Level box and click OK. You can specify a value from 10 to 400. How those values affect your display depends upon your monitor and graphics card. Ami uses 91% as the default Working View Level.

Standard view

Standard view is the standard that all Windows applications use. You will see less of your page in Standard view than you will in Working view.

Enlarged view

Enlarged view zooms in on a small portion of the page, so you can place frames and graphics precisely or edit text using a small font. Enlarged view is useful also when you create and edit equations. Equations use a smaller point size, and you can modify any portion of the equation easily when you use Enlarged View.

Facing pages view

Facing Pages view displays two facing pages (a left and a right page) as they will appear when printed. Facing Pages view is the only view in which you can neither edit your document nor select a command from Ami's menus or icon bar. You can only select Cancel from the Facing Pages dialog box. Facing Pages view is available only while you use Layout mode.

Selecting view preferences

No matter what view you select, Ami lets you choose from an assortment of elements that you can display on the screen. These include rulers, graphics, tabs, paragraph returns, and more. To specify what screen elements you want to display, select View Preferences from the View menu. Ami displays the View Preferences dialog box, as shown in Figure 4-2.

Column guides   Select Column guides to display a dotted border around column areas while you are using Layout mode. Column guides let you determine how many columns a page layout uses and the size of each column.

Margins in color   Select Margins in color to make page margins visible on the screen. Ami displays margins in color if you have a color monitor, or using a fill pattern if you have a monochrome monitor.

Pictures   Select Pictures to display any drawings, imported graphics, and equations in all three display modes. If you turn off the Pictures option, Ami displays an X in the frame. If the frame contains an imported graphic, Ami also displays the graphic's filename. Turning off pictures makes Ami perform more quickly, so if your PC is suffering from slow performance, turn off pictures to increase Ami's speed.

Tabs & returns   Select Tabs & returns to display tab and paragraph return markers in all three display modes.

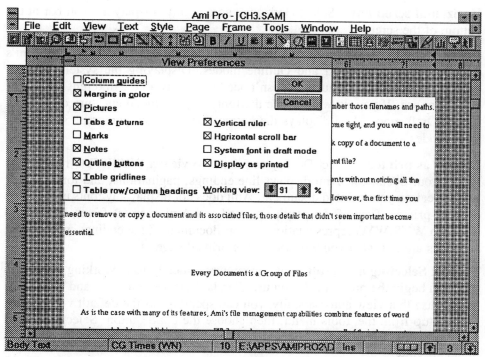

4-2 View Preferences puts many of your screen display choices at your fingertips.

Marks Select Marks to display markers for column and page breaks, inserted tab rulers, new page layouts, and floating headers and footers. Ami displays markers in all three display modes.

Outline buttons Select Outline buttons to display markers next to outline headings and text. Ami displays a plus sign for outline headings containing subordinate text and a minus sign for outline headings with no subordinate text. Ami displays a square next to subordinate text.

Table gridlines Select table gridlines to display borders around cells in a table. Table gridlines are display-only and do not print.

Table row/column headings Select Table row/column headings to display column letters and row numbers to identify each cell. The headings appear only when the cursor is inside a table cell and are display-only; they do not print.

Vertical ruler Select Vertical ruler to display a ruler along the left side of the document window. The default unit of measurement for the ruler is inches, but you can change it by modifying the unit of measurement for the horizontal ruler. Both rulers use the unit of measurement.

Horizontal scroll bar   Select Horizontal scroll bar to display a scroll bar at the bottom of the screen.

System font in Draft mode   Select System font in Draft mode to use Ami's default font in both Draft and Outline modes. Displaying the system font increases Ami's speed, because it doesn't need to display all the different fonts your document use. If you do want to see the fonts in your document, turn off System font in Draft mode. Ami displays the correct font for each paragraph style in all three modes.

Display as printed   Select Display as printed to view a WYSIWYG representation of your document. Ami displays line endings, paginations, and fonts as they will appear on your printed document. Ami does not display any fonts unavailable on your printer. Turn off Display as printed and Ami operates faster, but you do not see a WYSIWYG representation of your document. Line endings, pagination, and fonts are not what you will see on the printed page.

Tip 4-4: Selecting a Default view   Ami automatically uses Working view each time you begin the program. If you use Standard view extensively and would like Ami to use that view automatically, you can specify it as the default view. Select User Setup from the Tools menu, then choose the Load button. Select Standard view from the View box. The next time you load Ami, it automatically uses Standard view.

Tip 4-5: Using the Status Bar   No matter what view you choose, Ami always displays the Status Bar at the bottom of the screen. The Status Bar displays the current style, font, point size, default document directory, editing mode, and page number, if you are using Layout mode. The Status Bar also provides many shortcuts for performing tasks that would otherwise require a menu or an icon.

- Select a style by clicking on the style name and choosing a style from the list.
- Select a new font by clicking on the font name and choosing a font from the list.
- Select a different point size by clicking on the current point size and choosing a new point size from the list.
- Click on the default document directory to display the current date and time. Click again to display the current line and column numbers.
- Click on the word Ins to change to Typeover mode. Click again to turn on Revision Marking.
- Click on the small icons to toggle between showing and hiding the icon palette.
- Click on the up or down arrows to move up or down an entire page in the document.

Tip 4-6: Working view Level and SuperVGA If you use a SuperVGA graphics card, you can specify a higher Working view level to see more of your page. Because SuperVGA can fit more text and graphics on the screen, Ami's default of 91% might be too small to read text easily. Make sure you are using a SuperVGA driver by running Windows Setup from the Desktop, not from DOS. If you are using a SuperVGA driver, you can increase your Working View Level in Ami to a value of approximately 125% and still see a full line across the page.

Tip 4-7: Adding a Custom view to the View menu The CUSTVIEW macro lets you add another view to the View menu. This macro is useful if you use a custom page size, you work frequently with landscape pages, or if you switch between Working view's level of 91% and another percentage.

Once you run CUSTVIEW, Ami displays the Custom view dialog box, as shown in Figure 4-3. You can specify another view level for both Working view and the new Custom view. After you enter the new view levels and select OK, Ami adds two new menu items to the View menu: Custom and Custom View. The Custom menu item displays its view level percentage on the menu, and when you select it Ami changes to that view. The Custom View menu item displays the Custom View dialog box, letting you adjust the view levels for Working and Custom views.

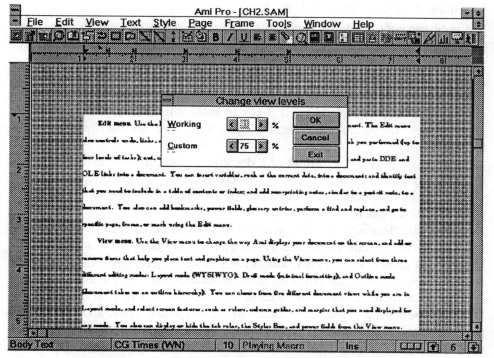

4-3 The Change View Levels dialog box, as displayed by the CUSTVIEW macro.

The Custom view you add is active only for your current work session. The next time you load Ami, the Custom and Custom View menu items do not appear on the View menu. You can specify CUSTVIEW as an AutoRun macro, so the Custom views are a permanent part of your menus. See chapter 13 for more information on the AutoRun option.

Creating a document's contents

You have four ways in which you can create text and graphics in a document: import them from another application, paste them from another application or from another document, load a style sheet with contents, or create them yourself in Ami.

Each method has its advantages over the others. The easiest method is to create original text and graphics using Ami's own word processing and graphics features. If you have a large collection of documents from another word processor, however, you don't want to recreate what you already have. If the external application is a Windows application, you can paste the text or graphic into Ami. Lastly, once you begin creating documents in Ami, you can save the ones you use repeatedly by saving a style sheet with its contents.

Creating text and graphics in Ami

Not only can you create text within Ami, you also can produce drawings and charts: you never need use an external drawing or charting application. Ami provides a rich assortment of word processing features that help you write eloquently, correctly, and in an organized manner. You can use Outline mode to begin with an outline of your document and build from the outline. Once you have a good amount of text, you can use spell check to make sure you haven't missed any glaring typos. If you can't find the word you want, you can use Ami's thesaurus for suggestions.

Once you have a rough draft of a document, you can use Find and Replace to make any global changes. You can insert notes to yourself or to others who will be editing the document, and you can mark changes using Revision Marking or Document Compare.

To create drawings in Ami, you can use the Drawing feature that lets you create lines, boxes, circles, arcs, polygons, and other shapes. You can modify the shapes, add colors, fill patterns, and arrows to the objects. You also can group and align objects on a grid. To learn more about drawing, refer to chapter 18.

You can create a chart from a table or other numbers in your document, or from an external file. You can choose from many chart types, and modify any part of the chart using the drawing feature. To learn more about Charting, refer to chapter 19.

Importing text and graphics from an external application

If you switched to Ami from another word processor, you probably have many files that you use regularly. Instead of recreating those files in Ami, you can import them. You can import both text and graphics created outside of Ami, as long as the files are in a format that Ami recognizes. To learn more about importing text files, refer to chapter 16. To learn more about importing graphics files, refer to chapter 17.

Pasting text and graphics from windows applications

You can copy text and graphics from another Ami document or from another application, then paste the contents of the Clipboard into the current document. The Clipboard is a common storage area for transferring text or graphics between Windows applications. You can cut a spreadsheet range from 1-2-3 for Windows and paste it into an Ami document. The opposite is also true: you can cut text from an Ami document and paste it into a 1-2-3 for Windows spreadsheet. You also can transfer information from one Ami document to another, or within the same document.

Before you can transfer text or graphics, you must place them in the Clipboard. To do so, select the text or graphic you want to transfer and then select Edit Cut or Edit Copy. Ami places the text or graphic in the Clipboard. You can see the contents of the Clipboard by minimizing Ami and selecting the Clipboard from the Main program group. The Clipboard displays its contents. The clipboard can hold only the last text or graphic you cut or copied. The next time you cut or copy an item, it overwrites the current contents of the Clipboard.

Once the Clipboard contains the text or graphics you want to transfer, open the document in which you want to paste the data. Position the cursor at the place in the document where you want to insert the text or graphic, and select Edit Paste. Ami inserts the data at the cursor's position.

Pasting text and graphics from DOS applications

You can transfer text between a DOS application and Ami if you run the DOS application in a window. You can transfer graphics from a DOS application to Ami only if you are running Windows in 386-enhanced mode.

Pasting text from a DOS application

If you are running Windows in real or standard modes, you can paste only a full screen of text into Ami. You cannot select a block of text and copy it to the Clipboard. You can do so if you are running Windows in 386-enhanced mode.

To copy a full screen of text from a DOS application, follow these steps:

1. Start the application and display the text you want to copy.

2. Make sure the application is running in a window. If it is not, press Alt-Enter to display the DOS application in a window.

3. Press PrtScr. Windows should copy the full screen of text to the Clipboard. If the text is not in the Clipboard, try Alt-PrtScr or Shift-PrtScr instead.

4. Exit the application and return to Ami.

5. Open the document in Ami into which you want to paste the text.

6. Position the cursor at the place in the document where you want to paste the text.

7. Select Edit Paste. Ami inserts the text from the DOS application at the cursor's position.

To copy a block of text from a DOS application, follow these steps:

1. Start the application and display the text you want to copy.

2. Make sure the application is running in a window. If it is not, press Alt-Enter to display the DOS application in a window.

3. Drag the cursor over the text you want to copy.

4. Select Edit from the window's Control menu.

5. Select Copy.

6. Exit the application and return to Ami.

7. Open the document in Ami into which you want to paste the text.

8. Position the cursor at the place in the document where you want to paste the text.

9. Select Edit Paste. Ami inserts the text from the DOS application at the cursor's position.

To copy a graphic from a DOS application, follow these steps:

1. Start the application and display the graphic you want to copy.

2. Make sure the application is running in a window. If it is not, press Alt-Enter to display the DOS application in a window.

3. Press PrtSer. Windows should copy the graphic to the Clipboard. If the graphic is not in the Clipboard, try Alt-PrtScr or Shift-PrtScr instead.

4. Exit the application and return to Ami.

5. Open the document in Ami that you want to paste the graphic.

6. Position the cursor at the place in the document where you want to paste the graphic.

7. Select Edit Paste. Ami inserts the graphic from the DOS application at the cursor's position.

Linking and embedding text and graphics

You can use DDE or OLE to paste text and graphics created in an external Windows application into your Ami document. Using DDE or OLE to create a document's content is advantageous if the content changes in the external Windows application, because Ami updates the content in your document automatically. The disadvantage is that few applications support DDE and OLE.

DDE and OLE are essentially the same, because they both update text and graphics in your document as they change in the external Windows application. DDE and OLE have three major differences:

- DDE asks your permission to start the application from which you created the original text and graphics. If you answer no, Ami does not update the text and graphics in your document to reflect the changes you made in the Windows application.

- OLE starts the Windows application on its own, without your permission, and automatically updates the chart in your document.

- OLE can link or embed information into an Ami document: a link pastes data from a saved file, while an embed can paste data from an unsaved file. DDE can link data only from a saved file.

Whenever you link or embed data into Ami Pro, whether the data comes into Ami as a link or an embed depends upon the application from which you are taking the data. Ami Pro accepts the data in the highest format available. The hierarchy for data formats is OLE embed, OLE link, DDE link, and finally Paste.

For example, if you are taking information from an application that supports the OLE embed format, Ami Pro accepts the data in that format. If the application does not support OLE embeds or OLE links, however, Ami Pro accepts the data as a DDE link. When an application does not support OLE or DDE, Ami Pro accepts the data as a regular paste operation.

The general procedure for linking or embedding a chart or chart data to an Ami document is as follows:

1. Open the Windows application and create the text or graphic.
2. Copy the text or graphic to the Clipboard using Edit Copy.
3. Minimize the application and start Ami.
4. Open the document into which you need to link the text or graphics.
5. If you are linking a graphic, create a frame to hold the graphic.
6. Link or embed the text or graphic data using either Paste, Paste Link, or Paste Special. Select Paste to accept the data in the highest data format available from the external application. Select Paste Link to link the data using the highest link format available: either OLE or DDE link. Select Paste Special to accept the data using the format you specify.

You can choose from the following formats: picture, Bitmap and DIB, and Rich Text Format. Picture pastes the data using the Windows Metafile format. Use this format to paste graphics. Bitmap and DIB paste the data using the Windows Bitmap format. Use these formats to paste graphics. Rich Text Format pastes text keeping its format. Select Link to create a DDE link. Select ObjectLink to create an OLE link. Select Native to create an OLE embed. Select Link Options to create a link or change existing links.

Using Link Options

Ami automatically creates a hot DDE or OLE link, meaning that each time you open a document containing a link, Ami will attempt to update it. A warm link updates the information only when you tell it to. Updating a link can be a slow process, and if your document contains more than one, you might want to use warm links to control when they update. You can use Link Options to change a hot link to a warm link, and vice versa. You also can change the link or create an entirely new one, but doing so is cumbersome, because Ami requires you to type a lot of information when it's easier to use one of the other commands on the Edit menu. Copying and pasting links is much easier; however, if you don't have enough memory to run both applications concurrently, Link Options is an alternative.

Once you select Link Options, Ami displays the Link Options dialog box. It displays the links in the current document. Each line displays the link number, type, status, application name, path name, and item description for one link.

Update Select Update to update any outdated or warm links in your document.

Unlink Select Unlink to delete an old link from your document.

Deactivate Select Deactivate to convert a hot link to a warm link.

Change Link Select Change Link to choose an new application, path (topic), and item (chart or cell range) in a link.

Create Link Select Create Link to create a new link in the document. Ami displays the Create Link dialog box. Specify the application name, path (Topic), and description (chart or cell range).

Loading a style sheet with contents

A style sheet contains a collection of paragraph styles that format the text in a document. However, a style sheet also can contain text and graphics if you save a style sheet using the With contents option. When you select the Save as a Style Sheet command from the Style menu, Ami displays the Save as a Style sheet dialog box, as shown in Figure 4-4. If you select the With contents option, Ami saves any text or graphics in the current document as part of the style sheet.

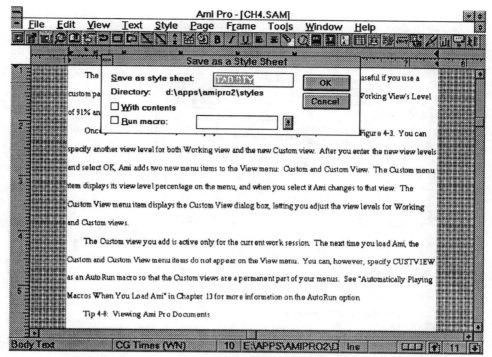

4-4 To save a style sheet's contents, you must choose the With contents check box on the Save as a Style Sheet dialog box.

The next time you choose that style sheet, you can decide whether to load the paragraph styles only, or load the style sheet's contents also. If you select a style sheet by choosing the Use Another Style Sheet command on the Style menu, you cannot load a style sheet with contents. You can do so only by selecting File New and selecting the With contents option from the dialog box. When you select the File New command, Ami displays the New dialog box as shown in Figure 4-5. Once you select a style sheet from the dialog box, you can select the With contents check box.

Deleting a document's contents

You can remove a document's text and graphics several ways. The method you choose depends on the contents you are deleting, how much you want to remove, and if you plan to reuse the contents later in the document.

- To delete text behind the cursor, press the Backspace key.
- To delete text in front of the cursor, press the Del key.
- To delete a block of text, highlight the text and press the Del key.

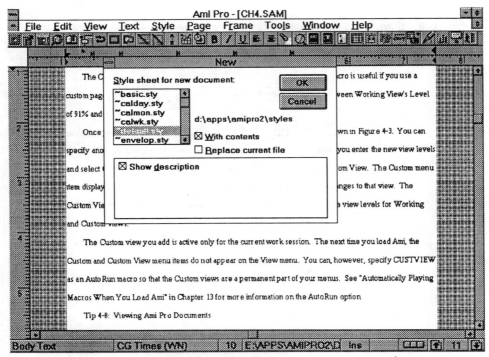

4-5 To load a style sheet's contents, select the With contents check box on the File New dialog box.

- To delete a block of text you plan to paste later, highlight the text and press the Shift-Del keys, or select the Edit Cut command.
- To overwrite a block of text, highlight the old text and begin typing the new text.
- To overwrite text character-by-character, press the Ins to change to Type-over mode and begin typing the new text.
- To delete a graphic, drawing, or equation, select the frame and press the Del key.

Tip 4-8: Moving a document's contents   The traditional method of moving text or graphics is to use the Edit Cut and Edit Paste commands. When you cut text or graphics to the Clipboard, however, Ami overwrites the current contents of the Clipboard. An easier method of moving a document's text is to use the Outline buttons displayed in Outline mode. Hide subordinate text underneath an outline heading. Then move the button next to the outline heading by dragging the button up or down to its new position in the outline. Ami moves the outline heading and all the subordinate text hidden underneath it. Outline mode is discussed in further detail later in this chapter.

Moving around in the document

Once your document is several pages long, you are ready to use Ami's cursor movement features. Ami lets you move to the next word, the next sentence, another page, or to the next item. Table 4-2 lists Ami's cursor movement shortcuts.

Tip 4-9: Moving to the next item   When you press Ctrl-G or select Go To from the Edit menu, Ami displays the Go To dialog box. You can choose to move to specific pages, but you also can move to the next item in the document. You can move to any of the following items using Go To:

- Bookmark
- Floating header/footer mark
- Footer
- Footnote mark
- Footnote text
- Frame
- Hard page break
- Header
- Layout change
- Next field
- Note
- Tab ruler
- Tab ruler mark.

Table 4-2.   Keyboard Cursor Movement Shortcuts

To move here:	Do this:
Previous word	Ctrl-Left Arrow
Next word	Ctrl-Right Arrow
Beginning of the line	Home
End of the line	End
Beginning of the sentence	Ctrl-Period
End of the sentence	Ctrl-Comma
Beginning of the paragraph	Ctrl-Up Arrow
End of the paragraph	Ctrl-Down Arrow
Beginning of the document	Ctrl-Home
End of the document	Ctrl-End
Previous screen	PgUp
Next screen	PgDn
Previous page	Ctrl-PgUp
Next page	Ctrl-PgDn

Once you move to that item and Ami closes the dialog box, you can press Ctrl-H to go to the next item of the same type in the document.

Tip 4-10: Moving to a specific bookmark Bookmarks are invisible points of reference you can use to move to a specific place, or highlight a section of your document quickly. You cannot see bookmarks, and you can create and remove them only by using the Edit menu. You can move to the next bookmark using the Go To command, or move to any bookmark in the document by using the Edit/ Bookmarks command or the Bookmark icon. Once Ami displays the Bookmarks dialog box, click on the bookmark you need and select Go To.

Tip 4-11: Creating a Bookmarks menu The MARKMENU macro creates a Bookmarks menu listing all the bookmarks in the current file. You can select a bookmark from that menu to move to that position in the document quickly. A typical Bookmark menu is shown in Figure 4-6. From the Bookmarks menu you also can add a new bookmark, update the menu to list new bookmarks, or remove the menu from the menu bar.

Adding special characters

You can add characters to your document that are not available on your keyboard by using the ANSI character set, displayed in Table 4-3. To create these characters, hold down the Alt key and type the appropriate numbers on your numeric keypad (not the top row of the keyboard), then release the Alt key. The character appears on your screen. Not all printers are capable of creating the ANSI characters; if your printer cannot print the character, it will substitute a mark such as a bullet instead.

Tip 4-12: Selecting ANSI characters from a menu Ami comes with a macro that lets you select ANSI without requiring you to remember their codes. The macro name is ANSI.SMM, and when you run it Ami displays the Chars menu that displays a dialog box from which you can choose ANSI characters. Figure 4-7 displays the ANSI Characters dialog box. You can choose from the following options:

OK Select OK to insert an ANSI character in the document and close the dialog box.

Insert Select Insert to add an ANSI character to the document and keep displaying the dialog box so you can choose additional characters.

Add to Menu Select Add to menu to display the ANSI character on the menu. You can insert the character in your document by displaying the menu and selecting the character.

Clear Menu Select Clear menu to delete all the characters from the Chars menu.

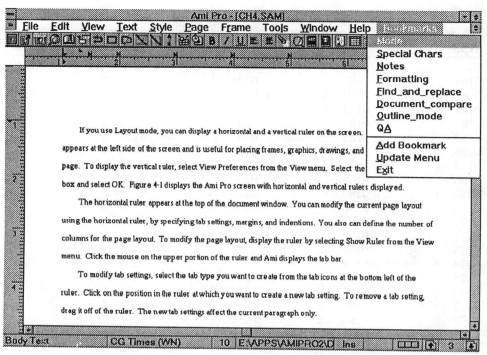

4-6 The Bookmarks menu, shown when you execute the MARKMENU macro, displays all the bookmarks in the current file.

Replace shaded   Select Replace shaded to replace highlighted text in the document with the ANSI character you selected. You also can choose to replace all other occurrences of the text you shaded with the ANSI character.

Shortcut Key   Select Shortcut Key to assign an ANSI character to a key combination.

Once you no longer need the menu displayed on the menu bar, select the menu and choose Exit.

Tip 4-13: Inserting the copyright symbol   The COPYRITE macro inserts the ANSI copyright symbol at the cursor's position in the document. If you create newsletters, books, or other material that needs to be copyrighted, you need to add the symbol to your documents, but you probably don't remember what ANSI code you use to generate the symbol. Next time, let the macro insert the copyright symbol for you. Ami includes a custom icon to which you assign the COPYRITE macro, so just click on the icon and the copyright symbol will appear in your document.

Tip 4-14: Inserting the registered trademark symbol   The REGMARK macro inserts the ANSI registered trademark symbol at the cursor's position in the document. If you create newsletters, books, or other materials that require a regis-

Table 4-3. ANSI character set

Type	Character	Type	Character	Type	Character	Type	Character	Type	Character
0160		0180	´	0200	È	0220	Ü	0240	ð
0161	¡	0181	µ	0201	É	0221	Ý	0241	ñ
0162	¢	0182	¶	0202	Ê	0222	Þ	0242	ò
0163	£	0183	·	0203	Ë	0223	ß	0243	ó
0164	¤	0184	¸	0204	Ì	0224	à	0244	ô
0165	¥	0185	¹	0205	Í	0225	á	0245	õ
0166	¦	0186	º	0206	Î	0226	â	0246	ö
0167	§	0187	»	0207	Ï	0227	ã	0247	÷
0168	¨	0188	¼	0208	Ð	0228	ä	0248	ø
0169	©	0189	½	0209	Ñ	0229	å	0249	ù
0170	ª	0190	¾	0210	Ò	0230	æ	0250	ú
0171	«	0191	¿	0211	Ó	0231	ç	0251	û
0172	¬	0192	À	0212	Ô	0232	è	0252	
0173	-	0193	Á	0213	Õ	0233	é	0253	ý
0174	®	0194	Â	0214	Ö	0234	ê	0254	þ
0175	¯	0195	Ã	0215	×	0235	ë	0255	ÿ
0176	°	0196	Ä	0216	Ø	0236	ì		
0177	±	0197	Å	0217	Ù	0237	í		
0178	²	0198	Æ	0218	Ú	0238	î		
0179	³	0199	Ç	0219	Û	0239	ï		

tered trademark, you need to add the symbol to your documents. Again, you might not remember what ANSI code you used to generate the symbol. Next time, let the macro insert the symbol for you. Ami includes a custom icon to which you assign the REGMARK macro, so all you have to do is click on the icon and the registered trademark symbol will appear in your document.

Tip 4-15: Inserting the trademark symbol   The TM macro inserts the ANSI trademark symbol at the cursor's position in the document. If you create newsletters, books, or other material that includes trademark material, you need to add the trademark symbol to your documents. Again, you might not remember what ANSI code you used to generate the symbol. Next time, let the macro insert the trademark symbol for you. Ami includes a custom icon to which you assign the TM macro, so all you need to do is click on the icon and the trademark symbol appears in your document.

Tip 4-16: Adding typographic ANSI characters   If you create manuals, books, newsletters, or other publications that use typographic characters such as em and en dashes, you can create those characters and more from the ANSI character set. These are codes and the characters they produce:

- 0145 open single quote
- 0146 closed single quote

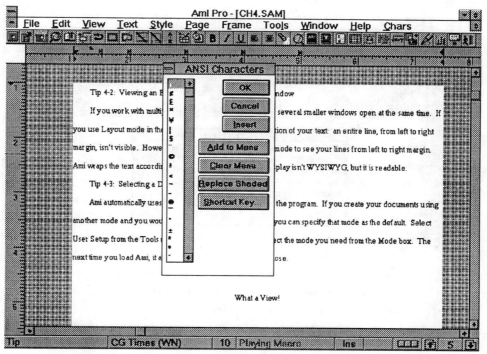

4-7 The ANSI Characters dialog box simplifies the task of inserting ANSI characters, because you don't need to remember their codes.

- 0147 open double quote
- 0148 closed double quote
- 0150 en dash
- 0151 em dash
- 0152 hyphen.

Tip 4-17: Inserting SMART quotes, dashes, and apostrophes If you need to use Smart quotes, dashes and apostrophes, use the SMARTYPE macro to convert them from regular format to the Smart format. Not all printers can print Smart typeset characters, so make sure your printer has that capability before running this macro. Ami displays the open and close quotes as vertical bars on the screen.

Adding notes

What did we ever do before those "Post-it" notes? They quickly became a staple in every office because they let us jot down to do lists, notes to coworkers, or even reminders to ourselves.

Ami has its own version of those "Post-it" notes that performs a similar function. Ami lets you create notes (displayed in Figure 4-8), that you can hide

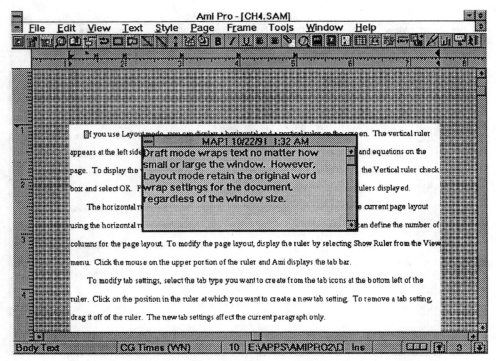

4-8 Note markers display only when you select Marks from the View Preferences dialog box.

and later redisplay. The notes are display-only, so that Ami does not print them with the rest of the document. Notes are useful if you have a question when you are editing a document, if you return to a section of a document and you forgot why you skipped it, or to explain how you created a document to the person responsible for updating it.

To create a note in your document, follow these steps:

1. Place the cursor at the position in the document where you want to create a note.

2. Select Insert from the Edit menu, and then select Note or click on the Note icon. Ami displays the Note dialog box displaying the current date and time.

3. Enter the text you need in the note.

4. Once you are ready to return to the document, click outside the note dialog box or select Close from the System menu to close it. Ami displays a note marker in your document.

Once you have created your note, you can redisplay the note dialog box by double-clicking on the note marker.

Tip 4-18: Adding your initials to and consecutively numbering note markers   You can distinguish your notes from those others have created by adding your initials or an identifying label to your note markers. Choose User Setup from the Tools menu, and type up to six characters in the Initials box. Select Display initials in tex to display the initials in the note marker. Now when you create a note, Ami displays your initials in the title bar of the note dialog box and before the number in the note marker. Ami also sequentially numbers note markers whenever you choose to display your initials in the note markers. Any notes you created previously are not affected.

Tip 4-19: Customizing the note's color   You can choose from 120 colors to display in the note dialog box and in the note marker. Choose User Setup from the Tools menu, and click on the color you need from the Note color list box. Initially the list box displays only 15 colors, but if you click on the down arrow button, Ami displays the full 120 colors. Once you select the color you need, click OK. Ami will display any notes you create in the color you chose. Any notes you created previously use the original note color.

Tip 4-20: Printing notes with the document   Normally Ami does not print the notes you create in the document. However, Ami does give you the option of printing the content of your notes when you print the document. When you display the Print dialog box, select the Options button. Select With notes. Ami prints the note markers, along with any numbers or initials displayed in the markers, at their locations in the document. Ami prints the notes' contents at the end of the document, similar to endnotes.

Tip 4-21: Deleting notes   You can delete a note by pressing Del, but you usually end up deleting text instead. Notes often cover up text on the screen, and when you press Del you delete the text, but not the note. A more exact method of deleting a note is to press Ctrl-G to display the GoTo dialog box. Select Note from the list box, and Ami will move the cursor to the next note in the document. Now you can press Del to remove the note without deleting any text. To remove all the notes in a document, double-click inside a note marker and select Remove All Notes from the System menu. Ami removes every note in the document, including those created by others.

Formatting words within paragraphs

Most text is formatted with style sheets, which contain a collection of paragraph styles that format all of the text in an entire paragraph. What if you need to emphasize a single character or word? Ami lets you format blocks of text smaller than a paragraph or irregular-sized blocks of text using the options in the Text menu, displayed in Figure 4-9.

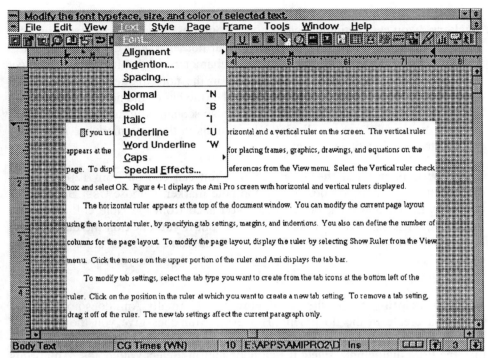

4-9 The Text menu lets you override any formatting specified in a paragraph style.

Using the Text menu

You can use the text attribute options in the Text menu to format a highlighted block of text. Any formatting you do with the Text menu overrides the formatting contained in the paragraph style. For example, if you use the Text menu to left-justify a block of text that is normally centered, the text remains left-justified until you select the Normal option from the Text menu. Even if you change the paragraph style's alignment to right-justified, the text you formatted with the Text menu remains left-justified.

Also, you can apply more than one attribute to a block of text. For example, if you need text to be both bold and italic, you can apply both attributes (or more, if needed).

If you choose the Caps option, Ami displays the Caps Options dialog box, listing four capitalization options: upper case, lower case, initial caps, and small caps.

Any text you modify using the Caps option uses that capitalization until you change it again using the Text menu. If you add new text to the block you changed, Ami converts the text to the capitalization you chose.

You can add text attributes at one of two points in your text creation process: as you type the text, or after you type the text.

Adding attributes as you type

To add text attributes as you type, select the text attribute you need from the Text menu. Type the text affected by the text attribute. Once you no longer need that text attribute, select the Normal option from the Text menu. All text you type from this point will reflect the formatting in the current paragraph style.

Adding attributes after you type

To add text attributes after you type your text, highlight the text you need to format. Table 4-4 lists the key combinations and mouse operations to select blocks of text. Select the text attribute you need from the Text menu. Ami formats only the text you selected, so you don't need to select Normal to specify when to stop using the text attribute.

Tip 4-22: Returning to the text's original display   If you apply a text attribute but you don't like the results, Ami has several ways you can return the text to its original display. If applying the text attribute was your last action, you can select Undo from the Edit menu or the icon bar. If you applied only one text attribute, or if you applied several but you want to turn off only one, you can highlight the text and select that attribute again from the Text menu. If you applied a font, alignment, indention, or spacing, highlight the text, select the attribute from the

Table 4-4.   Selecting Text Using the Keyboard or the Mouse

Use this tool:	To select this text:	Do this:
Keyboard	Previous word	Shift-Ctrl-Left Arrow
	Next word	Shift-Ctrl-Right Arrow
	Beginning of line	Shift-Home
	End of line	Shift-End
	Beginning of paragraph	Shift-Ctrl-Up Arrow
	End of paragraph	Shift-Ctrl-Down Arrow
	Previous sentence	Shift-Ctrl-, (comma)
	Next sentence	Shift-Ctrl-. (period)
	Beginning of document	Shift-Ctrl-Home
	End of document	Shift-Ctrl-End
	Previous screen	Shift-PgUp
	Next screen	Shift-PgDn
	Previous page	Shift-Ctrl-PgUp
	Next page	Shift-Ctrl-PgDn
Mouse	One word	Double-click
	Several words	Double-click and drag
	One sentence	Ctrl-click
	Several sentences	Ctrl-click and drag
	One paragraph	Ctrl-double-click
	Several paragraphs	Ctrl-double-click and drag

Text menu, and select the Revert to style option. If you want to turn off all the text attributes you applied to the text, highlight the text and select Normal.

Tip 4-23: Creating reverse text   Reverse text, white text on a black background, is useful for drawing attention to an area on a page. To create reverse text, select the Frame icon and draw a frame. Select Modify Frame Layout from the Frame menu. Select Square Corners as the frame's Display. Select the Lines & shadows attribute from the left side of the dialog box. Select Black for the Background color and select None for the Shadow. Double-click inside the frame. Select Font from the Text menu and select White as the font color. Type the text inside the frame, and Ami displays white text inside a black frame.

Tip 4-24: Creating a drop cap   The most effective way to create a drop cap in Ami is to draw a frame and include graphic text inside it. Because you can position graphic text freely inside a frame, you can place it against the top right edge of the frame, which you cannot do using normal text. To create a drop cap, select the Frame icon and draw a frame. Select Modify Frame Layout from the Frame menu. Select Wrap Around as the Text Flow Around option and Where Placed as the Placement option (In Line frames wrap only the first line of text around the frame. Subsequent lines appear below the frame). Select Square corners as the Display option. Select Size & position and select the Clear Margins button. Select Lines & Shadows and eliminate any lines and shadows around the frame. Select Drawing from the Tools menu and select the Text tool. Click inside the frame and type the letter you need to appear as a drop cap. Modify the graphic text's font and point size using the Text menu or the status bar. Choose the Selection Arrow from the Draw icon bar and position the text inside the frame.

Tip 4-25: Rotating text   Ami doesn't have a way of rotating normal text in a document. You can rotate any graphic text you create inside a frame, however. Refer to chapter 18 for more information about rotating text.

Tip 4-26: Changing the point size of selected text   Two of Ami's simplest macros are the FONTDN and FONTUP macros. They change the point size of any text you have selected by two points. The FONTDN reduces the text size by two points, while FONTUP increases the text size by two points. Ami supplies custom icons for both of these macros.

Finding and replacing text and styles

Most word processors limit Find and Replace to text and attributes only, and desktop publishing programs rarely offer any Find and Replace capability at all. Ami provides a full-featured Find and Replace that can search for text, attributes, and styles. Searching for styles lets you quickly scan all your major headings or globally change paragraphs using one style to another.

Performing a Find and Replace operation

After you select Find & Replace from the Edit menu, Ami displays the Find & Replace dialog box as displayed in Figure 4-10. The following paragraphs list guidelines for specifying the text or style you need to find and replace.

Find text box In the Find text box, type the text you want to search for. If you are searching for a style, type the style name exactly as it appears in the Styles Box or press the function key that assigns that style to a paragraph. You must also select the Style option button in the Find & Replace Options dialog box.

Replace with text box In the Replace text box, type the text that will replace the search text. If you need to replace a style, type the style name exactly as it appears in the Styles Box or press the function key that assigns that style to a paragraph.

Find Select the Find button to locate the first occurrence of the text or style you are searching for. Once Ami locates the occurrence, the Find & Replace dialog box changes its appearance and displays the text or style it found, the text or style that will optionally replace it, and what portion of the document it is checking. Ami also lists the options available for continuing the search, canceling it, or

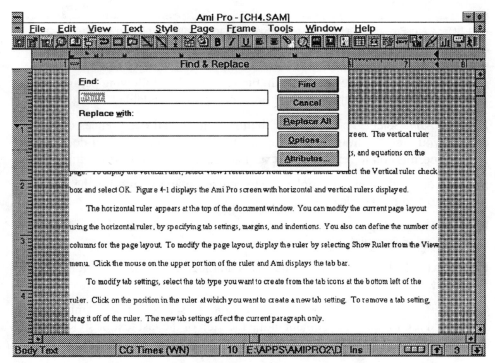

4-10 You must specify the text you want to find, but specifying replacement text is optional.

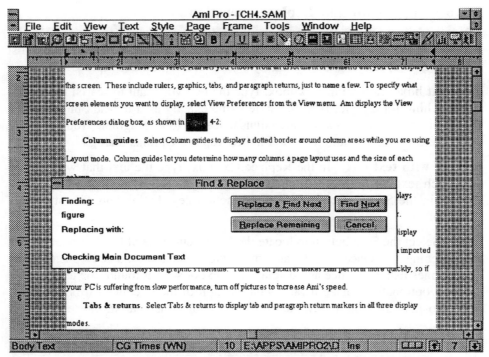

4-11 Once Ami Pro finds the text for which you are searching, the Find & Replace dialog box displays options you can choose.

replacing the text or style, as shown in Figure 4-11. The following paragraphs list guidelines for selecting the Find and Replace options available.

Replace All   Select the Replace All button to locate all occurrences of the text or style you are searching for and replace them automatically. Ami does not ask for your permission to replace any text or styles it finds if you select this option.

Replace & Find Next   To replace the occurrence and search for the next one, select Replace & Find Next.

Replace Remaining   To replace and all remaining occurrences in the document, select Replace Remaining.

Find Next   To leave this occurrence as is and locate the next occurrence, select Find Next.

Cancel   To stop the Find and Replace operation, select Cancel. Ami stops the search and returns to the document at the location of the last text or style it found.

Tip 4-27: Undo does not work on Find & Replace   You cannot use Undo to fix a Find and Replace gone wrong. If you choose Undo, Ami simply undoes the last editing change you made before you performed the Find and Replace. To prevent any disastrous results, always save your file before you begin Find and Replace. You can then select Revert to Saved from the File menu to restore your document to its original condition.

Tip 4-28: Copy and paste text into Find and Replace text boxes When you type the text you want to find incorrectly, your mistakes can foil Ami's best efforts at Find and Replace. To make sure you are using the exact spelling of the text you are searching for, copy it from the document and paste it into the Find or Replace with text boxes. Doing so ensures that Ami is searching for the text you need, and not text you typed in by mistake.

Tip 4-29: Continuing a cancelled search Ami doesn't provide an option for editing the text it finds, so if you need to change the text without replacing it, you have only two options: continue the search and hope you'll remember to return to that occurrence, or cancel the search and edit the search text. Cancelling the search is the best option, because you can correct immediately any problems with the search text. When you are ready to continue the search, just press Ctrl-F and Enter. Ami remembers the last Find and Replace text or style you specified.

Tip 4-30: Limiting Find and Replace to a block of text If you don't need to search an entire document for text or a style, you can speed up Find and Replace by searching only a specific block of text. Highlight the area you need to search and perform Find and Replace as you would normally. Ami searches only that area, thereby speeding up the Find and Replace process.

Tip 4-31: Using Find and Replace to delete text You can use Find and Replace to delete passages of text. To do so, specify the text you need to search for, but leave the Replace with text box blank. Select the Find and Replace button you need and Ami replaces the occurrences of the text with nothing, thereby deleting the text you specified. If you are confident that you want to delete all occurrences of the text, select the Replace All button. Otherwise, select Find so you can review each occurrence before Ami deletes it. You can also use Find and Replace to delete attributes such as bold or underline. Refer to Tip 4-38 for more information on deleting attributes.

Tip 4-32: Finding and Replacing ANSI characters, hard returns, tabs, and literal wildcard characters Not only can you find and replace text, styles, and attributes, but you also can specify ANSI characters, literal wildcard characters, hard returns, and tabs. To search for or replace an ANSI character, type the character in the text box, holding down the Alt key and typing the corresponding numbers using the numeric keypad. To search for or replace an asterisk, type an asterisk surrounded by angled brackets: <*>. You also must select the Whole word option button in the Find & Replace Options dialog box. To search for or replace a question mark, type a question mark surrounded by angled brackets: <?>. To search for or replace a hard return, press Ctrl-Enter. To search for or replace a tab, press Ctrl-Tab.

Tip 4-33: Do not use Find and Replace to locate marks   Find and Replace cannot locate bookmarks, tab rulers, footnotes, or other items identified by a mark in the document. To locate these items, use Go To instead. Go To can locate anything Ami identifies with a mark in the document. While Go To cannot move to a specific mark, it does cycle through them according to their locations in the document. So, if Go To doesn't locate the particular frame or other item you chose, continue selecting GoTo until it does.

Tip 4-34: Find and Replace Limitations   While Ami's Find and Replace feature can locate just about anything, it does have some limitations. You cannot search for fonts, alignment, indentions, superscript, subscript, or overstrike characters.

Tip 4-35: Performing a quick search for text in a document   If you need to search for text without replacing it, you can use the FIND macro to quickly find text, note its location, and continue the search. The FIND macro is useful if you need to locate text within a document, but you don't need to stop and edit the text once you locate it.

Once you playback the FIND macro, Ami displays the Macro Get String dialog box, as shown in Figure 4-12. Enter the text you need to search for and

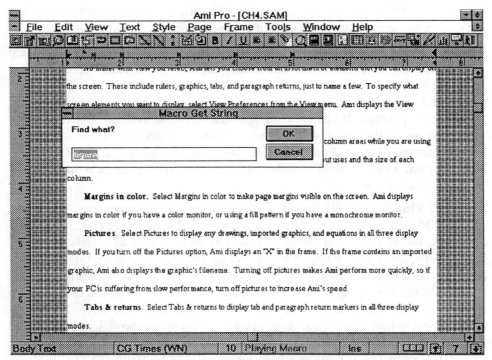

4-12   The FIND macro displays the Macro Get String dialog box so that you can enter the text you want to find only—not replace.

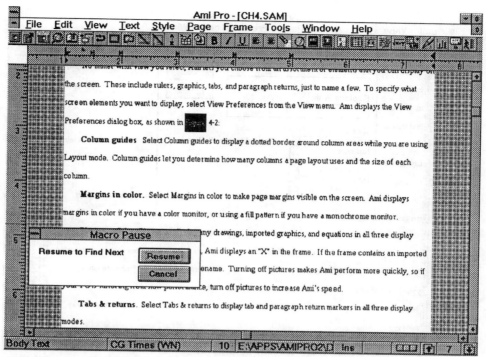

4-13 Once the FIND macro finds the search text, it pauses for you note the text's location.

select OK. Once Ami find the text, it displays the Macro Pause dialog box, as shown in Figure 4-13. Ami temporarily stops the search to let you note the text's location. You then can resume the search or cancel it.

Tip 4-36: Searching for text across documents   The FINDTXT macro lets you search for text among all documents in a directory. Ami scans each document's content, and displays the filenames of the documents that contain the text you needed to search for. You then can choose to open those files. If you have a large number of files in the directory you search, the FINDTXT might take anywhere from several minutes to an hour to search for the text, so make sure you have a block of time available to run this macro.

Tip 4-37: Finding and Replacing text across documents   If you write long documents made up of numerous smaller chapters, the FREPLACE macro is just what you need. It performs a search and replace across several documents. You specify the text Ami searches for and documents it should search in. Ami then finds and replaces all occurrences of the text without prompting you for any confirmation. So, before you use this macro, make sure you want to replace every occurrence of the text or you'll be surprised by the macro's results.

Once you playback the FREPLACE macro, Ami displays the Find & Replace Across Multiple Files dialog box, as shown in Figure 4-14. You specify the

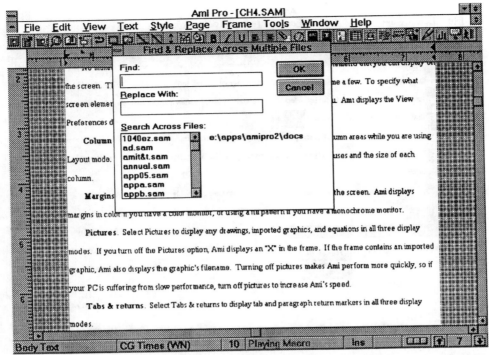

4-14 The Find & Replace Across Multiple Files dialog box lets you specify the find and replace text along with those files you need to search.

search text, the replace text, and the files Ami should search. Select OK and Ami opens each file, performs the find and replace operation, and closes the file. Ami does not stop to ask if it should replace or ignore the text.

Finding and Replacing text with attributes

Ami can find and replace text containing bold, italics, small caps, underline, and word underline. You can mix and match attributes to let Find and Replace do your editing. For example, if you included the title of a book in your document but forgot to italicize it, you can use Find and Replace to search for the normal text and replace it with italicized text.

To specify Find and Replace text attributes, select the Attributes button in the Find & Replace dialog box. Ami displays the Find & Replace Attributes dialog box as shown in Figure 4-15. You can choose from the following attributes to include in your Find or Replace text: normal, bold, italic, underline, word underline, and small caps. You can select one or multiple attributes for Find or Replace. Simply select the attributes you need and select OK.

Tip 4-38: Finding text attributes only   You can trick Ami into searching for a specific text attribute throughout your document. Type the asterisk wildcard char-

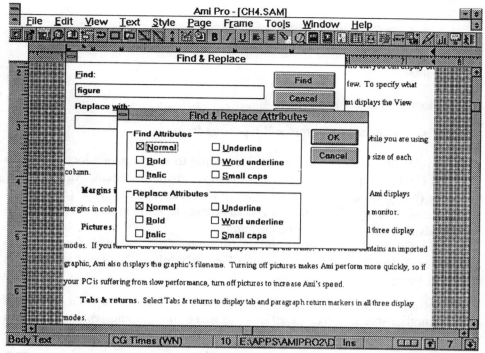

4-15 You can specify Find & Replace Attributes to perform global edits to your documents, such as replacing all bold text with italicized text.

acter in the Find text box and select the Attributes button. In the Find Attributes box select the attribute you need and click OK twice. Ami searches the document for that attribute. You can also specify a replacement attribute by selecting one or more from the Replace Attributes box in the Find & Replace Attributes dialog box.

Find and Replace options

Because Ami has many different search capabilities, you should decide on those you want to use. Then you must tell Ami the options you need to use. Ami lets you specify the following options for your search: forward or backward, the whole document or just specific areas, text or styles, whole words only, exact case, or exact attributes.

Normally Ami searches the main document text for text or styles. However, you can extend Ami's scope to find and replace text or styles in footnotes, frames, tables, headers, and footers. Ami searches the main document text only unless you specify a search text in other locations. Ami searches the areas in the following order:

1. main document
2. fixed frames

3. footnotes

4. floating frames

5. tables

6. floating headers and footers

7. fixed headers and footers and repeating frames.

Ami decides what areas to search according to your cursor's location when you start Find & Replace. If your cursor is in the main document, Ami searches that area (but you can specify to search other areas also). If your cursor is in another area, Ami searches that area and any others lower in priority. If you search backwards, Ami searches only the current area.

To specify Find and Replace options, select the Options button from the Find & Replace dialog box. Ami displays the Find & Replace Options dialog box as shown in Figure 4-16.

Find Options   Select Whole word only to ignore the find text when it appears as part of another word. Select Exact case to make the find and replace operation

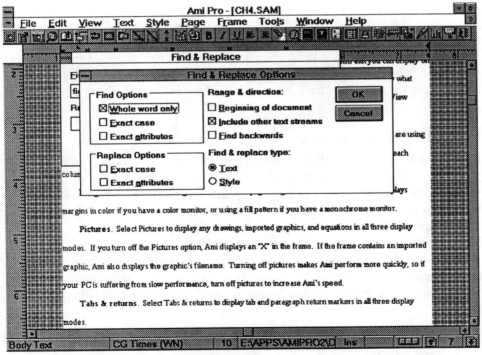

4-16   The Find & Replace Options dialog box lets you narrow or widen the scope of your search.

case-specific. If you select Exact case, Ami finds only occurrences of the text using the exact case you specified in the Find text box. Normally Ami finds all occurrences of the text, no matter what the case. Select Exact attributes to narrow the search to text using the attributes you selected in the Find & Replace Attributes dialog box. Normally Ami finds all occurrences of the text, no matter what their attributes.

Replace Options   Select Exact case to replace text using the same case you used in the Replace text box. Normally Ami replaces the text using the same case as the find text in the document. Select Exact attributes to replace the text using the attributes you selected in the Find & Replace Attributes dialog box. Normally Ami replaces the text using the same attributes as the find text in the document.

Range & direction   If your cursor is not at the beginning of the document but you need to start your search from that point, select Beginning of document. Select Include other text streams if your cursor is in the main document but you need to search all areas, including footnotes, tables, frames, headers, and footers. Select Find backwards to search from the cursor's location backward. If you select Find backwards, Ami searches only the current area.

Find & replace type   If you are using Find & Replace to search for or change styles, select the Style button. If you are searching for text, select the Text button. Text is the default option.

Inserting text from a glossary file

A glossary is a file that contains text used frequently in your documents. Instead of retyping that text each time you need it, you can type it once in a glossary and then retrieve it later. Examples of text you could store in a glossary are a salutation, a closing, standard copyright information, a disclaimer, and the company description included at the end of a press release. You also could use a glossary to create business cards, letterhead, or envelopes. When it comes time to insert your company's name and address, simply retrieve them from the glossary, rather than retyping it.

A glossary is an Ami Pro document containing only entries that you plan to retrieve later. Use these guidelines when creating a glossary file:

- Identify each entry using a unique name.
- If you use numbers to identify entries, use the same amount of digits in each number (001, 002, 003).
- Type a delimiter at the end of each entry name.
- Use the same delimiter for each entry name.
- Type another delimiter at the end of each entry.
- Use the same delimiter for each entry.

- Use any ASCII or ANSI symbol as a delimiter, as long as it doesn't appear in the glossary entries.
- Type the two delimiters, one for the entry name and one for entry, as the first line in the file.
- Do not include spaces between the delimiters on the first line.
- Type a field name for the entry name, the delimiter, a field name for the entries, and the delimiter on the second line.
- Each subsequent paragraph in the file should include the entry name, its delimiter, the entry, and its delimiter.
- Glossary entries can be several words, lines, or paragraphs long.
- Format the entry, using the Text menu, exactly as you want it to appear in its final document.

Figure 4-17 shows a sample glossary file.

To insert a glossary entry into a document, follow these steps:

1. Place the cursor at the position in the document where you need to insert the entry.

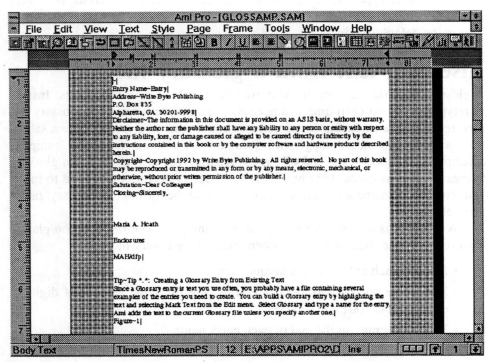

4-17 Sample entries in a glossary file. Notice that both the entry identifier and the entry end with delimiters.

2. Select Insert from the Edit menu.

3. Select Glossary Record. Ami displays the Insert Glossary Record dialog box, as shown in Figure 4-18.

4. Select the Data File button. Highlight the file containing the entries you need and double-click on it or select OK.

5. Select the glossary entry you need by highlighting it and selecting Insert. Ami adds the entry to the document and closes the dialog box.

6. Move to the next location in the document where you want to insert an entry.

7. Press Ctrl-K to display the Insert Glossary Record dialog box.

8. Repeat step five to add an entry to the file.

9. Continue adding entries until all the ones you need appear in the document.

Tip 4-39: Naming glossary entries   When you create entries in a glossary file, give each entry a descriptive name. When it comes time to insert the entry, you'll choose it from a long list of entry names contained in that file. If the entry names

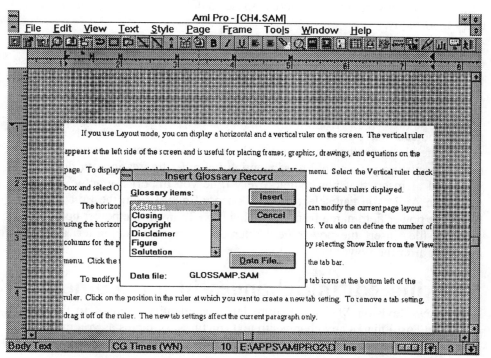

4-18   The Insert Glossary Record dialog box lets you choose the glossary entry you need from a list, so you don't have to remember the entry name.

aren't descriptive, you won't remember what each entry contains. For example, if you create a glossary file that contains disclaimers that you insert into a document, you need to identify the different disclaimers. DIS1, DIS2, and DIS3 are easy to enter, but they don't reveal much about their entry. If you have a disclaimer for a newsletter, name that entry DISNEWS. The name is short, yet it fully describes the glossary entry's contents.

Tip 4-40: Creating a glossary entry from existing text   Because a glossary entry is text you use often, you probably have a file containing several examples of the entries you need to create. You can build a glossary entry by highlighting the text and selecting Mark Text from the Edit menu. Select Glossary and type a name for the entry. Ami adds the text to the current glossary file unless you specify another one.

Tip 4-41: Limitations on delimiters   Even though you can use any ASCII or ANSI symbol as a delimiter, common sense calls for some precautions. Don't use wildcard characters, *, or ?, as delimiters, because you can run into problems when searching and replacing text. Also, don't use punctuation marks as delimiters, because you probably have them in one or more of your entries. If you have an entry several paragraphs long, for instance you probably used periods and commas, so you wouldn't want to use those as delimiters, or Ami will read your entry incorrectly.

Tip 4-42: Automatically inserting a specific glossary entry   You can use the Ctrl-K keyboard shortcut to insert a specific entry from a glossary file. To do so, type the name of the entry and press Ctrl-K. Ami replaces the entry name with its contents and without displaying the Insert Glossary Record dialog box.

Tip 4-43: Inserting custom power fields using a glossary   If you use power fields, you can insert them as entries in a glossary file. This method is efficient if you frequently insert the same power fields into a document. For example, if you created a custom power field to sequentially number figures in your documents, you need to insert that power field every time you import a graphic or draw a picture in Ami. You can select Insert Glossary Record from the Edit menu and select the power field name from the dialog box. To insert the power field into the glossary file, insert the power field after the entry name delimiter, and add a delimiter after the power field.

Marking editing changes in a document

Ami's new Revision Marking feature lets you identify changes to the current document. Ami marks any changes to text, pictures, or tables as you make them. When you are ready to save the document, Ami lets you review, save, or cancel the changes you made.

Revision Marking is similar to another new Ami feature called Document Compare. The difference between the two is that Document Compare reads two

ment, if someone else edits your document on-line, or if you have two versions of the same document, but you can't remember how they differ. Revision Marking is useful for marking changes as you make them. An editor could mark a writer's document with Revision Marking; when the writer reviews the document, he/she knows exactly what changes the editor suggests. Revision Marking also marks any inserted or deleted pictures or tables, while Document Compare does not. Refer to chapter 3 for more information on Document Compare.

Before you can tell Ami to mark changes to your document, you must specify how to display any insertions and deletions. You must distinguish these text changes so they stand out from the unchanged text. To do so, select Revision Marking from the Tools menu. Select the Options button and Ami displays the Revision Markings Options dialog box, as displayed in Figure 4-19. The choices you make in this box affect both Document Compare and Revision Marking. The following paragraphs discuss tips for using the Revision Marking Options dialog box.

Mark Insertions As   Select an appearance for text inserted into the document. You can choose from bold, italic, underline, or double underline. Ami also pro-

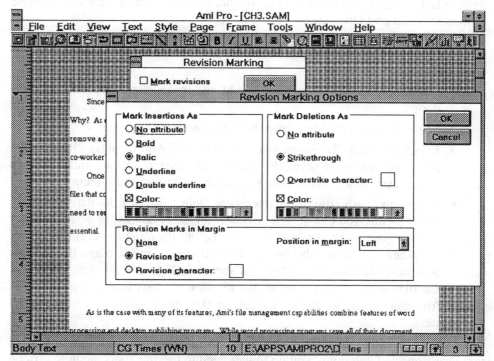

4-19   Choices you make in the Revision Marking Options dialog box affect both the Revision Marking and Document Compare.

vides No Attribute as a choice, but if you choose this option you cannot distinguish inserted text from unchanged text. You can also select from 120 colors to use for any text or pictures inserted into the document. If you do not see the color you need, double-click on the closest color and create a custom color.

Mark Deletions As   Select an appearance for text deleted from the document. Select from Strikethrough and Overstrike. If you select Overstrike, type the character in the text box that you wish to appear above the text. You can use any keyboard or ANSI character. Ami also provides No Attribute as a choice, but if select this option you cannot distinguish deleted text from unchanged text. You can also select from 120 colors to use for any text or pictures inserted into the document. If you do not see the color you need, double-click on the closest color and create a custom color.

Revision Marks in Margins   If other people frequently review your document, revision marks can guide them to places in the document that have changed. You can select None,Revision Bars (displays a vertical line in the margin next to any lines that have changed), or you can specify a unique character to appear in the margin. To do so, type the character in the Revision Character text box. You can use any keyboard or ANSI character.

Position in Margin   Use Position in Margin to position revision marks in the right or left margins. Select Left,Right, or Rt/Left for documents that use separate layouts for right and left pages.

Once you have specified how to display insertions and deletions, you must turn on Revision Marking for each document you want to review. To do so, follow these steps:

1. Open the document you want to edit and make sure it is the active window.

2. Select Revision Marking from the Tools menu.

3. Select the Mark Revisions box and click OK. Ami displays "Rev" in the status bar where it normally displays the current editing mode (Ins or Type). Ami marks changes to the document as you make them.

4. Once you finish editing the document, select Revision Marking from the Tools menu. You can accept or cancel all the revisions, or you can select Review Rev. to review each revision before deciding to accept or cancel it. When you select the Review Rev. button, Ami displays the Review Revision Marking dialog box, as shown in Figure 4-20. The options in the dialog box reflect whether the revision is a text insertion or deletion. You can choose to accept, cancel, or skip this revision and move to the next.

Tip 4-44: Activating Revision Marking   Once you define the appearance of text insertions and deletions, you no longer need to use the Tools menu to turn on

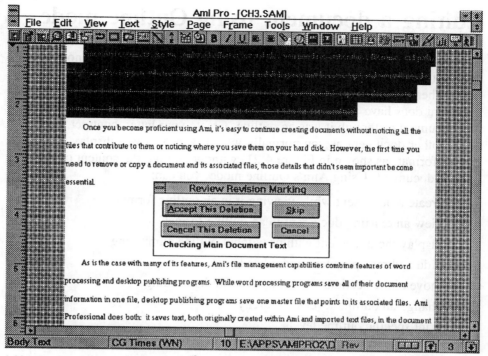

4-20 The Review Revision Marking dialog box lets you accept, cancel, or skip changes to a document individually.

Revision Marking. Instead, you can activate Revision Marking by clicking twice on the word Ins on the Status Bar. After you click the first time, Ins changes to Type. After you click the second time, Type changes to Rev displayed in red. Any changes you make to the document from this point on will contain the attributes you specified in the Revision Marking dialog box. To turn off Revision Marking, click once on Rev on the Status Bar. You still need to tell Ami whether to accept or cancel your changes by selecting Revision Marking from the Tools menu.

Tip 4-45: Revision Marking limitations   Revision Marking highlights text and frame insertions and deletions. It does not mark the contents of modified graphic frames, or any text modified with text attributes or style changes.

Tip 4-46: Use Revision Marking to display your latest revisions   If you save your document frequently as you write, you can use Revision Marking to display the editing changes you made since the last time you saved the document. Before you save the document, choose Revision Marking from the Tools menu and select Accept All Revisions. Select Save from the File menu. As you continue editing, Ami marks the changes you make to the document since the last time you saved it.

Editing a document using Outline mode

Your high school English teacher probably told you to create an outline before writing a large document. You had to make an outline and scribble notes next to each outline topic, before you could compile that information into a new document. There should have been an easier way.

Ami does have an easier way—an editable Outline mode that lets you view any document as though it was an outline. Create your letter, contract, brochure, or any other document as you normally would, and Ami will display it using an outline format, as shown in Figure 4-21, without altering the content or structure of your document. Using Ami's Outline mode, you can:

- create a document while viewing it in an outline format
- view an existing document in an outline format
- display the document with or without outline numbering
- hide and redisplay text under headings
- move entire sections of text by moving its heading
- change an outline level's hierarchy
- print specific outline levels.

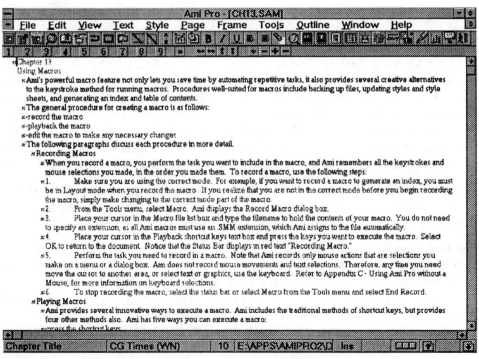

4-21 Outline mode displays a normal document as though you created it in an outline format.

Using Outline mode requires three steps: selecting Outline mode, specifying an outline hierarchy, and editing your document by moving or deleting outline levels.

Selecting Outline mode

Select Outline mode the same way you select Layout or Draft mode: choose the mode from the View menu or click on the icon in the icon palette. Outline mode uses the same font as Draft mode and doesn't separate the document into pages or display spacing or indentions, as shown in Figure 4-22. Additionally, Outline mode displays a button next to each paragraph, icons at the top of the window, and an Outline menu in the menu bar.

Creating an outline hierarchy

Ami lets you create an outline hierarchy using paragraph styles. You do not need to know how to create or modify styles to use Outline mode. However, you do need to understand how to assign a style to a paragraph (refer to chapter 5). When you view a document in Outline mode, Ami can display up to nine outline levels. To create an outline hierarchy, assign an outline level to your styles from 1 to 9.

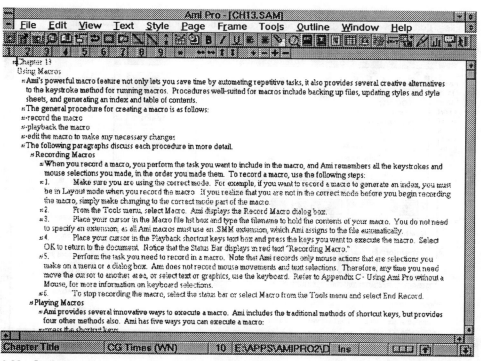

4-22   Outline mode is similar in appearance to Draft mode, but Outline mode does not display paragraph indentions or spacing.

Ami does not require you to assign an outline level to all the styles in your document. Generally, you should assign outline levels to headings and subheadings, and assign None to body text, lists, bullets, and other paragraphs making up the body of your document. However, you are free to make whatever assignments are appropriate for your document.

To create an outline hierarchy, follow these steps:

1. Use File Open or File New to open the document that you need to view in Outline mode.

2. Select the style sheet you want to use with the document. Ami comes with an Outline style sheet that has predefined outline styles, but if you need to use styles from another document, this style sheet is not of much use.

3. Select Outline Styles from the Style menu. Ami displays the Outline Styles dialog box, as shown in Figure 4-23, listing all the styles in the current style sheet and the outline levels available: 1–9.

4. Highlight the style that will use the first outline level. Drag the style to the left, or select the Promote button until the style is directly underneath the number 1. Release the mouse button. Ami moves the style to the top of the list and displays it under level 1.

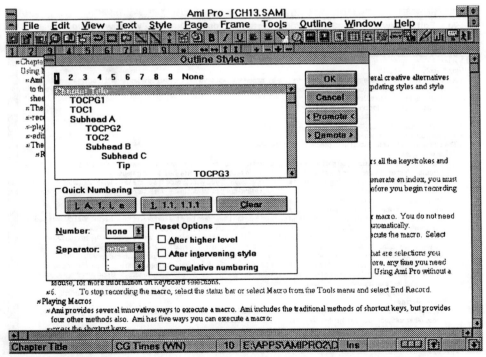

4-23   The first time you display the Outline Style dialog box, all styles use an outline level of None.

5. Repeat step four to assign subsequent levels to styles.

6. If you want to assign a numbering scheme to your outline, use the following options:

Quick Numbering   Select Quick Numbering to assign a numbering scheme to all the styles that were assigned a level. You can choose from traditional numbering (I, A, 1, a, i), or legal-style numbering (1, 1.1, 1.1.1). You also can choose to remove all numbering from your styles by selecting the Clear button.

Number   Select the type of numbering to assign to the highlighted style. Use Number when the Quick Numbering scheme isn't appropriate for your outline.

Separator   Select the punctuation to use as a separator between the text and its number.

Reset Option   Select After lesser level to restart numbering after a style using a lower numbering scheme. Select After intervening style to restarting numbering after a style that doesn't use a numbering scheme. Select Cumulative numbering to create a legal style numbering scheme (1.1, 1.1.1, 1.1.1.1).

7. Once you finish assigning outline levels to your styles, click OK. Ami returns to the document and displays it using the outline hierarchy you created.

8. If you plan to view other documents using this style sheet in Outline mode, save the changes to the style sheet. The styles to which you assigned outline levels are now document-only, but you can save them in the style sheet. Select Style Management from the Style menu. Highlight each style in the Styles in document list box and select >>Move>>. Click OK. Select Save as a style sheet from the Style menu and click OK to save the current style sheet under the same name. Select Yes when Ami asks you if you want to overwrite the current style sheet.

Tip 4-47: Creating a numbering scheme using outline styles   Even if you aren't creating an outline, you can use the numbering options in the Outline Style dialog box to create a numbering scheme that updates even after an intervening style. To do so, assign levels to two styles: the style to which you want to assign numbers, and a style that typically appears before the numbering style, such as a section title or body text. Assign a higher level to the body text or section title style, and assign the next lower level to the numbering style. Specify the Arabic Numbering option for the numbering style and choose After higher style as the Reset option.

Hiding sections of your document

Once you create an outline hierarchy and view your document in Outline mode, you can tell Ami what level of detail you need to view: the entire document, text in the first outline level only, or somewhere between the two. Hiding sections of your document is a great way to view your document's organization, because you can see all the headings of the same level on one screen. You can see easily if you omitted a topic by mistake, if you are concentrating too much on one area, or if you need to rearrange some topics.

You can hide portions of your document three ways: display only the outline levels you specify, hide subordinate text under a heading while displaying any subordinate headings, or hide all subordinate text and headings under a heading. Figure 4-24 show examples of each.

To display specific outline levels, follow these steps:

1. While you are in Outline mode, click on the numbered icon representing levels you need to display. Ami displays all the text in the level you specified along with any text in preceding levels. For example, if you want to see the first two outline levels, click on the number two icon. Ami displays the text in outline levels one and two. Any headings containing hidden text display a colored plus sign next to them. A blank plus sign indicates that no hidden text exists.

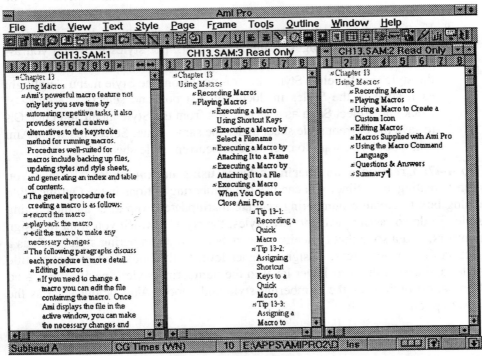

4-24 Outline mode lets you collapse text using a lower or no outline level underneath those paragraphs using a higher outline level.

2. Click on a higher number to see more detail. For example, to see the text up to outline level five, click on the number five icon.

3. To see the entire document, including any text not assigned to an outline level, click on the asterisk icon.

To hide only subordinate text under a heading, follow these steps:

1. Place your cursor in the paragraph under which you need to hide outline levels.

2. Click on the small minus sign icon. Ami hides all subordinate text under the current paragraph but displays any subordinate headings. The icon next to the heading is colored, indicating hidden text exists underneath it.

3. To redisplay the hidden text, click on the small plus sign icon.

To hide all subordinate text and headings under a heading, follow these steps:

1. Place your cursor in the paragraph under which you need to hide outline levels.

2. Click on the large minus sign icon. Ami hides all subordinate text and headings under the current paragraph. The icon next to the heading is colored, which indicates hidden text existing underneath it.

3. To redisplay the hidden text and headings, click on the small plus sign icon.

Tip 4-48: Hide subordinate text and headings quickly   A quick way to hide all the subordinate text and headings under a specific heading is to double-click on the plus sign next to the heading. Ami hides all the text and headings underneath. To redisplay the text and headings, double-click on the icon again. To achieve the same result using the keyboard, select Contract and Expand from the Outline menu.

Editing a document in Outline mode

While you view a document in Outline mode, you can move or delete entire sections of text. If text under level two would be more appropriate under level four, you can move all of the text associated with that level, and any underneath it. You also can change the outline level of a paragraph, so your original outline level assignments are not set in stone. Editing a large document in Outline mode is more convenient than using Cut and Paste because you can shrink the document to see the text's origination and destination simultaneously. You don't have to cut the text, scroll to the destination, paste the text, and scroll back.

Tip 4-49: Performing Spell Check and Find and Replace in Outline mode   Be careful when you check your spelling or try to find text while you are in Outline mode. Ami checks and searches only the displayed text; any collapsed text is ignored. Be sure to display all the text in a document before performing spell check and find and replace, or you might be unpleasantly surprised later.

Tip 4-50: Sorting in Outline mode   Sorting a document is especially powerful in Outline mode, because you can rearrange entire sections of a document. Hide subordinate text so that all Ami displays is the outline headings, as shown in Figure 4-25. Select the outline headings you want to rearrange and select Sort from the Tools menu. Specify the sort type (alphanumeric or numeric), the word on which to sort, and the sort order (ascending or descending). Ami rearranges the outline headings, moving their subordinate text also. Figure 4-26 shows the same document after sorting alphabetically in ascending order.

Moving sections of an outline

Ami has two ways you can move sections of text: you can move a paragraph up or down the outline, or move a heading and its subordinate text to a specific outline level.

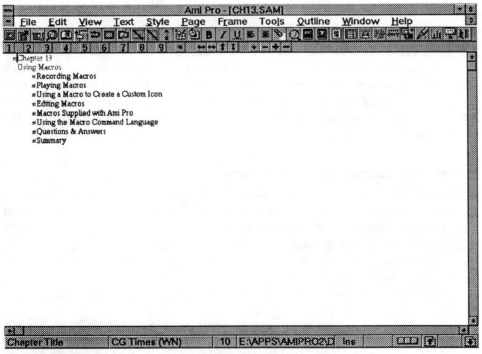

4-25   Sorting in Outline mode lets you sort blocks of text without sorting each line in the text, useful for sorting addresses and sections of a document.

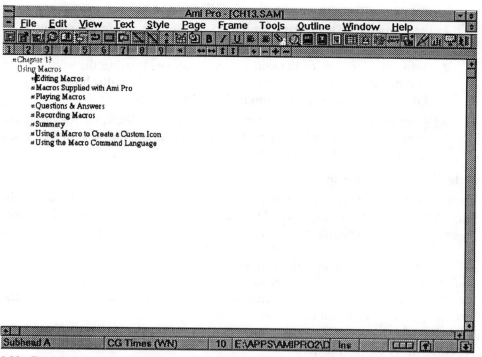

4-26 The left document displays the outline levels specified in the icon bar; the middle document displays document headings and subheadings; and the right document displays document headings only.

To move a paragraph up or down the outline, place your cursor in the paragraph you need to move, or if you need to move multiple paragraphs on the same level, highlight the paragraphs. Click on the up arrow or down arrow icon. Continue to click on the icon until the paragraph is in the location you need.

To move a heading and its subordinate text to a specific outline level, first identify the outline level of the paragraph you need to move. Click on the numbered icon representing the paragraph's outline level. For example, if you need to move a level two paragraph, click on the number two icon. Place the cursor on the plus button next to the paragraph and drag the button up or down the outline until the paragraph is in the position you need. Release the mouse button. Ami moves the heading and its subordinate text to the outline position you chose. Click on the asterisk icon to display all the text in document.

Changing an outline's level

To change a paragraph's outline level, place your cursor in the paragraph you need to change. Click on the left or right arrow icon until the paragraph is positioned at the level you need. Ami changes the paragraph's style to reflect that of the new outline level.

To change a paragraph's outline level, follow these steps:

1. Place your cursor on the plus button next to the paragraph you need to change.

2. Drag the plus sign to the outline level you need, using the vertical line Ami displays as a guide. You also can select the icon displaying a left or right arrow to change the paragraph's outline level.

3. Release the mouse button. Ami changed the outline level for the paragraph and any subordinating text. Ami also changed the paragraph's styles to reflect their new outline levels.

Deleting an outline level

You delete a single paragraph in an outline the same way you normally do: highlight the paragraph and press the Del key, or select Cut from the Edit menu. However, Ami has a simple way to delete an entire section of outline that is much easier than the traditional highlighting method.

To delete a heading and all of its subordinate text, hide any subordinate text underneath the heading that you need to delete. Then, highlight the heading and the paragraph mark. Press Del or select Cut from the Edit menu. Ami deletes the heading and all the hidden text underneath it.

Review of Outline mode

Ami's Outline mode is a powerful feature that simplifies editing long documents and aids in the creation new ones. Table 4-5 summarizes all the editing and viewing options you have in Outline mode, and how to perform them using the mouse, the keyboard, and the menu.

Creating a traditional outline

When you create a traditional outline in Ami, you use many of the same steps you use in Outline mode. Outline mode is a document management tool that lets you display any document using a hierarchy and expand and collapse text underneath headings. The document's appearance in Outline mode, however, does not reflect its final appearance on the printed page. Any indentation your paragraphs use in Outline mode does not carry over to Layout or Draft mode. To create a traditional outline, you should create paragraph styles to accommodate the number of levels you plan to use in the outline. You then can assign outline numbering schemes, and modify the styles to appear with indentions in Layout and Draft mode. You can display a traditional outline in Outline mode to collapse and expand outline levels and to move large sections of the outline quickly.

To create an outline, use these steps:

1. Select a style sheet to use with your outline. Ami provides several outline style sheets: ˉOUTLINE1.STY, ˉOUTLINE2.STY, ˉOUTLINE3.STY, and ˉOUTLINE.STY.

Table 4-5. Editing a Document in Outline Mode

Viewing/Editing Task	Mouse	Menu	Keyboard
Display specific outline level	Numbered icons Asterisk icon	Outline Expand Outline Contract	None available.
Hide subordinate text	Small minus icon	None available.	None available.
Reveal subordinate text	Small plus icon.	None available.	None available.
Hide subordinate text and headings	Large minus icon.	None available.	None available.
Reveal subordinate text and headings	Large plus icon.	None available.	None available.
Delete heading and subordinate text	Hide subordinate text.	Hide subordinate text.	Hide subordinate text.
	Highlight heading. Press Del.	Highlight heading. Press Del.	Highlight heading. Press Del.
Move one paragraph up the outline	Up icon	Outline Move Up	Alt-Up Arrow
Move one paragraph down the outline	Down icon	Outline Move Down	Alt-Down Arrow
Move heading and subordinate text up the outline	Plus button	Hide subordinate text.	Hide subordinate text.
		Outline Move Up	Alt-Up Arrow
Move heading and subordinate text down the outline	Plus button	Hide subordinate text.	Hide subordinate text.
		Outline Move Down	Alt-Down Arrow
Change one paragraph's outline level	Right or Left Arrow icons	Outline Promote	Alt-Left Arrow
		Outline Demote	Alt-Right Arrow
Change paragraph and subordinate text's levels	Plus button	Hide subordinate text.	Hide subordinate text.
		Outline Promote	Alt-Left Arrow
		Outline Demote	Alt-Right Arrow

2. Create a new style for each level you plan to use in the outline. Select Create Style from the Style menu. Type the new style name in the text box and select Modify. Select Save As and type the next style name. Continue selecting Save As until you create all the styles you need. Select OK or press Enter to return to the document.

3. Select Outline styles from the Style menu.

4. Highlight the style that will be the first level and drag it or select Promote until the style appears underneath the number one.

5. Continue assigning levels to the styles you created using step four.

6. Select one of quick numbering schemes to assign numbers to all levels or select the Number option to assign individual numbering options to each style.

7. Select a Reset Numbering option if you need to restart numbering within the outline. Ami normally does not restart numbering, and most outlines do not need to use this option.

8. Select OK or press Enter.

9. Type the text of the outline, assigning styles as you write.

10. Modify the outline styles, using the Modify Styles command on the Style menu, so that each style uses the appropriate indention when you use Layout or Draft mode. For more information on formatting styles, refer to Chapter 7.

You can use Outline mode to view more of your outline than you can see in Draft or Layout mode, to expand or collapse outline text, to rearrange sections of text, and to promote or demote outline headings.

Questions and answers

Q: Why do I always have an empty page at the end of my documents?

A: For some reason, Ami always adds a blank page to the end of a document. Because the page doesn't contain any text or graphics, however, it doesn't print or slow down the document in any way. The page doesn't have any content, so there is nothing to delete to rid your document of the page. It will always be there.

Q: I use Outline mode quite a bit to write and edit long documents. Sometimes when I switch to Outline mode from Layout mode, my text disappears.

A: If your cursor is in a footer, header, or a frame, Ami displays only the content of that item in Outline mode. If no content exists, the screen is blank. Even when your cursor is in the middle of your document and you change to Outline mode, it is possible that no text appears. When you change back to Layout mode, the cursor is the footer. The easiest way to display your text again is to change to

Layout mode, place the cursor in the middle of a paragraph, and change to Outline mode again.

Q: I am creating an outline, but am confused as to the difference between Outline mode and a regular outline. Must I use one to create the other?

A: No. Outline mode and creating an outline are two separate processes, but they are similar in several ways. Before you can display a document in Outline mode, you must assign levels to your styles using the Outline Styles command from the Style menu. Then you change to Outline mode to view your document.

Creating an outline is a similar process. You create the styles you want to include in your outline. Using Outline Styles from the Style menu, assign levels to the styles you created. From this dialog box you also create a numbering scheme. Then modify the styles so that each indents more than the one above it (Level 2 should use twice the indentation as Level 1).

You can use Outline mode to view and create an Outline, but it isn't necessary. Outline mode is useful when creating large outlines, because you can see more of the text and you can collapse and expand outline headings.

Summary

Ami provides word processing tools that let you efficiently create and edit a document. If you want to type all the text from scratch, Ami gives you a choice of display modes and views that let you customize your screen according to your editing tasks. You also can create or add to documents by pasting text from other Windows and nonWindows applications, loading a style sheet with contents, or inserting glossary entries. You can add special ANSI characters, and notes to serve as reminders to yourselves or others.

Once the document contents are in place, you can use Ami's editing tools to fine tune your document. Find & Replace lets you search for text, styles, and attributes, and lets you replace them if necessary. Revision Marking lets you mark changes to a document. Outline mode is a powerful tool for organizing documents, viewing long documents, and moving sections of text quickly. You can also use Outline mode to create outlines. All these tools let you make a smooth transition from document creation to editing and proofreading resulting in a polished document.

5
CHAPTER

Style sheets

The key to any desktop publishing software's usability lies in its style sheets. They give you the power to control every aspect of your document's appearance, from margins to fonts. However, understanding, using, and modifying style sheets traditionally has not been easy. To modify a paragraph style or create your own style sheet, you had to roam all over the screen making selections from several different menus and dialog boxes. How could you know if you made the right selections from the right menus?

Ami makes using style sheets easy. You don't have to use a style sheet at all if you don't need one. All the options for paragraph styles are located in one menu, the Style menu.

This chapter explains what a style sheet controls, how to select a style sheet, how to assign styles to paragraphs, how to create and delete styles, and the difference between document and global styles. Refer to chapter 7 to modify a style using the Style menu.

The foundation for any document

Ami's foundation for a document consists of three files: .SAM, .G00, and .STY. Ami stores text in the .SAM document file, graphic images in .G00 files, and formatting information in the style sheet, or .STY file.

When you create a new document, you must specify what style sheet to use. You cannot create a document without specifying a style sheet, because Ami will not know how to format your page or your text. Once you tell Ami what style sheet to use, it reads the page and paragraph formatting information and applies it to your document. When you are ready to save your document, you can tell Ami to continue referring to that style sheet, and update your document format as you make changes to the style sheet, or to stop referring to the style sheet, and use only its current formatting information.

You must specify one style sheet for each document, but you can reuse that style sheet with many different documents. You also can change your mind and select a different style sheet for a document. You can use any style sheet you want, but you can use only one at a time.

What does a style sheet control?

Ami's style sheets contain formatting information for a document's page layout and paragraphs. Each style sheet can contain formatting for one page layout and multiple paragraph styles. The style sheet controls the following page layout formatting:

- Margins and columns
- Page size and orientation
- Tab settings
- Lines around the page
- Lines between columns
- Header/footer margins and columns
- Header/footer tab settings

The style sheet controls the following paragraph formatting:

- Text font, size, color, and attributes
- Alignment and indentation
- Line and paragraph spacing
- Kerning
- Page breaks
- Lines above and below paragraphs
- Table format
- Hyphenation.

Choosing a style sheet

Ami comes with over 50 sample style sheets that are ready to use. You can select a style sheet when you select File New or when you select the Use Another Style Sheet command from the Style menu. Table 5-1 lists the sample style sheets that come with Ami. Ami automatically uses the ˉDefault style sheet for all your new documents, but you can choose another style sheet using the Use Another Style Sheet command on the Style menu.

You also can create your own style sheets using the sample style sheets as

Table 5-1. Ami Pro's Style Sheets

Filename	Description	Contents?
~Basic.sty	Contains only Body Text and Body Single styles.	Y
~Calday.sty	Appointment book table format for one day.	Y
~Calmon.sty	Landscape table for a one month calendar.	Y
~Calwk.sty.	Appointment book table format for one week.	Y
~Default.sty	Similar to ~Basic.sty, only contains more styles.	Y
~Envelop.sty	Landscape layout for an envelope.	N
~Envhp2p	HP IIP	Y
~Envhp3	HP III	Y
~Envhpdj	HP DT	Y
~Envpsii	HP II w/PS cartridge	Y
~Envtiml	Tl microlaser	Y
~Expense.sty	Table containing a weekly expense report.	Y
~Fax1.sty	Informal layout for a facsimile cover sheet.	Y
~Fax2.sty	Memo-style with reverse text heading for a facsimilie cover sheet	Y
~Fax3.sty	Memo-style with graphic heading for a facsimilie cover sheet.	Y
~Index.sty	One column layout for an index.	N
~Invoice.sty	Table, using invoice format, that calculates a total.	Y
~Label.sty	Contains a single label to be used with Merge.	N
~Letter1.sty	Block style for letters.	Y
~Letter2.sty	First line indented style with border around page for letters.	Y
~Letter3.sty	Block style with horiz ruler @ top.	Y
~Letter4.sty	First line indented style with horiz. ruler @ top	Y
~Memo1.sty	Informal memo with thick vertical line at left margin.	Y
~Memo2.sty	Block style with graphic for memos.	Y
~Memo3.sty	Block style with ruled heading for memos.	Y
~Memo4.sty	Block style with ruled heading for memos.	Y
~Memo5.sty	Block style with contemporary reverse text heading for memos.	Y

Table 5-1. Continued

Filename	Description	Contents?
~Memo6.sty	Block style with ornamental heading for memos.	Y
~Newset1.sty	Two column layout for newsletters or magazines.	Y
~Newslet2.sty	One column layout for newsletters or magazines.	Y
~Newslet3.sty	Three column layout for newsletters or magazines.	Y
~Newslet4.sty	Three column layout for newsletters or magazines.	Y
~Newslet5.sty	Two column layout for newsletters or magazines.	Y
~Outlin1.sty	Single column layout for simple outlines.	N
~Outlin2.sty	Indented single column layout for outlines.	Y
~Outlin3.sty	Indented single column layout with margin notes and border around page for outlines.	Y
~Outline.sty	For use with docs in outline mode.	N
~Overhd1.sty	Single column layout with graphic heading for overheads.	Y
~Ovrhd2.sty	Landscape layout with graphic at left margin for overheads.	Y
~Ovrhd3.sty	Landscape layout with graphic background for overheads.	Y
~Overhd4.sty	Single column layout with ruled heading for overheads.	Y
~Overhd5.sty	Single column layout with double ruled heading for overheads.	Y
~Press1.sty	Single column layout with double ruled heading for press releases.	Y
~Press2.sty	Single column layout with ruled heading for press releases.	Y
~Propos1.sty	Single column layout with ruled heading	N
~Propos2.sty	Two column layout for proposals.	Y
~Report1.sty	Two column layout with drop shadow heading for reports	Y
~Report2.sty	Two column layout with multiple reverse text headings for reports.	Y
~Report3.sty	Single column layout with ruled heading for reports.	Y
~Report4.sty	Single column layout with multiple ruled headings for reports.	Y

Table 5-1. Continued

Filename	Description	Contents?
~Title1.sty	Centered text with rule around title page.	Y
~Title2.sty	Centered text with double rule around title page.	Y
~Title3.sty	Centered text on a title page using a fill pattern.	Y
~Tutltr.sty	Style sheet used in tutorial.	Y
~Tutor.sty	Style sheet used in tutorial.	Y

templates. Choose the sample style sheet with the format closest to the one you need. Before you make any changes to the style sheet, save it under another name to ensure that the original remains unchanged. For examples of each style sheet, refer to Appendix D.

Tip 5-1: Selecting Show Description when selecting a style sheet   Ami has such a rich assortment of style sheets that it's hard to remember what each does. You don't have to remember if you select the Show Description option in the File New or Use Another Style Sheet dialog boxes. Ami will display a description of each style sheet, including whether or not it has contents, as shown in Figure 5-1.

Tip 5-2: Losing a document's association to its style sheet   If you select the Keep format with document option when you save a file, Ami no longer uses the style sheet or any styles associated with the document. When you keep the format with the document, the document loses its connection to the style sheet, but it does maintain the current formatting of those styles. Future changes you make to the style sheet do not affect the document. If you create a letter or a table that is unique and doesn't need to be updated, use the Keep format with document option. However, if you create several publications that need to appear consistent, or if your company uses a team of writers, the Keep format with document option is dangerous. The dangerous part is that Ami uses the Keep format with document option as the default, so you must turn it off to keep a style sheet and the styles with your document. You can lose a document's style sheet without realizing you did anything. When you use the Keep format with the document option, Ami displays "None" in the Styles Box, a shown in Figure 5-2. To begin using styles again, refer to Tip 5-15.

Tip 5-3: Create your own style sheets using ˜BASIC.STY   Occasionally you'll want to create your own style sheet from scratch, instead of using one of the style sheets designed for a specific purpose. The ˜BASIC.STY style sheet is

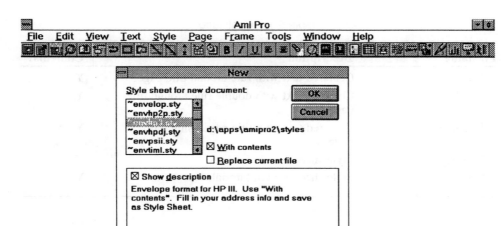

5-1 You can view a description of each style sheet by selecting the Show description check box in the File New dialog box.

the simplest style sheet available with Ami, because it comes with only two styles: Body Text and Body Simple. Use this style sheet to create your own.

Tip 5-4: Keep Ami's sample style sheets unchanged   You'll probably want to create your own style sheets using the samples as a foundation. So that you can reuse the original style sheets, always save them under another name before you make any changes. That way you can continue to use the originals for your documents to create additional style sheets. Refer to Tip 5-14 for information about making a style sheet read-only. If you accidentally overwrite a sample style sheet, you can copy the originals to your hard disk using the install procedure.

Tip 5-5: Selecting a Default style sheet   You can tell Ami to load the same style sheet each time you start the program. Normally, Ami automatically loads the ‾DEFAULT.STY style sheet, but you can specify a different one. Select User Defaults from the Tools menu. Select the Load button and highlight the style sheet you need. Click OK. The next time you start Ami the style sheet you chose will be loaded.

Tip 5-6: Using a style sheet with contents   Style sheets hold two types of formatting information: page and paragraph. Style sheets also can hold a third type of information, a document's contents. If you reuse the same style sheet for the

5-2 The Styles Box displays none when you saved the document using the Keep format with document option.

same type of documents, you can save text and/or graphics that remain constant, such as a newsletter masthead or logo, or a manual's copyright information and headers and footers. To save text and graphics so that you don't need to recreate them each time, save your style sheet using the Save as a Style Sheet command from the Style menu. Save the style sheet under the same name, and select the With Contents check box to save the document's contents with the style sheet. The next time you select the style sheet using File New, select on the With Contents check box, because Ami does not automatically load the contents with the style sheet. Figure 5-3 shows a style sheet that was loaded using the With contents option.

Tip 5-7: Selecting a Default style sheet with contents Specifying a default style sheet to use when you start Ami is a useful feature, but selecting a style sheet with contents is even better. Ami does not have the option of loading a default style sheet with contents under User Setup on the Tools menu, but you can achieve the same results using a macro. Select Macros from the Tools menu and select Record. Enter a filename for the macro and select OK. Select File New and choose the style sheet you want to use as the default. Select the With contents option. Select Macros from the Tools menu and select End Record. Select User Setup from the Tools menu. Select Program load and enter the macro's filename

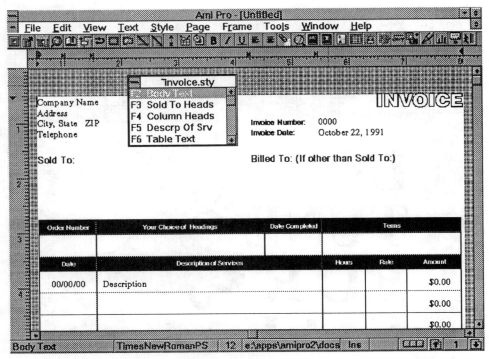

5-3 The entire expense report template is included as the ~EXPENSE.STY style sheet's contents.

in the text box. The next time you load Ami, it will run your macro and load the style sheet you chose with contents.

Tip 5-8: Creating a calendar   Ami comes with three calendar style sheets that create a calendar for you automatically. Ami can build a calendar for the current day, week, or month, using the system date as the basis for the calendar's dates. The ˜CALDAY.STY creates an appointment-style calendar for the day, the ˜CALWK.STY creates an appointment-style calendar for the week, and the ˜CALMON.STY creates a regular calendar for the month. Figure 5-4 shows an example of each calendar.

Assigning styles to paragraphs

Once you've created a new file, selected your style sheet, and created some text, you are ready to assign styles to your paragraphs. You can assign styles to entire paragraphs only. If you need to format a word or just a section of a paragraph, highlight the text you need to change and use the Text menu. You can assign styles using either the mouse or the keyboard. Refer to chapter 4 for more information.

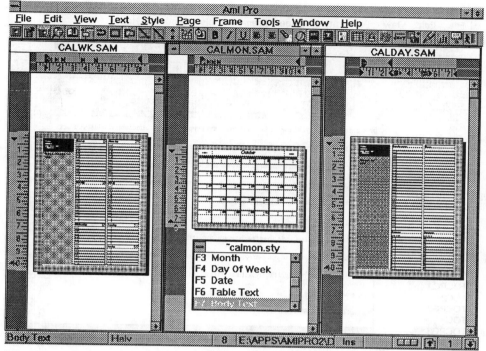

5-4 The ~CALDAY, ~CALMON, and ~CALWK style sheets loaded with contents.

Using the mouse

To assign styles using the mouse, click the cursor in the paragraph you need to format, and then select the style name from the Styles Box. You don't need to highlight the paragraph—Ami automatically assigns the style to the entire paragraph.

Tip 5-9: Select style names from the Status Bar   You can also select style names in the Status Bar at the bottom left of the screen. The Status Bar normally displays the style status of the current paragraph. Select the Status Bar and Ami displays all the styles available in the current style sheet (shown in Figure 5-5). Select the style you need and Ami returns the Status Bar to its normal display and formats your paragraph.

Tip 5-10: Create icons for styles   If your style sheet contains numerous styles, you need a quick way to access them. Only ten or twelve can be assigned to function keys, and scrolling through the Styles Box and Status Bar is too time-consuming. A better solution is to assign the styles you use most to icons and display them in the icon palette. To assign that style, insert the cursor in the paragraph and select the icon. Refer to chapter 13 for more about creating custom icons.

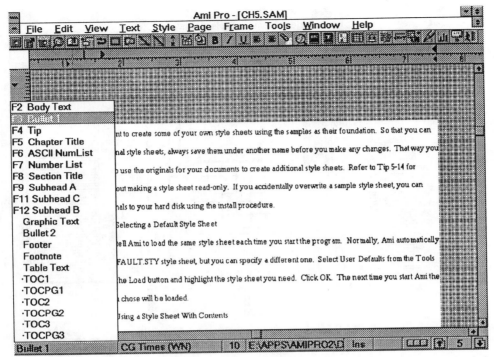

5-5 You can select a style by holding the mouse button down over the style name in the Status Bar.

Using the keyboard

You can assign styles using the keyboard by using the Styles Box or the function keys. To use the styles box, position your cursor in the paragraph you need to format and press Ctrl-Y. Your cursor moves to the Styles Box. Highlight the style you need and press Enter. To use the function keys, position your cursor in the paragraph you need to format and press the function key that corresponds to the style you need.

Ami preassigns styles in each style sheet to all available function keys. The number of available function keys depends on your keyboard—you could have ten or twelve function keys. You can reassign styles to function keys by selecting Style Management from the Style menu. Highlight the style you need to assign and select the function key you want. Figure 5-6 shows the Style Management dialog box and its function key assignments.

Tip 5-11: Assign styles to function keys in alphabetical order Ami lists styles in numerical order by function key in the Styles Box. Therefore, the style assigned to F2 appears first, then F3, F4, and so on. However, if you use the mouse to assign styles, you probably don't have the function key assignments memorized, so styles would be easier to find if they were listed in alphabetical order.

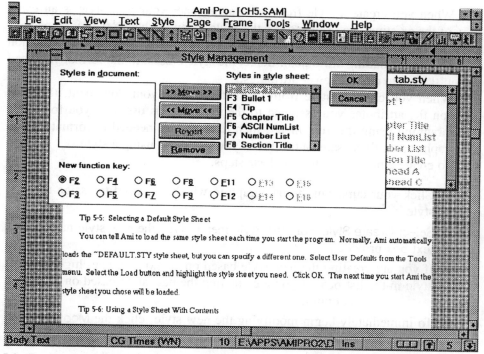

5-6 The F1 and F10 function keys are not displayed in the Style Management dialog box, because they are reserved for other Ami Pro functions.

Assign the styles to function keys in alphabetical order (F2 is Body Text, F3 is Bullet 1), so they appear the same way in the Styles Box.

Tip 5-12: Assign most-used styles to lowest function keys You also can assign the styles you use the most to function keys that appear first the Styles Box. That way the styles you need are always listed at the top of the Styles Box, and you don't have to scroll to find the style you want.

Tip 5-13: Assigning a style to several paragraphs If you use Ami for long documents, assigning styles to individual paragraphs can be cumbersome. Instead, you an assign a style to several paragraphs at the same time. Highlight the paragraphs you need to format and select the style. The paragraphs need to be consecutive and can span multiple pages.

Creating new styles

Each sample style sheet comes with useful styles, but eventually you'll need to create your own. When you create a new style, you will base it one of two items: an existing style, or formatted text.

When you create a style from an existing one, your new style is an exact copy of the existing one. You can use the Style menu to change the font, spacing, lines, and other features of your new style (refer to chapter 7 for more information on selecting formatting attributes). Select the style closest to the format you need so you'll have to change fewer attributes.

When you create a style from formatted text in your document, the style takes on the attributes you assigned to the text. This is useful if you formatted one paragraph using the Text menu, then realized you needed to format several paragraphs using those same attributes—you can do so using a style.

To create a new style, follow these steps:

1. Click your cursor in the paragraph to which you need to assign the new style.

2. Select Create Style from the Style menu. Type the new style name in the text box provided.

3. If you are creating the new style based on an existing one, highlight that style in the list box. If you are creating the new style based on formatted text, select that option.

4. To immediately begin modifying the new style, click the Modify button. To return to the document, select the Create button.

Ami returns to the document, but does not assign the new style to your paragraph. You must manually assign the style using the mouse or the keyboard.

Document styles vs global styles

A style sheet can have two types of paragraph styles: global styles or document styles. When you choose a sample style sheet to use with your document, all the styles in that style sheet are global. They affect all the documents that use that particular style sheet. The Body Text style in the ¯DEFAULT.STY style sheet is a global style. Document styles, however, do not come with the sample style sheets. When you create a new style or modify an existing one, it becomes a document style, meaning it affects only the current document. Ami does not add the new or updated style to the style sheet, but instead saves the formatting information in the document. If you change the Body Text style in the ¯DEFAULT.STY, it becomes a document style for this document only. All other documents using the same style sheet use the Body Text global style.

Document styles let you override the formatting in the style sheet. Without document styles, every change you made to a style would affect all other documents using that style sheet. Sometimes you don't need to change all your documents, you need to change only the current one. Without document styles, you would need to create a new style each time you needed a small change for one or two documents. You would end up with too many styles, eventually forgetting what many of them did.

How can you tell which styles are global and which are document? Document styles have a dot before their name in the styles box and global styles do not (shown in Figure 5-7). Table 5-2 summarizes the differences between document and global styles.

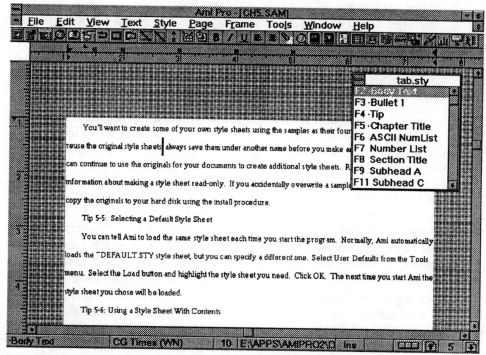

5-7 The Styles Box displays both documents and global styles: document styles appear with a dot before their names.

Table 5-2. Document Styles vs Global Styles

Document Styles	Global Styles
Affect current document only.	Affect all documents using the same style sheet.
Saved with the document file.	Saved with the style sheet file.
Appears in the Styles Box with a bullet before its name.	Appears in the Styles Box without a bullet before its name.
Created when you define a new style or modify an existing style. Also created when you convert a global style to a document style.	Come with style sheets supplied with Ami Pro. Also created when you convert a document style to a global style and save the style sheet.

Changing document styles to global styles

What if you modify a global style, but you need that change to affect all of your documents? At times, you'll change a global style but you don't intend for it to become a document style. Using the Style Management command in the Style menu, you can change document styles to global styles, and vice versa.

1. Select Style Management from the Style menu.
2. Highlight the document style in the Styles in Document list box you need to change to a global style.
3. Select the >>Move>> button. Ami moves the formatting information for the style you chose from the document file to the style sheet file. The style becomes a global style. Click OK.

You also can change a global style to a document style using the same steps. You simply would select the opposite Move button in step 3. A shortcut to changing all document styles to global styles is to save the style sheet. Every time you save the style sheet, Ami converts all document styles to global styles.

Tip 5-14: Protecting a style sheet from changes   You can make a style sheet read-only, so others can use it but they cannot save any modifications. Keeping a style sheet in its original form is important if you have a team of writers using the same style sheet. If each writer changes the style sheet to his or her own liking, your company's documents won't appear consistent. Making a style sheet read-only does not prevent you from making modifications to a style; however, it does prevent saving those changes to the style sheet. The style undergoing changes becomes a document style unable to be converted to a global style. You still can save the style sheet to another name and then modify the new style sheet. To make a style sheet read-only, select File Management from the File menu. Display the style sheet files, and highlight the file you need. Select Change Attributes from the File menu and select the Read only option. Select OK and close the File Manager window.

Using another style sheet

Choosing another style sheet is a tricky business. All styles sheets are not created equal: some have numerous styles, while others have just a few. Some style sheets are two columns, while others are just one column using a landscape orientation. Choosing another style sheet can elicit shrieks of horror when you use some applications, but not Ami. Ami has more flexibility when you select another style sheet than any other word processor or DTP application.

What happens when you change style sheets? Ami uses styles and the page layout from the new style sheet unless you have document styles or a document page layout in the current style sheet. Those override any formatting in the new

Table 5-3. Results of Using Another Style Sheet

Contents	Current Style Sheet or Document	New Style Sheet
More Styles	Global styles not in new style sheet use Body Text formatting. Document styles override styles in new style sheet.	Paragraphs can use new styles.
Document Page Layout	Overrides page layout in new style sheet.	No document page layout exists in a style sheet.
Standard Page Layout	Uses page layout attributes in new style sheet.	Document uses standard page layout unless it contains an overriding document page layout.
Document Styles	Override any global styles of the same name in the new style sheet.	No document styles exist in a style sheet.
Global Styles	Use attributes in new style sheet.	Format paragraphs in document unless they use an overriding document style.

style sheet, assuming that both style sheets contains the same styles. If they don't, paragraphs using styles not available in the new style sheet use Body Text formatting but retain their style associations. Even though the paragraphs look like Body Text, when you insert the cursor in the paragraph, Ami displays the style name they use in red on the status bar. Table 5-3 displays the results of choosing another style sheet.

When you change style sheets, you can choose which formatting to use in the new style sheet: page layout, styles, or a combination of both. You can choose the following formatting combinations when you change style sheets:

- page layout from a new style sheet, styles from previous style sheets
- page layout from a previous style sheet, styles from new style sheet
- page layout and styles from a new style sheet
- styles from the previous and the new style sheets.

To use these combinations, use the Save as a Style Sheet, Use Another Style Sheet, and Style Management commands from the Style menu. The key in choosing which styles and page layouts to use is the order in which you use these commands. Table 5-4 lists the commands to use to select page layouts and styles from the current or the new style sheet.

Table 5-4. Combining Settings from the Current and Another Style Sheet

PageLayout/Style Sheet	To Use New Style Sheet Settings	To Use Current Style Sheet Settings
Global Page Layout	Use another style sheet.	Modify the page layout. Use another style sheet.
Document Page Layout	Save style sheet. Use another style sheet.	Use another style sheet.
Global Styles	Use another style sheet.	Change global styles to document styles. Use another style sheet.
Document Styles	Use another style sheet. Revert document styles to global styles.	Use another style sheet.

Tip 5-15: Changing style sheets when the Styles box displays "None" If your Styles box displays "None" in the title bar, you had the Keep format with document option selected when you saved your file. When you keep the format with the document, it loses all connections to the style sheet and its styles, but it does maintain the formatting of those styles used. Because your document doesn't use styles anymore, using another style sheet has no effect. If you decide that you would like to begin using styles again, you must perform two steps: tell your document to begin using styles again; and select the style sheet you want to use. First, select the Save as a Style Sheet command under the Style menu. Enter a new style sheet name that no other style sheet uses. You are telling your document to begin using styles by associating the document with a style sheet, but you use a new filename to prevent overwriting any existing style sheets. Next, check the Styles box. If it displays the style sheet name you chose, your document is using styles again; however, its appearance hasn't changed yet. Select Use Another Style Sheet and choose the style sheet containing the styles you need. Ami formats your document using the style sheet you selected.

Tip 5-16: Creating a new style sheet from existing style sheets Rather than creating a style sheet from scratch or adapting a close relative, you can create a new style sheet by copying styles from existing style sheets. Select Use Another Style Sheet from the Style menu and select the first style sheet you want to use. Select Style Management from the Style menu. Highlight the styles in the Styles menu in style sheet list box you want to copy. Select the <<Move<< button to move the styles to the document. Continue choosing style sheets and moving styles from the style sheet to the document until all the styles you need are listed in the Styles in document list box. Ami uses the page layout attributes from the last style sheet you copied styles from, so use last the style sheet containing the page layout attributes you need. Select Save as a Style from the Style menu and enter a new filename for the style sheet. All the styles you copied are now document styles in your new style sheet. You can leave them as is or change them to global styles.

Deleting styles

If you've created too many styles, or if you haven't used a style in a while and you can't remember what it does, it's time to delete a few styles. Before you make the decision to delete a style from your style sheet, let's review what happens to the paragraphs using that style:

- If you remove a global style, all paragraphs using that style change to Body Text (in this document and in all other documents using the same style sheet).
- If you remove a document style that you modified (indicated by a bullet in front of it in the Styles Box), all paragraphs using that style change to the global style of the same name.
- If you remove a document style that you created (it also has a bullet in front of it in the Styles Box), all paragraphs using that style change to Body Text.

Now that you know what happens when you delete a style, review the steps to perform the deletion. First select Style Management from the Style menu. Highlight the style in either the Styles in Document or Styles in Style Sheet list box that you need to delete. Select the Remove button and click OK.

Questions and answers

Q: I tried to delete a style, but Ami will not let me. Why not?

A: Ami will not allow you to delete two styles: Table Text and Footnote. Ami automatically creates these when you insert a footnote or a table in your document, and as long as you have these items, Ami will not let you delete the needed styles from the document. Ami will allow you to delete the style only when you remove the footnote or the table.

Q: Can I add a description to my style sheets?

A: Yes. Select File New and choose the style sheet. Select Doc Info and type a description for the style sheet. Select Save as a Style Sheet and save the style sheet under the same name. The next time you choose File New or Use Another Style the description appears in the Show Description box.

Q: When I open my document, Ami displays the message "Cannot find style sheet."

A: Ami is telling you that it is looking in the directory for the style sheet attached to your document, but it cannot find it. Many changes can cause this message, including renaming a style sheet, moving the style sheet to a different directory, or deleting the style sheet. Also, if you change the style path in the User Setup dialog box or in the AMIPRO.INI file, Ami can't find your style sheet unless you copied it to the directory you specified in the file.

Q: *Why do some of my style names appear in red on the status bar?*

A: Styles that appear in red are not available in the current style sheet. Usually this happens when you use another style sheet or you are using an older version of the same style sheet. You have two options: create the style again, or copy the newer version of the style sheet over the old one.

Q: *Why does the title bar of my Styles Box say "None?"*

A: Either you had Keep format with document selected when you saved your file, or Ami could not find your style sheet. If you selected the Keep format with document option, Ami does not save the style sheet association with your document. It simply uses the current formatting from the style sheet. If Ami cannot find the style sheet, select another or copy the style sheet to the style directory specified in the AMIPRO.INI file.

Q: *I changed the style sheet I use with my document, but some of my styles lost their attributes.*

A: Styles in your old style sheet that don't exist in your new one lose their attributes and take on those of Body Text. You can keep their attributes by switching to your old style sheet, changing the missing styles to document styles, and then using the new style sheet. You can then keep the styles as document styles, or change them to global styles.

Q: *I changed one of my styles to a document style to prevent it from changing when I used another style sheet. However, I don't like the results. Do I have to return to my old style sheet?*

A: No, you can revert the document style to use the global settings in the current style sheet. To do so, select Style Management from the Style menu. Select the style in the Styles in document box and select Revert. The style then takes on the settings saved in the new style sheet.

Q: *When I modify my styles, Ami tells me I am using the wrong font.*

A: Ami's original style sheets are created using a specific printer. If you don't use that printer, Ami cannot use the fonts in those styles; it instead uses the closest font available. To avoid the message, you need to save all of your styles using a font available in your printer. You can do so using the Modify Styles dialog box, or by playing the CHGFONT macro supplied with Ami. The macro lets you change the styles in the current style sheet or in all style sheets.

Summary

The key to using Ami Pro to create professional-looking documents with a minimum of effort is style sheets. They let you achieve the appropriate design for a newsletter, a memo, a calendar, a book, or whatever document you are creating without having to define all the design details from scratch. You can even change the style sheet a document uses to achieve a totally different look.

Ami style sheets are quite flexible, letting you change styles to affect only the current document or all documents using that same style sheet. You can create your own style sheets by renaming one of Ami's original style sheets and then modifying its styles. You also can create a new style sheet by copying styles from existing style sheets. Overall, style sheets give you the power and ability to create professional-looking documents without requiring you to be a graphic designer or DTP expert.

6
CHAPTER

Using fonts

One of the most exciting aspects of the new generation of word processors is their support of fonts. The old Courier typewriter font looks ancient when you compare it to the Times Roman, Century Schoolbook, or Palatino that word-processed documents sport today. Even if your printer doesn't come with any special fonts, you can achieve professional results by using the Adobe Type Manager fonts supplied with Ami Pro.

Font terminology

A typeface is the distinctive look of an alphabet and its related characters. Common typefaces are Times, Univers, and Courier. A font is all the characters and punctuation marks of one size and style of type. For example, Times Bold and Times Italic are two different fonts within one typeface. A typeface family is all the different fonts that make up a typeface, such as obliqued (slanted), italic, black (extra bold), bold, light, book, roman (normal), compressed, and extended.

Each typeface is designed with a particular purpose in mind. Some typefaces are custom-designed for use in titles and headings. These are called display typefaces, and are usually bold and dramatic in appearance. Examples of display type include Bodoni and Franklin Gothic. Some typefaces are easily recognized because they appear exclusively on documents such as invitations and diplomas. These are called decorative typefaces, and are usually ornate and distinctive in appearance. Examples of decorative typefaces are Script and Caslon.

The most common typeface design is the text typeface used for the body of a document. Text typefaces provide an appearance that is pleasing to the eye, so that a document's audience doesn't have to strain to read the text. You would never use Script as the typeface for the body of a newsletter, because it would make it unbearable to read and inappropriate for the document's purpose. A serif typeface is commonly used for body text because it is one of the easiest to read. A serif typeface finishes each letter, number, or symbol with rounded or straight lines. A serif serves as a bridge from one letter to the next. Examples of serif typefaces include Times Roman and Courier. A typeface that doesn't uses serifs is called a sans serif typeface. Examples of sans-serif typefaces are Univers and Helvetica. Figure 6-1 displays an example of both serif and sans serifs typefaces.

Fonts are measured in points, which a unit of measurement equal to $\frac{1}{72}$ of an inch. The point size of a character is usually measured from the top of its highest point to the bottom of its lowest point. Points are a more convenient measurement to use than inches when measuring type, because you would be dealing constantly with fractions of inches, which would be confusing and cumbersome at best. Most body text is around 10 or 12 points (pts.). Headings are larger and captions are smaller.

Font types

The fonts available to you depend more on what printer you have than on Ami Pro. Printers have their own set of fonts that Ami lists in the Modify Style dialog box and the Status Bar. The types of fonts supplied with your printer determine the fonts available to you. In addition, Ami comes with Adobe Type Manager

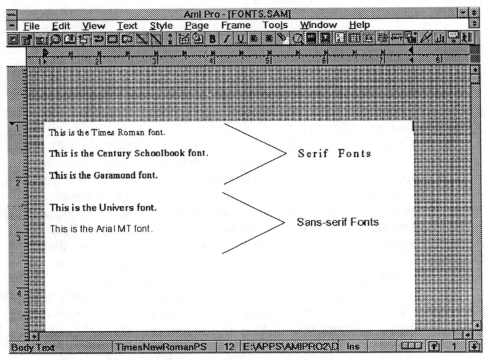

6-1 A Sample of serif and sans-serif typefaces.

fonts that you can install on your PC and use in your documents. Fonts come in three different varieties: vector fonts, bitmap fonts, and outline fonts.

Vector fonts

Vector fonts are built by drawing lines between the points and curves in a letter or number. Vector fonts can be scaled or rotated, but creating vector fonts requires additional PC power and memory. Consequently, vector fonts are slower to display and print than are bitmap or outline fonts; however, because you can scale a vector font, you need less storage space to hold them. You only need to store one font size, but you can scale that font up or down as needed.

Bitmap fonts

Bitmap fonts are built by combining a series of dots to form a character or number. Bitmap fonts cannot be scaled to a different size—you must store one file on your hard disk for every different point size and font you need to use in your document (Times Italic, Times Bold). As a result, bitmap fonts require a large amount of disk space. Also, you cannot rotate a bitmap font. Bitmap fonts usually come in the form of a printer cartridge or soft fonts.

Outline fonts

Outline fonts produce the sharpest, clearest result of all three fonts. Outline fonts are available on some laser printers, including PostScript and LaserJet III printers. Outline fonts are stored as sets of mathematical descriptions of the character outlines. When you use a 10-pt. Times Roman bold, the printer uses the outline to generate the font. Outline fonts can be scaled and rotated, so only one font of each typeface is required to create a range of sizes and variations of type.

Font sources

When you display the Modify Style dialog box and select the Font attribute, Ami displays a list of fonts available for your documents. The fonts listed in the dialog box come from a combination of three sources: your printer, your soft fonts, and your printer cartridge.

Printer fonts

Printer fonts come with your printer when you purchase it. All printers come with fonts, but not all have the same selection, quantity, or quality. Dot-matrix and letter-quality have the fewest number of built-in fonts, while laser printers have the most fonts from which to choose. PostScript printers come with 35 fonts, including Times Roman, Helvetica, Courier, Palatino, New Century Schoolbook, Avant Garde, Bookman, Chancery, Dingbats, and Symbol. Hewlett-Packard and compatible printers come with a variety of fonts, depending on the printer model.

HP LaserJet II printers come with only Courier 12-pt. medium and 8-pt. Line Printer, while HP LaserJet III printers come with scalable Times Roman and Universe, Courier 10 and 12-pt., and Line Printer 8.5-pt.

Soft fonts

Soft fonts are software files that come on floppy disks. Soft fonts usually supply two sets of fonts: printer fonts and screen fonts. Printer fonts format the appearance of the document on the printed page. The screen fonts format the appearance of the document on the screen. Not all soft fonts come with screen fonts, so you might not get a true WYSIWYG display. Even though printer fonts affect your document's appearance, you don't see the change in your document on the screen. The Adobe Type Manager fonts supplied with Ami Pro are soft fonts that you can install on your PC and use in your documents. The fonts supplied with ATM are Arial MT, Brush Script, Caslon OpenFace, Courier, Dom Casual, Franklin Gothic, Letter Gothic, Shelley Allegro Script, Symbol, and Times New Roman.

Cartridge fonts

Cartridge fonts come on a plug-in cartridge that you can insert into your printer. Cartridge fonts come in different varieties that are suitable for different applications. Some cartridge fonts carry very few fonts, such as the HP Tax 1 Font cartridge or HP Bar Codes cartridge, while others carry an entire library of fonts, such as the Pacific Data Products Complete Font Library cartridge, containing over 51 fonts. The fonts in the cartridge format only the printed document's appearance; they do not change the document's on-screen appearance to match the printed page. Some cartridge fonts come with screen fonts on a floppy disk that you can install for a true WYSIWYG appearance.

Installing fonts

How you go about installing fonts depends upon what font types you are using. Printer fonts don't require installation, because they are built-in to the printer. Soft fonts and cartridge fonts do require an installation process so that your printer and Ami can recognize and use them. However, each vendor uses a different installation process. Refer to your soft font or cartridge font manual for instructions on installing your fonts.

The installation process for Adobe Type Manager fonts is as follows:

1. Insert the ATM Fonts disk into drive A: and close the drive door.

2. Close Ami Pro by selecting Exit from the File menu or by selecting the Exit icon.

3. Open the File Manager by selecting the icon and choosing File Open or double clicking on the icon.

4. Select the A: drive to display the files on the ATM Fonts disk.

5. Highlight the INSTALL.EXE file and select Open from the File menu or double click on the file.

6. Specify a different target directory for the outline fonts and for the font metric files.

7. Select the Install button. ATM displays the percentage complete for the install process.

8. If your printer has less than 512K of memory and you want to install PCL fonts, specify a target directory and select Install. If you don't want to install PCL fonts select Skip.

9. Restart Windows so that it and Ami Pro will recognize the newly-installed soft fonts. The ATM Control Panel icon appears in the Main program group on the Windows desktop.

If at any time after you install the ATM fonts you don't want to use them, open the ATM Control Panel and select Off. Restart Windows to make it and Ami Pro ignore the soft fonts on your PC.

Selecting fonts in Ami Pro

Ami has three ways that you can select a font: from the Status Bar, from the Text menu, or from the Modify Style dialog box. Each method is designed for a different purpose and affects your documents differently.

Selecting a font from the Status Bar

You can use the Status Bar to select a new font and point size and apply them to one character or to an entire document. Any font changes you make using the Status Bar overrides the style's font assignment. Even if you change the style to use a different font, any paragraphs to which you applied new fonts using the Status Bar don't change.

Ami's Status Bar displays the font and the point size for the current paragraph. If you have a mouse, you can click on the font name to display the fonts available, as shown in Figure 6-2. You can highlight text to which you want to assign a different font, and select a new font and point size from the Status Bar. Ami assigns the new font and point size to the text you selected. If you did not select any text, Ami assigns the new font and size to the cursor's current position, so any new text you enter or import uses the new settings.

Selecting a font from the Text menu

Selecting a font from the Text menu gives you more choices than the Status Bar. Using the Text menu, you can select a new font, point size, or color. Also, font changes made to text using the Text menu override the style's font assignment.

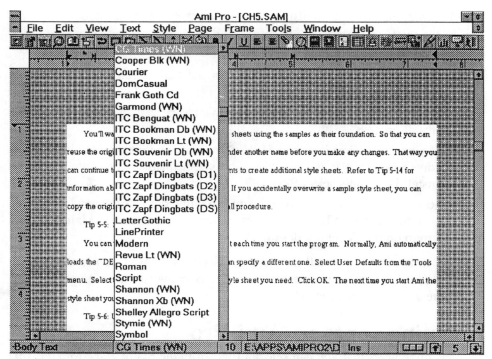

6-2 You can select a font by holding the mouse button down over the current font name in the Status Bar.

The only way you can change text is to use its original font is to select Revert to style in the Font dialog box or Normal from the Text menu. You can use the Text menu to assign a font to a block of text or to the cursor's current position to apply to any text you type or import.

Once you select the Font command from the Text menu, Ami displays the Font dialog box as shown in Figure 6-3. The following paragraphs list tips for using the options in the Font dialog box.

Face   The Face list box displays the fonts available to Ami Pro from your printer, printer cartridge, or soft fonts. Ami treats each font equally, no matter if it is a printer, cartridge, or soft font. However, if you use cartridge or soft fonts and you do not have screen fonts, Ami cannot display your font changes on the screen, although the font does appear when you print your document.

Size   Select the point size you want to use from the Size list box. If the point size you need isn't displayed in the list box, you can enter a custom point size in the Point text box.

Color   Select a color for your text from the color list box. Ami can print your text in color only if you have a color printer.

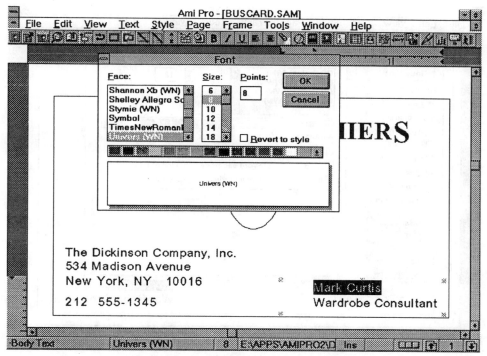

6-3 Selecting a font from the Font dialog box gives you more choices than doing so from the Status Bar.

Revert to style   Select Revert to style to undo any font, size, or color changes you made to your text. Ami formats the text according the settings in its style.

Selecting a font from the Modify Style dialog box

The Modify Style dialog box contains more font options than the Text menu or the Status Bar. Also, font changes you make in the Modify Style dialog box affect every paragraph using that style. Once you click on the Font style attribute in the Modify Style dialog box, Ami displays the options shown in Figure 6-4:

The Face list box displays the fonts available to Ami Pro from your printer, printer cartridge, or soft fonts. Ami treats each font equally, no matter if it is a printer, cartridge, or soft font. However, if you use cartridge or soft fonts and you do not have screen fonts, Ami cannot display your font changes on the screen, although the font does appear when you print your document.

Select the point size you want to use from the Size list box. If the point size you need isn't displayed in the list box, you can enter a custom point size in the Point text box.

Select a color for your text from the color list box. Ami can print your text in color only if you have a color printer.

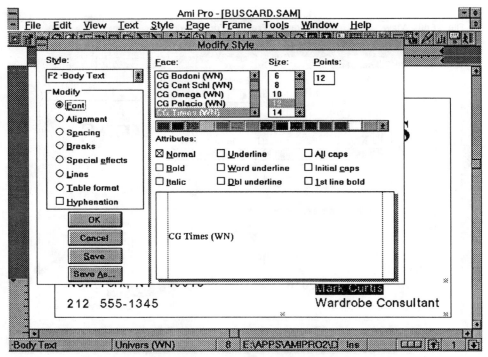

6-4 You can select the font, size, color, and attributes from the Modify Style dialog box.

Select the text attribute you want to assign to the paragraphs using this style. Any attribute you select applies to all the text in every paragraph using that style. You can select from Normal, Bold, Italic, Underline, Word Underline, Double Underline, All Caps, Initial Caps, and 1st Line Bold.

Tip 6-1: Display styles using different colors   When you display your document using Draft or Outline mode, it can be difficult to identify the styles your paragraphs use. Draft mode does show you the spacing, indention, and font for each paragraph, but Outline mode does not. It uses its own indention and spacing. The only style attribute you see in Outline mode is the font, and only if you turn off System font in Draft mode from the View Preferences dialog box. Even if you don't have a color printer, you can assign a different color to each style. You then can identify the styles you assign to your paragraphs by the colors they display. When you print your documents, Ami uses black for each style if you do not have a color printer.

Tip 6-2: Updating style sheets with fonts for default printer   How many times have you seen the message displayed in Figure 6-5? Ami displays this message because its style sheets were created with a different printer than the one you are using. The fonts your printer contains are not the same as those in the printer saved with the style sheet, so Ami is telling you to choose the appropriate font

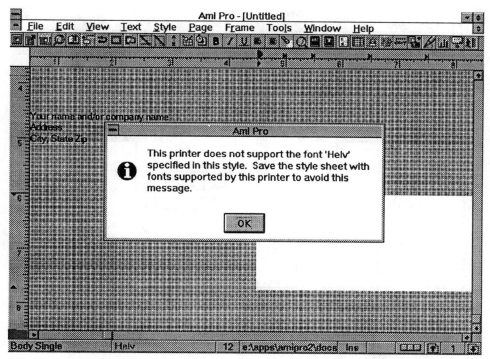

6-5 If you are not using the same printer that the document was saved with, Ami Pro displays this message.

from your own printer. However, selecting a font for every single style in every style sheet is very time-consuming. Fortunately, Ami provides a macro that lets you update your style sheets with the correct fonts for your printer. You can update the current style sheet or all style sheets.

The macro acts as a Find and Replace for fonts not available on your printer. Ami analyzes one or all style sheets, looks for fonts not available on your printer, and then asks you for replacements for each font.

When you playback the CHGFONT macro, you must have a document open. Otherwise, Ami Pro functions, the macro needs are greyed, and the macro cannot execute.

After you choose the CHGFONT macro, Ami displays the Select Style Sheets dialog box, as shown in Figure 6-6. You can choose one style sheet to update or select all style sheets to update at once. Ami then searches for the fonts specified in each style sheet. Ami tells you which style sheet it is analyzing in the Status Bar. If a font isn't available on your printer, Ami displays the New Font dialog box. You can then choose the font to replace the unavailable one.

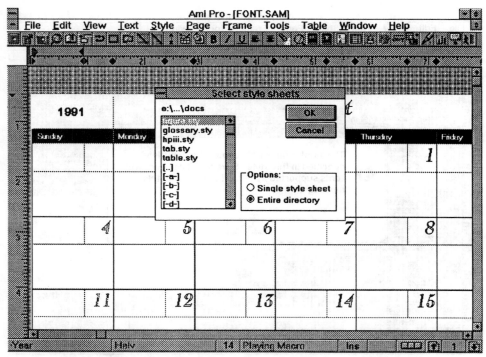

6-6 You can use the CHGFONT macro to update the fonts for all style sheets or just one style sheet to match those available on your printer.

Questions & Answers

Q: Why does my font name appear in red in the Status Bar?

A: If the Status Bar displays the current font in red letters, the font is not available. Either your printer, soft fonts, or print cartridge does not support that font. Ami's style sheets were created at Lotus Development Corporation using specific printers. If you don't use the same printer, or if you don't have ATM fonts installed, your fonts will not match those in the style sheet. You can change the style to use a font available in your printer, soft fonts, or printer cartridge using the Modify Style dialog box or by executing the CHGFONT macro.

Summary

Fonts are what make today's published documents look sleek. You no longer need to send a brochure to the print shop to use special typefaces, because they are now available for your own use. Three types of fonts are available: vector, bitmap, and outline. Fonts usually come from one of three sources: a printer, software (as in soft fonts), or in a printer cartridge. How you install those fonts depends upon the font source. Printer fonts require no installation, while soft fonts require you to select the fonts you need and to copy them to your hard disk. Once you install fonts, you use them to format the documents you create in Ami Pro. You select a font from the Status Bar, the Font command on the Text menu, or from the Modify Style dialog box. The method you use to select a font depends on the amount of control you need in formatting the document.

7
CHAPTER

Formatting text and pages

As you become more comfortable assigning styles to paragraphs and applying text attributes, you'll want to experiment with the options available to design your own look for your documents. To do so, you need to modify Ami's style sheets or create entirely new ones using commands on the Style and Page menus. All the formatting options available for your styles are located in the dialog box Ami displays when you choose the Modify Style command. All the formatting options available for the page are found in the Modify Page Layout dialog box on the Page menu.

Learning how to use all of the formatting options can be confusing and time-consuming. Creating and customizing styles and page layouts to produce your own style sheet is one of the most labor-intensive and time-consuming tasks in word processing and DTP. Fortunately, Ami simplifies the process by placing all formatting features in one dialog box for styles and in another dialog box for page layouts. Ami also shows you an example of how your text and page will appear while you are making formatting decisions. You aren't forced to return to your document to see your results, and then return to the dialog box for more tweaking if they aren't satisfactory.

Chapter 5 discusses style sheets, explains how to assign styles to your paragraphs, and explains how to create new styles. You need to understand how to perform those tasks before you tackle the advice in this chapter, which explains how to use the formatting options available in Ami to modify your own styles and page layouts.

Style attributes

Style attributes are similar to those commands located in the Text menu, such as font, alignment, and spacing. The difference between those commands and the style attributes discussed in this chapter is that you use the Text menu commands to format text within a paragraph. If you need only a few words of a paragraph in italics, use the Text menu to assign italics and override the current style. Use the style attributes in this chapter to change a style, affecting all of the paragraphs in all of the documents using the current style sheet. Also, style attributes are much more detailed and give you a greater control over your document's appearance than those formatting options stored in the Text menu.

Accessing Ami's style attributes

You can access the style attributes in one of two ways: by selecting Modify Style from the Style menu, or by creating a new style and selecting the Modify button. Either of these procedures displays the Modify Style dialog box as shown in Figure 7-1:

The Modify Style dialog box has a left and a right section. The left section contains style attributes. The right section displays the options available for the style attribute you chose in the left section. If you select the Alignment option button in the left section of the dialog box, the right section displays Alignment options. The dialog box displays two buttons in addition to the usual OK and Cancel buttons: Save and Save As. Select the Save button to record changes to the current style and remain in the dialog box to change additional styles. Select the Save As button to create a new style by saving the changes to the style under a new style name. Ami displays a dialog box in which you type the new style name.

At the top of the left section of the dialog box, Ami displays a list box that shows the name of the style you are modifying. If you want to modify additional styles, select the style name from the list box. If you have not saved the changes to the current style, Ami asks you if you want to do so.

The style attributes discussed in this chapter are:

- alignment and tabs
- line and paragraph spacing
- page and column breaks
- bullets and special effects
- lines above and below paragraphs
- hyphenation.

Tip 7-1: Work from top to bottom   Each style attribute's dialog box contains a rich assortment of options, but it can be confusing to know where to start. One method is to start from the top of the dialog box and work your way down. Begin

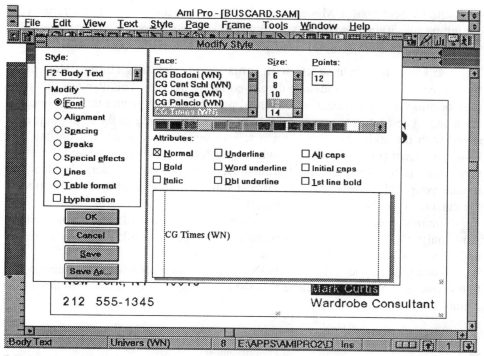

7-1 Use the Modify Style dialog box to change paragraph formatting.

by selecting the Font style attribute and making all the selections you need in the dialog box, then select the Alignment style attribute and do the same. Continue until you have selected all the style attributes. You probably don't need to use all the style attributes to modify a style, but working from top to bottom is an efficient method to use for both modifying and creating a style.

Tip 7-2: Use the unit of measurement appropriate for your document   In all dialog boxes except those for fonts, breaks, and table formats, you specify many options in a unit of measurement. Ami uses inches as its default unit of measurement, but for newsletters, books, brochures, and business cards, inches is too large of a unit for practical use. Specifying the amount of spacing between paragraphs, how far to indent the first line of a paragraph, and other attributes in fractions of inches is frustrating and time-consuming to calculate. You can change the unit of measurement for each style attribute by clicking on the inches button. Each time you select the button, a different unit of measurement appears. You can choose from inches, centimeters, picas, and points.

Tip 7-3: Use the dialog box examples as a guide   Ami displays an example in each dialog box of the effect your style attribute selections will have on your text. These examples save an incredible amount of time, because you don't need to return to your document each time you make a selection to see your results. You can actually see what a Modern font looks like or the effect of indenting your paragraph by .50 inches before you return to your document. You can experiment with each style attribute option and see the results immediately.

Tip 7-4: Updating style sheets with fonts for the default printer   How many times have you seen the message displayed in Figure 7-2? Ami displays this message because its style sheets were created with a different printer than the one you are using. The fonts your printer contains are not the same as those in the printer saved with the style sheet, so Ami is telling you to choose the appropriate font from your own printer. However, selecting a font for every single style in every style sheet is time-consuming. Fortunately, Ami provides a macro that lets you update your style sheets with the correct fonts for your printer. You can update the current style sheet or all style sheets.

The macro acts as a Find and Replace for fonts not available on your printer. Ami analyzes one or all style sheets, looks for fonts not available on your printer, and then asks you for replacements for each font.

When you playback the CHGFONT macro, you must have a document open. Otherwise, the Ami Pro functions that the macro needs are greyed, and the macro cannot execute.

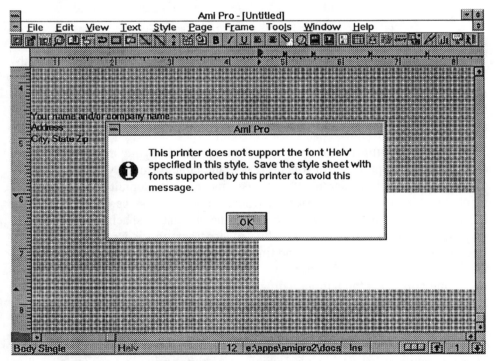

7-2   If you are not using the same printer that the document was saved with, Ami Pro displays this message.

After you choose the CHGFONT macro, Ami displays the Select Style Sheets dialog box, as shown in Figure 7-3. You can choose one style sheet to update or select all style sheets to update at once. Ami then searches for the fonts specified in each style sheet. Ami tells you which style sheet it is analyzing in the Status Bar. If a font isn't available on your printer, Ami displays the New Font dialog box. You can then choose the font to replace the unavailable one.

Alignment

Once you select the Alignment style attribute, Ami displays the options shown in Figure 7-4. Discussed below are tips on using the options for the Alignment style attributes:

Style Tab Ruler Create style tabs for the current style that will override the tabs in the page layout ruler. You can select from left, center, right, and numeric tab types. Each type can use an underline leader, a dash leader, or a period leader. To create a tab, select a tab icon and then select the top half of the ruler at the position where you need to add a tab. You also can specify a measurement in the text box and select Set Tab. To add a leader, select the leader icon to cycle through the leader options. The current leader type displays in the tab type icons. To delete a

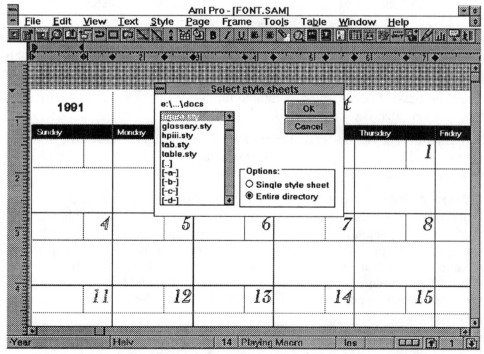

7-3 You can use the CHGFONT macro to update the fonts for all style sheets or just one style sheet to match those available on your printer.

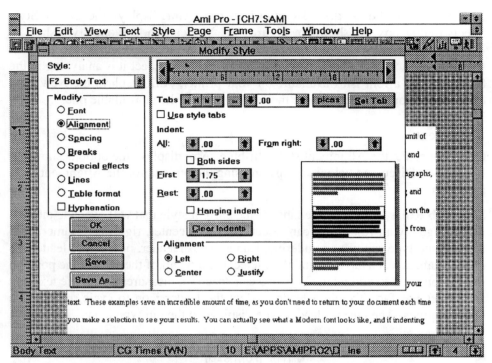

7-4 Alignment in the Modify Style dialog box controls style tabs, indentions, and alignment.

tab, drag the tab off the ruler. Table 7-1 displays the icons representing each tab type.

Use style tabs   Select Use Style Tabs to turn on the tab settings you created in the style tab ruler.

Alignment   The options available are Left, Center, Right, and Justify. You will base most of your own styles on Body Text, which uses left alignment, as do most of the styles in the sample style sheets.

Indent   All indents every line in the paragraph from the left edge of the column. Right indents every line in the paragraph from the right edge of the column. Both Sides gives the same effect as if you selected All and Right the same amount of times. First indents only the first line of the paragraph from the left edge of the column. Rest indents all lines in the paragraph except for the first from the left edge of the column. Hanging indent inserts a tab in the first line of the paragraph the same measurement you specified for Rest. Clear indents removes all indentions from the current style.

Tip 7-5: Identifying tab ruler types   Ami has three types of tab rulers: page layout, style tab, and inserted. You create each type of tab ruler using a different

Table 7-1. Tab Ruler Marks

Mark	Description	Mark	Description
	Left tab		Numeric tab
	Left tab with underline leader		Numeric tab with underline leader
	Left tab with dashed leader		Numeric tab with dashed leader
	Left tab with period leader		Numeric tab with period leader
	Right tab		Center tab
	Right tab with underline leader		Center tab with underline leader
	Right tab with dashed leader		Center tab with dashed leader
	Right tab with period leader		Center tab with period leader

method, and the tabs in each ruler have varying levels of control over the text in your document. Table 7-2 explains each type.

Tip 7-6: Displaying the tab bar   To create or modify tab settings in a dialog box or from the document, use the tab bar above the tab ruler, as shown in Figure 7-5. You can display the tab bar for the current tab ruler by clicking on the upper part of the tab ruler at the top of the screen. Select any part of the document or dialog box to close the tab bar.

Tip 7-7: Removing an inserted tab ruler   Don't try to delete an inserted tab ruler using the Del or Backspace keys. The only way Ami lets you delete an inserted tab ruler is using the Ruler Remove command from the Page menu. If the command is greyed, select Go To from the Edit menu or press Ctrl-G. Select Next Item and choose Ruler Mark.

Tip 7-8: Changing tab types   If you need to change a left-aligned tab to a right-aligned tab, you must delete it and then create a new one. Ami does not let you switch existing tabs. To delete the tab, drag it off of the tab ruler.

Tip 7-9: Using hard spaces instead of tabs   If you need to create a special tab for just one paragraph, use a hard space instead. A hard space is a fixed amount of space that you can use instead of creating new tab settings for a single paragraph. To insert a hard space, press Ctrl-Spacebar.

Table 7-2. Tab Ruler Types

Page Layout Tab Rulers	Style Tab Rulers	Inserted Tab Rulers
Create in the Modify Page Layout dialog box.	Create in the Modify Style dialog box.	Create by changing the ruler at the top of the screen or by selecting the Page Ruler Insert command.
Affect entire document.	Affect paragraphs using that style.	Affects current paragraph and all after it.
One ruler allowed per page layout.	One ruler allowed for each style.	One ruler allowed in each paragraph.
Lowest in hierarchy. Is overriden by style tab and insert tab rulers.	Overrides page layout tab rulers. Does not override inserted tab rulers.	Highest in hierarchy. Overrides both page layout and style tab rulers.

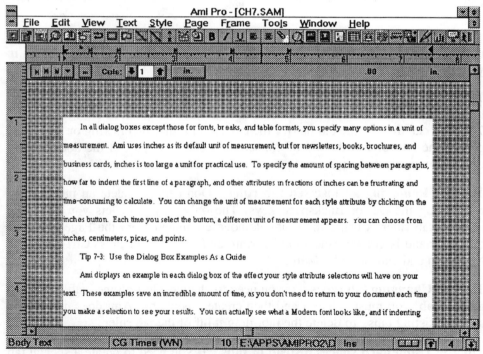

7-5 You can click on the upper portion of the tab ruler in the document or in the Modify Style dialog box to display the tab bar.

Tip 7-10: Creating signature lines using leader tabs   If you create forms with fill-in-the blanks or signature lines, create these items using a tab with an underline leader. Create a tab setting that includes the appropriate amount of space for the item, and select the tab type you need with an underline leader. When you press the Tab key, Ami precedes the tab with an underline.

Tip 7-11: Change first line and rest indents using tab ruler   You can move the marks for the First Line and Rest indents to change their settings. Position the mouse on the mark you need and drag it to its new position. Ami automatically enters the settings in the text boxes in the dialog box.

Tip 7-12: Measure indents and tabs from column edge   Ami measures any tabs or indents you create from the edge of the column, not the edge of the paper. You can display columns guides by selecting Column Guides from Edit/View Preferences. Column guides are dotted lines that surround your columns, making columns, gutters, and margins easier to see.

Tip 7-13: Using the alignment example box   The example box Ami displays when you select Alignment attributes displays three paragraphs: the top and bottom paragraphs never change, but the middle paragraphs reflects the attributes you select. The first line, displayed in blue if you have a color monitor, represents the First Line indent, while all subsequent lines, displayed in magenta, represent the Rest selection. The example box does not reflect any changes in justification or tabs.

Tip 7-14: Using hanging indents   Follow these rules when you create a hanging indent:

- Make sure the measurement you enter for Rest is the same or larger than the first tab setting in the ruler. Because Ami inserts a tab to create a hanging indent, it uses the tab settings in the ruler to determine where the text begins after the tab. If your measurement isn't as large or larger than the first tab setting, your second and subsequent lines will not be indented as much as the first.

- If you are using a first line indent along with the hanging indent, make sure to add the amount of the first line indent to the amount you need to indent the rest of the paragraph. If you don't, your second and subsequent lines will not be indented as much as the first. For example, if your first line indent is .50 inches, and you need to create a hanging indent about one inch from the term it describes, you would enter a measurement of 1.50 inches for Rest: one inch for the hanging indent, plus .50 inches to compensate for the first line measurement.

Spacing

Once you select the Spacing style attribute, Ami displays the options shown in Figure 7-6:

Line spacing controls the amount of space Ami inserts between lines on the page (also known as leading). Specify Single, 1½, Double, or a Custom amount. The rules for figuring spacing are in Table 7-3.

Paragraph Spacing   Good typography calls for extra spacing between paragraphs to make the text easier to read. Use paragraph spacing to insert additional space between each paragraph (in addition to the amount of line spacing you specified). However, when a paragraph appears at the top of a page, the extra space is not needed, so select When not at break under the Add in option to prevent a gap at the top of the page. The rules for figuring spacing are in Table 7-3.

Text Tightness   Use Text tightness to specify the amount of space you need between characters (also known as kerning). Tight text fits more words on a line, while loose text fits fewer words on a line.

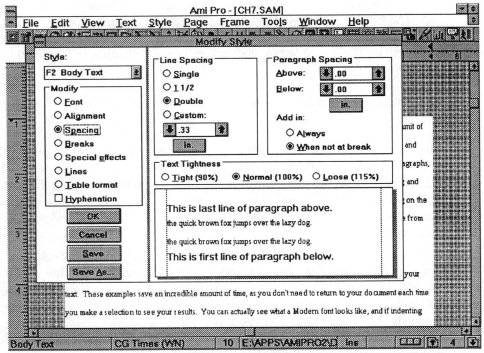

7-6 Spacing in the Modify Style dialog box controls line and paragraph spacing, and text tightness (kerning).

Table 7-3. Figuring Line Spacing Between Two Paragraphs

	Line spacing of current paragraph
+	Below paragraph spacing of current paragraph
+	Above paragraph spacing of next paragraph

Total space between paragraphs

Tip 7-15: Using line breaks instead of returns By pressing Ctrl-Enter, you can start a new line using a line break instead of a paragraph return. Line breaks let you start a new line without starting a new paragraph.

Tip 7-16: Creating em and en spaces Ami does not create em or en spaces used in typesetting, but you can create your own. A em space is the same width as the letter m, and an en space is the same width as the letter n. To create an em space, insert the em dash by pressing Alt-0151 (on the numeric keypad), highlight the dash, and change its color to white using the Font command on the Text menu. Ami does not print the character, and the letter is not visible on the screen, but you created a space the same width as an em space. Do the same for an en space by using the letter en dash, Alt-0150 on the numeric keypad.

Tip 7-17: Calculating custom line spacing When using the Custom option for line spacing, it should be at least two points larger than your font's point size. For example, if a style uses a 12-pt. font, its line spacing should be at least 14-pts. Any measurement less than this will not include enough white space between lines to make your text readable.

Tip 7-18: Using the spacing example box Ami displays four lines of text in the spacing example box. The two middle lines reflect the line spacing attributes you chose. The top and bottom lines reflect the paragraph spacing you chose.

Page and column breaks

Once you select Breaks style attribute, Ami displays the options shown in Figure 7-7:

If you need a style to be the first text on a page, select Before paragraph. If you need a style to be the last text on a page, select After paragraph. If you need a style to be the only text on a page, select both options. If you don't want to allow a paragraph to be divided by a page break, turn off Allow page/column break within. Ami moves the entire paragraph to the next page. If you need a style to be the first text in a column, select Column break before paragraph. If you need a style to be the last text in a column, select Column break after paragraph. If you want the style to be the only text in a column, select both options. If you don't want a paragraph divided by a column break, turn off Allow page/column break within.

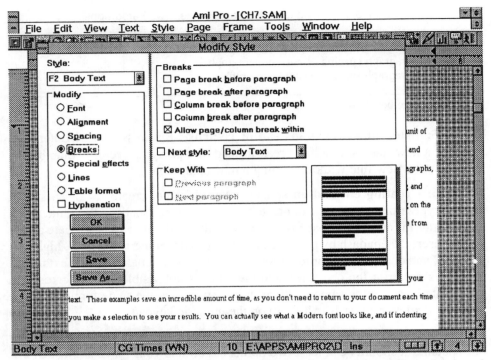

7-7 Breaks in the Modify Style dialog box controls column and page breaks, assigns a style based on the previous paragraph's style, and keeps a paragraph with the next or previous paragraph.

Next style   Wouldn't it be easy if Ami Pro knew our style sheets so well that it could predict the next style we need and activate it for us? Use the Next style option and you get exactly that. When you press the Enter key after using the current style, Ami changes to the style you specify in the Next style text box. Next style is useful for subheadings and the text that follows.

Keep With   If you need to keep two paragraphs together, select either Previous or Next paragraph. This option is useful for headings, subheadings, and paragraphs that follow. To use this option, make sure Allow Within is not selected. Ami will not let you use Keep Within if Allow Within is selected.

Special effects

Once you select the Special Effects style attribute, Ami displays the options shown in Figure 7-8.

Select Bullet to precede each paragraph using this style with a bullet. Select the bullet type from the list box.

Select Number to precede each paragraph using this style with a number. Ami automatically numbers the paragraphs, so if you insert or remove an entire

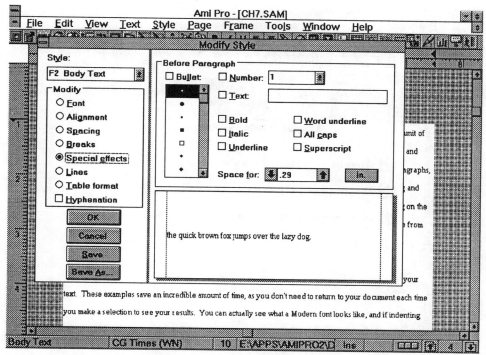

7-8 Special Effects in the Modify Style dialog box controls bullets, text, and numbering before paragraphs.

paragraph, Ami updates the numbering for you. Select the type of numbering style you need. Special effects numbering updates only paragraphs that are consecutive. If a paragraph using another style appears between two paragraphs using special effects numbering, the numbering does not update.

Select Text to insert a word or phrase before each paragraph using this style. In the text box, type the text you need to precede each paragraph.

Select an Attribute to apply formatting such as bold or italic to the text or number you insert before a paragraph.

Select Space for to insert a consistent amount of space after the text or bullet preceding the paragraph. Space for ignores tab settings and inserts the same amount of space each time.

Tip 7-19: Creating customized bullets Ami lets you choose from several bullet types, but you also can use graphics as bullets. Create a frame, import the graphic you need, and select the In line anchor type from the Modify Frame Layout command in the Frame menu. You can use graphic bullets to emphasize important text, such as warnings or cautions; you can include symbols that represent international signs or limitations; or you can include your company logo to mark official company policy. Graphic bullets are shown in Figure 7-9.

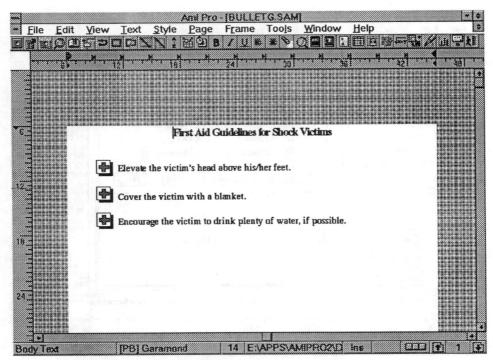

7-9 Anchor frames to paragraphs to create special effect bullets.

Tip 7-20: Creating bullets using ANSI characters   You can create bullets not available in the bullet list box by typing an ANSI character in the Text box in the Modify Style dialog box. Place your cursor in the text box, hold down the Alt key, and type the numeric code from the numeric keypad. Ami displays the ANSI character in the text box. Now each time you use that paragraph style, Ami uses the ANSI character as a bullet.

Tip 7-21: Create bullets using the Zapf Dingbat font   If you have a Postscript printer or additional fonts for your laserjet, you can create additional bullets using the Zapf Dingbat font. Follow the steps outlined in Tip 7-20, but change the font for the bullet to Zapf Dingbat. You cannot change the font while in the dialog box; you must make the change while you are in the document. An easy way to change the font for all your bullets is to create a macro rather than doing it manually.

Tip 7-22: Creating a to-do list using bullets   You can create a list that indicates action by selecting the checkmark when you choose the Bullet option. Select the Alignment option and remove all tabs from the ruler. Create a right tab using an underline leader. When you return to the document, assign the style to a new paragraph and press the Tab key. Ami inserts the bullet followed by an underline.

Tip 7-23: Present a list of choices using bullets If you use Ami to create brochures, invoices, or order forms, you can present the reader with a list of choices for products, shipping, and other options by selecting the hollow box bullet. As you list the choices on the form, assign the style using the hollow box to those paragraphs. Ami inserts a hollow box in front of the choices so readers can mark their selection. Figure 7-10 shows a sample order form that uses hollow box bullets.

Tip 7-24: Combining text and numbers to create special effects You can create specialized numbering schemes, such as *Fig 1-5,* by inserting both text and numbers in the Text box. Type the text in the Text box and specify the numbering scheme by clicking on Number. If you need numbers specific to each chapter of your document (Fig 1-x for chapter 1 and Fig 2-x for chapter 2), Ami cannot create them automatically; but you can create them manually by typing the number in the text box. Keep the style as a document style, and it always will be specific to the current chapter.

Tip 7-25: Creating a numbering scheme using outline styles Even if you aren't creating an outline, you can use the numbering options in the Outline Style

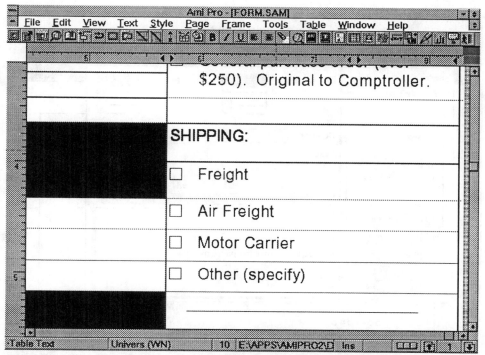

7-10 This form uses hollow box bullets as a place where you can check off your choice of several options.

dialog box to create a numbering scheme that updates even after an intervening style. To do so, assign levels to two styles: the style to which you want to assign numbers, and a style that typically appears before the numbering style, such as a section title or body text. Assign a higher level to the body text or section title style, and assign the next lower level to the numbering style. Specify the Arabic Numbering option for the numbering style and choose After higher style as the Reset option.

Lines

Once you select the Lines style attribute, Ami displays the options shown in Figure 7-11.

To place a line above the paragraph, select Line above. To place a lien below the paragraph, select Line below.

Select the line type you need from the Line style list box. Both Line above and Line below have their own Line style list boxes so you can select a different line style for each. Enter the amount of space you need between the paragraph and the line. Line above and line below each have their own text box for spacing. Depending on whether you chose Line above or Line below, Ami places the spacing you specify above or below the paragraph.

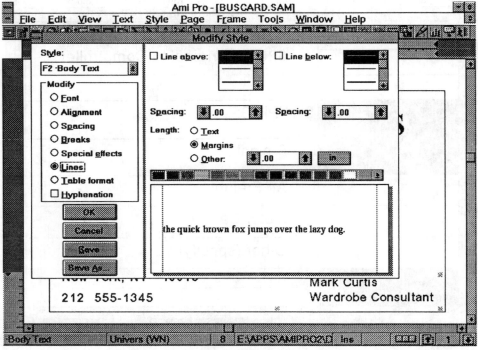

7-11 Lines in the Modify Style dialog box controls lines above and below a paragraph, line length, and line color.

The length options are Text, Margins, and Other. Select Text to make the line the same length as the paragraph. Select Margins to make the line extend from the left to the right margin. Select Other to create a line that extends to the length you specify in the text box.

You can select a color if you have a color printer. The color you choose affects both the Line above and the Line below.

Tip 7-26: Creating variable line lengths   What if you need a line that extends from the end of your text to the right margin? You can create one, but not using the Lines style attributes. Instead, use the Alignment style attribute. Change the style tab ruler for the style to include only one tab: a right-aligned tab with an underline at the right margin location. Select Use style tabs. Now when you need that line, simply type your text and press the Tab key. Ami creates a line that extends from your text to the right margin.

Hyphenation.

Normally Ami does not hyphenate words that do not fit at the end of the line. Instead, it moves the entire word to the next line. You do have the option of using hyphenation, however. Select Hyphenation to hyphenate words at the end of a line.

Tip 7-27: Rules for hyphenation   Once you turn on hyphenation, Ami uses the following guidelines:

- Ami will hyphenate no more than two consecutive lines.
- Ami does not hyphenate words connected with a nonbreaking space.
- Ami does not hyphenate words containing numbers.

Tip 7-28: Preventing hyphenation   If hyphenation is not appropriate for your text, you can turn it off. Simply highlight the text you do not want to be hyphenated, and select Mark Text from the Edit menu. Select No Hyphenation to remove existing hyphenation or to prevent Ami from hyphenating the text in the future.

Tip 7-29: Forcing hyphenation   You can force Ami to hyphenate text by inserting your cursor at the position in the text at which you need a hyphen and holding down the Ctrl key and pressing the hyphen key. Ami inserts a discretionary hyphen in your text.

Tip 7-30: Changing the hyphenation hot zone   You can increase or decrease the amount of hyphenation in your document by changing the hyphenation hot zone. Increasing the hot zone decreases the amount of hyphenation, while decreasing the hot zone increases the amount of hyphenation in your document. Ami's default hyphenation hot zone is five. To change the hyphenation hot zone, select User Setup from the Tools menu. Select Options. Type a new value, between two and nine, for the hyphenation hot zone in the list box.

Page layout attributes

Each style sheet has a standard page layout that contains the page specifications for the whole document. Changes you make to the standard page layout affect every page in the document.

You also can insert new page layouts throughout your document. However, Ami saves only the first page layout with the style sheet. Ami saves additional page layouts with the document.

Changing a page layout

To change a page layout, you must be in Layout mode. Ami lets you can change a page layout in one of three ways: by changing the standard page layout, by inserting a new page layout, or by returning to the standard page layout.

Ami manages page layouts the same way it manages styles in that it has document page layouts and global page layouts. Document page layouts affect only the current document, while global page layouts affect all documents using the same style sheet. How can you tell which page layouts are global and which are document? The first page layout is the global, while subsequent page layouts are document-only.

Ami saves all page layout changes to the document unless you save the style sheet with the new settings. Changes saved to the document affect only it and no other documents using the same style sheet. If you save the style sheet, Ami then considers the first page layout to be the global, and saves it in the style sheet. Ami saves subsequent page layouts in the document. The subsequent page layouts do not affect other documents using the same style sheet. When you use the style sheet with another document, the only page layout available is the global.

Accessing page layout attributes

You can access page layout attributes by selecting Modify Page Layout from the Page menu or Insert Page Layout from the Page menu. Either method displays the Modify Page Layout dialog box as displayed in Figure 7-12.

The Modify Page Layout dialog box has a left and a right section. The left section contains page layout attributes. The right section displays the options available for the style attribute you chose in the left section. If you select the Margins & columns option button in the left section of the dialog box, the right section displays Margins & columns options.

Pages

The Pages option appears at the bottom left of the Modify Page Layout dialog box. You can create a page layout for all pages, right pages, left pages, or mirrored pages.

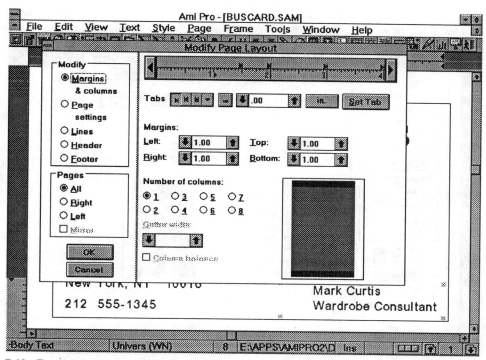

7-12 The Modify Page Layout dialog box lets you control page margins, columns, size, orientation, lines, headers, and footers.

Select All to create a page layout for every page in your document.

Select Mirror to create a layout for facing pages. Facing pages are a mirror image of each other because they contain exactly opposite page layouts. For example, if you have a larger left margin than right margin on your left page, your right page will have larger right margin than left margin. You specify only one page layout, and Ami will create the second set for the mirrored page.

Select Left to create a page layout for the left page that is different than the layout on the right page. Select Right to create a page layout for the right page that is different than the layout on the left page. When you select either left or right, you also need to create the page layout for the opposite page.

Margins & Columns

Once you select the Margins & columns page layout attribute, Ami displays the options shown in Figure 7-13.

Discussed below are tips on using the options for the Margins & columns page layout attributes.

Page Layout Tab Ruler   Use the page layout tab ruler to create tabs settings for the entire document. You can select from left, center, right, and numeric tab

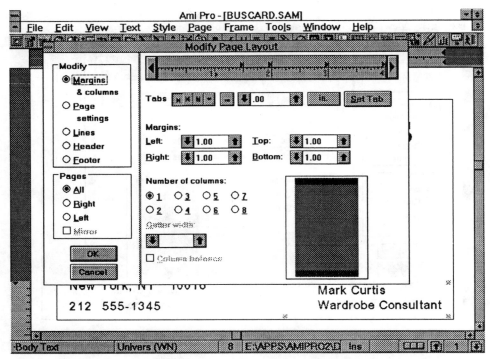

7-13 Margins & columns in the Modify Page Layout controls tab settings, margins, columns, and gutter widths.

types. Each type can use an underline leader, a dash leader, or a period leader. To create a tab, select a tab icon and then select the top half of ruler at the position at which you need to add a tab. You also can specify a measurement in the text box and select Set Tab. To add a leader, select the leader icon to cycle through the leader options. The current leader type displays in the tab type icons. To delete a tab, drag the tab off the ruler. Table 7-1 displays the icons representing each tab type. See Tips 7-5 through 7-11 for more information about tab rulers and tabs.

Margins   Enter the space you need for the left, right, top, and bottom margins. While you are in Layout mode, Ami displays margins in color (if you have a color monitor), or greyed if you have a monochrome monitor.

Number of columns   Select the number of columns you need for the document. You can have up to eight columns per page layout, but you rarely would need more than four. If you find that you need a large number of columns, consider using a table instead.

Gutter width   Gutters are the spaces between each column. Ami uses the figure you enter in the text box as the gutter width between all columns.

Column balance   Select column balance to place an equal amount of text in all of your columns. If you do not use column balance, Ami will fill the first column on the page with text before moving on to the next column.

Tip 7-31: Setting tabs for multiple columns   If you specify more than one column for your page layout, Ami creates tab settings for only the first column. You must manually create tab settings for each column using the tab ruler.

Tip 7-32: Creating uneven gutters   Ami automatically creates gutters of equal widths between your columns, but you can adjust the gutters to customized widths. Move the margin markers in the tab ruler to increase or decrease the gutter for each column. The example box will show the results of your changes.

Tip 7-33: Modifying tab settings for the current page and beyond   At first glance, there doesn't appear to be an easy way to modify tab settings for an entire section of a document, i.e. pages 4 through 11 of an eleven-page document. The page layout tab ruler would affect the pages before page 4, the style tab ruler would affect only one style, and the inserted tab ruler would affect only the current paragraph. However, you can do it by inserting a new page layout and modifying its tab settings. Make sure you insert the page layout at the end of page 3, because Ami inserts a page break before a new page layout.

Page size and orientation

Once you select the Page settings page layout attribute, Ami displays the options shown in Figure 7-14: You can select from seven sizes for your printed page:

- letter (8.5 × 11)
- legal (8.5 × 14)
- A4 (8.27 × 11.69)
- A3 (11.69 × 16.53)
- A5 (5.83 × 8.27)
- B5 (6.93 × 9.84)
- Custom.

Select whether to place text and graphics vertically or horizontally on the page. Portrait places text and graphics vertically on the page, while landscape places them horizontally. You also can select whether the page settings attributes affect all pages, right, or left pages.

Tip 7-34: Selecting page orientation before printing   Even though you told Ami what page orientation to use, you are not ready to print yet. You must also tell Windows what page orientation you are using. If you need to print using

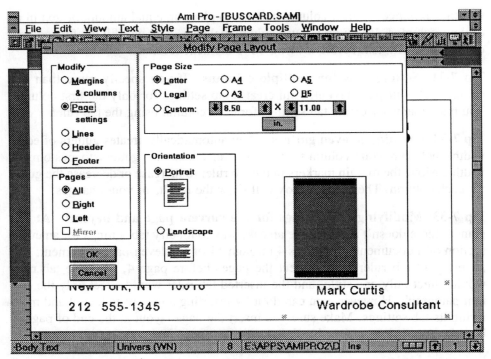

7-14 Page Settings in the Modify Page Layout dialog box controls the document's page size and print orientation.

landscape orientation or if you have changed the orientation, you always should check to ensure Windows is using the correct orientation before you print. To automate this process, you can attach a macro to the style sheet that automatically selects the correction orientation for the document. Refer to Tip 13-4 to learn about attaching a macro to a style sheet.

Lines

Once you select the Lines page layout attribute, Ami displays the options shown in Figure 7-15.

Select the line's position on the page. Select All to create a border around the page. Select Left to place a line on the left side of the page. Select Right to place a line on the right side of the page. Select Top to place a line on the top of the page. Select Bottom to place a line on the bottom of the page.

Select the appearance for the line around the page from the Style list box.

Position determines how close to the margin and to the edge of the paper your line appears. Position and Around Page work together to determine where the line appears on the page. Select Inside to place the line at the page margin. Select Close to inside to place the line near the page margin. Select Middle to

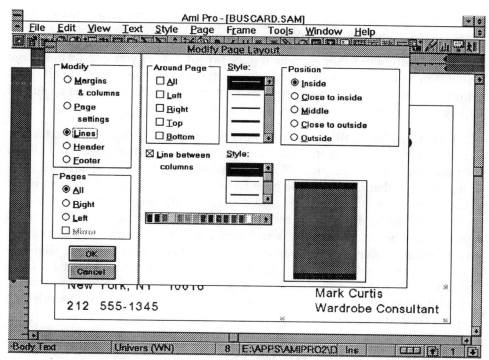

7-15 Lines in the Modify Page Layout dialog box controls lines around the page, the lines' position, lines between columns, line style and line color.

place the line between the margin and the edge of the paper. Select Close to outside to place the line near the edge of the paper. Select Outside to place the line at the edge of the paper.

Select Line between columns to place a line between the columns you specified in the Margins & columns dialog box.

Select the appearance for the line between columns from the Style list box.

If you have a color printer, you can select from 120 colors for your lines on the page. Your selection affects both lines around the page and between columns.

Tip 7-35: Removing an inserted page layout Don't try to remove a page layout using the Del or Backspace keys, because Ami will not let you delete a page layout using a keyboard shortcut. You must select the Insert Page Layout/Remove command from the Page menu to delete an inserted page layout. If you to try to select the command and it is greyed, your cursor is not positioned after the page layout marker. Use the GoTo command to move to the next page layout then select the Remove command.

Tip 7-36: Viewing a new page layout To view the specifications of an inserted page layout, place your cursor after the page layout marker and select Modify

Page Layout from the Page menu. The Modify Page Layout dialog box displays the settings for the new page layout.

Tip 7-37: Switching to the standard page layout   After you insert a new page layout, you can switch to the standard page layout without re-entering all of its settings. Select the Insert Page Layout/Revert command from the Page menu and Ami inserts a page layout that uses the standard settings.

Tip 7-38: Creating multiple page layouts on one page   When you insert a new page layout in your document, Ami automatically begins a new page. Ami allows only one page layout per page. What alternatives are there for documents, such as newsletters, that need multiple page layouts on the same page? You can insert a frame to create a new layout. Add a frame to the page that needs multiple layouts, making the frame large enough to hold the text. Then change the frame's layout using the Modify Frame Layout command on the Frame menu. You can create multiple columns, decide how text should flow around the flow, eliminate or enhance frame borders, along with other options discussed in chapter 17. Once you have created the frame, double-click inside the frame and either type the text or load it using the Open command from the File menu. Select the Insert button to insert the text inside the frame.

Questions and answers

Q: When I change a style in the Modify Style dialog box, should I select the Save *button before I choose* OK?

A: Not unless you plan to modify several styles at the same time. The Save button lets you save the changes to a style without exiting the dialog box. You then can select other style names from the list box and begin modifying their attributes. Use OK when you modify only one style; use Save when you modify several styles.

Q: I need to change the tab settings for my document. I modified the tab ruler at the top of the window, but only the current paragraph changed. My other paragraphs did not use the new settings.

A: Ami has several different tab rulers you can use: the page layout tab ruler, the style tab ruler, and the inserted tab ruler. To change the tab settings for the entire document, you need to use the page layout ruler, because it controls all paragraphs in the document. To access the page layout tab ruler, select Modify Page Layout from the Page menu. Change the settings in the tab ruler and select OK. Any paragraphs using a style tab ruler or an inserted tab ruler override the settings in the page layout ruler, so all the paragraphs in your document might not use your new settings.

Q: *I tried to modify my paragraph's tab settings using the tab ruler in the Modify Style dialog box, but now all my paragraphs that use this style have changed. I need special tab settings for only one paragraph.*

A: Use the inserted tab ruler at the top of the window, because it affects only the current paragraph. The style tab ruler in the Modify Style dialog box affects every paragraph using that style, not only in this document but in all others also. To insert a new tab ruler, place your cursor on the upper portion of the tab ruler and make the changes you need. When you finish, move the cursor outside the tab ruler and Ami inserts the tab ruler mark in the current paragraph.

Q: *I created an inserted tab ruler for a paragraph in my document, but it seems to follow me everywhere. Every time I press* Enter, *a new tab ruler shows up.*

A: Once you create an inserted tab ruler, Ami assumes you want it for each new paragraph you create. You can stop Ami from adding tab rulers to your paragraphs by deleting the tab rulers you don't need. Highlight the paragraphs that contain the rulers and select Ruler from the Page menu. Select Remove and Ami deletes the tab rulers, and more importantly, stops inserting them into your new paragraphs.

Q: *I created style tabs for my Body Text paragraphs, but they don't seem to be using the new settings. What did I do wrong?*

A: Make sure you selected the Use style tabs check box in the Modify Style dialog box. Even if you create tab settings on the style tab ruler, you must select that option for Ami to use them.

Q: *I am using a multiple column page layout, and I created tabs for my columns using the Modify Page Layout dialog box. However, the tabs appear only in my first column.*

A: When you create a multicolumn layout, you must set tabs for each column. Ami creates standard tab settings for the first column only. You must create additional tab settings for other columns or change the column settings in the first column.

Q: *How can I tell what tab ruler is in effect for my paragraph?*

A: There is no direct method, but you can perform a series of steps that tells you what tab ruler controls the current paragraph. First, do you have marks turned on in the View Preferences dialog box? If so, do you see an inserted tab ruler mark in your paragraph? If so, the paragraph uses the inserted tab ruler. If not, display the Modify Style dialog box and check if Use style tabs is selected. If so, the paragraph uses the style tab ruler. If not, the paragraph uses the page layout tab ruler.

Q: I created a style that inserted a number before the paragraph. However, when I assign the styles, the paragraphs are not updating; they all use the number one.

A: Paragraphs that use special effects numbering must be consecutive. If a paragraph using another style appears between two paragraphs using the special effects numbering, the second paragraph will not increase its number. The paragraphs must be adjacent to update their numbering scheme. However, you can create an outline numbering scheme (even though you are not creating an outline) that can consecutively number paragraphs even if they don't appear next to each other. Simply use the arabic numbering option and specify After higher level as the Reset option.

Q: I created reverse text, and it looks great on the screen. But when I try to print, the reverse text doesn't appear on the page.

A: If you use a 256-color display driver, Ami cannot print reverse text. Change to a display driver using a lower number of colors using Windows Setup. If you don't use a 256-color display driver, then your printer driver or your printer doesn't support reverse text. Call your printer manufacturer to ask if they can provide an updated printer driver.

Q: I inserted a column (or page) break in my document, but I no longer need it. No matter how I try to delete it, I can't remove the break.

A: The only way to remove a column break or a page break is to select Breaks from the Page menu. Then select Remove column or page break. You cannot remove a break by pressing Del or Backspace.

Q: When I modify my styles, Ami tells me I am using the wrong font.

A: Ami's original style sheets are created using a specific printer. If you don't use that printer, Ami cannot use the fonts in those styles; however, it uses the closest font available. To avoid the message, you need to save all of your styles using a font available in your printer. You can do so using the Modify Styles dialog box, or by playing the CHGFONT macro supplied with Ami. The macro lets you change the styles in the current style sheet or in all style sheets.

Summary

Formatting text and pages lets you design your own style sheets or modify those supplied with Ami. You can format paragraph styles by changing their fonts (discussed in chapter 6), alignment, spacing, page and column breaks, numbering, bullets, preceding text, lines and hyphenation. You can format pages by changing their margins, tabs, column, size, print orientation, and lines. Each change you make puts you one step closer to the final appearance of your printed pages. Follow the tips listed in this chapter and in chapter 5 to customize Ami's style sheets to suit your documents' needs.

8
CHAPTER

Tables

You might think of tables only when it's time to create a spreadsheet, but you can use them for many applications, including side-by-side text, resumes, lists, forms, invoices, and spreadsheets. You can include text, formulas, equations, DDE and OLE links, imported graphics, charts, and drawings in a table. When you create a table, Ami creates a Table Text style for use with any text you enter, paste, or link in it. However, you are not limited to using the Table Text style; you can use any style you wish inside a table.

Creating a table

You can create a table in the document or inside a frame. You can create a table in any mode, which is a new feature of Ami Pro 2.0. To do so, follow these steps:

1. Position your cursor inside the document or select the frame you want to hold the table.

2. Select Tables from the Tools menu or select the Table icon.

3. Enter the number of columns and rows you need in the table.

4. If you need to modify the table's layout before you enter any text, select Layout. If you want to enter text in the table before modifying its layout, select OK. Ami creates the table and displays the Table menu in the menu bar.

Tip 8-1: Displaying table gridlines and column/row headings When working with a table, you might find it useful to see the borders of individual cells and their cell addresses. You can display lines around the table and its cells, called gridlines, that are display-only. Gridlines are helpful in viewing cell and table

169

boundaries and they do not print. You also can display column and row headings that display the table's row numbers and column letters that make up a cell's address. The headings appear only when your cursor is inside the table. To display table gridlines and column/row headings, select those options from View Preferences in the View menu.

Tip 8-2: Displaying the table menu   Ami displays the Table menu only if you have created a table and your cursor is inside a table. Otherwise, Ami removes the Table menu from the main menu bar at the top of the screen.

Moving the cursor and selecting text inside a table

If you don't have a mouse, the keys you use to move about inside a table are different from those you use to move around normal text. Table 8-1 displays cursor movement keys in a table.

If you use the keyboard to select text inside a table, press Shift-Ctrl-Up Arrow or Down Arrow to highlight the cell above or below. Press Shift-Ctrl-Right Arrow or Left Arrow to highlight the previous or next cell.

Modifying a table's layout

You can access the Modify Table Layout dialog box in one of two ways: by selecting the Layout button from the Create Table dialog box, or by selecting Modify Table Layout from the Table menu. After you use either method, Ami displays the Modify Table Layout box as displayed in Figure 8-1. The following are pointers on using the options available in the dialog box:

Default Column Width   The measurement you enter here affects every column in your table. If you enter a measurement that is too large, Ami will not let you leave the dialog box until you reduce the measurement.

Default Column Gutter Size   Enter the amount of space you need between columns. Ami immediately updates the gutter width in the table and the gutter markers in the tab ruler as soon as you return to the document.

Default Row Height   Default Row Height is greyed if you have Automatic selected, because Ami will increase the row's height as text wraps to the next line. You can turn off the Automatic option to specify a custom row height in the Default Row Height text box. However, Ami will not increase the row's height proportionately if your text needs to wrap to the next line.

Default Row Gutter Size   Enter the space you need between each row in the table. Ami does not display the row gutter in the vertical ruler, so you will not see a change in the ruler when you return to the document.

Table 8-1.   Moving Around in a Table Using the Keyboard

To move to:	Press this:
Next cell	Tab or Ctrl-Right Arrw
Previous cell	Shift-Tab or Ctrl-Left Arrow
Cell above	Ctrl-Up Arrow
Cell below	Ctrl-Down Arrow
Beginning of line in cell	Home
End of line in cell	End
First cell in the row	Home, Home
Last cell in table	End, End
Tab setting in the current cell	Shift-Ctrl-Tab

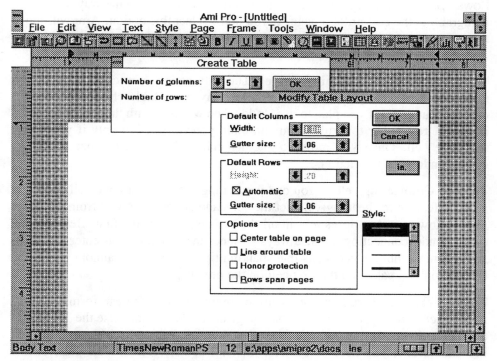

8-1   The Modify Table Layout dialog box is available only after you have created a table.

Center Table on Page   Ami normally places a table at the left margin, but you can center the table by selecting Center Table on Page.

Line Around Table   You can display a border around the entire table by selecting Line Around Table. Do not confuse the gridlines that display on the screen with lines you need to print. Gridlines are display-only for your reference when creating a table and entering text. To create lines and borders that will print, select

Line Around Table and the other line options available under the Lines/Shades option from the Table menu. If you create a table inside a frame, the Line Around Table option is not available.

Line Style Select the type of line you need to create the border around the entire table. If you create a table inside a frame, the Line Style option is not available.

Honor Protection If you select Protect from the Table menu without selecting Honor Protection first, Ami ignores your request to protect cells. You can turn off Honor Protection to place the cursor in cells that are normally protected. Ami displays a checkmark next to the Protect command in the Table menu when the cursor is in a protected cell.

Rows Span Pages To paginate a row that falls at the bottom of the page, select Rows Span Pages. Ami divides the text in the row similar to the way it breaks a paragraph at the bottom of a page. If you don't select this option, Ami will move the entire row to the next page, creating a gap at the bottom of the page. If you create a table inside a frame, the Rows Span Pages option is not available.

Tip 8-3: Using Undo within a table The only actions you can undo within a table are those changes you made to text. Any other table changes you make cannot be undone. If you plan to use Undo when working with the text or numbers in tables, remember this rule: Ami can undo your last action only if you are in the same cell. Once you move to another cell or highlight another cell, Ami cannot undo your last action.

Tip 8-4: Connecting cells You can join a range of cells into one cell, which is a handy feature for headings. Select the cells and choose Connect from the Table menu. However, Ami loses text in all the cells except for the first. Because you cannot undo connecting cells, always connect them before you enter any text. Also, Ami cannot connect cells that span multiple pages. You cannot connect the last cell on one page and the first cell on the next page.

Tip 8-5: Treat each cell as a separate page or frame You can format the text inside each cell as you would text on a page or inside a frame. Use the Text menu to change the text's or number's font, alignment, indents, spacing, or attributes. For example, if you need to center text, Ami centers it inside the cell, as if it were on its own page.

Tip 8-6: Positioning a table on the page Ami lets you choose from only two table placement options: left or center. You can place your table wherever you need it, however, by pasting the table into a frame. Then move the frame to appropriate location on the page.

Tip 8-7: Deleting a column or row quickly You don't need to highlight the entire row or column to delete it. Simply place your cursor in row or column and select Delete Row/Column from the Table menu. Select the option you need to delete (row or column) and Ami deletes the entire row or column for you.

Tip 8-8: Eliminate warning messages when you delete a row/column/ table   Every time you delete a row, a column, or an entire table, Ami reminds you that you cannot undo your action. Once you are familiar with tables, you don't need the reminder each time you delete a table item. You can turn off the warning message by selecting Disable Warning Messages from the User Setup dialog box on the Tools menu.

Tip 8-9: Adding margins around a table   Ami does not have direct way to add margins around a table, but you can add the appearance of margins using one of two methods:

- Place the table inside a frame and specify the frame's margins inside the Modify Frame Layout dialog box.
- Add empty rows to the top and bottom of the table, and add empty columns to both sides of the table. Do not place a line around the empty rows and columns, and it appears as though you have a margin.

Tip 8-10 Creating a table header   If your table spans multiple pages, you need to include a header at the top of the table on each page. Without the header, it's easy to forget what the information in each column or row represents. To create a header, simply highlight the row you need and select Header from the Table menu. Ami displays the header on the top row of each page.

Tip 8-11: Adding lines and shading to individual cells   The Modify Table Layout command lets you create a line around an entire table, but you also can add lines and shading to one or more cells. Select the cells that you want to add lines and shading to and select the Lines/Shades command on the Table menu. Select an option under Position to add lines to the cells, then select the lines' appearance from the Line Style list box and choose a shading color or fill pattern from the Fill color list box.

Tip 8-12: Adding bullets to table styles   You can create a check list for your customers to select their choice of products, shipping, or payment methods by adding the checkbox bullet to a style in your table. Because you don't want the bullet to appear in every cell, create a new style that you can use only for a list of choices. Select Create Style from the Style menu. Type the style name in the Name style text box. Highlight the Table Text style in the Based on list box. Select the Modify button. Select the Special effects attribute and select Bullet. Highlight one of the checkbox bullets from the Bullets list box. Return to the document and assign the new style to those cells listing a choice for your customers.

Tip 8-13: Creating custom fill pattern shades   You can select from 120 colors as a fill pattern for the cells in a table. If the color you need is not one of those colors, you can create a custom color for your fill pattern. Select Lines/Shades from the Table menu. To see additional colors, select the down arrow button. If the color you need is not displayed, double-select the color that is closest to the one you need. Ami displays the Custom Color dialog box. The dialog box contains two boxes from which you can customize a color. The large box affects the amount of red, blue, and green in the color, and the hue and saturation. The small box affects the amount of red, blue, and green in the color, and the luminosity. Drag the cursor in each box until Ami displays the color you need in the example box. You also can specify a setting for each element by typing a number in the appropriate text box, but dragging the cursor is more visual. Select OK to activate that color.

Tip 8-14: Cutting an entire table   If you block all the cells in a table and select Cut from the Edit menu, Ami cuts the contents of those cells, not the actual cells. To cut a table, place your cursor inside the table and press Esc. The cursor should appear to the right of the table and appear the same size as the table. Press Shift-Left Arrow to highlight the entire table and select Cut or Copy from the Edit menu. Ami cuts or copies the table instead of the table's content.

Tip 8-15: Importing a graphic or drawing inside a table   With version 2.0 of Ami Pro, you no longer need to draw a frame inside a table to import a graphic or use Ami's drawing feature. If you import a graphic, Ami sizes the graphic according to the size of the cell. You can adjust the graphic's size by selecting Graphics scaling from the Frame menu. To learn more about imported graphics, refer to chapter 17. To create a drawing, simply place your cursor inside the cell and select Drawing from the Tools menu. To learn more about creating a drawing, refer to chapter 18.

Changing the size of cells

You can change the size of a table's cells in three ways: using the Column/Row Size command from the Table menu, using the Default Column Width and Default Row Height options in the Modify Layout dialog box, or by dragging a column's border.

To change the size of all columns or rows in your table, use the option in the Modify Layout dialog box. Any changes you make in this box affect every column or row in the table.

To change the size of a range of columns or rows, highlight them and use the Column/Row Size command from the Table menu. The command affects only those columns or rows you selected.

To change the width of only one column, position the mouse on the column's border and drag it to stretch or shrink the column to its new size. You cannot change row height using the mouse.

Tip 8-16: Column width/row height hierarchy Any changes to columns and rows you make using the Column/Row Size command override the measurements you entered in the Layout dialog box when you created your table. Even if you need to change all the columns/rows again and you use the Layout dialog box, the changes you made using the Column/Row Size remain in effect. The only way to match those column/rows to the others in the table is to change them using the Column/Row Size command again.

Inserting and deleting columns and rows

The Table menu contains two commands that let you add or remove columns and rows: Insert Column/Row and Delete Column/Row. To use the commands, position the cursor in the table where you need to add or remove columns or rows. When you select the Insert Column/Row command, you can specify to insert columns or rows, how many, and whether to insert before or after the cursor's position in the table. The Delete Column/Row command works in the same way.

Tip 8-17: Quickly adding or deleting a row to a table If you need to insert or delete a row to a table, you can bypass the Table menu. Pressing Ctrl and the plus key on the numeric keypad inserts a row below the current one. If you select several rows, Ami inserts the same number of rows. Pressing Ctrl and the minus key on the numeric keypad removes the current row. If you select several rows, Ami deletes them all.

Creating text tables

How would you use a textual table? You can use text tables for comparisons, with rows and columns of comparative data, for a list of features in a product, for a resume, or for side-by-side text. You even can use a table for a merge: the table can be the standard or the merge document. Ami automatically uses the Table Text style for any text you enter into a table, but you can use any style. As a general rule, don't use styles inside a table that you also use for text outside a table. If you modify the style to change your text's appearance in the table, the style also affects text outside the table. Your table might look perfect, but the rest of your document probably won't look the way you hoped it would.

Creating a resume

To create a resume using a table, use each row for a specific career, educational, or professional accomplishment. Use two columns: the first to include the dates of your accomplishment, and the second to include the job title or educational/professional accomplishment name and description. Figure 8-2 displays an example of a resume created using a table.

Follow these guidelines when you create a resume using a table:

- Enter dates of each position, education, or accomplishment in the first column.
- Enter each position title, education, or accomplishment in the second column.
- Enter each paragraph of explanatory text in the second column in a separate cell.
- Use Row gutter space as paragraph spacing.
- Add rules to your text using styles or by adding lines to individual cells in the table.

Creating side-by-side text

Writers use side-by-side text for proposals, technical documentation, or any other long document that needs headings next to, rather than above, its corresponding text. You can create a limited amount of side-by-side text by specifying multiple columns in the Modify Page Layout dialog box; however, once you enter a column break in a column, no other text can appear below that paragraph. Column breaks limit writers to one topic per page. You don't have to waste a whole page

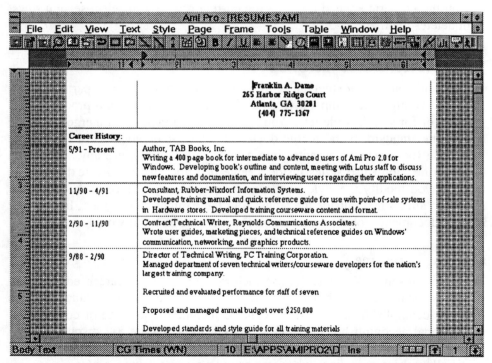

8-2 A table holding a resume, using rows as each accomplishment and columns to separate dates and the accomplishment.

if you have only a few lines in a paragraph. Using tables for side-by-side text lets you add as many topics as you want on a page. You are limited only by how much text fits on a page.

A typical proposal or technical manual uses two columns: the first column contains headings and the second column contains the body of the document. Figure 8-3 displays an example of documentation created using side-by-side text. Follow these guidelines when you create side-by-side text using a table:

- Create a table with the number of side-by-side columns you need.
- Specify the approximate number of paragraphs you expect to use as the number of rows.
- Enter each paragraph of explanatory text in the second column in a separate cell.
- Press Down Arrow to move to the next paragraph.
- Press Tab to move to the next column.
- Use Row gutter space as paragraph spacing.
- Add rules to your text using styles or by adding lines to individual cells in the table.

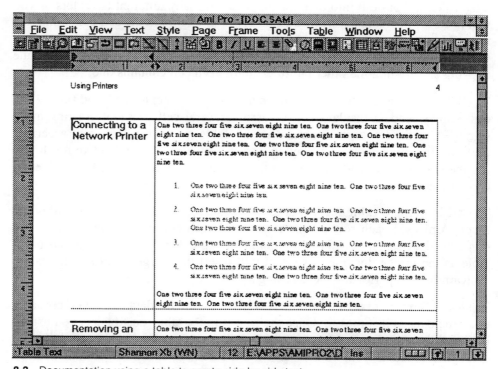

8-3 Documentation using a table to create side-by-side text.

Tip 8-18: Hide column/row headings when creating a text table   When you use a table for a resume or for side-by-side text, hide the column or row headings. You don't need to know cell addresses because you aren't using formulas, and Ami slows because it needs to display and refresh the headings. Unselect Column/ Row Headings in the View Preferences dialog box in the View menu.

Tip 8-19: Inserting page breaks into a text table   You can control how much text appears on a page using page breaks in a text table. To insert a page break into a table, move the cursor to the row that you need to move to the next page, and select Breaks from the Page menu. Select Insert page break. To remove a page break, select Go To from the Edit menu. Select Page break to move the cursor to the next page break in the document. If Ami does not move to the page break in the table, continue selecting GoTo until it does. Select Breaks from the Page menu and select Remove page break.

Tip 8-20: Creating tab settings for a table   Each cell in a table uses its own tab ruler, just as multiple columns do in a page layout. You can create one tab ruler and insert it into a range of cells, or create a tab ruler and copy and paste it into other cells. To create a tab ruler and insert it into a range or cells, select the cells that will use the tab ruler. Create the tab settings on the tab bar at the top of the screen and Ami inserts the tab ruler into each cell you have selected. To create a tab ruler and paste it into other cells, create as many different tab rulers as you will need for the table before you enter any text. Highlight the cell containing the first tab ruler, and select Copy from the Edit menu. Select the cells into which you need to insert the tab ruler and select Paste from the Edit menu. Continue copying and pasting the other tab rulers until each cell contains one.

Tip 8-21: Use leaders between cells to display the effect of leadered tabs   You can display leaders inside a cell or across several cells without creating a tab setting. Use the Leaders command in the Table menu to select from a period, dash, or underline leader. Displaying leaders between cells is effective for directing the reader's eye from one cell to the next in directories, price lists, tables of contents, an indexes.

Tip 8-22: Using a table for a merge   Tables simplify creating a standard document. Ami uses each row as one record and each column as one field, so you don't need to separate rows and columns using delimiters. You also can use a table as the merge document, so Ami will insert the merged data into the table. To learn how to perform a merge using a table, refer to chapter 12.

Tip 8-23: Sorting text in a table   If you use a table for data entry, you probably enter the data as it comes in. Once the data is in the table, sorting lets you list the data by zip code, last name, state, or by other entries. To sort data in the table, select the columns you want to sort (Ami sorts the entire row automatically). Select Sort from the Tools menu. Specify the sort field (column), whether to sort alphanumerically or numerically, the word in the column by which to sort, and whether to sort in ascending or descending order.

Creating numeric tables

You also can use tables to enter numbers and perform simple calculations. You can enter the data yourself by typing, or paste the data from the document. You can create the data using a DDE or OLE link, or you can import a file into the table. When you import a table, Ami imports the results of the imported table's calculations—Ami does not import formulas. So if you need to do "what if" projections or forecasting, enter the formulas directly into Ami. You choose the numeric format to use when displaying numbers and formula results using the Modify Style dialog box. Ami displays the numbers in your table using that format until you place your cursor in that cell. When you edit a cell, Ami displays the number without any formatting until you move to another cell or outside of the table.

Pasting, linking, or importing data into a table

When you insert data into a table by pasting, linking, or importing, Ami puts in only the data that can fit into the table. If the table doesn't contain enough rows or columns, Ami does not add them. If you add rows or columns after you paste the data, Ami will not insert the additional information into them. You must have the correct number of rows and columns when you initially paste the data. Position the cursor in the cell you want to use as the home position and paste the data.

Creating a formula

To create a formula, you can use the following operators: +, −, *, /, and sum(x..x). Sum(x..x) is a summary operator, and the x's represent cell addresses. Use the formula to add a series of numbers in a row or column.

You cannot create a formula by simply placing your cursor in a cell and typing. If you do, Ami reads your formula as text and will not calculate it. To create a formula, place your cursor in the cell that will display the result and select Edit Formula from the Table menu. Ami displays the Edit Formula dialog box as shown in Figure 8-4. Type the formula in the text box and click OK. Ami displays the formula results in the cell. You can identify the cells that use a formula, because Ami surrounds them with bold gridlines. To change the formula, double-select the cell or select Edit Formula again.

Tip 8-24: Entering numbers in a table   When you enter numbers into a table, do not add delimiters such as dollar signs or commas. Ami treats any entries using spaces, characters, commas, or paragraph returns as labels and will not calculate them in a formula. To format numbers in a table, modify the style the table uses.

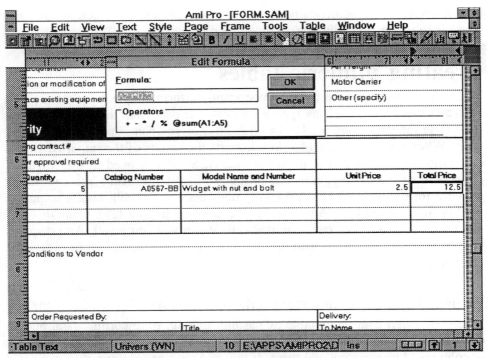

8-4 The only way to enter a formula into a cell is to use the Edit Formula dialog box.

If you need more than one numeric format in a table, create multiple styles and assign them to the numbers using a different format.

Tip 8-25: Specifying absolute cell addresses in a formula Normally when you cut or copy a formula to another cell, Ami changes the formula relative to its new cell. For example, if you copy a formula to a cell two rows above, Ami changes the formula to reference cells two rows above the old formula. You can specify absolute cell addresses that remain constant when you cut or copy a formula to a different cell. To specify an absolute cell address, insert a dollar sign before the row, column, or both addresses (A5, $A5, A$5 are all valid combinations of absolute cell addresses).

Tip 8-26: Displaying leading zeroes Ami does not let you display leading zeroes in a number, but it does display them in a label. If you don't need to use the number in any calculations, simply type a space after the number and Ami displays the leading zeroes. If you try to use the label in a formula, Ami ignores the label and any numbers preceding it in the formula.

Tip 8-27: Adding a row or column quickly To get a quick sum of a row or column, use Quick Add from the Table menu. Quick Add calculates the sum of the contents in the current row or column, placing the result in the current cell.

Tip 8-28: Creating a chart using table data Once you have a table using numbers and formulas, you can spruce up your document by adding a chart. Ami makes it easy to create a chart from a table. Simply select the data to use in the chart and select Charting from the Tools menu. To learn more about creating a chart, refer to chapter 19.

Modifying a style's numeric formatting in a table

Just like you can create styles that format text differently, you also can create styles that format numbers in a table differently. Not all numbers in a table need decimal places or dollar signs, and you can control a number's appearance by assigning it a style. You can assign a style to each cell containing text or numbers. The numeric options you select for the style do not affect any text in the table, only numbers. You can change the Table Text style, or create a new one, by selecting Modify Style from the Style menu and selecting the Table format attribute. Ami uses the following default numeric formatting options for the Table Text style:

- General numeric format
- Two decimal places
- A period as the decimal symbol
- A comma as the thousands separator
- A leading minus sign to indicate a negative number
- A leading dollar sign as the currency symbol.

You can change the Table Text options using the Table Format style attribute in the Modify Style dialog box, displayed in Figure 8-5:

Cell format Choose from General (450), Fixed Decimal (450.00), Currency ($450.00), and Percent (450.00%) numeric formats.

No. decimal places Enter the number of decimal positions you need when you use the Fixed Decimal numeric format.

Decimal symbol Type the symbol to use as the decimal point. You can type a character directly from the keyboard or type an ANSI symbol using the Alt key and the numeric keypad.

Thousand separator Type the symbol to use as the character to separate thousands from the remaining digits. You can type a character directly from the keyboard or type an ANSI symbol using the Alt key and the numeric keypad.

Negative format Choose from Leading minus (-450), Trailing minus ($450-$), Parentheses ((450)), or to display the number in red.

Currency Type the number to use as the currency symbol in the text box. You can type a character directly from the keyboard or type an ANSI symbol using

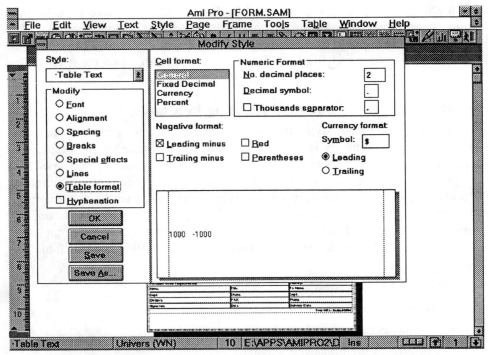

8-5 Control numeric formatting in a table by modifying the Table format of the Table Text or any other style you use in a table.

the Alt key and the numeric keypad. You also can choose whether to display the currency symbol in front of or behind the number.

Creating a form

You can use a table to create a form, as shown in Figure 8-6, or to fill out a preprinted form. Creating a table that serves as a form requires one extra step: you must tell Ami to protect the cells that serve as headings, so that others using the form cannot overwrite or alter them. Protecting cells in a form requires two steps: first tell Ami which cells to protect, and then turn on protection for the table.

To tell Ami which cells to protect in the form, follow these steps:

1. Select the cells you need to protect from being changed.

2. Select Protect from the Table menu.

3. Continue steps one and two until you have told Ami all the cells that need to be protected.

4. To turn on protection for the table, select Modify Table Layout from the Table menu. Select Honor Protection. Ami does not let you insert the cursor in the cells you protected. If you need to change the headings in

the table, turn off honor protection, edit the cells, and then turn on honor protection again.

Tip 8-29: Adding a company logo to an invoice or form You can add an imported graphic to any cell in your table. Simply select the cell and choose Import Picture from the File menu. Select the imported graphic filename and Ami inserts it in the table cell. Ami scales the graphic according to the cell's dimensions, but you can change the graphic's scaling. Select Graphics scaling from the Frame menu and select the appropriate setting.

Tip 8-30: Printing tables on preprinted forms One of the toughest tasks to do with a PC is filling in a preprinted form. Using Ami's table feature, you can recreate the form on your screen, fill in the blanks, and then print only the information you entered. You can turn off the shaded cells and lines you created for display purposes, so they won't print on the form. Choose On Preprinted Forms in the Print Options dialog box to print only the text in the table, not the lines and shading.

Tip 8-31: Saving a form as a style sheet vs an Ami Pro document Once you create a form, you can save it as a style sheet, with contents, or as an Ami Pro document. Saving the form as a style sheet is probably easier, because you don't have to worry about overwriting the style sheet—you must use Save As A Style

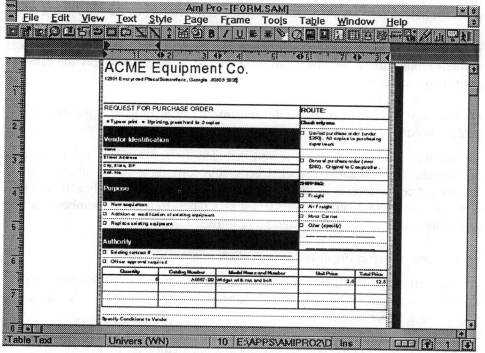

8-6 A form created by using a table.

Sheet to do so, and Ami warns you that you are about to overwrite your existing style sheet. Conversely, you can overwrite a form in an Ami Pro document easily—simply fill in the blanks and save the document. Ami doesn't display any warning messages. You would need to choose Save As once you fill in the form to avoid overwriting your blank form—a step that is easy to forget.

Questions and Answers

Q: *When I try to type text in my table, it doesn't appear in the cell. What am I doing wrong?*

A: If you cannot insert your cursor in a cell, it is protected and you won't be able to edit the cell. However, if you can insert your cursor in the cell and your text doesn't appear when you type, either your font or your spacing is too large. Decrease your font size and see if your text appears. If it does not, decrease the amount of spacing your style uses—especially if you are using 1½ or double-spacing. Change to single-spacing and your text should appear.

Q: *I am using a table to calculate values, but Ami isn't displaying the correct results. How can I tell where the problem is?*

A: The most common cause of a formula not displaying the correct result is one or more cells it refers to contains a number Ami reads as a label. If you enter any spaces, characters, or paragraph returns in a cell, Ami reads that entry as a label, even if it looks like a number. An easy way to distinguish a number that Ami reads as a label is to check its alignment in the cell. Ami right-aligns numbers and left-aligns labels. Numbers that appear left-aligned are probably the cause of your incorrect results.

Q: *I entered a formula in my table, but instead of displaying a number it says "REF." What does that mean?*

A: The REF message means that you included the result cell in the formula or one of your cells contains a label. Check your formula to make sure it refers to the correct cell addresses or that it contains a number and not a label. If Ami left-aligns a number in a cell, it considers it as a label. Retype the number omitting any spaces, characters, and paragraph returns.

Q: *Why are asterisks displayed in my cells?*

A: The cell is too small to display its content. Enlarge the cell by dragging the border to the right or by selecting Column/Row Size from the Table menu and specifying a larger column size.

Q: *When I connect cells, my text disappears. How can I get it back?*

A: Ami keeps only the text in the originating cell when you connect cells in a table. The originating cell is the one you start from when connecting cells. Once you connect the cells, you cannot redisplay the text. Next time you connect cells, do it before you type any text or begin connecting from the cell containing text.

Q: I locked some of the cells in my table by highlighting them and selecting Protect *from the Table menu; however, Ami still lets me edit the cells.*

A: Ami doesn't activate protected cells until you turn protection on for that table. To do so, select Modify Table Layout from the Table menu. Select Honor Protection to activate the protected cells.

Q: When I import text into a frame table, some of the text is missing. Do I need to enlarge the frame and then import the text again?

A: Frame tables can be only one page long. If your table should span more than one page, use a page table instead of a frame table. Also, Ami does not add extra rows or columns to accomodate your data if the current table isn't large enough. Enlarge the frame and more text should appear. If the frame extends the length and width of the page and you still don't see your data, delete the frame and create a page table to hold your text.

Q: Can I create tabs in my table?

A: Each cell in a table can have its own tab ruler. To set tabs for a cell, you must use an inserted tab ruler or set style tabs for the Table Text style (or whatever style you use in the table). An inserted tab ruler is more flexible than style tabs for Table Text, because they would require each cell in every table to use the same tab settings. To move to a tab in a cell, press Ctrl-Shift-Tab.

Q: I have to use numbers as the headings for some of my columns, but Ami treats them as numbers instead of labels.

A: Type a space before each numeric heading and Ami will recognize it as a label.

Summary

Most people think of tables only when they need to calculate numbers, but tables are actually an extremely versatile tool. You can create numeric tables that serve as simple spreadsheets or forms. You can create text tables to format a resume, to create side-by-side text, or to make a form. If you use tables to create forms, you can print the entire form, including all headings, lines, and shading, or you can print only the text on a preprinted form. If you create numeric tables, you can use the Table Text style or any other style you create to format the numbers in the table. Ami's table feature lets you present facts and figures that might otherwise be ignored in an inviting and readable format.

9
CHAPTER

Publishing details

The preceding chapters dealt with the process of creating and maintaining documents: managing files, creating text, using style sheets, selecting fonts, formatting text, and creating tables. All these items make up the body of your documents. Once you have these elements, you are ready to combine them and give them an identity of a chapter, a book, or a newsletter. You need to add the details that make professionally-prepared documents readable and polished. The following items are the publishing details that assemble your pages into a publication:

- headers and footers
- footnotes
- avoiding widows and orphans
- automatic numbers for paragraphs and headings
- frame anchoring
- automatically-inserted text
- page numbers
- indexes
- tables of contents
- cross references.

Headers and footers

Headers and footers let you navigate through a document without having to read each page. By looking at the top or bottom of the page, you typically can find out the page number, newsletter title, chapter title, book title, or topic covered, depending upon the publication. A header or footer lets you enter text and/or graphics just once, and Ami displays your entries on every page in your file. A header places the entries at the top of the page, and a footer places the entries at the bottom of the page.

Fixed vs floating

Ami has two types of headers/footers you can create: fixed or floating. Fixed headers/footers, shown in Figure 9-1, display the same text and/or graphics on every page of your file. You can alternate the contents of the left and the right page headers/footers, which is useful if you are creating a newsletter or a book. However, once you specify what is to appear on all left pages and all right pages, that's it. You cannot have another fixed header/footer in that file. Most people use fixed headers/footers 99% of the time.

Floating headers/footers, shown in Figure 9-2, let you insert more than one header/footer in a file. You also must complete an extra step when creating floating headers/footers. When you create a fixed header/footer, you insert your cursor in the top or bottom margin and start typing. When you create a floating header/footer, you do the same. Once you have the text in the margin, however, you

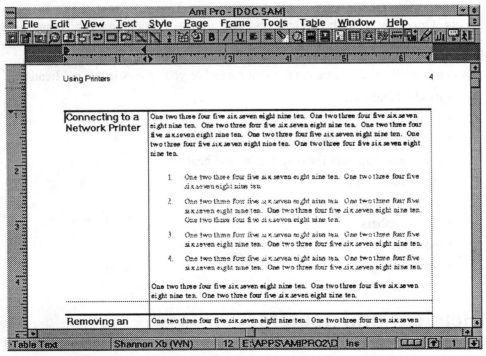

9-1 A fixed header in documentation.

File   Edit   View   Text   Style   Page   Frame   Tools   Table   Window   Help

Davis G — Day J

Glenda Davis	555-7070	Glenda Davison	555-7071	Glenda Day	555-7077
Gilbert Davis	555-0123	Gilbert Davison	555-0121	Gilbert Day	555-0127
Gwendolyn Davis	555-7839	Gwendolyn Davison	555-7831	Gwendolyn Day	555-7837
Harry Davis	555-1920	Harry Davison	555-1921	Harry Day	555-1927
Hugh Davis	555-2029	Hugh Davison	555-2022	Hugh Day	555-2027
Ivan Davis	555-2022	Ivan Davison	555-2023	Ivan Day	555-2027
J. B. Davis	555-3828	J. B. Davison	555-3821	J. B. Day	555-3827
J. C. Davis	555-4429	J. C. Davison	555-4421	J. C. Day	555-4427
J. D. Davis	444-1367	J. D. Davison	444-1361	J. D. Day	444-1367
J. E. Davis	335-2938	J. E. Davison	335-2931	J. E. Day	335-2937
James Davis	223-2903	James Davison	223-2901	James Day	223-2907
Jane Davis	555-9827	Jane Davison	555-9821	Jane Day	555-9827
Jimmy Davis	333-2918	Jimmy Davison	333-2911	Jimmy Day	333-2917
Jarrett Davis	555-6738	Jarrett Davison	555-6731	Jarrett Day	555-6737
Jay Davis	390-2093	Jay Davison	390-2091	Jay Day	390-2097
Joe Davis	555-6945	Joe Davison	555-6941	Joe Day	555-6947
Joseph Davis	555-8978	Joseph Davison	555-8971	Joseph Day	555-8977

Table Text   Shannon (WN)   10   E:\APPS\AMIPRO2\D   Ins   1

9-2   A floating header in a telephone directory.

place your cursor in the text of your document and select Floating Header/Footer from the Page menu. Ami attaches the header/footer to that text, so if the text moves to a different page, the header/footer moves with it. Floating headers/footers are ideal for directories, such as telephone books, in which the headers/footers change on just about every page. When you are looking for a name in the phone book, you look to the header to tell you what names that page starts and ends with. To create a floating header/footer for the current page, you must attach it to the first line of text on the page. Also, if you insert a new or standard page layout on the current page, Ami removes any floating headers for footers. You must retype them, but you do not need to select Floating Header/Footer from the Page menu.

Tip 9-1: Moving floating header/footer marks   If you need to cut and paste text that contains a floating header/footer mark, putting your cursor at the beginning of the text isn't enough. When you highlight the text and select cut (or press Enter to move the text down on the page), Ami moves the text but leaves the mark. The only way to include the mark is to move to it using the Go To command. Select Floating Header/Footer Mark and select Go To ^H. Highlight your text by placing your cursor at the end of the block and pressing the Shift key as you click your mouse. Ami highlights your text and the floating header/footer mark.

Tip 9-2: Identifying the floating header/footer attached to a mark   Editing a document that contains a different floating header/footer mark on each page can be frustrating. Although you began with one floating header/footer per page, after cutting and pasting text and graphics, you can end up with several floating headers/footers on one page and none on the next. How do you know which headers/footers belong to which marks? You don't. A good idea is to identify your floating header/footer marks by using notes or bookmarks. After you create the mark, create a short note or a bookmark identifying the header/footer to which the mark belongs. That way, if you have more than one floating header/footer mark on a page, you know which one to move.

Tip 9-3: Multiple floating headers/footers on a page   Even if you began with one floating header/footer per page, heavy editing of a document can result in several floating headers/footers on one page and none on the next. How does Ami decide which header/footer text to display? Ami uses the text tied to the last mark on the page.

Tip 9-4: Create floating headers/footers last   If you create floating headers and footers at the beginning of your publication process and your publication changes extensively, you could end up changing every floating header/footer in your document. Wait until the document is in its final stages before creating floating headers/footers, especially if you create floating headers/footers that serve as a guide for the information on a specific page (such as those in telephone directories).

Formatting headers/footers

You can format your headers and footers the same way you can format your documents: by changing their page layout and their styles. Each header and footer uses its own page layout. Just as you can control the margins, columns, and tabs for your page, you can control the same factors for your headers and footers. You also can change the style Ami uses in the headers and footers or create your own.

Modifying header/footer layout

Headers and footers have their own layout controls—even if you change a page's layout, the header and footer layouts are not affected. To access Ami's header/footer layout attributes, select Modify Page Layout from the Page menu. Select Header or Footer from the Modify Style dialog box and Ami displays the Header or Footer dialog box. Figure 9-3 displays the Header Layout dialog box. The following section list tips for using the Header/Footer layout attributes.

Tab Ruler   Use the tab ruler to create tab settings. You can select from 16 different tab types: left, center, right, and numeric are the main tab types. Then each tab type can be followed with a period leader, an underline leader, or a dash leader. Table 9-1 displays the icons representing each tab type.

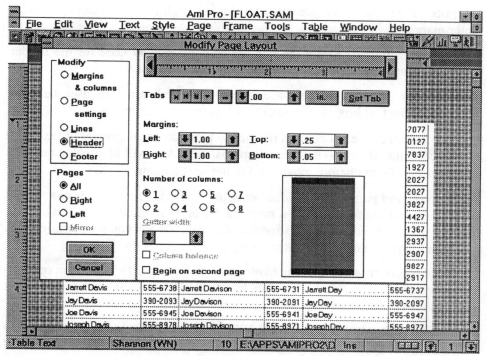

9-3 Header in the Modify Page Layout dialog box controls a header's tab settings, margins, columns, and gutter widths.

Table 9-1. Tab Ruler Marks

Mark	Description	Mark	Description
	Left tab		Numeric tab
	Left tab with underline leader		Numeric tab with underline leader
	Left tab with dashed leader		Numeric tab with dashed leader
	Left tab with period leader		Numeric tab with period leader
	Right tab		Center tab
	Right tab with underline leader		Center tab with underline leader
	Right tab with dashed leader		Center tab with dashed leader
	Right tab with period leader		Center tab with period leader

Margins   Enter the space you need for the left, right, top, and bottom header/footer margins.

Number of columns   Select the number of columns you need for the header/footer. You can have up to eight columns per header/footer.

Gutter width   Gutters are the spaces between each column. Ami uses the figure you enter in the text box as the gutter width between all columns.

Column balance   Select column balance to place an equal amount of text in all of your columns. If you do not use column balance, Ami will fill the first columns on the page with text before moving on to the next column.

Begin on second page   Many documents, such as newsletters and books, do not use a header on the first page of a new chapter or issue. Select begin on second page to omit the header or footer from the first page. When you select this option, you cannot type in the top or bottom margin of the first page.

Tip 9-5: Setting tabs for multiple columns   If you specify more than one column for your page layout, Ami creates tab settings for only the first column. You must manually create tab settings for each column using the tab ruler.

Tip 9-6: Creating uneven gutters   Ami automatically creates gutters of equal widths between your columns, but you can adjust the gutters to customized widths. Move the margin markers in the tab ruler to increase or decrease the gutter for each column. The example box will show the results of your changes.

Tip 9-7: How much text can you put into a header or footer?   Ami doesn't set a limit on the amount of text that can fit in a header or a footer; however, what you can fit into your header/footer depends on a combination of these factors: page margins, header/footer margins, header/footer style, and font size and spacing used in style. The larger the page margins, the larger your header/footer can be. Conversely, the larger the header/footer margins, the smaller your header/footer will be. Also, the font size and spacing your style uses determines how much text you can fit—the larger the font and the spacing, the less text will fit in the header/footer. Once you have text in your header/footer, changing the page or header/footer margins affects the text differently. Increasing your page margins adds space below the text in both the header and footer. Increasing your header/footer margins add space above text in the header, but adds space below text in your footer.

Formatting text in headers and footers

Ami assigns the Body Text style to any text you place in the header or footer. You can change the Body Text style to suit the header or footer, but any text in the body of your document that uses Body Text will be affected also. A better solution is to create a new style exclusively for use in a header or footer. If you use alternating headers/footers (a separate header/footer for right pages and left pages), you can create separate styles for each. Right page header/footers usually have their text right-aligned, and the text in left-page headers/footers is usually left-aligned.

Tip 9-8: Save headers/footers in a style sheet   If you create a style sheet for use in a periodical or one that you reuse regularly, save your headers/footers with the style sheet using the With contents option. You then eliminate the need to retype a newsletter name and page numbers for each new issue, or the need to enter the same copyright information for each periodical you publish.

Tip 9-9: Use repeating frames for graphics in headers/footers   Although text you enter in a header or footer appears on every page in your document, the same rule does not apply to graphics. A frame in a header or footer appears only on one page unless you make a repeating frame that appears on every page of your document. If you need the frame to appear in a different position on right and left pages, or if you need to use a different graphic on right or left pages, specify the frame as a repeating frame for right/left pages. The frame you created on a right page appears only on right pages, and the frame you created on a left page appears only on left pages. You must specify both frames as repeating frames for right/ left pages.

Footnotes

Creating footnotes in Ami is easy: place the cursor at the position in the document where you need the footnote, and select Footnote from the Tools menu. Select Insert Footnote, and Ami creates two items: a footnote reference number in the main body of the document, and an area at the bottom of the current page for the footnote text. Type the reference information in the footnote text area and return to your document. As you create additional footnotes in the same document, Ami sequentially numbers the footnotes for you.

Tip 9-10: Making endnotes instead of footnotes   Many word processors are limited to footnotes only; however, Ami lets you create endnotes easily. To specify endnotes rather than footnotes, select the Make endnotes option in the Footnote Options dialog box. Ami places all footnotes on the last page of the document.

Tip 9-11: Cutting and pasting footnotes   To move a footnote reference number and its related footnote text, cut and paste the reference number only. Ami automatically moves the footnote text along with the number to its new location in the document.

Tip 9-12: Deleting a footnote   To delete a footnote, remove the footnote reference number by highlighting it and pressing the Del key. Ami deletes the related text along with the number, but only after warning you that a footnote is in the text you chose to delete.

Tip 9-13: Moving to the next footnote mark or footnote text   You can use the GoTo command to move to footnote marks and footnote text. You cannot specify a particular footnote, but Ami does move the cursor to the next footnote mark or footnote text in the document. Ami does not let you move to footnote text while you are in Draft or Outline mode using the GoTo command.

Tip 9-14: Moving to a specific footnote mark or footnote text   If you created endnotes, moving between your document and the endnote text for editing can be a cumbersome process at best. However, you can move directly to a specific footnote mark or footnote text using the Tools Footnote command. When your cursor is on a footnote reference number, select Edit Footnote from the Footnotes dialog box to move directly to the corresponding footnote text. When you finish editing, select the Tools Footnote command again and select Return to Text to move back to the footnote text's reference number in the document.

Tip 9-15: Creating footnotes across documents   Ami's new Master Document feature is wonderful for creating an index and table of contents, but you cannot use it to number footnotes across chapters. You can get around this limitation by starting each chapter's first footnote reference number as one more than the previous chapter's last footnote reference number. Select the Tools Footnote command and select Options. Type the footnote reference number in the Starting number text box, and Ami consecutively numbers footnotes beginning with that number. Wait until your document is relatively stable before you begin specifying starting numbers. Otherwise, you end up changing the numbers for each chapter each time you add or remove a footnote.

Tip 9-16: Formatting footnote text   Ami uses the Footnote style for footnote text, which uses the same font and point size as Body Text. However, traditional typesetting formats footnotes so they are italicized and use a smaller point size than the text in the body of the document. You can modify the Footnote style or create a new style for your footnotes to follow traditional formatting. The footnote reference number assumes the same style as the text in which you inserted it.

Widows and orphans

Word processors define widows and orphan differently: what one calls a widow another calls an orphan. With Ami, it doesn't matter how you define them, because Ami controls them both the same way: either you have them or you don't. You can turn them on or off in the User Setup Options dialog box under the Tools menu. You cannot control the minimum number of lines at the top or bottom of page: Ami uses one line as its barometer for widows and orphans.

Automatic numbering

Ami can automatically generate numbers before your paragraphs or lines. You have four types of numbering schemes to choose from: simple list numbering, legal numbering, outline numbering, or line numbering. Use simple list numbering to number sequentially items in a list, and legal numbering to number sequentially paragraphs using a legal numbering format (1.1, 1.2, 1.3, etc.). Use outline numbering to create traditional outlines, and line numbering to number lines, rather than paragraphs, in your document.

Creating a simple list numbering style

Ami comes with its own simple list numbering style called Number List. The easiest method of creating a numbering style is to modify Number List or to create a new style based on it. To create a simple list numbering style, follow these steps:

1. Create a new style or place your cursor in a paragraph using Number List.
2. Select Modify Style from the Style menu. Select Special Effects from the dialog box.
3. Select Number option. Select the numbering style you need from the list box.
4. Type any punctuation you need in the Text box. Number List uses a period, but you can delete that and insert a parenthesis or any other symbol.
5. Select the appropriate attributes if you need the number to appear bold, underline, italic, word underline, capitalized or superscript. Click OK.
6. Select Alignment from the Modify Style dialog box and adjust the alignment to accommodate the number Ami inserts before your paragraph. Click OK.
7. Click OK to return to the document.

Creating legal numbering and outline numbering styles

The process for creating legal and outline numbering schemes is similar. When you create outline styles to generate a numbering scheme, you use many of the same steps in using Outline mode. Outline mode is a document management tool that lets you expand and collapse text underneath headings and display any document using a hierarchy. However, the document's appearance in Outline mode does not reflect its final appearance on the printed page. Any indentation your paragraphs use in Outline mode does not carry over to Layout or Draft mode. To create styles using outline or legal numbering, you should create paragraph styles to accommodate the number of levels you plan to use in the outline. You then can assign outline or legal numbering schemes and modify the styles to appear with indentions in Layout and Draft mode. You can display documents using these styles in Outline mode to collapse and expand outline levels and to move large sections of the outline quickly.

To create outline or legal numbering schemes, use these steps:

1. Select a style sheet that you will use in the documents that need the numbering scheme. Ami provides several style sheets that use numbering schemes: ˉOUTLINE1.STY, ˉOUTLINE2.STY, ˉOUTLINE3.STY, and ˉOUTLINE.STY.

2. Create a new style for each level you plan to use in the document. Select Create Style from the Style menu. Type the new style name in the text box and select Modify. Select Save As and type the next style name. Continue selecting Save As until you create all the styles you need. Select OK or press Enter to return to the document.

3. Select Outline styles from the Style menu.

4. Highlight the style that will be the first level and drag it, or select Promote until the style appears underneath the number one.

5. Continue assigning levels to the styles you created using step four.

6. Select one of the quick numbering schemes to assign numbers to all levels, or select the Number option to assign individual numbering options to each style.

7. If you need to restart numbering within the document, select one of the following Reset Numbering options:

After higher level   If you want outline styles to restart their numbering scheme after a higher level in the outline, select After higher level. You must select this option for each outline style you create. Most outlines use this type of numbering.

After intervening style   If you want outline styles to restart numbering any time they follow an outline style using a different level or a outline level set to None, select After intervening style.

Cumulative numbering   If you want to create legal numbering or numbering you often see in contracts, select Cumulative numbering. Instead of increasing the number or letter displayed in front of the paragraph, Cumulative numbering inserts another number, as in 1, 1.1, 1.11, 1.111.

8. Select OK or press Enter.

9. Type the text of the document, assigning styles as you write.

10. Modify the outline styles, using the Modify Styles command on the Style menu, so that each style uses the appropriate indention when you use Layout or Draft mode. For more information on formatting styles, refer to chapter 7.

You can use Outline mode to view more of your document than you can see in Draft or Layout mode, to expand and collapse text, to rearrange sections of text, and to promote or demote headings and subordinate paragraphs.

Generating line numbers

Ami can count the number of lines in your document and insert the line number at the left margin. You can customize Ami's line numbering scheme to one of the following options:

- number every line
- number every other line
- number every five lines
- number every *n* lines (you insert the number for *n* in the text box)
- restart numbering on each page.

Ami asks you to base line numbering on a style. Ami applies the formatting that style uses to the line numbers in the margin. However, Ami does not add paragraph above or below spacing between the numbers. So, line numbers will not align with the sentences they represent unless the style you chose does not use paragraph above and below spacing. No matter what style you choose, Ami numbers the lines in your document regardless to the style they use. Figure 9-4 displays a legal document using line numbering.

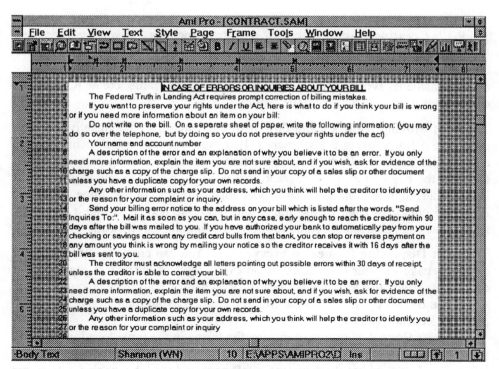

9-4 Line numbering in a legal contract provides easy reference to specific citations.

Frame anchoring

Frame anchoring lets you attach a frame to its surrounding text so that when your text moves, the attached frame moves also. Ami has three types of frame anchors: page anchors, paragraph above anchors, and text anchors.

Use page anchors to keep the frame on the page exactly at the position you placed it. When the text moves, the frame stays put. Ami uses this frame anchor as the default. Select Where placed from the Position box in the Modify Frame Layout dialog box to keep the frame on the same page and position as you originally placed it.

Use paragraph above anchors to keep the frame with the paragraph above it. Ami attaches the frame to the last character of the preceding paragraph. As the text moves, Ami moves the frame, keeping it below the paragraph at all times. When you select With para above in the Modify Frame Layout dialog box, you cannot flow text around the frame—only beside it, or you can turn off text wrap.

Use text anchors to keep the frame between the text in which you placed it. Ami attaches the frame to the character preceding it. Text anchors are useful for frames that contain graphics that need to remain next to or inside a block of text, not below it. When you select Flow with text as the anchor type, Ami automatically selects Wrap Around as the text flow type. No other text wrap selection is available.

Tip 9-17: Creating frames with flow with text anchors   If you try to create a frame within an existing paragraph using a text anchor, Ami moves the frame to the end of the paragraph. Don't wait until you type the entire paragraph to place a frame inside it. Type the text to appear in front of the frame, create it, place the cursor after the frame and continue typing.

Tip 9-18: Moving frames using flow with text anchors   Technically you cannot move a frame using a text anchor. However, you can use a technique that achieves the same result, by moving the text instead. For example, if you have a frame at the beginning of a paragraph that needs to be in the middle of the first line instead, highlight the text that should appear in front of the frame and cut it. Place the cursor in front of the frame and paste the text. You didn't move the frame, but you achieved the same result by moving the text instead.

Tip 9-19: Displaying frames on every page   You can create frames to appear on every page of your document, or on every right or every left page of your document. If you use a frame in a header or as part of your page layout, you can select one of two options from the Modify Frame Layout dialog box: Repeat all pages or Repeat right/left.

Choose Repeat all pages to display the frame in the same location on every page. Choose Repeat Right/Left to display the frame on only right pages or only left pages. If you create the frame on a left page and you choose this option, the frame appears only on left pages. To display a frame on all right pages, you must create the frame on a right page and select this option.

Tip 9-20: Placing frames in the margin   Ami lets you place a frame in the margin just as you can place one in the usable portion of the page. You could place a frame in the margin to serve as a tab for locating a specific chapter. If you use the frame in all of your documents, save the style sheet using the With contents option. Make sure the frame does not appear in the unprintable zone for your printer, because few printers can print to the very edge of the page. Refer to your printer manual to make sure your frame doesn't appear in the unprintable zone.

Tip 9-21: Using frames as bullets   Ami has a limited selection of bullets, but you can create your own using frames. Simply draw or import a graphic you would like as a bullet into a frame and place the frame in front of the paragraph. Attach the frame using a text anchor by selecting the Flow with text option in the Modify Frame Layout dialog box. Indent the entire paragraph so that it appears to the left of the frame.

Tip 9-22: Numbering frames in a document   The SEQ power field is designed to sequentially number figures, tables, or any other items you need to list in a document. You insert the SEQ field as part of the figure or table caption, and Ami inserts the figure or table number in the caption. If you remove figures or tables and their accompanying SEQ power fields, Ami automatically renumbers the remaining figures or tables (when you choose Update All.) If you have more than one figure or table on a page, Ami reads them in order first from left to right, and then from top to bottom.

The SEQ power field uses the following syntax:<SEQ expression [= [expression]] [− [expression]] [+ [expression]] [% format option]

Expression can be the name of a variable, or a mathematical operation, such as Figure = Figure + 1.

The format option controls the appearance of the power field's result. For more information, refer to chapter 15.

Automatically inserting text

You can insert a standard block of text in front of a paragraph using a specific paragraph style. This feature is a great shortcut for figure and table captions, because each must begin with *Table* or *Figure*. Use the auto insert text feature for notes, warnings, cautions, or for any text that appears repeatedly as the first part of a paragraph. Type the text in the Text box in the Special Effects dialog box. You can type up to 40 characters in the text box. Select any text attributes, such as bold or italic, and click OK. Remember the text appears in front of every paragraph using the style.

Page numbering

Ami lets you place page numbers in the header or footer of your document, ensuring they appear on every page. You can specify any leading text to precede the page number, on what page numbering should start, and what number it should start with. The following tips help you achieve special effects with page numbering.

Tip 9-23: Placing page numbers in the right or left margins   Ami does not let you insert a page number, or any other text, in the right or left margin. To get around this limitation, create a repeating frame in the margin and insert the page number in the frame. Enhance the frame with any borders or shading you would like. Ami updates the page number and it appears on every page of your document.

Tip 9-24: Create page references using a power field   Use the PageRef power field to insert a page reference to any text or graphics you are discussing in your document. The PageRef power field displays the page on which a bookmark appears, so you must create a bookmark at the location of the text or graphic you need to reference. Insert your cursor at the place where you need the page reference and insert the power field. For example, the power field PageRef Logo frame would insert the page number on which that frame appears. Refer to chapter 15 for more information on the PageRef power field.

Tip 9-25: Create "Page X of X" page numbers   If you need to display the total number of pages in your document as part of the page number, use the power field NumPages in your header/footer. Insert the power field and preceding text, and it appears on every page, automatically updating as your page total changes. Refer to chapter 15 for more information on the NumPages power field.

Tip 9-26: Numbering pages across chapters   You can continue to number pages consecutively across pages using the Master Document feature.

Master document

The Master Document is a file that contains references to other Ami Pro files you would like to include in one publication, such as a book, a directory, or any other long document. The advantage of using a Master Document is that you can perform tasks on one file (the Master Document) instead of performing the same task repeatedly on individual files. You can create a table of contents, an index, number figures or lists, and print using a Master Document.

To create a Master Document, follow these steps:

1. Open a new file using File New.
2. Select Master Document from the File menu. Ami displays the Master Document dialog box as shown in Figure 9-5.

3. Highlight the first file to appear in the master document and select the Include button. Ami displays the filename in the Master doc files list box.

4. Continue highlighting files and clicking on Include until all the files you need appear in the Master doc files list box. Click OK to return to the document.

5. Save the file.

Tip 9-27: Reorganizing files in a master document   You cannot move files up or down inside the Master doc files list box, but you can delete the file and insert it at a new location. Highlight the file you need in the Files list box, and highlight the file to precede it in the Master doc files list box. Click Include, and Ami places the file after the file you highlighted in the Master doc files list box.

Tip 9-28: Viewing files in a master document   The MASTRDOC macro lets you view the documents in master document, and move to the previous or next file in a master document. You must have a master document open when you playback the MASTRDOC macro. Once you do execute the macro, Ami adds a new menu item to the File menu called Master Browser, as shown in Figure 9-6. From the Master Browser menu item, you can display the initial file, or the next

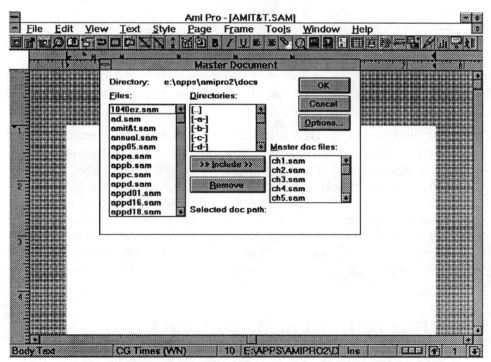

9-5 The Master Document dialog box lets you add, remove, and rearrange files in a master document.

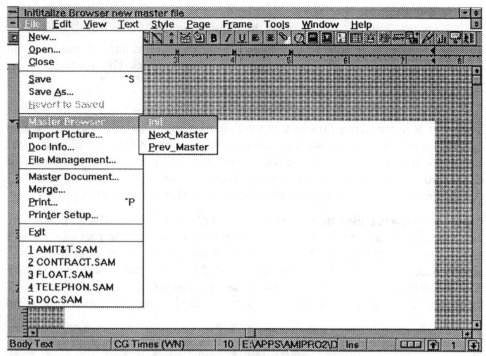

9-6 The MASTRDOC macro adds the Master Browser command to the File menu. It remains on the File menu until you exit Ami Pro.

or previous file in the master document. Once you open several files in a master document, you can use the Next Master and Previous Master to move among the files.

Tip 9-29: Inserting page references across files in a master document The PageRef power field inserts the page number of a bookmark, letting you building cross references to other text and graphics in the same file. However, you cannot use the PageRef power field with bookmarks in other files. Ami has two macros, CROSREF9 and CROSSREF, that let you use PageRef with bookmarks in other files. The macros create global variables by the same name as the bookmarks it finds, and uses the global variables to generate page references. Use the CROSS-REF macro for a master document containing nine or fewer files, and use the CROSREF9 macro to generate cross references for a master document containing more than nine files.

Generating a table of contents

Ami creates a table of contents that has up to three levels of entries. Ami pulls the entries from the document from which you create the table of contents—either a regular document or a master document. You specify up to three styles in the document Ami should use to create the table of contents. Ami searches for every occurrence of those styles in or among the documents, and inserts the text using the styles into your table of contents.

Creating the table of contents requires two major steps: generating the TOC text file and formatting the TOC text file.

Generating the TOC text file

To generate the table of contents text file, follow these steps:

1. Decide on the chapter titles and subheadings you need to include in the table of contents. You can include up to three levels of headings.

2. Open the file for which you need to create a table of contents. The file can be a regular document file or a master document. If you are using a master document, make sure all the files you need appear in the Master Document dialog box and that they are in the correct order. Make any necessary changes and save the file.

3. Select TOC, Index from the Tools menu. Select the Table of Contents check box and type the output file to which you need send the table of contents entries. Ami will create the file if you have not created it previously. Select the TOC Options button to display the TOC Options dialog box, as shown in Figure 9-7.

4. Enter the styles you need to include in the table of contents. You can specify the style name by typing it or by selecting it from a list box. You also can specify a separator to use between the entry and the page number, whether or not to include page numbers, and if they should be right-aligned.

5. Click OK twice to return to the document. Ami creates the table of contents, and places the cursor in the table of content's text file when finished. Ami puts the table of contents in a table in the output file. Ami creates three new styles in the output file: TOC1 for Level 1 entries, TOC2 for Level 2 entries, and TOC3 for Level 3 entries. The TOC styles, however, do not use the same style attributes as the styles from which the entries came. TOC1 uses the font of the Level 2 style, and TOC2 uses the font of the Level 3 style. Because there is no style under the Level 3 styles, those entries use the Body Text font. Figure 9-8 illustrates the font assignments.

Formatting the TOC text file

Once Ami displays the table of contents text file, you can modify the TOC styles to create your own design. Use the same process to modify TOC styles as you would any other styles in a document. Ami uses the !TOC.STY style sheet for all tables of contents, but you can load any style sheet you want to use.

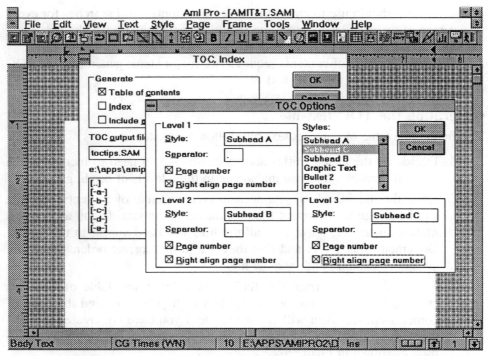

9-7 Selecting style names from the list boxes in the TOC Options dialog box prevents spelling or capitalization errors in creating the table of contents.

Indexing

Ami automatically generates an index. Sounds great, doesn't it? Well, you have a much larger stake in the process than you might imagine. Ami does compile a list of index entries, but it does so only for the index entries you create by paging through the document and marking each entry. You must tell Ami what text to reference, whether the text is a primary entry or a secondary entry (appearing underneath another entry, such as Icons, or Creating), and if it should use any cross reference such as See or See Also. Creating an index is a three step process: marking index entries, generating the index, and formatting the index.

Marking index entries

The first step in creating an index is to decide what to include, called marking index entries. To do so, follow these steps:

1. Open the document for which you need to create an index. If you are using a Master Document, you must create index entries in each of the documents listed in the Master Document, not in the Master Document itself.

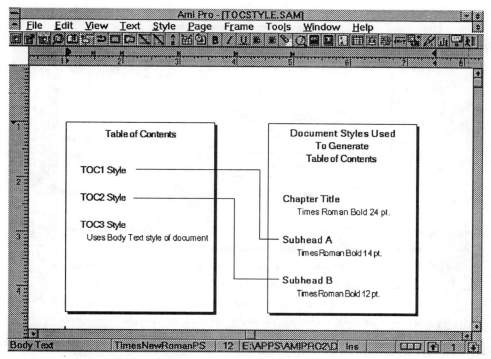

9-8 The formatting rules Ami Pro uses to format the table of contents for one or more documents.

2. Move to the first text in the document you need to appear in the index. Highlight the text and select Mark Text/Index Entry from the Edit menu. Ami displays the Mark Index Entry dialog box as displayed in Figure 9-9. Each index entry must contain a primary entry. You also can specify a secondary entry that Ami indents underneath the primary entry. You must specify if you need the index entry to use a page number or other type of reference. Other is for See and See Also references, which you type in the Other text box.

3. Once you finish specifying the index entry, select the Mark button. Ami creates the index entry.

4. Click OK when you are ready to return to the document.

5. Repeat steps 2 through 4 to create the index entries for your document. Once you have completed the entries for the document, save it. If the document is one of several of a Master Document, open the next document and repeat the process.

Tip 9-30: Use the Mark Index Entry example box   The Mark Index Entry dialog box displays an example of how your index entry will appear in the index.

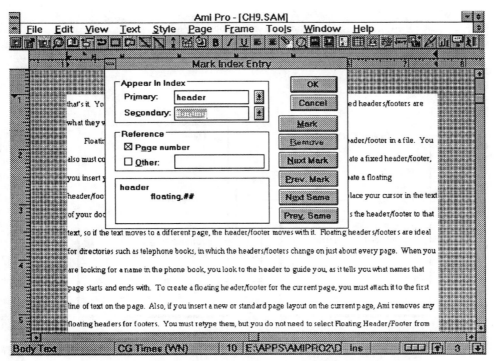

9-9 The Mark Index Entry dialog box lets you specify a primary, secondary, and See Also references for a block of text.

As you create your primary and secondary entries, use the example box to make sure you are achieving the results you need.

Tip 9-31: Changing index entries   When you need to change an index entry, use the Mark Text/Index Entry command on the Edit menu. The dialog box has five buttons you can use to change your entries: Next Mark, Previous Mark, Next Same, Previous Same, and Remove.

Use Next/Previous Mark to move to the next or previous index entry in the document. Use Next/Previous Same to move to the next or previous index entry using the same primary or secondary entry displayed in dialog box. Once you move to the entry, you can make any editing changes necessary or you can select Remove to delete the entry.

Tip 9-32: Including chapter numbers in page numbers   If you need to include chapter numbers as part of the page numbers appearing in the index (2-5, 7-34, etc.), you can do so by adding the chapter numbers to the page number in the documents. Type the chapter number in the Leading text box in the Page Numbering dialog box. The chapter numbers appear in the page numbers in the document and in the index. If you manually type the chapter number in front of the page number in the documents' headers or footers, the index will not include the chapter numbers.

Tip 9-33: Marking all occurrences of a word as index entries   The INDEX-ALL macro lets you mark every occurrence of specified text in the current file as an index entry. The INDEXALL macro adds a new menu item to the Edit menu: Mark Index All after you select Mark Text. Once you select this command, Ami marks the text you selected as an index entry. It then continues to search for every occurrence of the text, even if the text occurs as part of another word, and marks each occurrence as an index entry. This is a powerful macro that can save you hours when creating an index. However, be certain that you want to mark every occurrence of the text, because Ami does not ask for your permission to mark—it just does it.

Tip 9-34: Marking index entries using the INDEX power field   The INDEX power field marks an entry for inclusion in the index, just as you do when you select Mark Text Index Entry from the Edit menu. You can specify a primary entry, a secondary entry, a *See also* reference, and whether to display a page number in the index or not.

You can use the Mark Text Index Entry from the Edit menu to locate and edit any index entries you create using the INDEX power field.

The INDEX power field uses the following syntax:<Index "Primary" [#] "Secondary" "other"

Primary is the primary heading for the index entry. The pound sign [#] tells Ami to include the page number with the index entry. *Secondary* is the secondary heading to appear under the primary heading. *Other* is any type of miscellaneous reference, such as See or See Also.

Generating the index

To generate the index text file, follow these steps:

1. Open the file for which you need to create an index. The file can be a regular document file or a master document. If you are using a master document, make sure all the files you need appear in the Master Document dialog box and that they are in the correct order. Make any necessary changes and save the file.

2. Select TOC, Index from the Tools menu. Select the Index check box. If you want to include letter headings above each index section, select the Include alphabetical separators check box. Type the output file to which you need send the index. Ami will create the file if you have not created it previously.

3. Click OK to return to the document. Ami creates the index, and places the cursor in the index text file when finished.

Formatting the index

Once Ami displays the index text file, you can modify the index styles to create your own design. Use the same process to modify index styles as you would any other styles in a document. Ami uses the !INDEX.STY style sheet for all tables of contents, but you can load any style sheet you want to use.

Cross references

You can create cross-references to pages containing items you need to refer to in a document. The PAGEREF power field inserts the page number on which a specified bookmark is located. The PAGEREF uses the page numbering inside the current document, and not any page numbering across documents created by the Master Document feature. To use the PAGEREF field to insert cross-references for figures, you would need to insert a bookmark at each figure's location.

The PAGEREF power field uses the following syntax:

<PageRef [bookmark name]>

Bookmark name is the bookmark for which the power field finds its location in the document and inserts its page number.

However, you cannot use the PageRef power field with bookmarks in other files. Ami has two macros, CROSREF9 and CROSSREF, that let you use PageRef with bookmarks in other files. The macros create global variables by the same name as the bookmarks it finds, and uses the global variables to generate page references. Use the CROSSREF macro for a master document containing nine or fewer files, and use the CROSREF9 macro to generate cross-references for a master document containing more than nine files.

For more information on using Power Fields, refer to Chapter 15, chapter 13 for more information on using macros.

Questions & Answers

Q: I printed several documents by including them in a Master Document and printing it. But my page numbers changed. Ami updated the page numbers as though the files were all one document.

A: The Master Document feature is designed to combine several smaller files into one large publication. Books, manuals, directories, and other long documents are ideal for a Master Document. If, however, your documents are not related and you do not want Ami to consecutively number their pages across files, do not use the Master Document feature to print multiple documents. Instead, use the PRNBATCH macro to print several documents at a time.

Q: My document uses chapter and page numbers in the footer, but when I generate a table of contents and an index, the chapter numbers don't appear.

A: If you manually type a chapter number in your footer, Ami will not include it in the table of contents or index. Instead, you must add the chapter number as leading text before the page number. Insert the cursor in the footer of the first page that uses page numbers. Select Page Numbering from the Page menu. Type the chapter number in the Leading text box and Ami will add the chapter number and include it with the page number the next time you generate a table of contents or index.

Q: I use a Master Document to combine my smaller files into one large document. I also use power fields in each file to insert cross-references to pages within the file. However, the power fields do not pick up on the numbering scheme created by the Master Document.

A: Power fields do not use the consecutive page numbers created across files by the Master Document. Instead, power fields use the page number within the chapter that appears at the bottom right of your screen.

Q: How can I remove floating headers or footers if I have marks turned off?

A: Select GoTo and choose Next item. Select Floating Header/Footer mark from the Next item list box. Ami moves to the next mark in the document. If that is the mark you need to remove, select Floating Header/Footer from the Page menu and select Remove. If the mark is not the one you need to remove, continue selecting GoTo until Ami locates the appropriate mark.

Q: I am creating a long document, but I am using smaller files for each section of the document. I am not using the Master Document feature, because I am using page numbers that restart in each chapter. Is there any way I can generate a table of contents or index one time and include all the files?

A: No. You need to generate a table of contents or index for each file, then combine the tables from each file into one large table for the entire document. The table of contents will be in the correct order, but you should sort the index so that the entries appear in alphabetical order.

Summary

Ami provides a wide variety of tools that let you give an identity to your documents. Headers and footers let you identify the contents of a document, chapter, or individual pages. Footnotes and endnotes reference a source of information in your document. You can avoid widows and orphans to make your documents more readable and create simple, outline, and legal numbering schemes. You can attach frames to their surrounding text or paragraphs and sequentially number frames in a document. Several chapters can be combined into one larger publication using a Master Document. Your pages can include page numbers independent of other chapters, or you can number pages consecutively across chapters. You can include cross-references to pages in the current or other chapters. Ami also lets you create a table of contents or index for the current file or multiple files in a master document. All of these tools let you make your publications easier to read and understand.

10
CHAPTER

Putting a document together

Ami is so flexible, you can use it to create virtually any document. Creating a book, however, requires a different strategy than creating a legal contract, a flyer, or a business card. This chapter details how to flow from putting together a newsletter to putting together an ad, using the most efficient and effective procedure in each case.

You can use one of three main strategies when creating your documents: foundation-page strategies building-block strategies or free-form strategies. Each strategy is appropriate for certain types of documents, but not for others.

Foundation-page strategies

The foundation-page strategy uses the page as the document's foundation, differing from the building-block and free-form strategies that use frames or tables as the foundation. Most documents use the foundation-page strategy, in which you place text and graphics directly on the page. As you add text and graphics, Ami adds the number of pages necessary to hold the new items. These documents use only one page layout throughout the entire document, ensuring consistency among its pages. Documents using this type of layout strategy are manuals, directories, books, advertisements, flyers, and short newsletters.

Building-block strategies

Documents that require more variety and flexibility than the foundation-page strategy allows use the building-block strategy. Newsletters often use multiple layouts on the same page, using a three-column layout for one story and switching to a two-column story for the next. Stories often start on one page and continue on to another. They also insert *floating* items, such as pull-quotes and table of contents within an article.

Although Ami lets you use multiple page layouts in one document, you cannot use them on the same page. To create these documents, make frames to hold each story, pull-quotes, or headline. Each frame uses its own layout, so one frame holds a two-column story and another contains a three-column story, but you use only one page layout for the document. Once you create your frames and arrange them on the page, add your text and graphics to each frame. The building-block strategy is used for newsletters, newspapers, and magazines.

Free-form strategies

What about documents that don't fit into either the foundation-page or the building-block strategies? These documents have blocks of text, individual words, and graphics scattered on the page, or they might have a grid of rows and columns, but too many individual *boxes* for frames. For these documents, use a free-form strategy, created with either frames or with tables. Documents that have an *open* appearance, such as advertisements and flyers use frames to place their text and graphics. Create the first frame, modifying its layout, borders, and shading, and make that frame the default. Each new frame you create uses those same attributes. Documents that have a structured appearance, such as forms or grids, use tables to place their text and graphics. The free-form strategy is used for flyers, advertisements, business cards, letterhead, and forms.

Designing documents

Ami gives you more options and flexibility than any other word processor or desktop publisher. After all, what other program lets you create multiple page layouts for one document and the ability to customize styles within each of your documents without affecting others? However, along with that flexibility comes the responsibility to design your documents wisely.

Many people don't realize they are designing a document. They simply choose a page size, create and modify a few styles, and make adjustments as they go along. Unfortunately, making choices without an overall plan is designing haphazardly, and the documents tell the real story.

Before you create your first document in Ami, plan your design. Look at documents others have designed and note your likes and dislikes. One of the best ways to create your own design is to borrow ideas that worked well in other documents. Once you have a basic idea of what you want, draw a sample page and think of the paragraph styles you would use on the page. Decide on your document's design before you create a document in Ami, not after.

As you plan your design, think of your document's function, whether people want to read it, or if they need to read it. Documents fall into three categories:

- documents people like to read. Designs should be pleasant and interesting, including newspapers, periodicals, and books
- documents people must read, whether they want to or not. Designs should be clear and understandable, including tax forms, tables, formal papers, and reports
- documents people must be encouraged to read. Designs should be luring and strive to keep the readers' attention, including press releases, advertisements, and flyers.

This book does not attempt to cover all the aspects of good design for all documents. Rather, the following paragraphs list design basics for all documents, and then detailed design guidelines for several document types.

General design guidelines

The following design rules apply to all types of documents, from business cards to books. Keep these basics in mind when you draw your sample page and create a page layout for your document.

- Use the page's optical center as a focal point, placing a headline or a graphic in that position to draw attention. The document's optical center is slightly above and to the left of the mathematical center, as shown in Figure 10-1.
- Arrange text and graphics in a "Z" pattern, beginning from the optical center, as shown in Figure 10-2. A reader's eye travels from the optical center to the bottom of the page in a Z pattern, so take advantage of that pattern by placing your type and art accordingly.
- Place multiple graphics throughout the page to balance it, rather than putting them only in the bottom or top of the page. Don't mix heavy typestyles and graphics that will make the document top or bottom heavy.
- Stay within one or two typefaces, mixing fonts within one or two families.
- Don't mix all caps with lowercase letters. Avoid using all caps because they are difficult to read.
- Use boldface and italics sparingly.
- Break up long blocks of text with subheads.

Press release, advertisement, and flyer design guidelines

Figure 10-3 shows a sample advertisement that follows these design guidelines:

- Specify your product in the headline.
- Stress benefits rather than product features.

- Identify your product in the body copy.
- Clearly state the product's price and any discount.
- Use a distinctive logo.
- Put body copy next to a graphic.

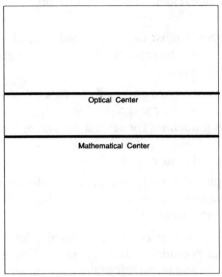

10-1 A document's optical center is slightly above its mathematical center. The reader's eye hits the optical center first.

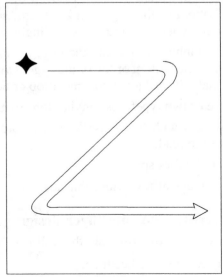

10-2 Readers scan a document in a "Z" pattern starting from the top left corner of the page.

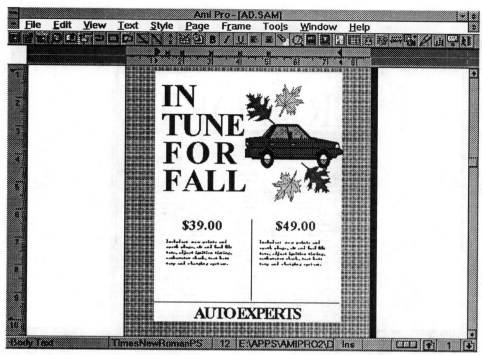

10-3 An advertisement created in Ami Pro.

Newsletter and magazine design guidelines

Figure 10-4 shows a sample newsletter that follows these design guidelines:

- Use ample white space and margins, because they serve as a frame for your text and graphics.
- Make the table of contents easy to read.
- Use drop caps to begin a story—they draw attention. Use drop caps consistently, but do not mix them with subheads: too many items draw attention away from the story.
- Use a different font for headlines, subheads, and bylines, but use the same font consistently for each.
- Be consistent in your design of headings, captions, bylines, and page numbers.
- Use reverse type sparingly. Use a sans-serif typeface in reverse type, because it is easier to read than when you use a serif typeface in reverse type.
- Avoid jumps as much as possible. Usually stories that are continued on another page are not read.

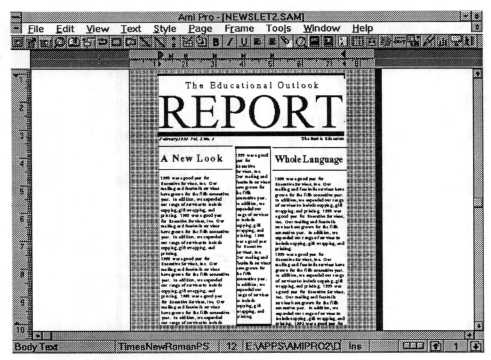

10-4 A newsletter created in Ami Pro.

Brochure design guidelines

Figure 10-5 shows a sample brochure that follows these design guidelines:

- Design brochure pages in the order you read them.
- Use ample margins.
- Place coupons or registrations where readers can detach them without removing necessary information they will need later.
- Use ample boldface if the brochure doubles as a flyer.

Letterhead design guidelines

Figure 10-6 shows a sample piece of letterhead that follows these design guidelines:

- Letterhead design shouldn't interfere with the page's active area (the space on which you write the letter).
- Choose colored paper carefully.
- Be conservative: letterhead is not the place for obtrusive text, spacing, or graphics.

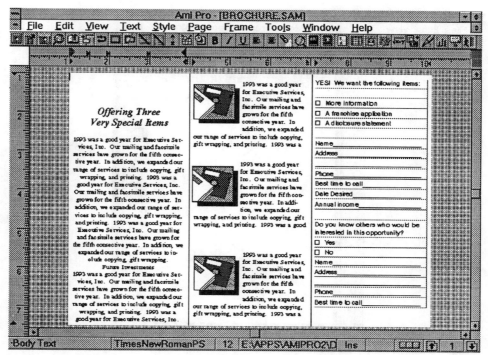

10-5 A brochure created in Ami Pro.

- Display long lists of names (officers, partners in a law firm, doctors in the same office) down the right or left margins. Displaying the names at the top or bottom requires too much space.
- Achieve a traditional layout by placing text and a logo in a square or inverted pyramid pattern. Center any graphics.
- Achieve a modern layout by placing a logo in an invisible horizontal or vertical line.

Business card design guidelines

Figure 10-7 shows a sample business card that follows these design guidelines:

- Use the standard 2 × 3½″ size. Irregularly-shaped cards don't fit well in a filing system and end up in the trash.
- Traditional layouts use landscape orientation.
- Modern layouts use portrait orientation.
- Use ample margins: 12 to 18 points.
- The card's active area should be at least 18 picas wide.

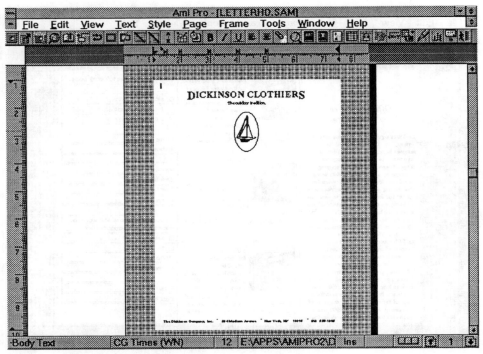

10-6 A piece of letterhead created in Ami Pro.

Forms design guidelines

Figure 10-8 shows a sample form that follows these design guidelines:

- Exclude the company's logo or make it small enough not to draw attention. Don't waste precious space for advertising.
- Use a box design for columns with left-aligned titles.
- Date forms to prevent using obsolete versions.
- Use large left margins so forms can fit into a binder without losing information when three-hole punched.
- Fill-in space should be large enough to accommodate the information requested.
- Align check boxes vertically.
- Use shading to separate sections.
- Put instructions below the form's title.
- Make the form's title descriptive and place it at the top left of the form.

10-7 A business card created in Ami Pro.

Book and manual design guidelines

Figure 10-9 shows a sample page from a book that follows these design guidelines:

- Avoid widows and orphans.
- Don't hyphenate a word from one column or page to the next.
- Avoid three consecutive hyphenated lines.
- Use a larger top margin than bottom margin.
- Use a smaller inner margin than outer margin.
- Use headers to identify a book's title and chapters.
- Start page numbering with the inside title page.
- Use arabic page numbers from the title page forward. Use roman numeral page numbers before the title page (table of contents, copyright page, etc.).

Laying out a document

Now that you have a basic idea of your document's design, you are ready to begin laying out and creating your document. The basic process is the same no matter

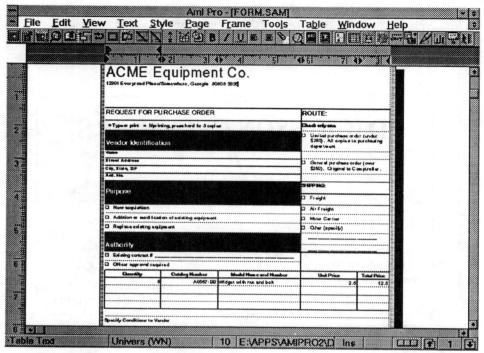

10-8   A form created in Ami Pro.

what type of document you are creating. The following steps list the order in which you should layout and create all of your documents:

1. Create a directory structure to hold your document's files, as discussed in chapter 3.

2. Design the document as much as possible, drawing a sample page and listing the paragraph styles you need to create. Expect to do some fine-tuning later.

3. Start Ami, loading the style sheet you need.

4. Save the style sheet under a new name (before you make any changes).

5. Change to Full Page view so you can see your page as a whole.

6. Modify the style sheet to fit your design, changing the page size, orientation, margins, and columns as discussed in chapter 7.

7. Remove any extraneous ruling lines, borders, or boxes that came with the style sheet (if you used the With contents option).

8. Draw the frames that will hold the text and graphics for your newsletter, discussed in chapter 17. Draw the frames or create the table that will hold your form or flyer.

9. Design your paragraph styles as discussed in chapters 5 and 7.

10. Save the style sheet using the With contents option. Your frames or table are now saved with style sheet, so you can reuse them.

11. Make your current style sheet the default using the User Setup command under the Tools menu. Select the Load button and highlight the file in the Style sheet list box. Now, anytime you select File New, Ami automatically uses the current style sheet.

12. Create and edit your text as discussed in chapter 4.

13. Create headers and footers as discussed in chapter 9.

14. Add logos, graphics, and drawings to your document, discussed in chapter 17.

15. Add any power fields necessary to update figure or page references, discussed in chapter 15.

16. Add enhancements, such as lines and arrows, to your imported graphics, discussed in chapter 18.

17. Save your document.

18. Print your document for review.

19. If you are creating a multichapter document, such as a book, select File New and restart the process.

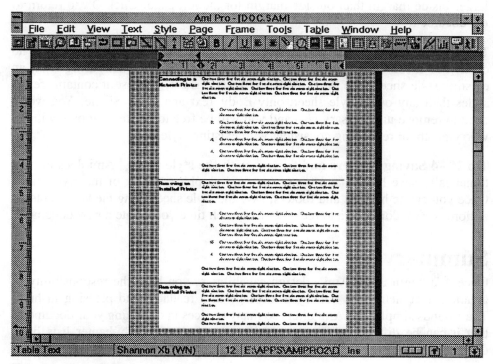

10-9 A book created in Ami Pro.

Tip 10-1: Adding crop marks to your pages   First, do you need crop marks? If your final trim size is 8½ × 11, you don't need them. If your final trim size is smaller, such as 7 × 10 or 5½ by 8½, you need crop marks. Crop marks tell your printer where to cut excess space on the page. If you created a custom page size using the Page Setting option in the Modify Page Layout dialog box, you need crop marks to tell the printer what size your final page should be. Ami does not display crop marks on the screen, but it will print them if you select the Crop Marks check box under Print Options. Ami prints crop marks a half-inch outside the margins.

   If for some reason you are using an 8½ × 11 trim size but you still need crop marks, you can draw them in a frame, and make the frame repeating so it appears on every page of your document.

Tip 10-2: Creating a binding margin   If your document will be bound, you need to create a larger inside margin than outside margin. Although the margins are unequal, binding takes up about ¼", so the margins will appear equal once the document is bound. Most bound documents begin on a right page and use a odd page numbers (1, 3, 5). From the Page menu, select Modify Page Layout and select Margins & columns. Select the Right page, and make the left margin ¼" larger than the right margin (on a right page, the left margin is the inside margin and the right margin is the outside margin). Select Mirrored and Ami creates a larger inside margin than outside margin for the left page. Click OK to return to the document.

Tip 10-3: Starting a new style sheet   Some documents use a design like no other. For those documents, creating an original is easier than basing it on an existing style sheet. Use the ‾BASIC.STY style sheet, because it contains fewer styles than any other style sheet: only Body Text and Body Single. You won't need to remove unnecessary tags and you will be free to create your own without worrying about remaining consistent with existing styles.

Tip 10–4 Saving headers and footers with the style sheet   Ami does not automatically save header and footer text and graphics as part of the style sheet. Once you create headers and footers, save the style sheet using the With contents option, so you don't have to recreate them each time you create a new document.

Summary

Once you begin using Ami's design capabilities, you have the responsibility of creating documents that convey a message in a readable and pleasing fashion. That sounds simple, but Ami offers so many choices in designing your documents that it can be difficult to decide which option is best. This chapter lists basic design guidelines for the most common documents and publications people create when using word processing and DTP, including press releases, advertisements, newsletters, magazines, brochures, letterhead, business cards, forms, and books and manuals. Take notice of what you like and dislike about the designs of other documents, and, most importantly, plan your design. Before you begin creating and modifying styles and page layouts, decide on your document's appearance so you have a plan to guide you.

11
CHAPTER

Checking your spelling & grammar

Ami lets you proof your document using its own spell check and thesaurus tools. You also can use an outside grammar checker from within Ami. These tools help ensure that your documents look and read professionally.

How Spell Check works

Ami spell checks the portion of your document where your cursor is positioned. If your cursor is in the main document text, then that is what Ami spell checks. If your cursor is in a frame, Ami spell checks the frames in your document. Ami spell checks the these items in your document separately: main document text, text in frames, footnote text, and header/footer text. Ami calls each of these pieces of text a text stream, and checks the main document text stream separately from other text streams unless you specify otherwise.

To begin checking the main document text, place your cursor in the document text and select Spell Check from the Tools menu. If you need to spell check the other text streams at the same time, select the Include other text stream check box. To spell check only the text in frames, footnotes, or header/footers, place your cursor inside one of those text streams. Ami checks each occurrence of text in a frame, footnote, and header/footer, in that order. Ami does not check the main document text if you begin spell check from inside a different text stream.

You also can include spell check options, as shown in Figure 11-1.

Check for repeated words   If you want Ami to flag any words that appear twice in succession, select Check for repeated words.

Check for words with numbers   If you want Ami to flag any words that include numbers, select Check for words with numbers.

Check words with initial caps   If you want Ami to flag any words that have only the first letter capitalized, select Check words with initial caps.

Include user dictionary alternatives   If you have added words to the user dictionary, either by editing the dictionary or selecting Add to Dictionary, you must select Include user dictionary alternatives for Ami to supply those words as alternatives.

Tip 11-1: Editing as you check spelling   What happens when Ami finds a misspelled word but doesn't supply a suitable alternative? Your first reaction might be to cancel the spell check, edit the word, and continue with spell check. However, you can edit the word directly from the Spell Check dialog box. When Ami displays the word in the Replace With text box, you can edit the word by placing

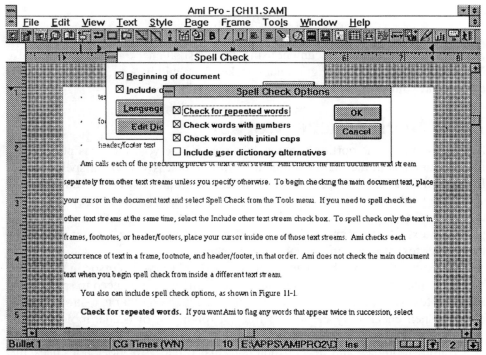

11-1   The Spell Check Options dialog box lets you customize your spell check according to your document's needs.

the cursor in that box and making the appropriate changes. Once you finish editing the word, select Replace, and Ami changes the word to the edited version you supplied. This procedure also works well when Ami finds two occurrences of the same word (i.e. the the). It highlights the word and places it in the Replace With text box. You can delete the word from the text box and select Replace. Ami deletes the word, leaving only one of the original two words in the document.

Tip 11-2: Spell checking across documents The FPSELL macro was made with writers of long documents in mind. Usually you perform tasks on groups of files, such as spell checking all the files in a book, printing all the files, backing up all the files, and so on. The FPELL macro performs a spell check across multiple documents, letting you review all the files making up a long publication at the same time.

Once you playback the FSPELL macro, Ami displays the Spell Check Multiple Files dialog box, as shown in Figure 11-2. You can specify the same options when spell checking across several document as you can when you spell check a single document. Select the files you want to spell check from the list box and select OK. Ami performs the spell check, opening each document and displaying alternatives for each word it doesn't find in its dictionary. You can replace the

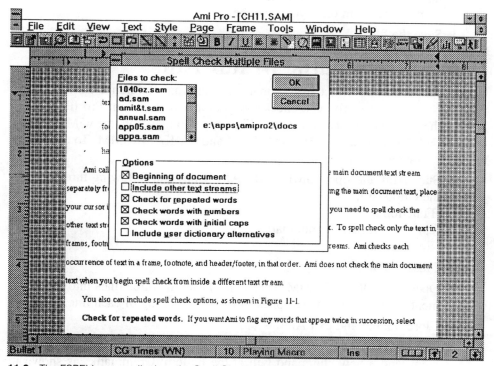

11-2 The FSPELL macro displays the Spell Check Multiple Files dialog box.

word, skip it, skip all occurrences of the word, add it to the dictionary, or cancel the spell check. Once Ami completes the spell check, it closes and saves the file and continues to the next one.

Editing the dictionary

Ami has over 130,000 words in its dictionary, but sometimes that isn't enough. You have words you use everyday that don't appear in Ami's dictionary, such as employee names, your company name, and your products. You can add those words to Ami's user dictionary so that Ami won't consider those words mistakes.

To add words to Ami's user dictionary, follow these steps:

1. Select Spell Check from the Tools menu. Select the Edit Dictionary button from the Spell Check dialog box. Ami opens the user dictionary file (VEAMAB51.LEX if you are using the English version), as shown in Figure 11-3. Anytime you spell check a document and click on the Add to Dictionary button, Ami adds the word to the user dictionary. Ami lists the words and numbers appearing in the dictionary file in this order: numbers, symbols (in order by ANSI values), uppercase words, and finally lowercase words.

2. Change the dictionary by adding or removing the words you need. You do not need to add the words in alphabetical order, because Ami will alphabetize them once you save the file.

3. Save the file.

Using Grammatik within Ami

Grammatik Windows 2.0, the grammar checker from Reference Software, can run from within Ami. You can check the grammar of any Ami Pro file without leaving the program. To install Grammatik, copy two files from the \GM directory to the \AMIPRO directory: GMKAMI.SAM and GMKAMI.SMM. To use Grammatik, follow these steps:

1. Start Ami and open GMKAMI.SAM. Copy the following three lines to the Clipboard:
   'Function auto ()
   'call gmkami.smm!grammar()
   'End Function

2. Close the file.

3. Open AUTOEXEC.SMM macro file. Paste the three lines into the document. Remove the apostrophes from the beginning of each line.

4. Close the file and exit Ami.

5. Restart Ami and open the file you need to proofread. Click on the Tools menu and a new command will at the bottom: Grammatik, as shown in

Figure 11-4. Simply click on Grammatik to start the grammar checker without leaving Ami.

Tip 11-3: Save editing changes to Ami files before starting Grammatik
Before you select the Grammatik command from the Tools menu, always save any editing changes you made to the document. Grammatik checks the version of the current file on disk, rather than the one you have open. If you have not saved the latest changes, Grammatik cannot check them with the rest of the file.

Summary

Ami's spell check tool lets you verify that words in your document are spelled correctly. You can choose to spell check the main document, text in frames, footnotes, and headers and footers, or all of them at once. You also can choose to spell check optional words, such as repeated words, words including numbers, words that begin with a capital letter, and words you included in the user dictionary. In addition to the spell check tool, you can run Grammatik from inside Ami, so you can check your grammar too.

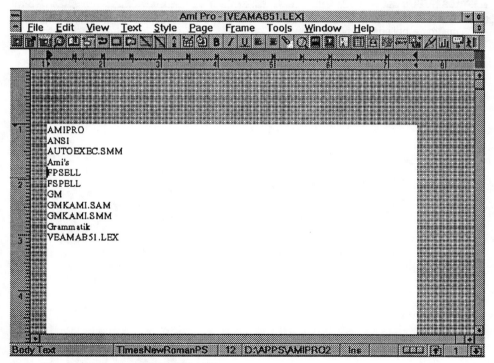

11-3 The user dictionary: VEAMAB51.LEX

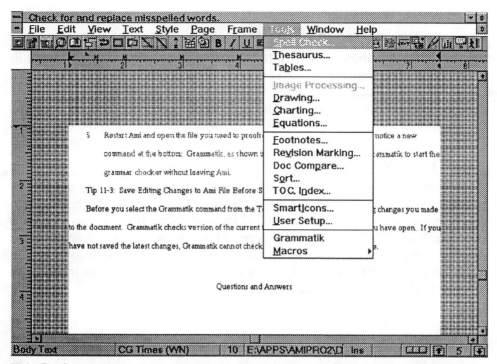

11-4 The Grammatik command appears on the Tools menu after you install Grammatik and run the macros supplied for Ami Pro.

12
CHAPTER

Merging and sorting text

Performing a merge is similar to exercising: you know you need to do it, but you never look forward to it. Traditionally, merge has been a complicated procedure that few people mastered. Ami's merge feature is powerful, yet simple enough that you won't need to sweat it when you create your labels or form letters.

Ami also has a sorting feature that lets you arrange the text in your document in alphabetical or numeric order. Sorting is the perfect compliment to merge, in that you can sort addresses by zip code and then merge them to label sheets.

Merging text

When Ami performs a merge, it takes text from two separate documents to create a new document. The two documents you need to perform a merge are a data document and a standard document. The data document contains the text Ami inserts into a letter, label, or form. The standard document contains the letter, label, or form into which Ami inserts the text from the data document. Figure 12-1 displays a data document and a standard document that create form letters. Figure 12-2 displays a data document and a standard document that create labels.

The general process for merging two documents involves first creating the data document and the standard document. Then use the File Merge command to merge the two documents into a new file.

Creating the data document

The Ami Pro documentation tells you to create a data document using field and record delimiters. Forget it. It's too difficult to remember which delimiters to use,

231

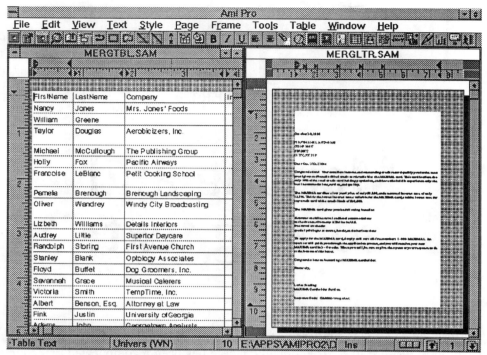

12-1 A form letter's data and standard documents: the top document is the data document; the bottom document is the standard document.

it's difficult to read the file, and the documentation doesn't tell you that you cannot use certain characters as delimiters (such as the asterisk and the question mark symbols). A much easier way of creating a data document is by creating a table to hold your text. The rules for using a table as your data document are as follows:

- The document must not contain any text outside the table.
- Each column in the table represents one field in a record.
- Each row in the table represents one record.
- The first row of the table must contain the field names.

To create a table as your data document, follow these steps:

1. Count the number of fields you need in your data document. This is the number of columns you will need in your table. Count the number of total records you need to enter into the data document. Add one to that number for the total number of rows you need in your table (the additional row is for the field names at the top of the table).

2. Create a table with the correct number of columns and rows using the Tables command from the Tools menu.

3. Enter the field names for the data in the first row of the table. Enter one field name per row.

4. Enter the data into the table.

5. Save the file.

Tip 12-1: A tutorial for creating a data document If you have never created a data document, the MERGDATA macro takes you through the process step-by-step, from specifying field names, to adding and deleting records, and even searching for specific values in a field. The MERGDATA macro is an excellent tutorial for those who are not comfortable with creating a data document. However, the MERGDATA does not use a table to create a data document; the macro uses field and record delimiters instead.

Once you execute the MERGDATA macro, Ami adds a new command to the File menu: Merge Create/Edit. When you select this command, Ami displays a message telling you that the current document (whether you have one open or not) is not a records file, and it asks if you want to create one? Select OK and Ami opens an untitled document and displays the Create Record File dialog box, as shown in Figure 12-3. Specify the number of fields you want in the data doc-

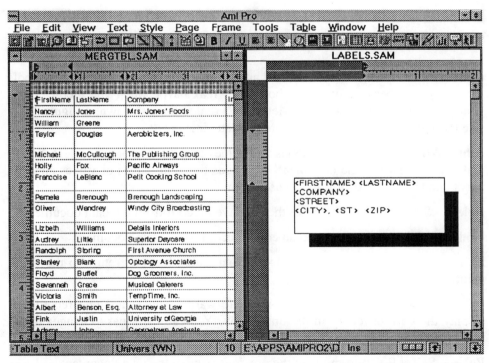

12-2 A label sheet's data and standard documents: the top document is the data document; the bottom document is the standard document.

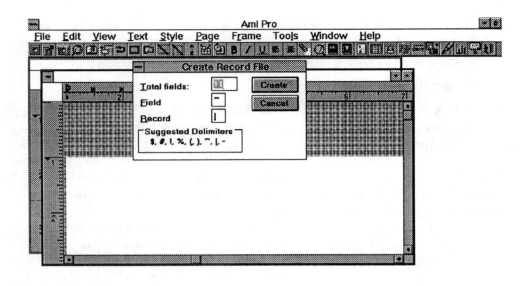

12-3 The MERGDATA macro displays the Create Record File dialog box to assist you in creating a data document.

ument and the symbols to use as field and record delimiters. Stick to the symbols Ami suggests, because other symbols can wreak havoc when you merge. Once you select OK, Ami displays the Merge Data dialog box as shown in Figure 12-4. Use these command buttons to create the data document:

Add   When you enter field names and values into the text boxes, select Add to make them a part of the document. Ami adds the field names or values and displays empty text boxes for you to use again.

Delete   Select Delete to remove the displayed record from the data document.

Update   Select Update to add an edited record to the data document.

Exit   Select Exit to remove the Merge Data dialog box and return to the document.

< < or > >   The arrow buttons move forward or backward one record and display the current record in the dialog box. You can then make changes to the record and select Update to add the changes to data document.

PgUp   Select PgUp to move to the previous page in the data document.

PgDn   Select PgDn to move to the next page in the data document.

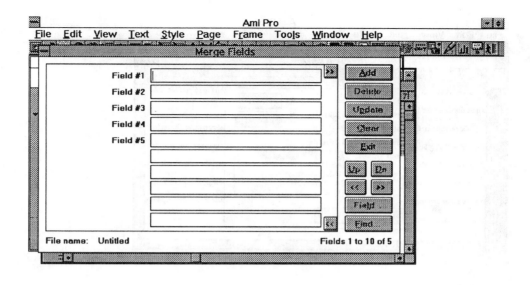

12-4 The MERGDATA macro displays the Merge Fields dialog box to let you enter, search for, and remove records.

Field Select Field to move to a specific field. Ami displays the GoTo Field dialog box, from which you select a field name and select OK. Ami moves to the field you chose.

Find Select Find to move to a field containing a specific value. Ami displays the Find dialog box. Select the field name you want to search, and enter the value you want to find in that specific field. Select OK and Ami searches the data document for the specified value.

Tip 12-2: Viewing and selecting a dBASE file for a merge If you use dBASE files as merge data documents, you can use the DBASVIEW macro to view information about the database file's structure. You also can have Ami create a data description file so you can use the file as a data document for merge.

Once you run the DBASVIEW macro, Ami displays the dBASE File Info dialog box, as shown in Figure 12-5. The dialog box shows the file's name, the date the file was last edited, the number of records it contains, the number of fields it contains, and a list of all the field names in the file. You can select the Create Description File button and Ami creates a data description file in an untitled document. A description file lets you use a file from another application as a data document for the merge.

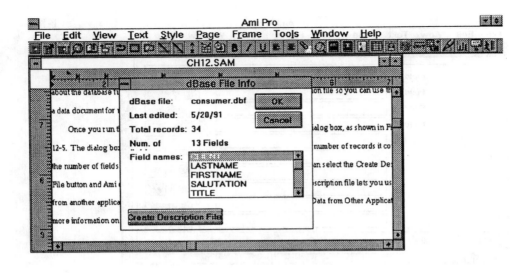

12-5 The DBASVIEW macro displays the dBASE File Info dialog box to let you view the structure of a dBASE file.

Creating the standard document

The process for creating a standard document is the same for any other document. Choose a style sheet, create a page layout, modify your styles, and add the text to the document. When you come to a place in the document where you need to insert text from the data document, follow these steps:

1. Select Insert from the Edit menu. Select Merge Field. Ami displays the Insert Merge Field dialog box, as displayed in Figure 12-6.

2. Select the Data File button to tell Ami the data document from which it should merge. Type or highlight the data document filename and click OK. Ami returns to the Insert Merge Field dialog box. Ami lists all the field names you created in the data document in the Field names list box.

3. Highlight the field you need to insert into the standard document and click Insert. Ami inserts the field at the cursor's position in the standard document.

4. Continue typing text in the standard document without closing the Insert Merge Field dialog box.

5. When you are ready to insert the another field into the standard document, repeat steps three and four.

6. When you finish inserting fields into the standard document, click Cancel.

7. Save the standard document.

Tip 12-3: Using a table as the standard document   Just like you can use a table as a data a document, you can do the same with the standard document. However, you have even more flexibility using a table as a standard document, because you can include text outside the table. You can create a letter containing a table, or create the entire standard document inside the table. Create the document and the table as you normally would. When you are ready to insert merge fields, place the cursor inside the table. Select Edit Insert Merge Field and choose the field to insert into the cell. Continue positioning the cursor and inserting merge fields until every field you need is in the table. Save the file and perform the merge. One note of caution: if both the data and the standard documents use tables, Ami slows considerably when performing a merge.

Merging the data and the standard documents

Once you have created the data and the standard documents, you are ready to merge them. Before you do so, however, you need to plan what to do with the

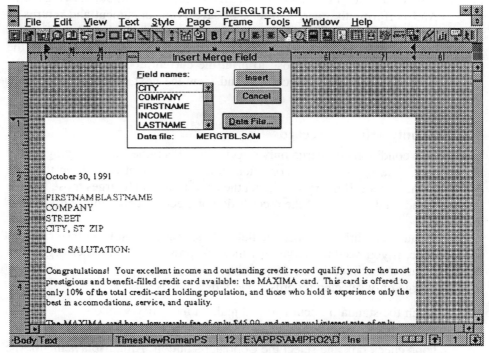

12-6   The Insert Merge Field dialog box lets you select merge fields to place into a standard document.

new documents Ami creates during the merge process. Ami gives you three choices: you can print the documents without reviewing them, review the documents first and then print them, or you can save the documents to a new file. Ami saves the new documents only if you choose the last option; otherwise you can print them only.

To merge a data and a standard document, follow these steps:

1. Open the standard document and make it the active window. Make sure you are in Layout mode, because Ami does not let you merge documents while you are in Draft mode.

2. Select Merge from the File menu. Ami displays the Merge dialog box, as displayed in Figure 12-7.

3. Select the Data File button to specify what file to use as a data document. Type or highlight the data document filename and click OK.

4. Select from three merge options: Merge & print; Merge, view & print; or Merge & save as.

5. If you selected to save the document to a new file, type the filename in the text box.

6. Click OK to perform the merge.

7. If you chose to only print or to save the documents without viewing them, Ami performs the merge, prints, or saves your document and returns to the standard document. If you chose to view the document, Ami displays the first merged document along with the Merge dialog box. From the dialog box, you can choose to print the current document and view the next, skip the current document and view the next, print all the merged documents, or cancel the merge.

Merging only selected records

You can use conditions to merge only selected records rather than merging all the records in a data document. A condition is a criterion that records in the data document must meet. If the records meet the condition, Ami merges those records into the standard document. If the records do not meet the condition, Ami ignores the records.

To create a condition, choose the field whose values must meet the criterion. For example, if you need to merge only those records in the state of Georgia, you need to create a condition in the State field.

To merge only selected records, follow these steps:

1. Open the standard document and make it the active window.

2. Select the Merge command from the File menu. Select the With conditions check box and select the Conditions button. Ami displays the Merge Conditions dialog box as displayed in Figure 12-8.

3. Place the cursor inside the Field name text box and select the field name from the list box on the right. Once you select the field name, Ami selects the If check box and places the cursor inside the Operator text box.

4. Select an operator from the list box on the right. Once you select an operator, Ami places the cursor inside the Value text box.

5. Type the value that the field must meet for Ami to merge the record. Values are case-specific, so make sure the value you type in the text box matches the values in the field.

6. If you need to use more than one set of criteria for the field, select AND or OR. You can specify up to three sets of criteria for one field.

7. Repeat steps three through six for each additional set of criteria you need.

8. Once you finish specifying the condition for this field, click OK to return to the Merge dialog box.

9. Select the merge action you need and select OK to perform the merge.

Figures 12-9 through 12-11 display several examples of merge conditions.

Tip 12-4: Select field names and operators from list boxes When you create a condition, you can type field names and operators or you can choose them from

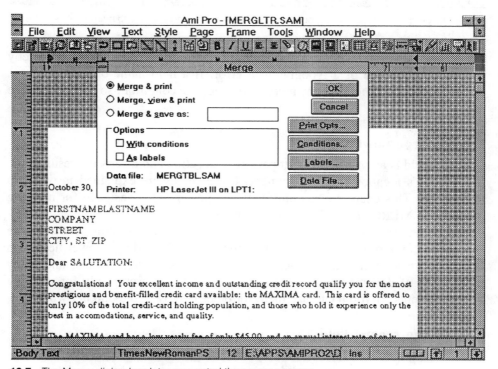

12-7 The Merge dialog box lets you control the merge process.

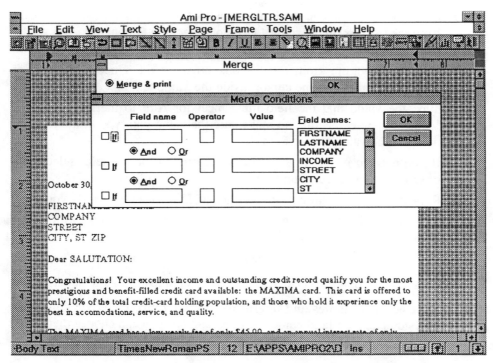

12-8 The Merge Conditions dialog box lets you narrow the merge process to merge only selected records.

a list box. Always select field names and operators from the list box, thereby reducing the chance of a typographical error. If a field name or an operator is incorrect, Ami will not find any records to match the condition, so it cannot merge any records.

Using merge power fields

A power field is an instruction that performs an action and inserts the result at the power field's location in the document. Power fields are explained in detail in chapter 15. This chapter deals only with the power fields designed for merging documents: MERGEREC, NEXTREC, and SKIP.

Ami lets you use these three Merge power fields to customize the merge process of combining standard and data documents. The Merge power fields can help you create form letters, telephone lists, rosters, address labels, and many other types of documents. The Merge power fields are useful only for merging two documents. If you try to use them for other purposes, they do not work.

The Merge record field

The MERGEREC field returns the number of the current merge record. MER-GEREC does not count any records skipped during a merge, because they did not

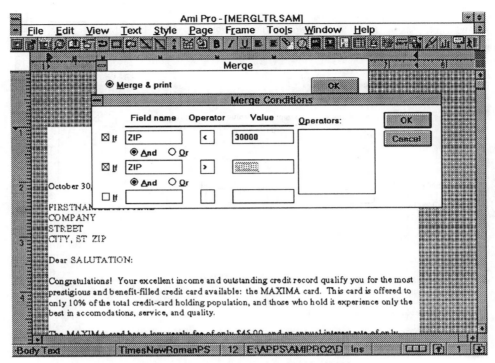

12-9 A condition that merges only a range of zip codes: 30000–40000.

meet conditions in the Merge Conditions dialog box or because of the SKIP power field. You can combine the MERGEREC power field with decision-making power fields to perform actions when the MERGEREC value reaches a certain amount.

The MERGEREC power field is useful for determining which records were printed, for identifying records that don't print properly, or if you need the record number for particular records on the standard document. For example, if you were creating a marketing mailing and you had a response code on the letter, the code could be a standard document filename and the addressee's record number could be in that file. A sample response code could be: GA0992.SAM-2. The "GA0992.SAM" is the standard document filename (including the state and date of the mailing), and the number two is the result of the MERGEREC power field. Figures 12-12 and 12-13 show a standard document containing the MERGEREC power field and of one the merged documents containing the MERGEREC result.

The MERGEREC power field uses the following syntax:

```
<MergeRec>
```

The next record field

Normally Ami places only one record on a page when it prints merged records. Using the NEXTREC power field, you can place multiple records on one page of

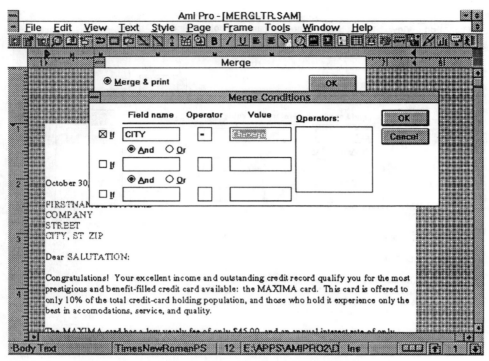

12-10 A condition that merges only records that incomes of $25,000.

the standard document. Technically, the NEXTREC advances to the next field during a merge. The result, however, is that you can print more than one record on a page.

To create a standard document using the NEXTREC power field, insert the merge fields on the second line of the document, adding the NEXTREC power field at the end of the line. Copy the line and paste it as many times as it takes to fill the page, or stop pasting when you reach the number of records you want to appear on the page. When you perform the merge, Ami places the records on the page.

The NEXTREC would be useful if you had a data document containing a list of conference speakers to whom you were sending confirmation letters, but if you also needed to create a list of speakers by their session time. You need all the records to appear on one page, rather than one record per page. Figure 12-14 shows a standard document containing the NEXTREC power field. The power field appears at the end of each line except for the last.

The NEXTREC power field uses the following syntax:

<NextRec>

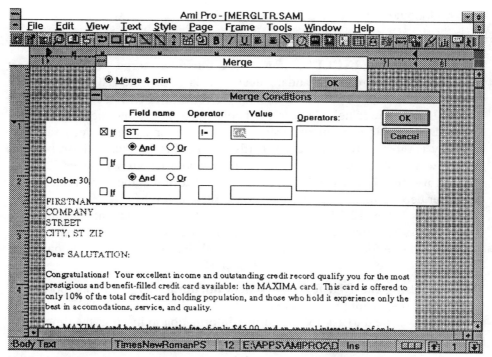

12-11 A condition that does not merge records in the state of Georgia.

The skip record field

The SKIP power field skips the record you specify and continues to the next record. The SKIP power field is really the equivalent of specifying conditions in the Merge Conditions dialog box. You can combine SKIP with IF to create conditions even more powerful than those you can create using the Merge Conditions dialog box. Using SKIP and IF, you can create conditions based on the current record number, identified by the MERGEREC field, which you cannot do using the Merge Conditions dialog box, because you are limited to conditions based on the values in the merge fields.

The SKIP power field uses the following syntax:

```
<Skip>
```

The SKIP and IF power fields also let you create target mailings that you can save in a standard document. Each time you want to send a mailing to a specific target group, merge the standard document with the data document containing the target audience you need. For example, if your company is offering a new credit card for people with incomes over $25,000, you could use the IF and SKIP power fields to send the mailings to those people only. The power field you would create would look like this:

<If Income <25000 Skip Else NextRec EndIf>

Figure 12-15 shows a standard document that uses the SKIP and IF power fields.

Tip 12-5: Using the INCLUDE power field during a merge   One of the most powerful ways to create a standard document is to use the INCLUDE and IF power fields. The IF power field evaluates the contents of each merge record, and the INCLUDE power field decides what contents to insert into the standard document depending on the merge record's contents. For example, let's say your company is offering two new credit cards: one card is for those whose incomes are below $25,000; the other card is for those whose incomes are over $25,000. You can use the IF and INCLUDE power fields to insert the appropriate credit card offer depending on each merge record's income level.

Figures 12-16, 12-17, and 12-18 show the standard document containing the power fields, and two resulting merge documents: one for the income below $25,000 and one for the income above $25,000. For more information on the IF and INCLUDE power fields, refer to chapter 15.

Tip 12-6: Using the QUERY power field during a merge   If one portion of the standard document changes often, such as a toll-free number, you can use the QUERY power field to ask for the current information to insert at the time of the

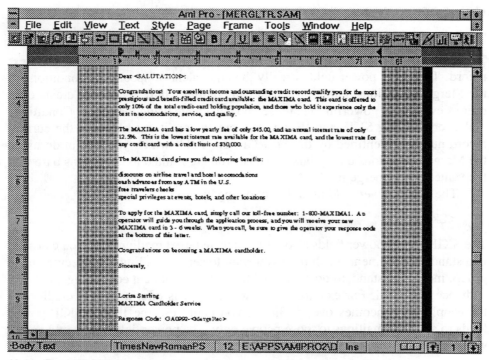

12-12   The MERGEREC power field used as a response code in a standard document.

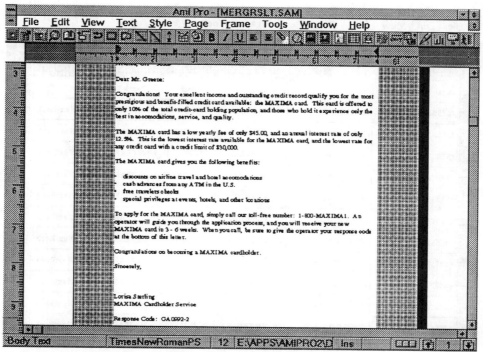

merge. Using the QUERY power field, you can insert variable information into the standard document without editing it each time you perform a merge. You could use the INCLUDE power field to insert a toll-free number, but you would need to edit the power field or the bookmark it inserts each time the toll-free number changes. Instead, you can use the QUERY field to ask for the most current toll-free number, and Ami inserts it into the standard document. You also can specify a default toll-free number with the QUERY field, so that if the number hasn't changed, you don't have to specify a new one.

A power field that inserts a variable toll-free number into the standard document looks like this:

```
<Set Min Query$("What is the toll-free number for MINIMA clients?")>
<Set Max Query$("What is the toll-free number for MAXIMA clients?")>
```

Then, insert the <Min> and <Max> fields in the bookmarks in the file containing the bookmarks.

Merging data from other applications

Ami lets you merge records you created in another application. The records must be in one of the following file formats:

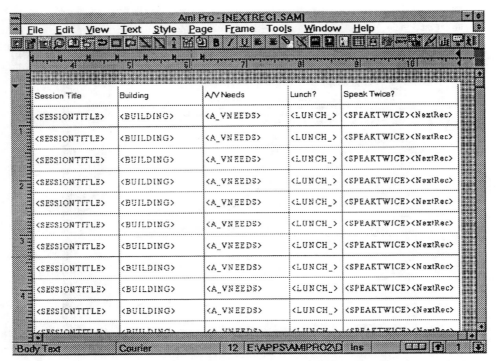

12-14 Place the NEXTREC power field at the end of each record in the data document.

- ASCII (fixed field)
- ASCII (comma delimited)
- DIF
- 1-2-3 versions 1 and 2.x (.WKS and .WK1)
- 1-2-3 versions 3 and 3.1 (.WK3)
- dBASE versions III, III+, and IV (.DBF)
- Excel versions up to 3.0c (.XLS)
- Paradox versions up to 3.5
- SuperCalc versions 3 and 4.

Ami has two methods you can use to merge external records: you can import the records into a table, or import the records nto the document and create a document description file.

Importing external records into a table

Use the same table format for external records as for internal records: each column represents one field, and each row represents one record. Field names oc-

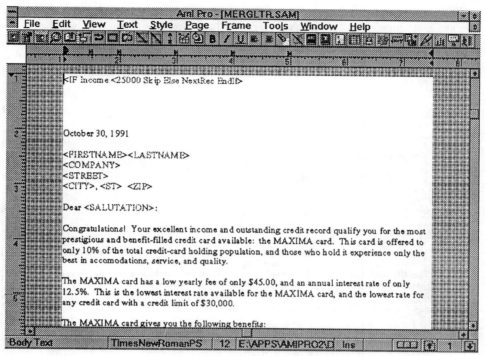

12-15 The SKIP and IF fields used to created merge conditions in a standard document.

cupy the first row and data occupies the remaining rows. To import external records into a table, place the cursor in the first cell of the table and choose File Open. Select the file type and filename you need and click OK.

Importing external records into the document

To import external records, follow these steps:

1. Open a new file by select File New.
2. Create a data description file by following these guidelines:
   On the first line, include the name of the application. You must spell the application name exactly as it appears under the File Type list box in the File Open dialog box. For example, if you want to use a Lotus 1-2-3 file, you would type "1-2-3" at the top of the file.
   Each subsequent line should list the name of a field in the file. Each line should contain one field name only, as shown in Figure 12-19.
3. Save, name, and close the file using the File Close command.
4. Open the standard document using the File Open command.
5. Begin the merge process by selecting the File Merge command.

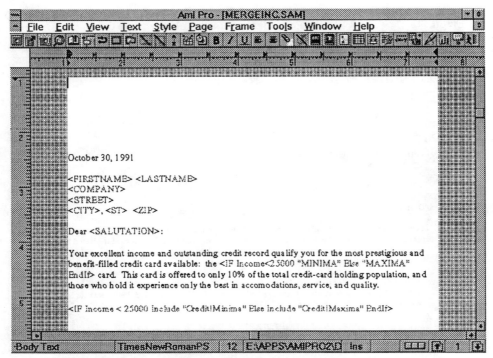

12-16 The INCLUDE field, along with the IF field, used to create a condition in a standard document.

6. Select the Data File button.

7. Specify the name of the external application file you want to use as the data document and select OK. Ami displays a message stating that the file is not an Ami document.

8. Select OK to remove the message. Ami displays the Description of NonAmi Data File dialog box.

9. Specify the name of the data description file you created in steps 1–3 and select OK. Ami returns to the Merge dialog box.

10. Select OK to merge the two files.

Ami merges the two files just as it would if you had used an Ami Pro file as the data document.

Creating labels

To create mailing labels, follow the standard merge process of creating a data and a standard document. When you are ready to merge, however, you tell Ami what type of labels you are using and it creates the labels for you.

Before you create mailing labels, you need to measure the size of your labels. Take the following measurements of your labels: label height, label width, space from top of page to the first label (for laser printer labels), and space from left of page to the first label (for laser printer labels).

The process for creating mailing labels is as follows:

1. Create a data document containing the names and addresses to appear on the labels.

2. Create an empty standard document. Modify its page size to be the same size as one mailing label. If your mailing labels measure $1'' \times 2\frac{5}{8}''$, make your page layout the same size using the Modify Page Layout command. Save the standard document.

3. While in the standard document, select Merge from the File menu. Select the data file that contains the names and addresses to appear on the mailing labels.

4. Select the As labels check box to tell Ami you need to print labels.

5. Click Labels to display the Merge Labels dialog box. In the Labels across page list box, enter the number of labels that appear across your label

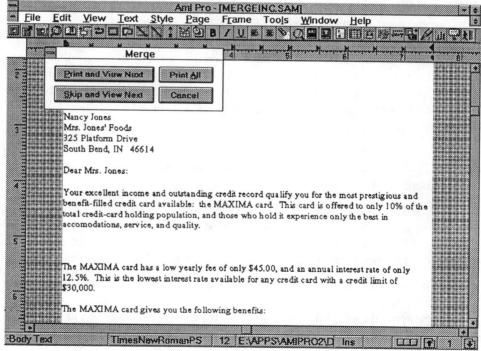

12-17 One result of the INCLUDE power field in a merged document.

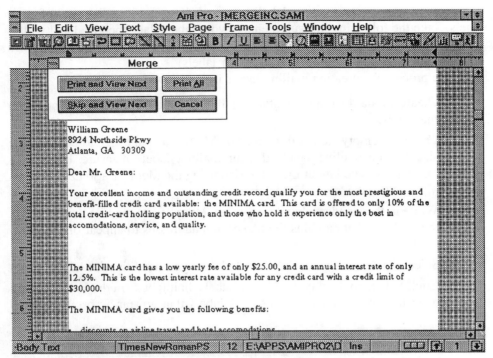

12-18 Another result of the INCLUDE power field in a merged document.

sheet. In the Labels down page enter the number of labels that appear down your label sheet. In the First label indent box, enter the how far down and to the right to indent the first label (the amount of space between the top/left edge of the sheet and the first label for laser printer labels).

6. If you need to print multiple copies of your labels, specify how many copies to print in the Print each label x times list box.

7. Click OK to return to the Merge dialog box. Click OK to perform the merge and create labels.

Tip 12-7: Fitting more text on a label   If you aren't able to fit as much text as you would like onto a label, you can change the label's margins. Because the page layout equals the dimensions of one label, simply reduce the margins for the page layout and you increase the amount of space available for text on the label.

Tip 12-8: Formatting label text   If you want to change the appearance of the text on the label, you can do so by modifying the style you use for label text. You can choose special fonts, lines, and other attributes that call attention to the labels. You also can modify the page layout by adding borders and shadows.

Tip 12-9: Printing a list of all merged records   By tricking Ami into thinking it's printing labels, you can get a handy reference of all records in your data document. Simply follow the merge process as if you were printing labels, but insert regular paper into your printer instead of labels. Ami performs the merge and prints the records in label format on your regular paper. You also can specify conditions to print a list of those records that meet certain criteria.

Tip 12-10: Print an entire sheet of return address labels   If you use labels for your return address, here's an easy way to print an entire sheet of them. Specify a condition so that only your return address meets the criterion. Count the number of labels on one label sheet, and tell Ami to print the label the same number of times. For example, if your label sheet holds 30 labels, enter 30 in the Print each label x times list box. Ami fills the entire sheet with your return address record.

Sorting text

Before you sort text in your document, review the following sort guidelines:

- You can sort an entire document, a portion of a document, or a table.
- Undo does not work on a sort, so if you aren't satisfied with the sort results, you cannot revert to the original document unless you saved it.
- Ami sorts text based on values in a field.

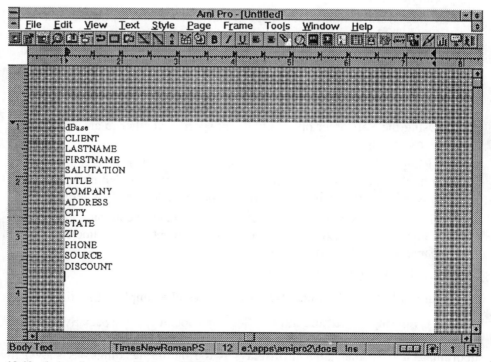

12-19   A data description file for a dBASE data document.

- If your text is in a table, Ami considers each column as a field. If your text is not in a table, you must separate your text by tabs or some other delimiter for Ami to recognize each as a separate field.

- You can sort text based on a maximum of three fields.

- You must specify at least one field by which to sort. Use a second and third field if you need to sort in more detail. For example, if you sort a table by state and more than one record has the same state, use the second level criterion to sort those records by zip code.

To perform a sort, follow these steps:

1. Select the text you need to sort. If you need to sort the entire document, don't select any text. Ami will ask you if you want to sort the entire stream. If the text is in a table, you do not need to select the entire row for each record. Ami sorts the entire record automatically.

2. Select Sort from the Tools menu. Ami displays the Sort dialog box.

3. In the Field list box, select the field on which Ami should base the sort. Identify the field numerically by its order of appearance in the record, not by its filename. If your text is in a table, count each column as a field.

4. Using the Type option buttons, specify whether to sort the text alphabetically or numerically.

5. Using Word option buttons, specify whether to sort using the first word in the field, the second word, or all words. All words is useful if you have more than one piece of information in a field, such as a last name and a first name.

6. Repeat steps three through six for each additional sort level you need to specify.

7. Using the Sort order options buttons, specify whether to arrange the text in ascending or descending order.

8. Using the Delimiter options buttons, specify whether the text uses tabs or a field delimiter. If you select field delimiter, type the delimiter in the text box. If your text is in a table, you do not need to specify a delimiter.

9. If your records contain multiple paragraphs, enter the amount each record contains in the text box. All records must contain the same number of paragraphs for this option to work correctly.

10. Click OK to perform the sort.

Figures 12-20, 12-21, and 12-22 display several examples of sorting.

Tip 12-11: Sorting in Outline mode   Sorting a document is especially powerful in Outline mode, because you can rearrange entire sections of a document. Hide subordinate text so that all Ami displays is the outline headings, as shown in

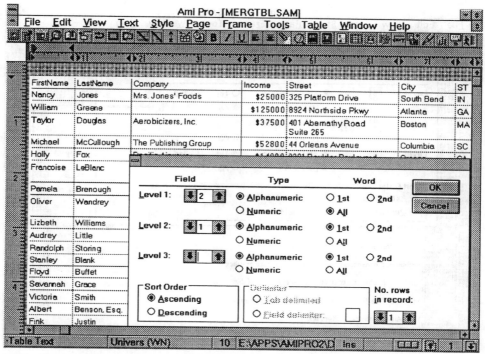

12-20 The Sort dialog box used to sort a table.

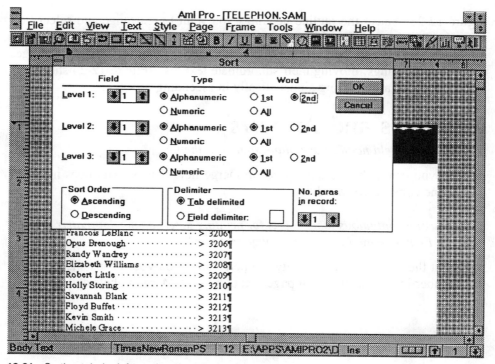

12-21 Sorting tabular information: the telephone extension in a phone list.

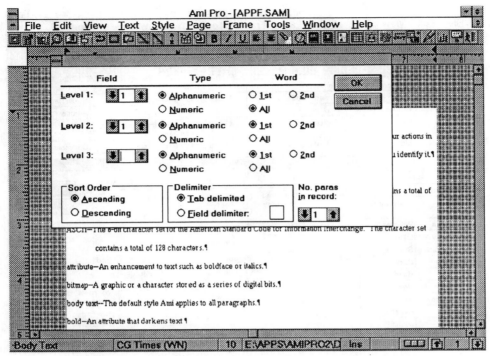

12-22 Sorting paragraphs using hanging indents.

Figure 12-23. Select the outline headings you want to rearrange and select Sort from the Tools menu. Specify the sort type (alphanumeric or numeric), the word on which to sort, and the sort order (ascending or descending). Ami rearranges the outline headings, moving their subordinate text also. Figure 12-24 shows the same document after sorting alphabetically in ascending order.

Questions and Answers

Q: Can merge field names have blank spaces in them?

A: Yes, you can include blank spaces in merge field names. Ami does not limit you to one consecutive word.

Q: I am using continuous label sheets for printing labels on my dot-matrix printer. What do I enter in the Labels down page text box?

A: Count the number of labels between perforations on your labels sheets. Enter that number in the Labels down page text box in the Merge Labels dialog box.

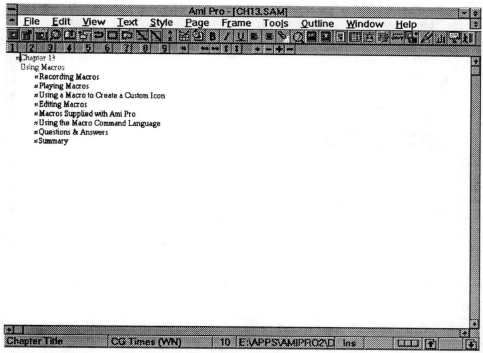

12-23 Sorting a document in Outline mode.

Summary

Merge and sort let you you take text that you enter only once, and manipulate it to produce unlimited results. From one data document, you can create form letters, tables, and labels. You can sort the data document so that the records are in order by zip code, income, or any other criterion you choose. You can even exclude records you don't need to merge this time. Ami is flexible in its merge standards, so you can use an Ami Pro document or a document from an external application as a data document. You can use a regular document or a document containing a table as the standard and data documents. Ami lets you make your merge process even more powerful by including merge power fields that control the merge process.

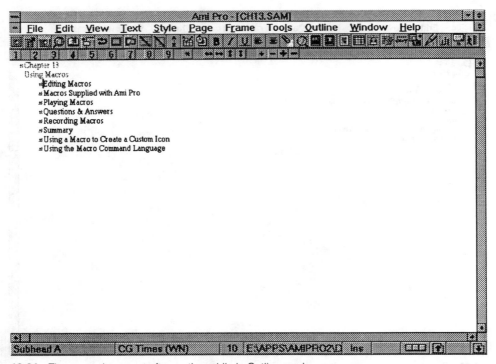

12-24 The same document after sorting while in Outline mode.

13
CHAPTER

Using macros

Ami's powerful macro feature not only lets you save time by automating repetitive tasks, it also provides several creative alternatives to the keystroke method for running macros. Procedures well-suited for macros include backing up files, updating styles and style sheets, and generating an index and table of contents.

The general procedure for creating a macro is as follows: first, record the macro and play it back. Then edit the macro making any necessary changes.

Recording macros

When you record a macro, perform the task you want to include in it for Ami, and Ami remembers all the keystrokes and mouse selections you made, in the order you made them. To record a macro, use the following steps:

1. Make sure you are using the correct mode. For example, if you want to record a macro to generate an index, you must be in Layout mode when you record the macro. If you realize that you are not in the correct mode before you begin recording the macro, simply make changing to the correct mode part of the macro.

2. From the Tools menu, select Macro. Ami displays the Record Macro dialog box.

3. Place your cursor in the Macro file list box and type the filename to hold the contents of your macro. You do not need to specify an extension, because all Ami macros must use an .SMM extension, which Ami assigns to the file automatically.

4. Place your cursor in the Playback shortcut keys text box and press the keys you want to execute the macro. Select OK to return to the document. The Status Bar displays "Recording Macro" in red text.

5. Perform the task you need to record in a macro. Ami records only mouse actions that are selections you make on a menu or a dialog box. Ami does not record mouse movements and text selections. Therefore, any time you need to move the cursor to another area, or select text or graphics, use the keyboard. Refer to Appendix C for more information on keyboard selections.

6. To stop recording the macro, select the status bar or select Macro from the Tools menu and select End Record.

Playing macros

Ami provides several innovative ways to execute a macro. Ami includes the traditional methods of shortcut keys, but it also provides four other methods. Ami has five ways you can execute a macro:

- press the shortcut keys
- select a filename from the Playback Macro dialog box
- attach the macro to a frame
- attach the macro to a file (either a document or a style sheet)
- attach the macro to Ami's start or end.

Executing a macro using shortcut keys

To run a macro using the shortcut keys, simply press the keys you specified when you recorded the macro.

Executing a macro by selecting a filename

To run a macro by selecting a filename first select Macro from the Tools menu. Select Playback and then a filename from the Macros list box. Select OK and Ami runs the macro you selected.

Executing a macro by attaching it to a frame

Once a frame contains a macro reference, select the frame and Ami runs your macro. Attaching a macro to a frame requires you to first select the Run frame macros option in the Document Description dialog box. Selecting this option activates all frame macros in the file. Turn off this feature to modify the frame without activating the macro. With the frame selected, choose the Modify Frame Layout command from the Frame menu. Type the name of the macro you need in the Frame macro drop-down list box and select OK. When you select the frame, Ami runs the macro you specified. A frame macro is a great way to simplify a complex task. For example, you could create a macro that performs a merge, then assign the macro to a frame. Anyone using that file could perform the merge by selecting the frame—prior knowledge of how to merge files wouldn't be necessary.

An example of a file that uses frame macros is the GOODIES.SAM file. It has three frames that you can select to execute macros.

Executing a macro by attaching it to a file

Another way to run a macro is to attach it to a document or style sheet file. Each time you open or close a document file or load the style sheet using File New, Ami executes the macro. To specify a macro that you want to attach to a document file, follow these steps:

1. Open the file to which you want to attach a macro.
2. If you have not created the macro, do so.
3. Select Macros from the Tools menu.
4. Select Edit; Ami displays the Edit Macro dialog box.
5. Select the Assign button. Ami displays the Assign Macro to Run Automatically dialog box, as shown in Figure 13–1.
6. Select either the File open or File close check box. In the text box next to the option you chose, type the macro filename you want to execute or select it from the list box.
7. Select OK to return to the Edit Macro dialog box.
8. Select Close to close the dialog box without editing the macro. The next time you open or close the file, Ami executes the macro you selected.

To attach a macro to a style sheet, select Save as a Style Sheet from the Style menu. Type the style sheet filename and select the Run macro check box. Type or select the macro filename from the drop-down list box and select OK. Now, anytime you choose File/New and select that style sheet, Ami runs the macro you chose.

Executing a macro when you open or close Ami Pro

The last way to automatically execute a macro is to do so whenever you open or close Ami Pro. To attach a macro to the program's start or end, select User Setup from the Tools menu. From the Run Macros box, select either Program load or Program Exit. In the list box next to the option you chose, type or select from the list box the macro filename you want to execute automatically. Select OK until you return to the document. The next time you open or close Ami Pro, the macro you specified runs automatically.

Tip 13-1: Recording a quick macro   You can record a macro without specifying a filename or any shortcut keys. Use the Quick Record and Quick Playback commands to record and run the macro. Ami saves the macro under the filename

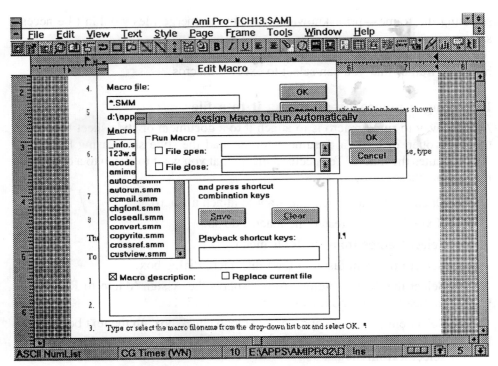

13-1 Attaching a macro to a file using the Edit Macro command.

UNTITLED.SMM. You can edit this file like you edit other macro files, which is discussed later in the chapter. You can record only one quick macro; once you record another, Ami overwrites the contents of the UNTITLED.SMM file, replacing the old quick macro with the new one.

Tip 13-2: Assigning shortcut keys to a quick macro Ami doesn't ask you for any shortcut keys when you record a quick macro. Playing back the macro by selecting Quick Playback from the Tools menu isn't exactly a quick option. Instead, you can assign shortcut keys to the quick macro, which can be done in one of two ways. The first method is to select Macro from the Tools menu. Select Record. Ami displays the Quick Record Macro Options dialog box, as shown in Figure 13-2. You can enter the shortcut keys to start and stop recording a quick macro, and to playback the macro. Select OK once you specify the shortcut keys you need. Select Close. Now you can press the shortcut keys to record and run the quick macro instead of selecting a menu command.

Tip 13-3: Assigning a macro to the default style sheet If you assign a macro to the style sheet you specified in the Load Defaults dialog box, the result is the same as if you assigned a macro to run when you start the program. When Ami loads a new file at the start of the program, it runs the macro you specified when

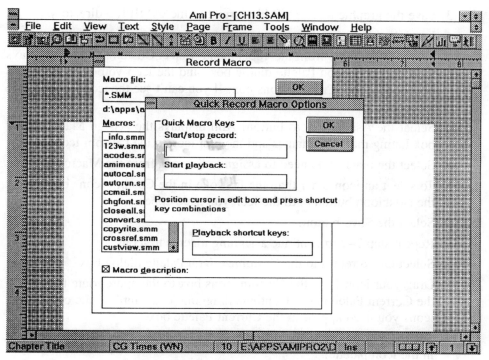

13-2 Assigning shortcut keys to recording and playing a quick macro.

you saved the style sheet. If you specified macros to run when you load Ami, and with the default style sheet make sure they don't conflict.

Using a macro to create a custom icon

One of the most powerful features in Ami is the ability to create your own icons. This feature overcomes the biggest shortfall of Windows programs: a cumbersome menu system that advanced users find limiting and inflexible. Creating a custom icon requires two major steps. You must first create a graphic to use in the icon, and then assign a macro to the icon.

To create a custom icon, follow these steps:

1. Create the graphic to use in the icon using Ami's drawing tool or an external graphics application.

2. If you have an EGA display, make the picture 24 × 24 pixels. If you have a VGA display, make the picture 32 × 32 pixels. If you do not scale the picture according to your display, the icon will be too small to see in Ami. (In Windows Write, select the Image Attributes command under the Options menu. Select pels as the unit of measurement, and make the width and height the appropriate measurements.)

3. Save the graphic to a .BMP file format in the \AMIPRO directory.

4. Load Ami Pro.

5. Select SmartIcons from the Tools menu. Select Customize. Ami displays the Customize Icon Palette dialog box, and the icon you created appears at the end of the Custom icons box. If you can't see the icon, scroll to the end of the icons.

6. Select the Assign macro button. Ami displays the Assign Macro dialog box listing macro filenames and the first icon in the Custom Icons box.

7. Select the macro you need to assign to the icon from the Macros list box.

8. To select an icon other than the first one in the Custom Icons box, select the Next Icon button until the icon you need appears.

9. Select the Save button.

10. Repeat step 7–9 to continue assigning macros to icons.

11. Select OK to return to the Customize Icon Palette dialog box.

12. Drag your icon from the Custom icons box to the appropriate location in the Current Palette box. Continue dragging icons until all the customized icons you need appear in the Current Palette box.

13. Select OK to return to the document. Ami displays your customized icons in the icon palette.

Editing macros

If you need to change a macro, edit the file that contains it. Once Ami displays the file in the active window, you can make the necessary changes and save the file.

To edit a macro, follow these steps:

1. Select Macro from the Tools menu. Select the Edit command. Ami displays the Edit Macro dialog box.

2. Select the file you need to change from the Macros list box and select OK. Ami opens the file and displays it in the active window.

3. Make the editing changes you need. Refer to the *Macro Command Language* documentation or the Macro Documentation help menu for more information on the commands displayed in the file.

4. Save and close the file.

Tip 13–4: Changing a macro's shortcut keys   You can modify or clear the shortcut keys you assigned to a macro. To do so, follow these steps:

1. Select Macro from the Tools menu. Choose either the Edit, Record, or Playback command. Any of these commands display a dialog box with the shortcut key text box inside.

2. If you need to clear any shortcut keys associated with the macro, select Clear (this option is useful if you want to execute a macro by selecting on a frame instead of using shortcut keys).

3. If you need to assign new shortcut keys, insert your cursor in the text box and press the new shortcut keys. Select Save to update the macro file. The dialog box no longer displays a Cancel button: the buttons are OK and Close. If you chose OK, Ami would begin recording, playing back the macro, or it would display the file in the active window, depending on which command you chose: Record, Playback, or Edit.

4. Select Close to save your shortcut key changes without recording a new macro or editing the macro file.

Macros supplied with Ami Pro

Ami Pro comes with over 40 macros that let you customize your screen, files, style sheets, fonts, and perform tasks you might have thought previously weren't possible. For example, when you select Tile from the Window menu, Ami tiles any open documents vertically. Did you ever want to tile the documents horizontally? Using a macro you can do just that and even more. Some macros perform the simplest of tasks, but save you from displaying menus and making selections from dialog boxes. Two such macros are FONTDN and FONTUP, which change selected text up or down two point sizes. Other macros perform complicated tasks in a few minutes or seconds that would take you hours to perform, such as marking every occurrence of a word as an index entry.

If you become a macro fan and want to get more of them, Lotus' Word Processing Division continually creates additional macros to extend Ami Pro's functionality. To receive additional macros, contact Lotus Word Processing Technical Support, or download the latest macros from the Ami Pro forum in CompuServe (type GO LOTUSWP).

Auto run option

Some macros are so useful they will become second nature to you. For the macros you cannot do without, you can run them each time you load Ami by selecting the AutoRun option. However, not all macros are suitable for the AutoRun option. To select the AutoRun option, open the GOODIES file or playback the INFO or AUTORUN macros.

Using the Goodies file

The GOODIES.SAM file is a gem: it describes all the macros shipped with Ami, and lets you "test drive" each macro (the same as executing the macro). Select the AutoRun option for a macro, and display all the macros for which you selected AutoRun. If you are new to Ami Pro's macros, this file is an excellent tutorial, because it explains each macro, who developed it, what commands are in the macro from the Macro Command Language, and what programming skill is required to write the macro. Not everyone wants the command language information, but it is useful for those interested in writing their own macros. Figure 13-3 displays a sample page from the GOODIES.SAM file.

Viewing descriptions of Ami Pro's macros

You can use the INFO macro to view a description of all the macros supplied with Ami Pro. When you playback the INFO macro, Ami displays the Information on Macros dialog box, as shown in Figure 13-4. On the left side of the dialog box is a list of all the macros supplied with Ami. The rest of the dialog box displays information on the macro you select from the list box. Ami displays a description of the macro, who developed it, whether the macro requires beginning, intermediate, or advanced programming skills, and what types of Macro Command Language functions and statements are included in the macro.

You can select the following options within the Information on Macros dialog box:

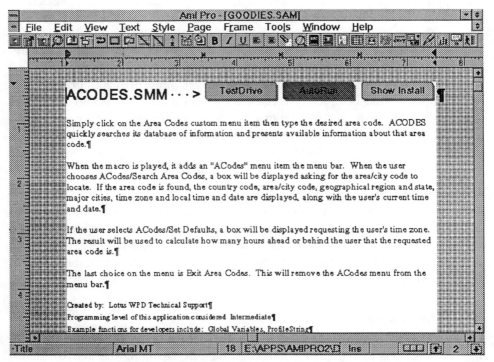

13-3 A page from the GOODIES.SAM file that describes each Ami Pro macro in detail.

Auto Run   Select the >>Move>> button to automatically start the highlighted macro when you load Ami. Select the <<Move<< button to remove a macro from the Auto Run list.

Details   Select this button to open the GOODIES.SAM file and move to the description of the highlighted macro. You can view a more detailed macro description, run the macro, or add the Auto Run option to the macro from the GOODIES.SAM file.

Run   Select Run to execute the highlighted macro.

Custom icons supplied with Ami Pro

Ami ships 33 custom icons for use with the macros that come with Ami, and suggested macros you can assign to these icons; however, you can use them for whatever macros you wish. More information on assigning macros to an icon is discussed later in this chapter. Table 13-1 lists the custom icons shipped with Ami and the macros with which they are designed to be used.

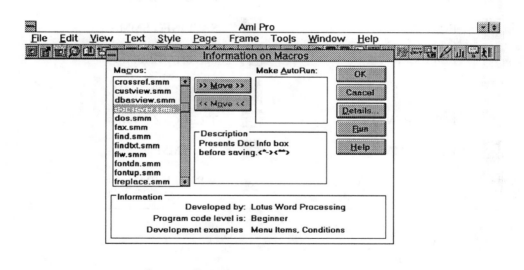

13-4   Playing the INFO macro displays the Information on Macros dialog box.

Table 13-1. Custom Icons

Icon	Macro	Icon	Macro
	123W.SMM		NOTES.SMM
	AMIMENUS.SMM		OPENBOOK.SMM
	AUTORUN.SMM		OPENDOCS.SMM
	CCMAIL.SMM		PHONBOOK.SMM
	CLOSEALL.SMM		PRNBATCH.SM
	COPYRITE.SMM		PRNPAGES.SMM
	CUSTVIEW.SMM		PRNSHADE.SMM
	DOS.SMM		REGMARK.SMM
	FAX.SMM		SAVEBOOK.SMM
	FINDTXT.SMM		SAVEINFO.SMM
	FLW.SMM		SAVSHADE.SMM
	FONTDN.SMM		SMARTYPE.SMM
	FONTUP.SMM		TILEHORZ.SMM
	GAME.SMM		TM.WMM
	KEYWORD.SMM		WINFILE.SMM

Starting other applications from Ami Pro

Ami Pro provides macros you can use to start other Lotus applications from Ami. The macros are 123W to start 1-2-3 for Windows, CCMAIL to run cc:Mail, FLW to start Freelance for Windows, and NOTES to start Lotus Notes. Ami also provides custom icons to which you can assign these macros. You can create your own macros to starts41other applications using the Macro Command Language.

Displaying geographic information by area code

The ACODES macro adds an ACodes menu to the end of the Ami Pro menu bar. Select the Find Area Code command from the menu and Ami displays a dialog box in which you type an area code. Ami then displays that region's country code, country, major cities, the state or province, time zone, current time and date, as shown in Figure 13-5. You can then choose to enter additional area codes or exit the dialog box. Select Exit Area Codes from the ACodes menu and Ami removes the menu from the menu bar.

Customizing Ami's menus

The AMIMENUS macros lets you customize Ami's menus by adding and removing menu items. The menu items can be existing Ami Pro functions that you want to place on another menu, or they can be selections inside a dialog box that you make easier to access by placing them directly on a menu. You also can add commands to menus that execute macros shipped with Ami or macros you create.

Once you play the AMIMENUS macro, Ami displays the Customize Menus dialog box, as shown in Figure 13-6. The dialog box lists the menus in a list box,

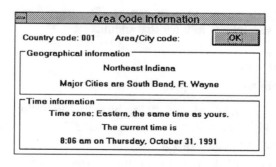

13-5 Use the ACODES macro displays geographical and time zone information for an area code you supply.

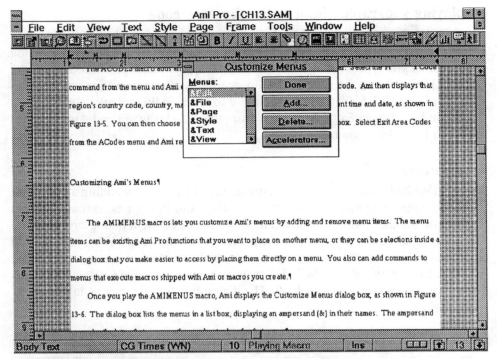

The ACODES macro adds an [...] command from the menu and Ami [...] ode. Ami then displays that region's country code, country, ma[...] nt time and date, as shown in Figure 13-5. You can then choose [...] ox. Select Exit Area Codes from the ACodes menu and Ami re[...]

Customizing Ami's Menus¶

The AMIMENUS macros lets you customize Ami's menus by adding and remove menu items. The menu items can be existing Ami Pro functions that you want to place on another menu, or they can be selections inside a dialog box that you make easier to access by placing them directly on a menu. You also can add commands to menus that execute macros shipped with Ami or macros you create.¶

Once you play the AMIMENUS macro, Ami displays the Customize Menus dialog box, as shown in Figure 13-6. The dialog box lists the menus in a list box, displaying an ampersand (&) in their names. The ampersand

13-6 Use the AMIMENUS macro to customize Ami Pro menus.

displaying an ampersand (&) in their names. The ampersand precedes the letter that serves as the accelerator key for that menu.

Adding a menu item

To add a menu item to Ami's menus, follow these steps:

1. From the Customize Menus dialog box, highlight the menu to which you want to add a menu item and select Add. Ami displays the Add Menu Item dialog box, as shown in Figure 13-7.

2. Type the name of the new menu item in the Appear on menu text box. If you plan to add an accelerator key to the menu item, place an ampersand before that letter in the menu item name. Ami will underline that letter when it appears on the menu.

3. Select where to place the new menu item from the Insert before list box. Highlight the name of the item that you want to appear after your new menu item.

4. If you want to add an accelerator key, type the letter or number of the keystroke in the Keystroke text box, and select the key combinations to

use with it. For example, if you want to use Ctrl-Shift-A as the accelerator key, type A in the Keystroke text box and select the Ctrl and Shift check boxes.

5. Select the command button representing the action you want to include as a menu item. If you want to place an Ami Pro function on a menu, select Function. If you want to place a macro on a menu, select Macro.

6. Select the function or the macro you want to include on a menu and select OK. Ami displays the following message: "Do you want to make this permanent?"

7. If you want the menu item to appear every time you load Ami, select Yes. If you want the menu item only for this work session, select No. If you select Yes, Ami creates an AUTOEXEC.SMM macro that adds your new menu item to the menu you selected. Each time you start Ami Pro, it runs this macro, activating your new menu item.

8. Select OK and then select Done from the Customize Menu dialog box.

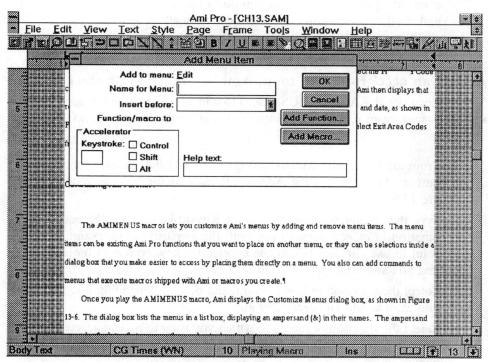

13-7 The Add Menu Item dialog box lets you add a macro or an Ami Pro function to any menu on the menu bar.

Deleting a menu item

You can delete a regular menu item or one you added using the Customize Menus dialog box. Deleting a menu item is never an irreparable step, because you always can replace it later using the Customize Menus dialog box.

To delete a menu item from Ami's menus, follow these steps:

1. From the Customize Menus dialog box, highlight the menu from which you want to delete an item and select Delete. Ami displays the Delete Menu Item dialog box, as shown in Figure 13-8. Ami displays the menu items available on the menu you selected.

2. Highlight the menu item you want to delete and select OK. Ami displays the following message: "Do you want to make this permanent?"

3. If you want the menu item omitted every time you load Ami, select Yes. If you want the menu item omitted only for this work session, select No. If you select Yes, Ami updates the AUTOEXEC.SMM macro to remove the menu item. Instead of deleting the previous reference to the menu item, Ami adds an additional section to the macro removing the menu item. The result is that the macro adds, then deletes, the menu item each time you start Ami, but you don't see these steps. You see only the end result, which is omitting the menu item altogether.

4. Select Done from the Customize Menu dialog box.

Adding an accelerator key to an Ami Pro function or macro

You also can use the AMIMENUS macro to add an accelerator key to any menu item or macro, even if the macro doesn't appear on any menu. To do so, follow these steps:

1. From the Customize Menus dialog box, select the Accelerator command button. Ami displays the Add Accelerator dialog box, as shown in Figure 13-9.

2. Type the accelerator keystroke in the Keystroke text box. Select the combination keys you want to use with the keystroke. For example, if you want to use Ctrl-Shift-A as the accelerator key, type A in the Keystroke text box and select the Ctrl and Shift check boxes.

3. Select the Function or Macro command button, depending upon to which you want to add an accelerator key.

4. Select the function or macro to which you want to add an accelerator key. Ami displays the following message: "Do you want to make this permanent?"

5. If you want to use the accelerator key every time you load Ami, select Yes. If you want to use the accelerator key only for this work session,

selectNo. If you select Yes, Ami updates the AUTOEXEC.SMM macro to include the new accelerator key.

6. Select Done from the Customize Menus dialog box.

Creating a calendar

When you select New from the File menu and choose the ~CALMON.STY style sheet, Ami runs the AUTOCAL macro to create dates for the calendar. Ami displays a dialog box listing the current month and year, but you can choose any month and any year from 1980 to 1999. Once you select the month and year, Ami creates a calendar for that month.

Automatically playing macros when you load Ami

Some macros are so useful you just can't do without them, so Ami lets you specify macros you want to run every time to start Ami. When you playback the AUTORUN macro, Ami displays the AutoRun Macro Installer dialog box, as shown in Figure 13-10. AutoRun is an option that automatically executes the macro each time you load Ami. To specify a macro as an autorun macro, highlight its filename from the Macros list box and select >>Move>>. Ami displays the macro filename in the Installed Macros list box.

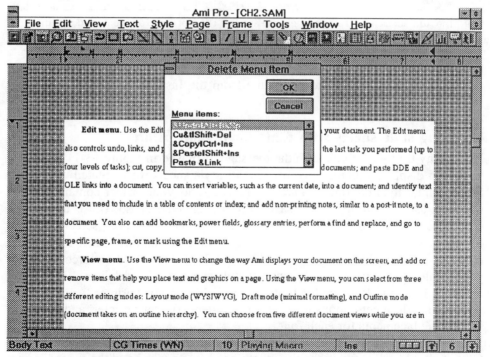

13-8 The Delete Menu Item dialog box lets you remove a macro or an Ami Pro function from any menu on the menu bar.

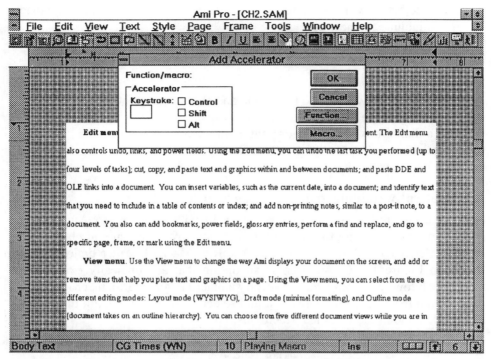

13-9 The Add Accelerator dialog box lets you assign a shortcut key to any command on a menu.

Not all macros are suitable for the Autorun option, and Ami does not activate the >>Move>>button when you select those macros. You also can uninstall an autorun macro by highlighted its name from the Installed Macros list box and selecting <<Move<<.

Updating style sheets with fonts for default printer

How many times have you seen the message displayed in Figure 13-11?

Ami displays this message because its style sheets were created with a different printer than the one you are using. The fonts your printer contains are not the same as those in the printer saved with the style sheet, so Ami is telling you to choose the appropriate font from your own printer. However, selecting a font for every single style in every style sheet is time-consuming. Fortunately, Ami provides a macro that lets you update your style sheets with the correct fonts for your printer. You can update the current style sheet or all style sheets. The macro acts as a Find and Replace for fonts not available on your printer. Ami analyzes one or all style sheets, looks for fonts not available on your printer, and then asks you for replacements for each font.

When you playback the CHGFONT macro, you must have a document open. Otherwise, Ami Pro functions the macro needs are greyed and the macro cannot execute.

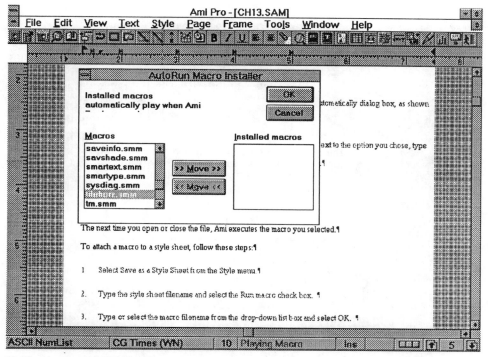

13-10 Use the AUTORUN macro to designate macros to run each time you load Ami Pro.

After you choose the CHGFONT macro, Ami displays the Select Style Sheets dialog box, as shown in Figure 13-12. You can choose one style sheet to update or select all style sheets to update at once. Ami then searches for the fonts specified in each style sheet. Ami tells you which style sheet it is analyzing in the Status Bar. If a font isn't available on your printer, Ami displays the New Font dialog box. You can then choose the font to replace the unavailable one.

Closing all open documents simultaneously

If you have more than one document displayed on the screen, saving and closing each file becomes repetitive. You can automate that process by using the CLOSEALL macro that saves and closes all open documents simultaneously. When you playback the macro, Ami saves all documents and closes them without any prompts or messages. Be sure you want to save the changes in all the documents before you use this macro.

Converting several word processing files into Ami Pro format

If you used another word processor before changing to Ami Pro 2.0, you probably have an entire library of documents you need to import into Ami. You would need to specify the file format, the filename, the file's drive and path, and any import

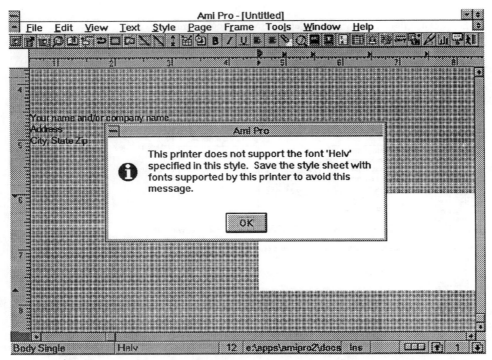

13-11 If you are not using the same printer that the document was saved with, Ami Pro displays this message.

options, such as Ignoring Styles or Keeping Styles every time. An easier way is to use the CONVERT macro that lets you specify multiple files to convert to Ami Pro format.

Inserting the copyright symbol

The COPYRITE macro inserts the ANSI copyright symbol at the cursor's position in the document. If you create material that must be copyrighted, you need to add the symbol to your documents, but you probably don't remember what ANSI code you use to generate the symbol. Next time, let the macro insert the copyright symbol for you. Ami includes a custom icon to which you assign the COPYRITE macro, so that all you need to do is select the icon and the copyright symbol appears in your document.

Inserting page references across files in a master document

The PageRef power field inserts the page number of a bookmark, letting you build cross-references to other text and graphics in the same file. However, you cannot use the PageRef power field with bookmarks in other files. Ami has two macros, CROSREF9 and CROSSREF, that let you use PageRef with bookmarks in other files. The macros create global variables by the same name as the bookmarks it

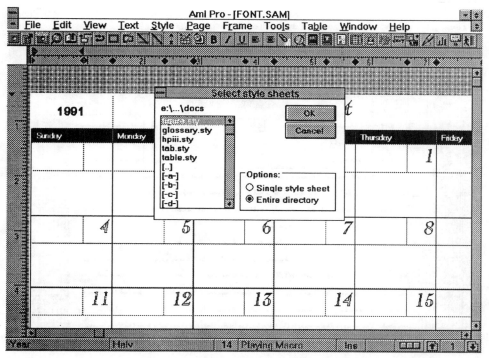

13-12 You can use the CHGFONT macro to update the fonts for all style sheets or just one style sheet to match those available on your printer.

finds, and uses the global variables to generate page references. Use the CROSS-REF macro for a master document containing nine or fewer files, and use the CROSREF9 macro to generate cross-references for a master document containing more than nine files.

Adding a custom view to the View menu

The CUSTVIEW macro lets you add another view to the View menu. This macro is useful if you use a custom page size, if you work frequently with landscape pages, or if you switch between Working view's level of 91% and another percentage.

Once you run CUSTVIEW, Ami displays the Custom View dialog box, as shown in Figure 13-13. You can specify another view level for both Working view and the new Custom view. After you enter the new view levels and select OK, Ami adds two new menu items to the View menu: Custom and Custom View. The Custom menu item displays its view level percentage on the menu, and when you select it Ami changes to that view. The Custom View menu item displays the Custom View dialog box, letting you adjust the view levels for Working and Custom views.

The Custom view you add is active only for the current work session. The

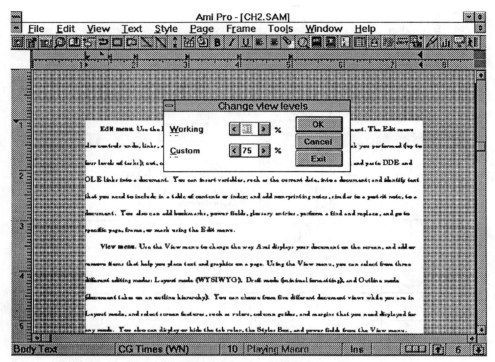

13-13 Use the CUSTVIEW macro to customize Working view and to create an additional view on the View menu.

next time you load Ami, the Custom and Custom View menu items do not appear on the View menu. You can, however, specify CUSTVIEW as an AutoRun macro so that the Custom views are a permanent part of your menus.

Viewing and selecting a dBASE file for a merge

If you use dBASE files as merge data documents, you can use the DBASVIEW macro to view information about the database file's structure. You also can have Ami create a data description file so you can use the file as a data document for merge.

Once you run the DBASVIEW macro, Ami displays the dBASE File Info dialog box, as shown in Figure 13-14. The dialog box shows the file's name, the date the file was last edited, the number of records it contains, the number of fields it contains, and a list of all the field names in the file. You can select the Create Description File button and Ami creates a data description file in an untitled document.

Temporarily exiting to DOS

If you ever needed to exit to DOS, you know that you had to minimize Ami Pro and then select DOS from the Windows Main program group. Now you can exit

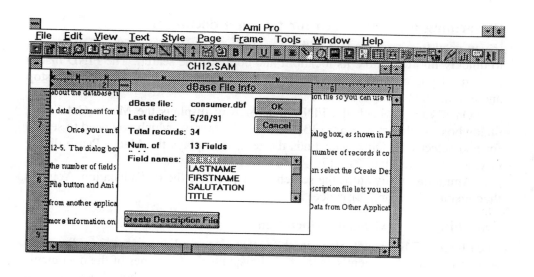

13-14 The DBASVIEW macro displays the dBASE File Info dialog box to let you view the structure of a dBASE file.

to DOS directly from Ami Pro using the DOS macro. Ami Pro exits to DOS, and you can return to Ami Pro by typing "Exit." Your document remains in its original condition, and you can resume working on it as you did before you exited to DOS. Ami supplies a custom icon to which you can assign the DOS macro.

Generating and attaching files to a FAX cover sheet

The FAX macro lets you generate a FAX cover sheet and attach Ami Pro files to it for printing. Once you run the FAX macro, Ami displays the FAX Cover Sheet Options dialog box. From it, you can select a style sheet to use as the basis for the FAX cover sheet. Ami also adds a Compose FAX command to the File menu. The Compose FAX command lets you generate a cover sheet, print the current file or other files along with the cover sheet.

Once you select Use Current Doc or New FAX Doc, Ami displays the FAX Cover Sheet Information dialog box, as shown in Figure 13-15. You can enter recipient's company, name, to whom a carbon copy goes to, a FAX number, a telephone number, and any special comments. If you want to print files other than the current document when you print the FAX cover sheet, select Files and choose the filenames.

Performing a quick search for text in a document

If you need to search for text without replacing it, you can use the FIND macro to quickly find text, note its location, and continue the search. The FIND macro is useful if you need to locate text within a document, but you don't need to stop and edit the text once you locate it.

Once you playback the FIND macro, Ami displays the Macro Get String dialog box, as shown in Figure 13-16. Enter the text for which you need to search for and select OK. Once Ami finds the text, it displays the Macro Pause dialog box, as shown in Figure 13-17.

Ami temporarily stops the search to let you note the text's location. You can then resume the search or cancel it.

Searching for text across documents

The FINDTXT macro lets you search for text among all documents in a directory. Ami scans each document's content, and displays the filenames of the documents containing the text for which you needed to search. You can then choose to open those files.

If you have a large number of files in the directory you search, the FINDTXT might take several minutes to an hour to search for the text, so make sure you have a block of time during which you can run this macro.

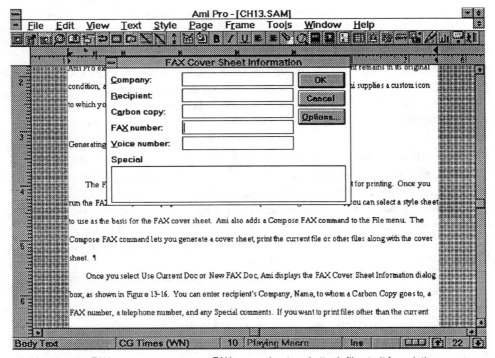

13-15   Use the FAX macro to generate a FAX cover sheet and attach files to it for printing.

Changing the point size of selected text

Two of Ami's simplest macros are the FONTDN and FONTUP macros. They change the point size of any text you have selected by two points. The FONTDN reduces the text size by two points, while FONTUP increases the text size by two points. Ami supplies custom icons for both of these macros.

Finding and replacing text across documents

If you write long documents made up of numerous smaller chapters, the FRE-PLACE macro is made for you because it performs a search and replace across several documents. You specify the text for which Ami searches and the documents it should search. Ami then finds and replaces all occurrences of the text without prompting you for any confirmation. Before you use this macro, make sure that you want to replace every occurrence of the text or you'll be surprised by the macro's results.

Once you playback the FREPLACE macro, Ami displays the Find & Replace Across Multiple Files dialog box, as shown in Figure 13-18. Specify the search text, the replace text, and the files that Ami should search. Select OK and Ami opens each file, performs the find and replace operation, and closes the file. Ami does not stop to ask you if it should replace or ignore the text.

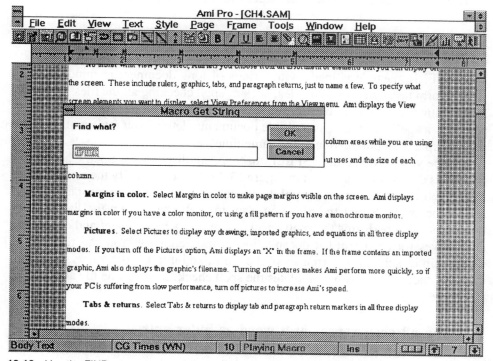

13-16   Use the FIND macro to search for, but not replace, text in a document.

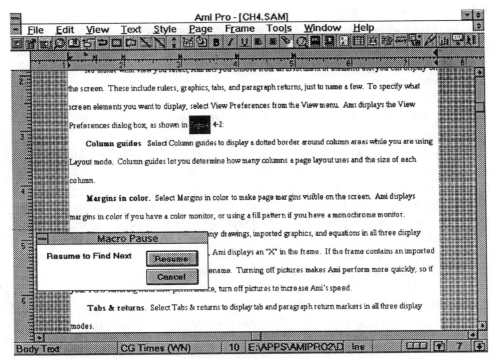

13-17 The FIND macro pauses after it finds the search text to let you note the text's location.

Spell checking across documents

The FPSELL macro was made with writers of long document in mind. Usually you perform tasks on groups of files, such as spell checking all the files in a book, then printing all the files, backing up all the files, and so on. The FPELL macro performs a spell check across multiple documents, letting you review all the files making up a long publication at the same time.

Once you playback the FSPELL macro, Ami displays the Spell Check Multiple Files dialog box, as shown in Figure 13-19. You can specify the same options when spell checking across several document as you can when you spell check a single document. Select the files you want to spell check from the list box and select OK. Ami performs the spell check, opening each document and displaying alternatives for each word it doesn't find in its dictionary. You can replace the word, skip it, skip all occurrences of the word, add it to the dictionary, or cancel the spell check. Once Ami completes the spell check, it closes the file and continues to the next.

Marking all occurrences of a word as index entries

The INDEXALL macro lets you mark every occurrence of specified text in the current file as an index entry. The INDEXALL macro adds a new menu item to the Edit menu: Mark Index All after you select Mark Text. Once you select this command, Ami marks the text you selected as an index entry. It then continues to search for every occurrence of the text, even if the text occurs as part of another word, and marks each occurrence as an index entry. This is a powerful macro that can save you hours when creating an index. Be certain that you want to mark every occurrence of the text, however, because Ami does not ask for your permission to mark—it just does it.

Searching for keywords among documents

If you ever wondered what the Keywords text box was for in the Doc Info dialog box, this is it. When you enter keywords for the document in that text box, you can use the KEYWORD macro to search the contents of the Keyword text box for multiple documents.

Ami displays a dialog box listing those documents it finds using the keywords.

Creating a Bookmarks menu

The MARKMENU macro creates a Bookmarks menu listing all the bookmarks in the current file. You can select a bookmark from that menu to move to that posi-

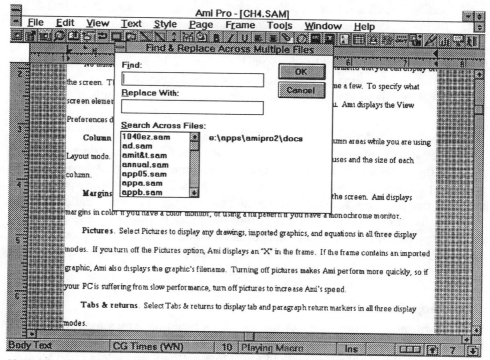

13-18 The Find & Replace Across Multiple Files dialog box lets you specify the find and replace text along with those files you need to search.

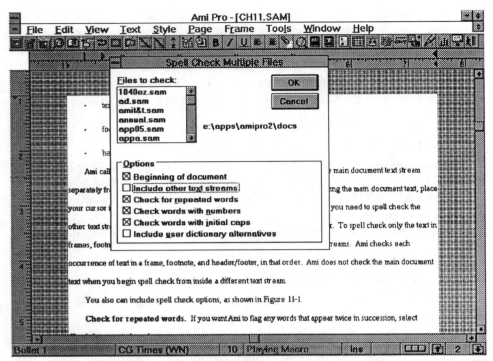

13-19 The FSPELL macro displays the Spell Check Multiple Files dialog box.

tion in the document quickly. A typical Bookmark menu is shown in Figure 13-20. From the Bookmarks menu you also can add a new bookmark, update the menu to list new bookmarks, or remove the menu from the menu bar.

Viewing files in a master document

The MASTRDOC macro lets you view the documents in a master document, and move to the previous or next file in a master document. You must have a master document open when you playback the MASTRDOC macro. Once you do execute the macro, Ami adds a new menu item to the File menu called Master Browser, as shown in Figure 13-21. From the Master Browser menu item, you can display the initial file in the master document, or the next or previous file. Once you open all the files in a master document, you can use the Next Master and Previous Master to move among the files.

Displaying Ami's Short menus

If you don't need to use many of the functions listed on Ami's menus, you can run the MENULITE macro to change to Ami's short menus. Ami displays a new menu item on the View menu called Short Menus. When you select Short Menus, Ami displays only basic document creation and editing tasks. The Short Menus

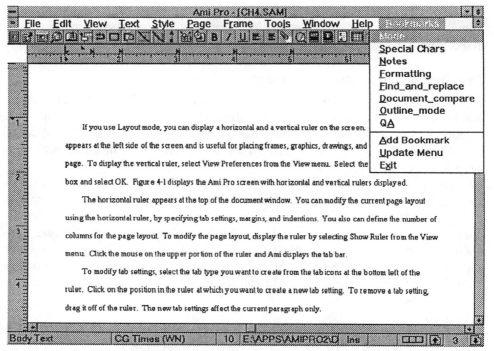

13-20 The Bookmarks menu, shown when you execute the MARKMENU macro, displays all the bookmarks in the current file.

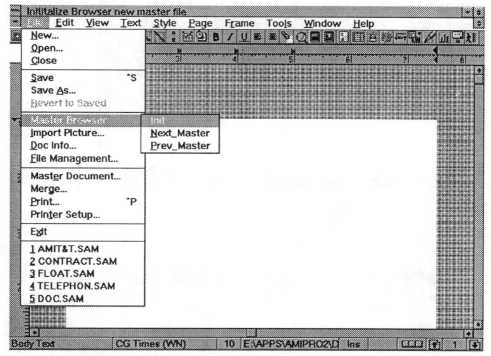

13-21 The MASTRDOC macro adds the Master Browser command to the File menu. It remains on the File menu until you exit Ami Pro.

command is a toggle; once you select it, Ami changes to display Long Menus. Switching between short and long menus is as easy as selecting the command from the View menu.

Creating a merge data document

If you have never created a merge data document, the MERGDATA macro takes you through the process step by step, from specifying field names, to adding and deleting records, and even searching for specific values in a field. The MERGDATA macro is an excellent tutorial for those who are not comfortable with creating a data document.

Once you execute the MERGDATA macro, Ami adds a new command to the File menu: Merge Create/Edit. Once you select this command, Ami displays a message telling you that the current document (whether you have one open or not) is not a records file, so it asks if you want to create one? Select OK and Ami opens an untitled document and displays the Create Record File dialog box, as shown in Figure 13-22. Specify the number of fields you want in the data document and the symbols to use as field and record delimiters. Stick to the symbols

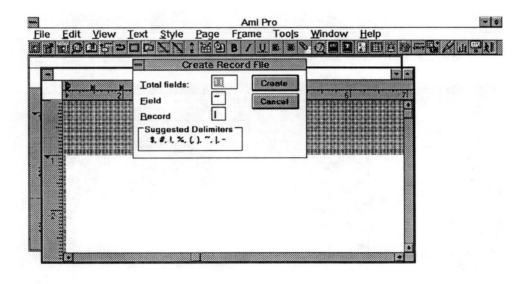

13-22 The MERGDATA macro displays the Create Record File dialog box to assist you in creating a data document.

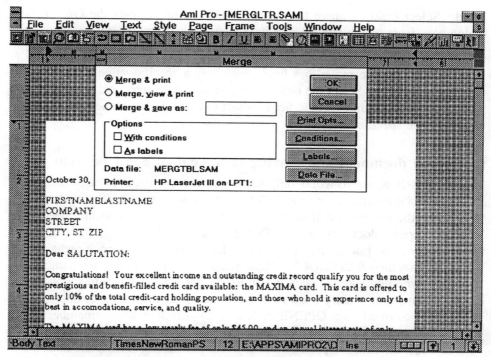

13-23 The MERGDATA macro displays the Merge Fields dialog box to let you enter, search for, and remove records.

Ami suggests, because using other symbols can wreak havoc when you merge. Once you select OK, Ami displays the Merge Data dialog box, as shown in Figure 13-23. Use the command buttons to create the data document:

Add   When you enter field names and values into the text boxes, select Add to make them a part of the document. Ami adds the field names or values and displays empty text boxes for you to use again.

Delete   Select Delete to remove the displayed record from the data document.

Update   Select Update to add an edited record to the data document.

Exit   Select Exit to remove the Merge Data dialog box and return to the document.

<<or>>   The arrow buttons move forward or backward one record and display the current record in the dialog box. You can then make changes to the record and select Update to add the changes to data document.

PgUp   Select PgUp to move to the previous page in the data document.

PgDn   Select PgDn to move to the next page in the data document.

Field   Select Field to move to a specific field. Ami displays the Go To Field dialog box, from which you select a field name and select OK. Ami moves to the field you chose.

Find   Select Find to move to a field containing a specific value. Ami displays the Find dialog box. Select the field name you want to search, and enter the value you want to find in that specific field. Select OK and Ami searches the data document for the specified value.

Opening a document and moving to the cursor's last position

The OPENBOOK macro works only when you also use the SAVEBOOK macro. If you save a document using the SAVEBOOK macro instead of File Save, Ami remembers the cursor's position in the document when you execute the macro. When you open a document using OPENBOOK instead of File Open, Ami opens the document and places the cursor in its last position—the position it was in when you executed SAVEBOOK. These macros are quite handy for authors and writers of long documents. Even if you use bookmarks to move to a position in the document, you usually need to do some scrolling or paging through to find your last place of editing. OPENBOOK and SAVEBOOK help remember where you left off, so you can begin there without searching through the document.

To mark the cursor's position in the document, the SAVEBOOK macro creates two bookmarks—| and °—which you can see if you select the Bookmarks icon or the Edit Bookmarks command. Do not delete these bookmarks, because the OPENBOOK and SAVEBOOK macros need them to locate the cursor's position in the document. Ami provides two custom icons to which you assign the OPENBOOK and SAVEBOOK icons.

Opening multiple documents simultaneously

Ami lets you have nine documents open at the same time, but you have to open each one individually using the File Open command. If you can edit documents simultaneously, why can't you open them in the same way? Using the OPEN-DOCS macro, you can open up to nine documents at the same time. When you execute OPENDOCS, Ami displays the Multiple File Open dialog box , as shown in Figure 13-24. You can choose to cascade the documents or minimize all nine to icons. Ami provides a custom icon to which you can assign the OPENDOCS icon.

Using Ami as a phonebook database

The PHONBOOK macro lets you build, search, and maintain a name and address directory in Ami Pro. This macro is handy for sales and marketing staff who constantly need quick access to client's and contact's names and telephone num-

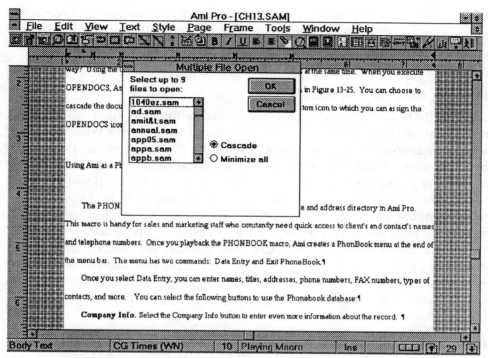

13-24 The OPENDOCS macro lets you open several files simultaneously.

bers. Once you playback the PHONBOOK macro, Ami creates a PhonBook menu at the end of the menu bar. The menu has two commands: Data Entry and Exit PhoneBook.

Once you select Data Entry, you can enter names, titles, addresses, phone numbers, FAX numbers, types of contacts, and more. You can select the following buttons to use the Phonebook database:

Company Info Select the Company Info button to enter even more information about the record.

Add Select the Add button to save the current record and add it to the phonebook.

Save Select the Save button to save the current record.

Next Select the Next button to move to the next record in the phonebook.

First Select the First button to move to the first record in the phonebook.

Previous Select the Previous button to move to the previous record in the phonebook.

Clear   Select the Clear button to remove the current record from the phonebook.

Close   Select the Close button to save the currently displayed record and end the macro.

Printing multiple documents

The PRNBATCH macro adds a desperately needed feature to Ami Pro—the ability to print multiple documents. Until now, neither Ami Pro nor Windows had a way to print more than one document. You can do so using a Master Document, but Ami numbers pages across files, making the assumption that all the documents belong to one publication that uses consecutive numbering. If you are printing chapters of a publication that use chapter numbering, or if the documents are not related, the Master Document feature does not provide an effective means of printing multiple documents. However, the PRNBATCH macro does.

When you playback PRNBATCH, Ami displays the Select Files to Print dialog box, as shown in Figure 13-25. From this dialog box, choose the files you want to print. You can choose to print the files now, or at a later time that you specify. Use the command buttons to specify a later print time and print options for each document.

Options   Select Options to specify individual print options for each document you chose to print. The print options available are the same as those listed in the Print Options dialog box when you choose Print from the File menu. Once you specify options for the highlighted file in the Select Files to Print dialog box, you can save them by selecting the Save button, and you can specify options for the next file you chose to print by selecting the Next File button.

Time   If you chose to print later rather than now, select Time to specify a print time. You can specify how many hours and minutes from the current time to print the documents. You can specify more than 24 hours in advance to set the print time to tomorrow or later in the week. Once you select OK, you can reselect the Time button and Ami displays the print day and time in the dialog box. The time option is especially handy if you share a printer, because you can tell Ami to print your documents at night when no one else has scheduled print times.

Printing nonconsecutive pages

When you select the Print command from the File menu, you can specify a range of pages to print, but that range must include consecutive pages, such as pages 5–11. What if you need to print 1–3, 5–9, 21, 43, and the last five pages of the document? Previously, you would have selected the Print command five different times, specifying a different page range each time. Now you can use the PRNPAGES macro to print nonconsecutive pages of a document.

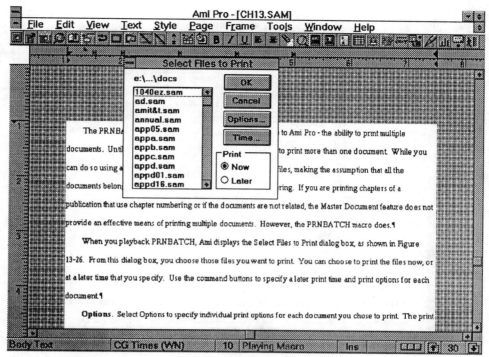

13-25 The PRNBATCH macro lets you print several files simultaneously.

Once you playback the PRNPAGES macro, Ami displays the Select Pages to Print dialog box, as shown in Figure 13-26. Using this dialog box, you can specify to print the first *x* pages, the last *x* pages, two page ranges, and individual page numbers. You can type the page numbers yourself or you can select them from the list box at the left.

Printing only selected text or graphics

The PRNSHADE macro lets you print only the text or graphics you have selected in the current document. This macro is handy for proofing a block of text or a graphic without printing the entire document or page. Once you playback the PRNSHADE macro, it copies the text and graphics you selected and pastes them into an untitled document. Ami displays the Print dialog box, letting you select any print options. Once you select OK, Ami prints the selected text and gaphics and closes the untitled document without saving it.

Inserting the registered trademark symbol

The REGMARK macro inserts the ANSI registered trademark symbol at the cursor's position in the document. If you create newsletters, books, or other material

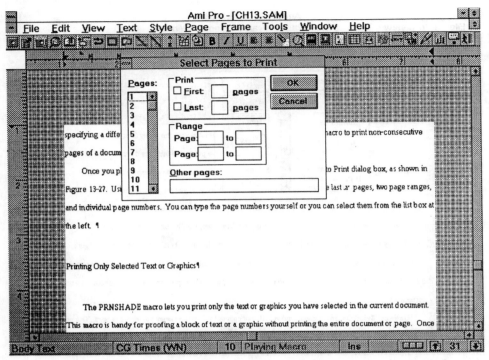

13-26 The PRNPAGES macro lets you print nonconsecutive pages, page ranges, and the first and last several pages of a file.

that should include a registered trademark, you need to add the symbol to your documents, but you probably don't remember what ANSI code you use to generate the symbol. Next time, let the macro insert the symbol for you. Ami includes a custom icon to which you assign the REGMARK macro, so that all you need to do is select the icon and the registered trademark symbol appears in your document.

Saving a document and remembering the cursor's position

The SAVEBOOK macro works only when you also use the OPENBOOK macro. If you save a document using the SAVEBOOK macro instead of File Save, Ami remembers the cursor's position in the document when you execute the macro. When you open a document using OPENBOOK instead of File Open, Ami opens the document and places the cursor in its last position—the position it was in when you executed SAVEBOOK. These macros are quite handy for authors and writers of long documents. Even if you use bookmarks to move to a position in the document, you usually need to do some scrolling or paging through to find your last place of editing. OPENBOOK and SAVEBOOK help remember where you left off, so you can begin there without searching through the document.

To mark the cursor's position in the document, the SAVEBOOK macro creates two bookmarks—| and °—which you can see if you select the Bookmarks icon or the Edit Bookmarks command. Do not delete these bookmarks, because the OPENBOOK and SAVEBOOK macros need them to locate the cursor's position in the document.

Ami provides two custom icons to which you assign the OPENBOOK and SAVEBOOK icons.

Updating Doc Info when you save a document

You know you should complete the Doc Info dialog box for all your documents, but you never get around to it, right? Well, now you can remind yourself to update the Doc Info before you save a document by using the SAVEINFO macro. It adds a new command to the File menu called Save with Doc Info, which displays the Doc Info dialog, prompting you to enter the information instead of relying on your sense of "I know I should do but I don't have time right now." After you update the Doc Info and select OK, Ami saves the document. Ami Pro supplies a custom icon to which you can assign the SAVEINFO macro.

Saving selected text to a file

The SAVSHADE macro saves any text you have selected to a file. When you execute the SAVSHADE macro, Ami copies the selected text to an untitled document and displays the Save As dialog box. Enter the filename, any options, and a description and select OK, and Ami saves and closes the new document.

Using Smart quotes, dashes, and apostrophes

If you need to use Smart quotes, dashes, and apostrophes, use the SMARTYPE macro to convert them from regular format to the Smart format. Your monitor and graphics card might not be able to display the characters, but your printer might still be able to print the characters. Not all printers can print Smart typeset characters, so make sure your printer has that capability before running this macro.

Tiling documents horizontally

When you select the Tile command from the Window menu, Ami tiles all open documents vertically on the screen, so that each document displays next to each other. If you use Layout mode in those documents, you cannot see an entire line of text on the screen.

The TILEHORZ adds a Tile Horizontally command to the Window menu. When you select Tile Horizontally, Ami places the open documents on top of each other, making it easier to see an entire line of text in each document. Figure 13-27 shows documents after selecting Tile Horizontally from the Windows menu. Ami provides a custom icon to which you can assign the TILEHORZ macro.

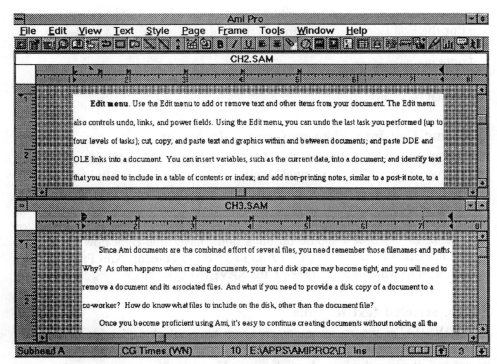

13-27 The TILEHORZ macro tiles documents horizontally and ads the Tile Horizontally command to the Windows menu.

Inserting the trademark symbol

The TM macro inserts the ANSI trademark symbol at the cursor's position in the document. If you create newsletters, books, or other material that includes material that is a trademark, you need to add the trademark symbol to your documents, but you probably don't remember what ANSI code you use to generate the symbol. Next time, let the macro insert the trademark symbol for you. Ami includes a custom icon to which you assign the TM macro, so that all you need to do is select the icon and the trademark symbol appears in your document.

Selecting ANSI characters from a menu

Ami comes with a macro that lets you select ANSI without requiring you to remember their codes. The macro name is TYPECHAR.SMM, and when you run it Ami adds the Chars menu to the menu bar. When you choose Select Chars from the menu, Ami displays the ANSI Characters dialog box from which you can choose ANSI characters, as shown in Figure 13-28. You can choose from the following options:

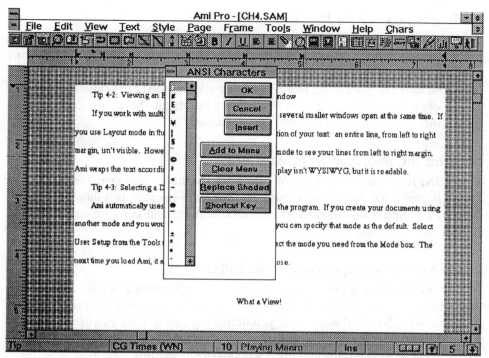

13-28 The ANSI Characters dialog box simplifies the task of inserting ANSI characters, because you don't need to remember their codes.

OK   Select OK to insert an ANSI character in the document and close the dialog box.

Insert   Select Insert to add an ANSI character to the document and keep displaying the dialog box so you can choose additional characters.

Add to Menu   Select Add to menu to display the ANSI character on the menu. You can insert the character in your document by displaying the menu and selecting the character.

Clear Menu   Select Clear menu to delete all the characters from the ANSI menu.

Replace Shaded   Select Replace shaded to replace highlighted text in the document with the ANSI character you selected. You also can choose to replace all other occurrences of the text you shaded with the ANSI character.

Shortcut Key   Select Shortcut Key to assign an ANSI character to a key combination.

Once you no longer need the menu displayed on the menu bar, select the menu and choose Exit.

Adding a task list to the menu bar

The WINAPPS macro adds a menu of active applications, both Windows and nonWindows, to the menu bar. You can use the Active Apps menu to move among currently active Windows applications, in the same way you do the Windows Task List. You also can update the menu to add newly activated applications or remove closed ones by selecting Update Apps from the menu. Selecting Exit Apps removes the Active Apps menu from the menu bar.

Starting file manager from Ami Pro

The WINFILE macro starts the Window File Manager and switches to it. This macro is useful for doing the preparatory work before creating a large document, such as creating a document and backup directory, and copying any necessary files to that directory.

Creating workgroups from related files

Most word processing users work with the same files over and over again. They might be templates for new documents, or files that you simply cannot do without. The WORKGRUP macro lets you define a group of files you use together as a workgroup, or a group of files that you can open and edit simultaneously. You can build new workgroups and open workgroups using this macro.

Once you playback the WORKGRUP macro, Ami adds a Workgroup command to the bottom of the View menu.

Using the *Macro Command Language*

When you record a macro, Ami remembers the keystrokes and mouse selections you made and includes those in the file you specified. Ami records your keystrokes and mouse selections into a file using its macro command language, consisting of programming statements, macro functions, and Ami Professional functions. The macro command language is explained in the Macro Documentation portion of the Help menu, and in the documentation titled *Macro Command Language*.

When you edit a macro, you are editing the programming statements or functions that Ami used to write your macro. As you edit your macro, refer to the help menu or the *Macro Command Language* manual to help you understand the different statements and functions.

Using the command language, you can write original macros that perform tasks not available as Ami commands, such as starting another application from within Ami (useful for DDE links), sending an E-mail to people on a cc: list in an Ami document, and backing up files using Windows or DOS without ever leaving Ami.

Questions & Answers

Q: When I edit a macro, the dialog box has an OK *and a* Close *button, but no* Cancel *button. Which do I use?*

A: Use OK when you want to open the macro file and change its content. Use Close when you change the macro's shortcut keys but you don't need to open the macro file to edit it.

Q: Is there a way to change shortcut keys without rerecording the macro?

A: Yes, select Edit from the Tools Macro menu. Highlight the macro filename, insert the cursor in the Shortcut key text box and press the new keys. Select Close and Ami reassigns the shortcut keys.

Q: I attached a macro to a frame, but when I select the frame nothing happens.

A: Even though you attached a macro to a frame, you also must turn on frame macros for the document. Select Doc Info from the File menu. Select Run frame macros and the next time you select the frame, Ami should execute the macro attached to it.

Q: Can I create a macro to start an application?

A: Yes. Use the Exec function from the Macro Command Language to execute a program within Ami. You also can assign the macro to an icon so that you can execute the application by selecting an icon.

Summary

Ami's macro facility is easy to use and flexible enough that you can tailor the way you execute the macros according to your document's purpose. You can execute macros by pressing their shortcut keys, selecting their filename from the Macro Record dialog box, attaching the macro to a file or the start or end of the program. Also, you can execute a macro by assigning it to a custom icon.

The macros supplied with Ami Pro enable you to perform tasks not normally available from Ami's menus. Learning about the macros is easy, because Ami provides a file that describes each macro and how you use it. Using the macros supplied with Ami you can perform many operations across files, such as find and replace, spell checking, and printing without a master document. These are just a few of the tasks available to you from Ami's assortment of macros.

14
CHAPTER

Creating equations

Ami's Equation Editor makes building an equation so easy that even people suffering from math phobia can do it. Building an equation is as easy as creating a frame and adding equation elements by selecting icons. You don't have to learn a complicated equation language to build your mathematical and scientific equations. Table 14-1 displays the icons Ami displays in the equation icon bar.

Before you begin using the Equation Editor, you need to install a symbol font that Ami recognizes. Windows automatically installs a symbol font, but Ami does not recognize it, and you cannot use it to build equations. The ATM fonts bundled with Ami come with a Symbol font you can use to build equations. If you don't use a Symbol font, you cannot properly view your equations or print them. Refer to chapter 6 for more information on installing ATM fonts.

Creating a sample equation

To demonstrate how easy creating an equation is, let's go ahead and build one:

1. Select Equations from the Tools menu. Ami displays the Equation Icon Bar, as displayed in Figure 14-1.

2. Select Enlarged View from the View menu.

3. Select the Fraction template icon.

4. Select the Radical template icon.

5. Type the following as the formula under the radical:
   4ab

6. Press Tab to move to the root portion of the Radical template.
7. Select the plus/minus ± icon. Press the spacebar to move outside of the Radical template.
8. Press Tab to move to the denominator portion of the Fraction template.
9. Type *b* as the denominator.
10. Select the Superscript template icon.
11. Type *2* as the superscript.
12. Press Esc to stop building the equation.

You just created a rather complex equation, but building it was easy, because Ami didn't require you to use a programming language. Just point to the equation element you want and Ami creates it for you.

Table 14-1. Equation Icons

Icon	Equation Tool	Icon	Equation Tool
	Fraction Template		Functions
	Radical Template		Spaces
	Superscript Template		Revise Character
	Subscript Template		Label Position
	Parentheses Template		Over/Under
	Brackets Template		Lowercase Greek Alphabet
	Summation		Uppercase Greek Alphabet
	Integral		Binary Operators
	Math/Text Mode		Binary Relations
	Show/Hide Input Boxes and Matrix Lines		Arrows
	Operators		Miscellaneous Characters
	Brackets		Delimiters
	Matrix		

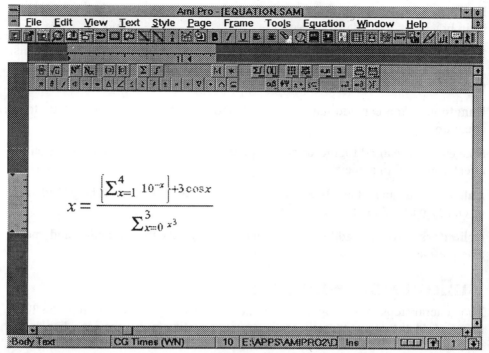

14-1 The Equation icon bar displays only after you select Equations from the Tools menu.

Parts of an equation

Equations are a combination of several mathematical elements. Each serves a different purpose in your equation, and you select each from the icon bar. Not all equations use every element, but if you do scientific and mathematical writing frequently, you probably will use each element at some time.

Templates Templates are fill-in-the-blank equations, and are the heart of the equation editor. Use templates to add a fraction, a radical (square root), a superscript, a subscript, or a formula surrounded by parentheses or brackets. When you select a template icon, Ami displays an input box to which you add the equation, and it displays a symbol if appropriate, as with fractions, square roots, parentheses, or brackets. Ami also lets you nest templates within each other. For example, to create a superscript under a radical, you would add the Radical template, and then add the Superscript template.

Operators Operators are mathematical symbols that perform an action on numbers or variables in an equation. You can type operators available from the keyboard, such as plus, minus, and equals. You can select an operator icon for the operators not available from the keyboard, such as summation and integral operators.

Brackets　You can choose to surround the entire equation, or just a portion of it, in brackets.

Matrices　A matrix is similar to a table, because it is made of rows and columns. Although not its sole purpose, you can use a matrix to build a multiple line equation.

Functions　You can add mathematical functions such as cos, tan, and arc to an equation.

Spaces　You can add large or small spaces to your equation, depending on the effect you need to achieve.

Labels　You can add labels above or below your equation. Labels help to identify or clarify parts of an equation.

Delimiters　You can add special symbols that signify the beginning and end of an equation.

Building an equation

The general steps to build an equation include selecting Equations from the Tools menu. Add the elements you need in your equation using the icon bar or the Equation menu. Press Esc to leave the Equation Editor.

Tip 14-1: Don't create a frame before using the equation editor　Ami creates a frame automatically when you select Equations from the Tools menu. The frame's size adjusts as equations grow or shrink. However, if you add a frame and then select Equations from the Tools menu, Ami does not adjust the frame's size according to the equation's size. The result is a big gap or a frame too small to hold the equation, and you'll have to resort to manually changing the frame's size.

Tip 14-2: Use Enlarged View to build an equation　Working View is too small to see what you're doing when building an equation. Switch to Enlarged View before you create the equation, and you'll get a much better view of your results.

Choosing Math or Text mode

Ami uses two different equation editing modes: Math and Text. While you are in Math mode, Ami assumes you are entering only mathematical characters and symbols. All text you type is italicized and displayed in red to represent a variable. Even though the characters and symbols display using a red color, they print using black. When you are in Text mode, Ami assumes you are entering only text, and all text you type displays normally. Ami's default mode is Math mode. To switch between Math and Text mode, select the Toggle Math/Text mode icon or select Math/Text from the Equations menu. Table 14-2 displays text as it appears when entered in Text vs Math mode.

Table 14-2. Text vs. Math Mode

Character Entered	Text Mode Result	Math Mode Result
4	4	4
a	a	*a*
x	x	*x*

Tip 14-3: Changing a character from math to text   If you enter a portion of an equation using the wrong input mode, it's not too late to change it. To change a part of the equation, highlight it and select the appropriate mode from the Equation icon bar or the Equation menu.

Adding a template

A template is a fill-in-the-blank equation, into which you can enter mathematical characters and symbols, operators, functions, text, or other templates. For example, in the sample equation you created earlier, you nested a square root (radical) template inside a fraction template.

To add a template to an equation, follow these steps:

1. Position the cursor at the place in the equation at which you need a template.
2. Select the template icon. Table 14-3 displays the icons and the templates they represent.
3. Fill in the content for the template, using the keyboard or the equation icons.
4. Press Tab to move to the next input box in the template.
5. Repeat steps 2 through 4 until you fill in all input boxes in the template.
6. Press the spacebar to move outside the template.

Tip 14-4: Hiding input boxes   The input box that appears as part of a template does not print—it is a display-only guideline for the template's content. If you find the box distracting, you can hide it on the screen by selecting Show/Hide Input Boxes from the Equation menu.

Tip 14-5: Deleting a template's content   You can remove a template's content without removing the template itself. To do so, use one of the following methods. Highlight the content and press Del. Place the cursor to the right of the content and press Backspace. Place the cursor to the left of the content and press Del.

Table 14-3. Equation Icons

Icon	Description	Icon	Description
	Fraction Template		Bracket Template
	Radical Template		Matrix Template
	Superscript Template		Label Template
	Subscript Template		Over/Under Template
	Parentheses Template		

Adding an operator

An operator is a symbol that denotes a mathematical operation, such as addition, multiplication or division. To add any operator available from the keyboard, type it while you are in Math mode. To add an operator that is not available from the keyboard, such as a summation or integral operator, follow these steps:

1. Position the cursor at the position in the equation where you need an operator.
2. Select the Operator icon, or select Insert Operator from the Equation menu. Ami displays the Operator dialog box, as shown in Figure 14-2.
3. Choose from the following options:

Operators Select a symbol from the Operators box. Table 14-4 lists the operators and their names.

Limit position If you add a limit to the operator, you can specify its position in relation to the operator. Ami does not automatically add limits to an operator. You must add a superscript or subscript template to do so. The Limit position option controls the placement of that template. Auto uses the settings in the Limits & Size dialog box. Above/Below places the limits above and below the operator. At right places the limits to the right of the operator.

Size The Size option controls how large or small an operator is. Auto uses the size settings in the Limits & Size dialog box. Big creates a large operator, similar to 14 pt. text, and Small creates a small operator, similar to 10 pt. text. Use Small if you want to create an equation within a line of text. Use Big if you want to place the equation outside a paragraph, such as between two paragraphs or in a margin.

4. Select OK to exit the dialog box and return to the equation.

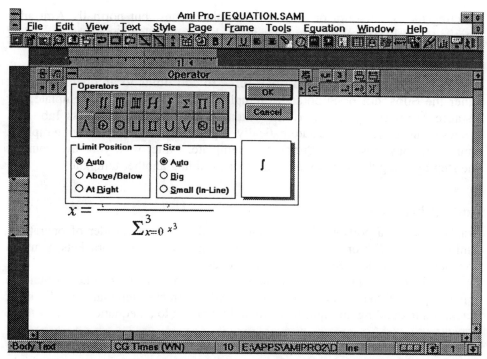

14-2 The Operators dialog box lets you select from several operators to include in an equation.

Table 14-4. Equation Editor Operators

Operator	Name	Operator	Name
$\int$	Integral	$\wedge$	Infimum
$\iint$	Double Integral	$\oplus$	Direct sum
$\iiint$	Triple Integral	$\odot$	Bigodot
$\iiiint$	Quadruple Integral	$\sqcup$	Big Square Cup
$\int \cdots \int$	Multiple Integral	$\amalg$	Coproduct
$\oint$	Circular Integral	$\cup$	Union
$\sum$	Summation	$\vee$	Supremum
$\prod$	Product	$\otimes$	Tensor Product
$\cap$	Intersection	$\uplus$	Disjoint Union

Tip 14-6: Quickly adding summation and integral operators If you want to add a summation or integral operator to your equation, you can do so without having to display the Operator dialog box. Simply select the Summation icon or the Integral icon from the equation icon bar. You can add limits to the operator by

selecting the Superscript or Subscript template icons, but normally Ami adds them to the right. If you want to place them above and below the operators, select Limits & Size Big from the Equation menu.

Tip 14-7: Adding limits to an operator   To add limits to an operator, select either the Subscript or Superscript template. Once you add one template, for instance, the Superscript, insert the content of the input box and press Tab. Ami creates a Subscript template automatically. If you had added a Subscript template, Ami would have inserted a Superscript template. Either way, you save yourself one step by using the Tab key as a shortcut to adding another template.

Adding brackets

Brackets define a portion of an equation and determine the order of operation. Ami's Equation Editor lets you choose from an abundance of brackets; you can even select different opening and closing brackets.

You have two options when adding brackets: you can add brackets around an existing part of the equation, or you can add a bracket template, made up of brackets surrounding an input box. To add a bracket to an equation, follow these steps:

1. If you want to place brackets around existing part of the equation, highlight the characters to be placed inside. If you want to add a bracket template, place the cursor at the position in the equation at which you need the template.
2. Select the Brackets icon or choose Insert Brackets from the Equation menu. Ami displays the Brackets dialog box, as shown in Figure 14-3.
3. Select the opening bracket from the first set of brackets. Ami displays an opening and a closing bracket in the example box. Ami assumes you want two brackets of the same type. If so, move to step 5.
4. Select the closing bracket from the second set of brackets
5. Select OK to return to the equation
6. If you inserted a bracket template, add the content to the input box.

Tip 14-8: Adding only one bracket instead of a pair   Normally Ami assumes that you want add a pair of brackets: one opening and one closing bracket. At times, however, you need to add only one. To do so, select the row of dots from the appropriate set of brackets in the Brackets dialog box. For example, if you need only a closing bracket, select the row of dots from the first set before you select a closing bracket. If you need only an opening bracket, select the row of dots from the second set after you select an opening bracket.

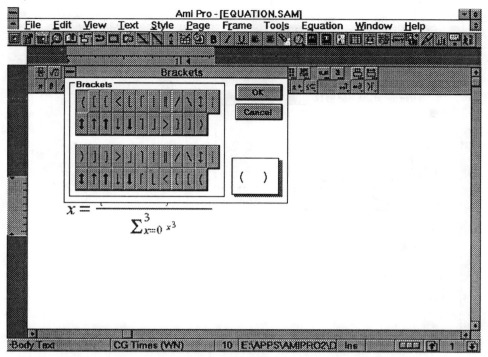

14-3 The Brackets dialog box lets you select from several brackets to include in an equation.

Adding a matrix template

A matrix is an array with two dimensions: rows and columns. Ami asks you how many you need in the matrix, but this figure is flexible because you can insert and remove rows and columns later. To add a Matrix template to an equation, follow these steps:

1. Position the cursor at the place in the equation where you need a matrix.
2. Select the Matrix icon or select Insert Matrix from the Equation Editor. Ami displays the Create Matrix dialog box, as shown in Figure 14-4:
3. Specify the number of rows and columns you need and select OK. Ami adds the matrix to the equation, adding an input box for each cell.
4. Add the content to each input box.

Once you add the content to the Matrix template, you might find that you don't have enough cells or you need more. To split an existing cell into two, press Enter. To combine two cells, press Del (combining cells works only if you have a one-column or one-row matrix). To delete an entire row or column, highlight it and press Del or Backspace.

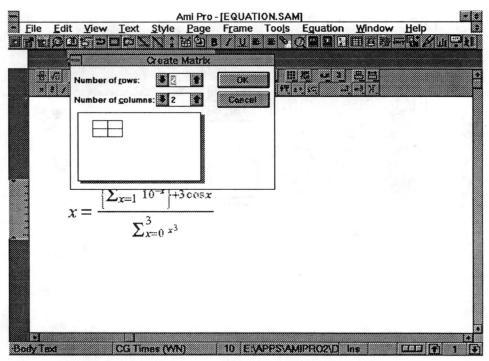

14-4 The Create Matrix dialog box lets you build a matrix to include in an equation.

Tip 14-9: Wrapping an equation using a matrix   Some equations don't fit on one line or are not appropriate for only one line. Although Ami does not let you wrap an equation to the next line, you can achieve the same results using a matrix. Create a matrix containing as many rows as you need lines, and containing only one column. Insert the content for the first line in the input box on the first row. When you are ready to create the equation on the second line, move to the second row. Continue adding to the matrix until all the rows are filled.

Tip 14-10: Hiding matrix lines   The lines that appear inside a matrix do not print—they are for your display only. If you find the lines distracting, you can hide them on the screen by selecting Show/Hide Matrix Lines from the Equation menu.

Adding a function

Ami has over thirty functions you can add to your equation. If you don't find the one you need in Ami's list, you can design your own custom function to use in an equation. To insert a function in an equation, follow these steps:

1. Place the cursor in the position in the equation where you need a function.

2. Select the Function icon or Insert Function from the Equation menu. Ami displays the Function dialog box, as displayed in Figure 14-5.

3. Select from the following options:

Insert   Select the function name from the Insert list box. Once you select a function, Ami makes available the options in the Limits box, if it can use limits.

Limits   Select the position where the limits for the function should be. Auto uses the settings in the Limits & Size dialog box . Above/Below places the limits above and below the operator. At right places the limits to the right of the operator.

Custom Function   If the function you need is not listed in the Insert box, select Custom Function. Ami displays a text box in which you can type the function name and select OK.

4. Select OK to return to the equation.

Ami inserts the function, using roman text and a grey color, in the equation.

Tip 14-11: Changing functions' display color   Normally Ami displays all functions in grey on the screen, although they print using black. Ami uses a different color for functions than it does for other mathematical characters so you

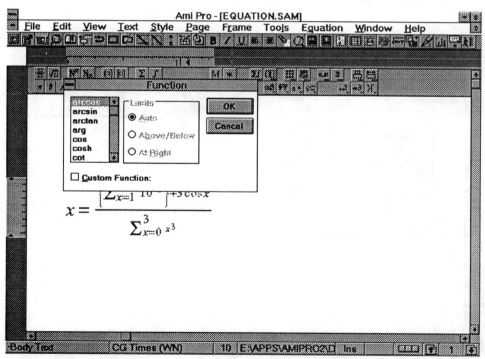

14-5   The Function dialog box lets you select from several functions to include in an equation.

can distinguish one from another. However, you can change the color used for functions in the display by selecting Preferences from the Equation menu. Select a new color from the Functions color set and select OK You cannot change the font or the attributes the function uses.

Adding spaces

Usually you don't need to add spaces to equations, because Ami does it for you. Each time you add a template, mathematical character, symbol, or function, Ami inserts a space that adheres to mathematical typesetting rules. If you need to customize your equation by adding an additional space or one of a different size, you can do so using the Spaces icon or the menu command.

To add custom spaces to an equation, follow these steps:

1. Place the cursor at the position in the equation where you need a custom space.

2. Select the Space icon or select Insert Space from the Equation menu. Ami displays the Spaces dialog box, as shown in Figure 14-6.

3. Select the custom space you need to insert. Table 14-5 lists the custom spaces available and their results.

4. Select OK to return to the equation.

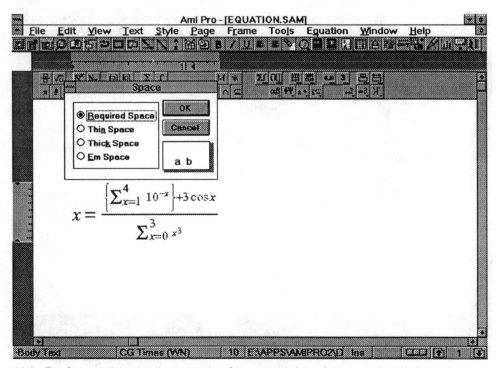

14-6 The Spaces dialog box lets you select from several sizes of spaces to include in an equation.

Table 14-5. Custom Spaces Available for Equations

Space Name	Size	Results
Required Space	1/6 em wide	$e = mc^2$
Thin Space	2/9 em wide	$e = m\ c^2$
Thick space	5/18 em wide	$e = m\ \ c^2$
Em space	1 em wide	$e = m\ \ \ c^2$

Tip 14-12: Quickly adding a required space   Most custom spaces you add will be required spaces. You can add a custom space without using the dialog box by pressing Ctrl-Spacebar. Ami adds the required space to the equation without forcing you to select the space from the dialog box.

Adding accents, negate marks, and bold to characters

Most mathematical characters and symbols appear directly to the right or left of the expression they modify. You can place limits above and below their operators, but what if you have a character other than a limit that needs to appear above the expression? Ami lets you add several accents, a negate mark, and even bold to any character using the Revise Character icon.

To assign an accent, negate mark, or bold to one or more characters in an equation, use these steps:

1. Highlight the portion of the equation where you need to add a mark.
2. Select the Revise Character icon. Ami displays the Revise Character dialog box, as displayed in Figure 14-7.
3. Select from the following options:

Accent on Top   Select this check box if you need to place an accent character on top of the highlighted character. Select the accent character from the drop-down list box.

Negate   Select this check box to add a slash through the highlighted character.

Bold   Select this check box to add boldface to the highlighted character.

4. Select OK to return to the equation.

Adding labels

Sometimes equations themselves aren't enough to get the message across. Complicated equations, or those requiring additional clarification, can use labels to help the reader understand the equation. A label template adds two input boxes: one for the equation and one for the label. You can add a label to a new or existing equation, and you can place the label above or below the equation.

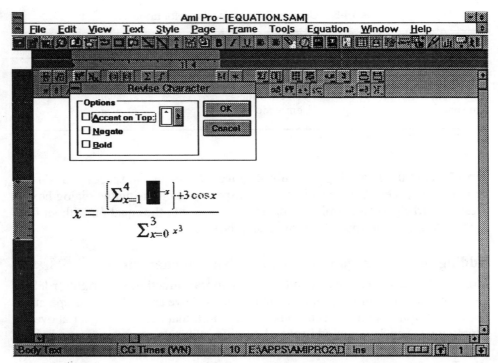

14-7 The Revise Character dialog box lets you add a revise character, a negation character, or bold to an existing symbol in the equation.

To add a label template to an equation, follow these steps:

1. If you want to add a label to an existing equation, highlight the equation. If you want to create a new equation and label at the same time, select Equations from the Tools menu.

2. Select the Label Position icon or select Insert Label from the Equation menu. Ami displays the Label Position dialog box, as shown in Figure 14-8.

3. Select the icon representing the label placement you need: either above or below the equation input box. The smaller input box represents the label input box.

4. Select OK to return to the equation. Ami inserts the label template containing two input boxes: the larger input box is for the equation; the smaller input box is for the label.

5. Insert the cursor in the equation input box and build the equation.

6. Press Tab to move to the label input box. Type the label, which can be either text or another equation, in the label input box.

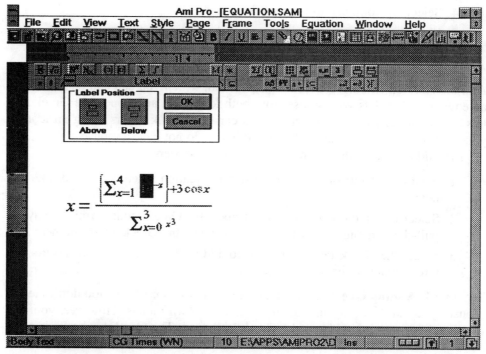

14-8 The Label dialog box lets you insert a template either above or below the equation that holds a label.

Adding marks over or under an equation

You can add arrows, bars, or braces above or below an equation. You can add a mark template, which includes a mark over or under an input box, or you can add the mark to an existing equation, both to individual characters or to the entire equation.

To add arrows, bars, or braces above or below an equation, follow these steps:

1. If you want to add the mark to an existing equation, highlight the characters in the equation where you need to add the mark. If you want to add a mark template, insert the cursor at the position in the equation where you need to insert the template.

2. Select the Over/Under icon, or select Insert Over/Under from the Equation menu. Ami displays the Over/Under dialog box, as shown in Figure 14-9.

3. Select the icon representing the mark you need to add to the equation from the Over or Under boxes. Table 14-6 lists the over/under marks available.

4. Select OK to return to the equation.

5. If you added a mark template, add the equation to the input box.

Adding Greek symbols

Ami provides an extensive Greek alphabet from which you can add characters to an equation. Ami lets you choose from both lowercase and uppercase Greek letters. As with the Accent characters, you can add Greek letters using an icon if you have a mouse, or using the keyboard if you do not have a mouse.

To add a Greek letter to an equation, use these steps:

1. Position the cursor at the place in the equation where you need a Greek letter.

2. Select either the Lowercase or Uppercase Greek icons. Ami displays a pull-down menu from which you can select the Greek letter you need.

3. Select the Greek letter you need to add to the equation. Ami inserts the Greek letter in the current equation.

Tip 14-13: Adding Greek characters using the keyboard   If you don't have a mouse, you can't display the Greek letter pull-down menus. However, you can use the characters available on the Greek keyboard. The Greek keyboard is a set

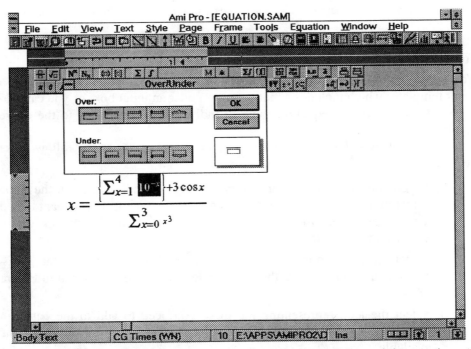

14-9 The Over/Under dialog box lets you insert an Over or Under mark to an existing equation or to a new equation.

Table 14-6.   Equation Editor Over/Under Marks

Mark	Name	Mark	Name
$\overline{\Box}$	Over Bar	$\underline{\Box}$	Under Bar
$\overset{\leftarrow}{\Box}$	Over Left Arrow	$\underset{\leftarrow}{\Box}$	Under Left Arrow
$\overset{\rightarrow}{\Box}$	Over Right Arrow	$\underset{\rightarrow}{\Box}$	Under Right Arrow
$\overset{\leftrightarrow}{\Box}$	Over Left and Right Arrow	$\underset{\leftrightarrow}{\Box}$	Under Left and Right Arrow
$\overset{\frown}{\Box}$	Over Brace	$\underset{\smile}{\Box}$	Under Brace

Table 14-7.   Greek Keyboard Characters

Key	Greek Character	Key	Greek Character
a	α	k	κ
b	β	l	λ
c	ψ	m	μ
d	δ	n	ν
e	ε	o	ο
f	φ	p	π
g	γ	q	χ
h	η	r	ρ
s	σ	F	Γ
t	τ	G	Λ
u	υ	L	Λ
v	ν	L	Λ
w	ω	S	Σ
x	ξ	U	Υ
y	θ	W	Ω
z	ζ	X	Ξ
C	Ψ	Y	Θ
D	Δ		

of characters normally not available on a regular keyboard. By selecting the Greek Keyboard command from the Equation menu, or by pressing Ctrl-G, Ami activates the Greek keyboard. The next character you type will be from the Greek Keyboard character set; however, the keyboard is active for one letter only. If you need to add several letters, you must select the Greek Keyboard command for each letter you want to add. Table 14-7 lists the Greek letters and keys you press to add them.

Adding binary operators and relations

Ami lets you add operators and relations not normally available from the keyboard. To do so, use these steps:

1. Position the cursor at the place in the equation where you need an operator.
2. Select the Binary Operators or Binary Relations icon. Ami displays the pull-down listing the operators or relations you can add to the equation.
3. Select the operator or relation that you need to add to the equation. Table 14-8 lists the binary operators and relations available.

Ami adds the operator or relation you selected. If you do not have a mouse, use the Symbol Keyboard command from the Equation menu to add a binary operator or binary relation not available from the keyboard.

Adding arrows

Ami lets you add arrows not normally available from the keyboard. To do so, position the cursor at the place in the equation where you need an arrow. Select the Arrows icon. Ami displays the pull-down listing the arrows you can add to the equation. Select the arrow that you need to add to the equation. Table 14-9 lists the arrows available.

Ami adds the arrow you selected. If you do not have a mouse, use the Symbol Keyboard command from the Equation menu to add an arrow not available from the keyboard.

Table 14-8. Equation Editor Binary Operators and Relations

Symbol	Name	Symbol	Name
$\pm$	Plus or Minus	$\leq$	Less Than Or Equal
$\cdot$	Centered Dot	$\geq$	Greater Than Or Equal
$\times$	Times	$=$	Equivalent
$\div$	Divide	$\cong$	Congruent
$\cap$	Intersection	$\approx$	Approximate
$\cup$	Union	$\sim$	Similar
$*$	Asterisk	$\subset$	Subset
$\diamond$	Diamond	$\subseteq$	Subset or Equal
$\bullet$	Bullet	$\supseteq$	Superset or Equal
$\vee$	Logical Or	$\supset$	Superset
$\wedge$	Logical And	$\perp$	Perpendicular
$\otimes$	Tensor Product	$\propto$	Proportional
$\oplus$	Direct Sum	$\notin$	Not In
$\in$	In	$\neq$	Not Equal

Table 14-9. Equation Editor Arrows

Arrow	Name	Arrow	Name
→	Right Arrow	⇑	Double Up Arrow
⇒	Double Right Arrow	↓	Down Arrow
←	Left Arrow	⇓	Double Down Arrow
⇐	Double Left Arrow	↔	Right and Left Arrow
↑	Up Arrow	⇔	Double Right and Left Arrow

Table 14-10. Equation Editor Miscellaneous Characters

Symbol	Name	Symbol	Name
ℵ	Aleph	¬	Logical Not
℘	Script P	ℑ	Imaginary
∂	Partial	ℜ	Real
∞	Infinity	. . .	Ellipses
∫	Small Integral	· · ·	Centered Ellipses
∇	Nabla	⋮	Vertical Ellipses
∠	Angle	⋰	Diagonal Ellipses
∀	For All	∅	Empty Set
∃	Exists	′	Prime

Adding miscellaneous characters

Ami lets you add miscellaneous characters, such as infinity, gradient, and partial derivative symbols, not normally available from the keyboard. To do so, position the cursor at the place in the equation where you need a miscellaneous character. Select the Miscellaneous icon. Ami displays the pull-down listing the miscellaneous characters you can add to the equation. Select the miscellaneous character you need to add to the equation. Table 14-10 lists the characters available.

Ami adds the character you selected. If you do not have a mouse, use the Symbol Keyboard command from the Equation menu to add a miscellaneous character not available from the keyboard.

Adding delimiters

Ami lets you add delimiters not normally available from the keyboard. Position the cursor at the place in the equation where you need a delimiter. Select the Delimiters icon. Ami displays the pull-down listing the delimiters you can add to the equation. Select the delimiter you need to add to the equation.

Ami adds the delimiter you selected. If you do not have a mouse, use the

Symbol Keyboard command from the Equation menu to add a delimiter not available from the keyboard.

Customizing the Equation icon bar

The lower left portion of the icon bar displays what Ami considers the most commonly used math symbols and characters. These symbols originally came from the pull-downs on the lower right side of the Equation icon bar. If you don't use the symbols or characters in the lower left portion of the icon bar, you can customize it to display any character or symbol from the pull-downs in the icon bar. To do so, follow these steps:

1. Display the pull-down menu on the icon bar containing the math symbol or character you want to add to the icon bar.

2. Hold the Shift key down and click on the symbol or character you want to add to the icon bar. Release the Shift key.

3. Hold the Shift key down and click on the symbol you want to replace on the icon bar. Ami adds the new symbol or character over the old one in the icon bar.

4. Continue with steps 1–3 to add other math symbols or characters to the icon bar.

Using the TeX language

If you are familiar with the TeX mathematical typesetting language, you can use those commands to build equations instead of using the Equation icon bar. When you select an icon from the Equation icon bar, Ami uses the TeX language to build the operator, template, function, character, or symbol. You can bypass the icon bar and use the TeX commands to build the equation directly. To do so, use these steps:

1. Position the cursor at the place in your document where you need to add an equation.

2. Select Equations from the Tools menu.

3. Select theInsert TeX command from the Equations menu or press Ctrl-Tab. Ami displays the TeX Command dialog box, as shown in Figure 14-10.

4. Select the command you need from the Commands list box.

5. Select OK to return to the equation. Ami translates the TeX command into an operator, template, function, character, or symbol and inserts it into the frame.

6. Repeat steps 3–5 to continue building the equation.

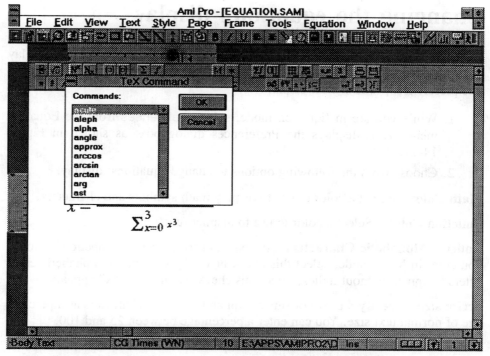

14-10 The TeX Command dialog box lets you build an equation using TeX commands.

Saving and importing equations

You can save the equations you build in Ami as TeX files so that they can be reused in other files or applications. You also can import equations from TeX files that were created in Ami or using other applications.

To save an equation to a TeX file, follow these steps:

1. Select the frame containing the equation you need to save to a TeX file.
2. Select Equations from the Tools menu.
3. Highlight the portion of the equation that you need to save to a TeX file.
4. Select Save As Equation from the File menu.
5. Type the equation filename in the text box and select OK. You do not need to add a file extension, because Ami automatically adds a .TeX extension to the file you save.

To retrieve an equation from a TeX file, position the cursor in your document at the place you need to insert the equation. Select Equations from the Tools menu. Select Import Equation from the File menu. Type the filename of the equation you need to retrieve into the frame and select OK.

Changing the equation's display

Normally Ami displays math characters and symbols in red and functions in black. You can change the colors Ami uses to display equations and the display and print size of the characters in equations. To change equations' display and size preferences, follow these steps:

1. While you are in Equation mode, select Preferences from the Equation menu. Ami displays the Preferences dialog box, as shown in Figure 14-11.

2. Choose from the following options to change equations' display:

Math Color   Select a color to use to display math symbols and characters.

Function Color   Select a color to use to display functions.

Italicize Alphabetic Characters   If you want to italicize alphabetic characters you enter in Math mode, select this check box. If you want the alphabetic characters to appear without italics, select this check box until no "x" appears.

Script size   Specify the size of superscript and subscript characters as a percentage of normal text size. You can enter a percentage between 25 and 100.

Scriptscript size   Specify the size of superscripts and subscripts that appear within another superscript or subscript as a percentage of normal text size. You can enter a percentage between 25 and 100.

Operator size   Specify the size of operators as a percentage of normal text size. You can enter a percentage between 100 and 200.

Big operator size   Specify the size of large operators, such as summations and integrals, as a percentage of normal text size. You can enter a percentage between 100 and 200.

3. Select OK. Ami uses the preferences you chose to format all equations you create in the future. Any equations you created previously are not affected.

Questions & Answers

Q: How can I leave a template? I press Tab to move around the template, but I can't get out of it.

A: To move outside a template, you can use one of several keys. The Spacebar should move the cursor outside the template input box, but it sometimes produces unexpected results. You also can use the Right and Left arrow keys to move before or after an input box.

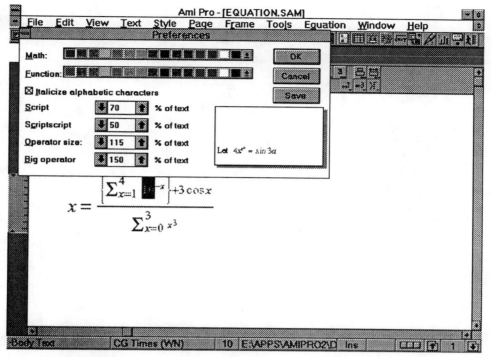

14-11 The Preferences dialog box lets you control the color, size, and formatting of equations.

Q: I tried to cut and paste an equation in my document, but when I pasted it Ami inserted codes instead of the equation.

A: If the cursor is not in a frame and if you are not in Equation mode, Ami inserts the TeX commands that it uses to create the equation. Make sure you have a frame selected and that you are in Equation mode before you paste an equation.

Summary

Ami's equation editor lets you concentrate on mathematics, finance, or statistics, instead of spending time on formatting your equations. Ami doesn't require you to know a complicated programming language to create equations: instead, you simply click on the symbol you need, and Ami builds the equation for you. The equation editor includes intelligent templates that expand as you add symbols and values. You can create and save your equations in the industry standard format, TeX if you are familiar with it.

15
CHAPTER

Power fields

A power field is an instruction that performs an action and inserts the result at the power field's location in the document. You can use power fields to consecutively number figures, insert cross-references, prompt users for information, and insert document statistics (number of pages, date created, etc.) into your document, along with many other uses. Once you insert a power field, Ami continually updates the information contained in the field. For example, a power field that inserts the current date into the document looks like this:<CreateDate>. It inserts the current date into the document and updates when you tell it to.

This chapter begins with an overview of power fields and how they operate. It continues with an explanation of how to insert, view, update, print, edit, and delete power fields. Finally, the chapter lists all the power fields supplied with Ami and an explanation of how to use each one.

Power field overview

Power fields bring to Ami Pro 2.0 a way of generating a variety of information that previously required you to use a different procedure for each type of information you required. For example, power fields can generate form letters, use merge data and standard documents, and mark index entries, all at the same time. Before power fields, however, you had to generate each one separately.

Use power fields to generate whatever document contents you wish. Tasks especially well suited for power fields are those that:

- insert document contents that change frequently
- insert different types of document contents at the same time that would otherwise require a separate procedure for each
- repetitive procedures that you would need to do using a menu command

• procedures that require you to execute a macro.

Power fields are the most efficient way of creating a document's content, because you use the same procedure to insert any type: you insert the power field with the instructions and then tell it to produce the text or graphics. Ami has four types of power fields that you can use in your documents.

Ami Pro function   Automate Ami Pro features at a specific location in your document. Think of these functions as location-specific macros. A power field that inserts the current date is an Ami Pro function power field.

Document description function   Insert document statistics into a specific location in your document. A power field that inserts the number of pages in the document is a document description function power field.

Field functions   Automate features normally not available as an Ami Pro features. A power field that sequentially numbers frames in a document is a field function power field.

Macro functions   Use Ami's macro command language to perform an action at a specific location in your document. A power field that executes an application is a macro function power field.

Ami provides over 40 power fields, but you can create additional ones by saving existing power fields with your own instructions.

Power field syntax

A power field consists of three elements: angled brackets, the field name, and instructions. The angled brackets define the beginning and the end of the power field. You do not type the angled brackets; Ami automatically inserts them when you insert the power field into the document. The field name tells Ami what type of power field it is and what action to perform. The instructions further clarify and detail what type of action to perform and how to do so. A power field's syntax is extremely important, because any spelling errors or typographical mistakes you make in inserting a power field can produce the wrong results.

Field name

The first element in the power field is most often the field name, which identifies the power field and tells Ami what action to perform. You can precede a field name with a space, for readability, without affecting the power field's performance. You also can insert a macro function as the first element in the power field to manipulate the results of the power field.

Instructions

Many power fields require instructions to define, clarify, or provide further details about the action to be performed. For example, to insert the contents of another file or a bookmark into the current document, you can use the INCLUDE power field. However, it needs further instructions to determine whether to insert a file's content or a bookmark's content into the current file. Instructions can take on different forms, including bookmarks, global variables, macro functions, merge fields, numbers, other power fields, quoted text, and variables.

Bookmarks A bookmark identifies a selection of text, graphics, table cells, or a position in a document. Identify a bookmark by giving it a name using the Edit Insert Bookmark command or by using the Bookmark icon. Many fields use bookmarks to identify the contents or location you want to use as the field's result.

Global variables A global variable is a storage place that holds information to use as an instruction in a power field. Global variables differ from normal variables in that more than one power field can use a global variable. Several power fields can use the same global variable to get their results.

Macro functions A macro function is an instruction that comes from Ami's Macro Command Language. These instructions are not available as part of Ami's menus, but only from the command language. Thus, you can perform tasks normally not available in Ami. You can use macro functions as part of the instructions in a power field.

Merge fields Merge field names identify the contents of a merge record. Many power fields can manipulate the contents of a merge field, but you must first tell Ami which field in the record to use. Merge fields serve as part of the instructions in that they identify the portion of the merge record on which the power field should act.

Numbers You can enter one or more numbers as instructions for a merge field. The numbers can be part of an expression, such as REVENUES < 500, they can specify the number of characters in a word on which the power field should act, or they can tell the power field which word to act on in a phrase.

Power fields You can use power fields for instructions for other power fields. A power field that commonly uses others as instructions is IF, which evaluates a condition. The other power field tells IF what action to perform should the result of the condition be true or false.

Quoted text Power fields use text appearing in quotes as literal strings in dialog boxes or other messages that prompt users for information. If you want the text to appear exactly as you type it, enclose it quotation marks. Otherwise, Ami will not use it in the power field.

Options Options are instructions that tell a power field how to format its results. Power fields that use options most often generate a date, time, or number as their result, and you can tell the power field how to format that result.

Variables A variable is a storage place that holds information the power field uses to generate its result. Most variables are good for only the one power field that uses them. Global variables hold information that is accessible to more than one power field.

Inserting a power field

Power fields are one of the most versatile tools in Ami, but they can be intimidating at first. Because they are a new and extremely powerful feature to Ami Pro, you might not feel comfortable with them. Fortunately, inserting a power field is simple, because Ami provides you with a list of available fields, tells you what instructions you need to insert, and gives you help every step of the way. You don't have to remember the exact name or syntax of every power field, because Ami displays them in a list box from which you can choose.

To insert a power field into a document, use these steps:

1. Place the cursor at the position in the document where you need to insert a power field.

2. Select Power Fields from the Edit menu.

3. Select Insert. Ami displays the Insert Power Fields dialog box as shown in Figure 15-1.

4. Select the power field you need to insert from the Fields list box. Once you highlight the field, Ami places it in the Insert box.

5. Place the cursor in the insert box and type any instructions for the power field. Use the Description box as a guide, because Ami shows a description of the power field and its syntax.

6. If the power field has any options available, select the option you want from the Options list box. Options usually are formatting switches for date, time, and numeric results.

7. Select OK to insert the power field into the document.

Table 15-1 lists the power fields available and their syntax.

Tip 15-1: Editing the power field syntax After you type the instructions for the power field in the Insert box, you might need to change them. You can do so by selecting the part of the instruction you need to change and typing new text or by pressing Del or Backspace.

Tip 15-2: Inserting a power field using a macro If you find yourself returning to the Insert Power Field dialog box to select the same power field, you can create a macro to insert it instead. Select Macros from the Tools menu and select Record. Type a filename for the macro and assign shortcut keys. Select Power Fields from the Edit menu and select Insert. Select the power field you need, adding any instructions or options necessary, and then stop recording the macro. The next

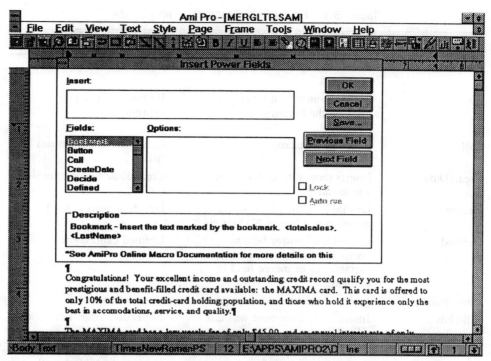

15-1 The Insert Power Fields dialog box lets you select from a list of available power fields.

time you need to insert the same power field in this or another document, press the shortcut keys for the macro.

Tip 15-3: Inserting a power field using an icon   If you create a macro to insert a power field you use often, you can assign the macro to an icon. Shortcut keys can be difficult to remember, especially because Ami uses many of the Ctrl combinations. You cannot use the Alt combinations because they let you access menus, as outlined in IBM Common User Access standards. To make inserting the same power field easier to do and to remember, create a custom icon and assign to it the power field macro you created in Tip 15-2.

Saving a custom power field

If you use the same power field again and again, you can save it to a power field file so that Ami displays it in the Insert Power Field dialog box. To save a power field to a file, use these steps:

1. Select Power Fields from the Edit menu.
2. Select Insert.
3. Select the power field from the Fields box.

Table 15-1. Power Field Descriptions and Syntax

Power Field	Description	Syntax
Bookmark	Inserts contents of the specified bookmark.	[Bookmark name]
Button	Performs an action when you click on the button in the document.	Button "display text" expression
Call	Executes a macro.	Call filename(!function) (p1, ..)
CreateDate	Inserts date or time document was created.	CreateDate %[date/time option]
Decide	Displays a dialog box with a question and Yes or No buttons.	Decide (question text)
Defined	Use with IF power field to check if a bookmark, global variable, or or merge field is defined.	Defined expression
Description	Inserts document description.	Description
EditDate	Inserts date document was last edited.	EditDate [%date/time option]
Exec	Executes an application.	Exec("program [,parameters]" [,show])
FileSize	Inserts size of current file in kilobytes.	FileSize
FormatNum$	Displays a number in the defined format.	FormatNum$(prefix, suffix, decimals, expression)
If	Performs an action based on conditions.	If condition expression [ElseIf condition express] [Else express] EndIf
Include	Inserts contents of a document, ASCII file, or bookmark.	Include "filename [!bookmark]"[%P][$W]
Index	Marks an index entry.	Index "Primary" [#] ["Secondary"] ["other"]
LCase$	Converts a string to lowercase.	LCase$(expression)
Left$	Displays a specified number of character from the left of the expression.	Left$(expression, count)
Len	Displays the number of characters in a string.	Len(expression)
MergeRec	Inserts the number of the current merge record.	MergeRec
Message	Displays a dialog with a message.	Message ("Message text")

Table 15-1. *(Continued)*

Power Field	Description	Syntax
Mid$	Displays a specified number of characters from the middle of the expression.	Mid$(expression, start, count)
NextRec	Advances to the next record during a merge.	NextRec
Now	Inserts the current time.	Now
NumChars	Inserts the document's character count.	NumChars
NumEdits	Inserts the number of edits for the document.	NumEdits
NumPages	Inserts the document's page count.	NumPages
NumWords	Inserts the document's word count.	NumWords
PageRef	Inserts the page number of the specified bookmark.	PageRef [Bookmark name]
PrintEscape	Inserts printer escape sequences.	PrintEscape "[027]text"
Query$	Displays a dialog box with a question, a text box, OK, and Cancel buttons.	Query$("Question text")
Right$	Displays the specified number of characters from the right of the expression.	Right$(expression, count)
Seq	Inserts a sequential number.	Seq expression[= [exp]][+ exp]
Set	Defines a global variable.	Set [global variable] expression
Skip	Skips the specified record during merge.	Skip
StrCat$	Appends strings and inserts them in the document.	StrCat$(expression, expression, [expression..])
StrField$	Inserts an item from an expression.	StrField$(expression, fieldnum, separator)
Total Editing Time	Inserts the total number of minutes document has been open.	EditTime
UCase$	Converts a string to uppercase.	UCase$(expression)
Void	Performs an action without inserting a value in the document.	Void [expression]

4. Type the instructions in the Insert box.

5. Select any options from the Options box.

6. Select the Save button. Ami displays the Save Power Field dialog box, as shown in Figure 15-2.

7. Type the name for power field in the Field text box. Power field names can be up to 24 characters and they can include spaces.

8. Type a description for the power field in the Description text box. The description appears when you highlight the power field in the Insert Power Field dialog box, so you should include the same type of descriptive information as Ami does for its own power fields. Include a description of the field and the field syntax.

9. Select OK to return to the Insert Power Field dialog box.

10. Select OK again to insert the power field in the document, or select Cancel to leave the dialog box without inserting the power field. Either choice does not affect the power field you saved previously.

The next time you display the Insert Power Field dialog box, Ami displays your new power field in the Fields box. You can insert it by highlighting the field and selecting OK.

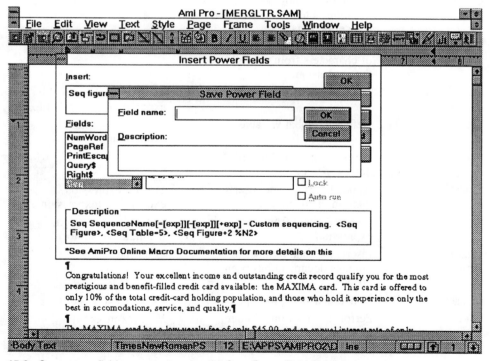

15-2 Save power fields you create using the Save Power Field dialog box.

Viewing power fields or their results

When you insert a power field into a document, Ami does not display the power field code. Instead, Ami displays the result of the power field's actions. Normally you want to view the power field's results, so you can see the document statistics, index, or other data it inserted into the document. If you ever need to delete or edit a power field, however, you need to view its codes rather than its results. You can use the Show/Hide Power Fields command on the View menu to toggle between displaying a power field's results and its codes.

Tip 15-4: Selecting a power field   Editing a power field is the same as editing any text or graphic outside a power field. Select the portion of the power field you need to change and make the modifications. However, you need to select the Show Power Fields command from the View menu before doing so, otherwise all you see in the document is the power fields' results. If you accidentally delete a portion of the power field's results, such as the year from a date power field, updating the field returns the entire result to the file.

Tip 15-5: Editing a power field   You can edit a power field's results just as you do normal text or graphics in the document. This is especially useful if the power field does return the result you expected. You can add, delete, or modify any text or graphics that appear as a result of a power field. However, anytime you update that power field or all power fields in the document, Ami replaces your modifications with the new results of the power field.

Viewing both power fields and their results

Correcting mistakes in a power field is much easier when you can see the field result and the field codes at the same time. Otherwise, you would need to display the codes, correct any errors, and display the results to see the change in the power field. Repeating this process for each power field you need to correct would soon become tedious. Ami doesn't have a direct way to display a power field's codes and results at the same time, but you can achieve the same effect by displaying the same document in two windows: one window shows the power fields' results, while the other window shows the power fields' codes.

To display a document's power field codes and results at the same time, follow these steps:

1. Use File Open to retrieve the document into the active window.
2. Select New Window from the Window menu. Select OK when Ami tells you that you cannot save any changes to the second window.
3. Select Tile from the Window menu to display each window side by side.
4. Place the cursor in the Read Only window and select Draft mode from the View menu.

5. Place the cursor in the original window and select Draft mode from the View menu.

6. Select Show Power Fields from the View menu. You display the codes in this window because you cannot edit the Read-Only window.

7. Edit the power fields as necessary. The Read-Only window won't update to show you the results of the power field changes immediately, but you can see the original power field code.

8. To display the results of your changes, save the file using Save from the File menu.

9. Close the Read-Only window and redisplay it to display the power fields' new results.

To show the same view in both windows, turn on or off the Show Power Fields command from the View menu.

Anytime you save a file containing power fields, Ami changes their display to show results instead of codes. Ami also changes power fields' display when you update them. If you update a single power field, Ami changes the display for that field only. If you update all power fields, Ami changes the display for all fields.

Tip 15-6: Printing power fields   You can print the power field codes in your document by selecting Show Power Fields from the View menu, then selecting Print from the File menu. Ami prints the document, including any power field codes. Do not save the file before you print, or Ami will change the power fields to display results rather than codes.

Tip 15-7: Moving to a power field   You can move to a power field using one of two methods. You can select Power Fields from the Edit menu and select Next Field or Previous Field. You also can select Go To from the Edit menu or press Ctrl-G, select Next Item, and select Next Field. Either way, Ami moves the next or previous field in the document, depending on the selection you made.

Updating power fields

Updating a power field displays that field's latest results. Ami automatically updates the results of power fields at these times: when you insert them in the document, when you generate a table of contents or index, and when you print the document using the Update fields option.

Additionally, you can control which power fields update and when they do so. You can update one field, all fields, only certain fields each time you open the document, or prevent a field from updating at all.

Updating one power field

If you have several power fields in a document, you might not want to update all of them simultaneously, especially if any of them prompt you for information. You can update power fields individually without affecting other power fields in the document. To do so, position the cursor on the power field that needs to be updated. If you cannot place the cursor precisely on a field, select Power Fields from the Edit menu then select Next Field or Previous Field until Ami places the cursor on the correct field. Select Power Fields from the Edit menu, and select Update. Ami updates the power field on which the cursor is located, but does not affect other power fields in the document.

Updating all power fields

If you want to update every power field in the document, you can do so simultaneously rather than one by one. It doesn't matter where the cursor is in the document when you update all power fields. No matter if it is at the beginning, middle, end, or not on a power field at all, Ami updates every power field in the document. To do so, select Power Fields from the Edit menu. Select Update All. Ami updates each power field in the document and displays their new results.

Updating fields when you open the document

You can tell Ami to update individual power fields each time you open the document by using the Auto Run feature. Auto Run is especially useful for power fields that reference information outside the current file that has changed since the last time you updated the power field, or for power fields that prompt the user for information.

To turn on the Auto Run feature for an individual field, place the cursor in the power field where you want to activate the feature. Select Power Fields from the Edit menu and select Insert. Select the Auto Run check box. Select Cancel to exit the Insert Power Field dialog box without inserting a power field. Ami turns on the Auto Run feature for the power field you selected. Repeat steps 1–5 for any other power fields that need to use Auto Run. The next time you open the file, Ami updates the results of any power fields using Auto Run.

Preventing fields from updating

If you have a power field that takes too long to update, or if it is not necessary to update the field often, you can lock the field so that Ami does not update its results.

To lock a power field, place the cursor in the power field you need to lock. Select Power Fields from the Edit menu, and select Insert. Select the Lock check box. Select Cancel to exit the Insert Power Field dialog box without inserting a power field. Ami locks the power field you selected. Repeat steps 1–5 for any other power fields that need to lock. The next time you update the power fields in the document, Ami does not refresh the power field's result.

Tip 15-8: Updating locked power fields   Even if you have locked a power field, you can update it periodically by turning on Auto Run for that field. Ami updates the field only when you open the file, but not at any other time. To turn on Auto Run for a locked field, place the cursor in the field and select Power Fields from the Edit menu. Select Insert and select the Auto Run check box. Select Cancel to leave the dialog box and turn on the Auto Run feature.

Deleting power fields

You can delete a power field from the document, and you also can delete a custom power field from the Insert Power Field dialog box. You cannot remove predefined power fields from the dialog box. Deleting old power fields from the document lets you clean up outdated fields that you no longer use. Deleting custom fields from the dialog box lets you remove any power fields that have been replaced with more efficient ones.

Deleting a power field from the document

To remove power fields from the document, select Show Power Fields from the Edit menu to display the codes of all power fields in the document. Select the power field you need to delete, including both angled brackets surrounding the field. Press the Del key. Ami removes the field from the document.

Deleting a custom power field from the Insert power field dialog box

If you created a custom power field that you no longer use, you can remove it from the Insert Power Field dialog box. To do so, however, you must edit the AMIPRO.INI file.

1. Select Open from the File Menu.
2. Change the drive and directory to C:\WINDOWS or your Windows directory.
3. Select ASCII as the File Type.
4. Highlight the AMIPRO.INI file from the Files list box.
5. Select the ASCII Options button.
6. Select CR/LF at paragraph ends only from the ASCII File Option box.
7. Select OK. Ami opens a new window containing the AMIPRO.INI file.
8. Select Find & Replace from the Edit menu.
9. Type [Fields] and select Find.

10. Locate the line that defines the field you want to delete and highlight the entire line.

11. Press Del.

12. Select Save As from the File menu and select OK. When Ami prompts you whether to overwrite the file, select OK. Ami removes the custom field from the Insert Power Field dialog box, but does not remove any power fields you inserted using the custom field. The power fields, and their results, remain in the document.

Power field types

Ami Pro 2.0 offers over 40 different power fields. This section explains power fields and includes explanations so that you can see its syntax and available options. The power field explanations are grouped in order by their purpose, so you can find the field that creates the results you need in your document.

Date and time power fields

Most of Ami's date and time power fields deal with when the document was created. If you need to insert the current date or time in a document, you can use the Insert Date and Time command from the Edit menu to do so, and depending on your choice, Ami can update the field automatically. You can control the appearance of the date and time Ami's power fields create using options.

The creation date field

The CREATEDATE field inserts the date or time the document was created. You choose whether to display the date or time by adding a switch to the power field. The date and time the document was created appears in the Doc Info dialog box.

The CREATEDATE field uses the following syntax:

CreateDate [% date/time option]

The edit date field

The EDITDATE field inserts the date or time the document was last edited. You choose whether to display the date or time by adding a switch to the power field. The date and time the document was created appears in the Doc Info dialog box.

The EditDate field uses the following syntax:

EditDate [% date/time option]

The total editing time field

The EDITTIME field inserts the total number of minutes the document has been open, as of the last update of the Doc Info dialog box or since the last update of the power fields in the document. The total editing time information appears in the Doc Info dialog box.

To update the EDITTIME field, you must select Update All from the Edit menu, print the document with the Update fields option selected, or generate a table of contents or index.

The EDITTIME field uses the following syntax:

EditTime

Date and time options

You can add options to format the appearance of the date and time. If you don't add options to the fields, Ami inserts a series of numbers that will not resemble a date or a time. Make sure you add a switch to every date and time field you use. Table 15-2 lists the options available for formatting date and time power fields. All options begin with a backslash (\), followed by two letters: the first letter determines whether the field produces a date or a time; the second letter determines the appearance of the date or time.

User interaction power fields

User interaction fields require you to perform an action so that the power field can return a result or complete a task. Some fields request information by displaying a dialog box with a question inside, and you must type an answer or select a button. Ami has four power fields that interact with the user: the DECIDE field asks for a yes or no answer, the Message field displays a message but does not return a value, the QUERY field asks you to type an answer to the question; and the BUTTON field requires you to double click on the field so that it can complete its action. QUERY fields are especially useful when you use them with data-entry forms.

The Decide power field   The DECIDE field displays a question inside a dialog box with Yes and No buttons. The DECIDE field returns a true or false result, depending upon whether you select yes or no from the dialog box. A true result returns a one, while a false result returns a zero. You can combine the DECIDE field with the IF field to evaluate a condition, and perform an action based on whether the DECIDE field returns a true or false answer. Each time you update the DECIDE field or all fields in the document, Ami displays the dialog box requesting a response. To enter the question Ami displays in the dialog box, type the text enclosed in quotes. The DECIDE power field uses the following syntax:

<Decide("Question text")>

Question text is the question you want to appear in the dialog box. Always enclose the question in quotation marks.

Table 15-2. Date and Time Power Fields Formatting Options

Code	Format Type	Format
Da	Date	5/1/93
Db	Date	May 1, 1993
DB	Date	MAY 1, 1993
Dc	Date	1 May 1993
DC	Date	1 MAY 1993
Dd	Date	Monday, May 1, 1993
DD	Date	MONDAY, MAY 1, 1993
De	Date	May 1
DE	Date	MAY 1
Df	Date	Monday May 1
DF	Date	MONDAY May 1
Dg	Date	5/1
Dh	Date	5/1/1993
Di	Date	1.May
DI	Date	1.MAY
Dj	Date	1.May.1993
Dk	Date	1993 May 1
DK	Date	1993 MAY 1
Dl	Date	May 1993
DL	Date	MAY 1993
T0	Time	7:15
T2	Time	7:15 AM
T3	Time	07:15 AM
T4	Time	7:15A
T5	Time	07:15A
T6	Time	7:15am
T7	Time	07:15am
T8	Time	7:15a
T9	Time	07:15a

The Message power field   The MESSAGE field displays a message inside a dialog box with an OK button. The Message field does not return a result; instead it displays the dialog box until the user acknowledges the message by selecting the OK button. The MESSAGE field is useful for displaying help messages, warnings, or to otherwise catch the user's attention.

To enter the message Ami displays in the dialog box, type the text enclosed in quotes.

The MESSAGE field uses the following syntax:

```
<Message("Message text")>
```

Message text is the message you want to appear in the dialog box. Always enclose the message text in quotation marks.

The Query Field   The QUERY$ field displays a question inside a dialog box with a text box and OK and Cancel buttons. The answer you type in the text box is the power field's result. Each time you update the QUERY$ field or all fields, Ami displays the dialog box requesting a response. QUERY$ fields are perfect for filling in forms, because they can request the information for each cell in a table. If the form contains a lot of QUERY$ fields, however, you probably don't want to update each one every time, especially if you have already filled in most of the form. QUERY$ fields are great candidates for the Auto Run option, because you usually need to fill in a form when you first open the file.

The QUERY$ power field uses the following syntax:

```
<Query$("Message Text" [,"Default Text"])>
```

Message text is the question you want to display inside the dialog box. Always enclose the message text in quotation marks.

Default text is the text that Ami uses as the default answer should the user select the OKbutton without typing an answer in the text box. Always enclose the default text in quotation marks.

Tip 15-9: Using the Query power field during a merge   If one portion of the standard document changes often, such as the toll-free number clients should call, you can use the QUERY power field to ask for the current information to insert at the time of the merge. Using the QUERY power field, you can insert variable information into the standard document without editing it each time you perform a merge. You could use the INCLUDE power field to insert a toll-free number, but you would need to edit the power field or the bookmark it inserts each time the toll-free number changes. Instead, you can use the QUERY field to ask for the most current toll-free number, and Ami inserts it into the standard document. You also can specify a default toll-free number with the QUERY field, so that if the number hasn't changed, you don't have to specify a new one.

A power field that inserts a variable toll-free number into the standard document looks like this:

```
<Set Min Query$("What is the toll-free number for MINIMA clients?")>
<Set Max Query$("What is the toll-free number for MAXIMA clients?")>
```

Then, insert the <Min> and <Max> fields in the bookmarks in the file containing the bookmarks.

The Button field   The BUTTON field displays text in the document. When you double click on the text, the Ami performs the action you specified in the BUTTON field. You can use the BUTTON field along with the MESSAGE field to display help text in a document, and when you double click on the help text, Ami displays a help message. Ideally, you would place the BUTTON field inside a frame with a colored background to draw attention to the BUTTON power field.

The BUTTON power field uses the following syntax:

```
<Button "Display Text" expression>
```

Display text is the text in the document on which you double click to perform the action. Always enclose the display text in quotes. The action you want the power field to perform when you double click on the display text is the expression. The expression can be another power field or a macro function.

Numbering power fields

Ami lets you perform two types of numbering using power fields: sequential numbering of figures, tables, or other items, and cross-reference numbering. The PAGEREF power field inserts the page number of a bookmark in the current document. The SEQ power field sequentially numbers items in a document.

Page Reference field   The PAGEREF inserts the page number where a specified bookmark is located. PAGEREF uses the page numbering inside the current document, and not any page numbering across documents created by the Master Document feature. To use the PAGEREF field to insert cross-references for figures, you need to insert a bookmark at each figure's location.

The PAGEREF power field uses the following syntax:

```
<Page Ref [bookmark name]>
```

Bookmark name is the bookmark for which the power field finds its location in the document and inserts its page number.

Sequence field   The SEQ power field is designed to sequentially number figures, tables, or any other items you need to list in a document. Insert the SEQ field as part of the figure or table caption, and Ami inserts the figure or table number in the caption. If you remove figures or tables and their accompanying SEQ power fields, Ami automatically renumbers the remaining figures or tables (when you choose Update All). If you have more than one figure or table on a page, Ami reads them in order first from left to right, and then from top to bottom.

The SEQ power field uses the following syntax:

```
< SEQ expression [ = [expression]] [ – [expression]] [ + [expression]] [%
format option] >
```

Expression can be the name of a variable or a mathematical operation, such as Figure Figure + 1.

The format option controls the appearance of the power field's result. Table 15-3 shows the format options available for the SEQ field.

Index power field   The INDEX power field marks an entry for inclusion in the index, just as you do when you select Mark Text Index Entry from the Edit menu. You can specify a primary entry, a secondary entry, a "See also" reference, and whether to display a page number in the index.

Table 15-3. Formatting Options for the SEQ Power Field

Code	Format Type	Format
N1	Number	1, 2, 3
N2	Number	I, II, III
N3	Number	i, ii, iii
N4	Number	A, B, C
N5	Number	a, b, c

You can use the Mark Text Index Entry from the Edit menu to locate and edit any index entries you create using the INDEX power field.

The INDEX power field uses the following syntax:

<Index "Primary" [#] ["Secondary"] ["other"]>

Primary is the primary heading for the index entry. The pound sign [#] tells Ami to include the page number with the index entry. Secondary is the secondary heading to appear under the primary heading. Other is any type of miscellaneous reference, such as See or See Also.

Imported contents power fields

Power fields that import contents let you create sections of a document by importing its content from bookmarks, files, and variables. The BOOKMARK power field imports the content of a bookmark into the document. The INCLUDE power field imports the content of an Ami Pro or ASCII file into the current document. These power fields let you compile a document from existing text— you don't need to retype blocks of text that exist in other locations. The SET power field defines a variable and assigns it a value that you can insert repeatedly in the document. You can combine these power fields with decision-making power fields to import different bookmarks or files, depending on the client to whom you are sending a letter or whether a figure is above or below its explanatory text.

Bookmark power field The BOOKMARK power field inserts the content of the bookmark as the power field's result. You can choose from bookmarks in the current file only. To do so, simply highlight the BOOKMARK power field from the Insert Power Field dialog box. Ami displays the available bookmarks in the Options box. Highlight the bookmark you need and select OK. The BOOKMARK power can return a result only if you selected text and then named the bookmark. If you choose a bookmark you created to mark a position, but you do not highlight any text when you add the bookmark, the power field returns nothing.

If you need to insert the contents of a bookmark in another file, use the INCLUDE power field.

The BOOKMARK power field uses the following syntax:

<Bookmark name>

Include power field   The INCLUDE power field inserts the content of an Ami Pro, or an ASCII file into the current document. The INCLUDE power field also can insert a bookmark from the another document into the current document.

The INCLUDE power field uses the following syntax:

<Include "filename[!bookmark]" [%P] [%W]>

Filename is the Ami Pro or ASCII file you want to insert into the current document. Bookmark is the bookmark from the Ami Pro file you specified that you want to insert into the current document. The %P option imports an ASCII file with carriage return/line feeds at the end of every paragraph, rather than the default setting of carriage return/line feeds at the end of every line. The %W option imports an ASCII file using the 8-bit PC-ASCII format, rather than using the 7-bit default format.

SET power field   The SET power field defines a global variable that you can insert into several locations in the document. You also can insert the SET power field into other documents and it will return the same value. The SET power field is useful for inserting text across documents and changing it at one time by redefining the variable. In doing so, Ami changes the text at each occurrence of the power field in every document.

The SET power field uses the following syntax:

<Set global variable expression>

Global variable is the name of the global variable you are defining. Expression is the value you assign to the global variable. The expression can be a number, a mathematical operation, or a string. If you assign a string to the variable, enclose it in quotation marks.

Comparison fields

Comparison fields evaluate a condition, and perform one action if the condition is true or another if the condition is false. Comparison fields are helpful in deciding what text or graphics to insert into the document depending on the result of the condition. For example, if you are sending a letter to a client, the comparison field can ask for the name of the client, look up the client's correct address and phone number, and insert them into the letter.

IF field   The IF field evaluates a condition and chooses an action to perform based on the condition's result: if the condition is true, the power field performs one action; if the condition is false, the power field performs a different action. You can combine the IF field with mathematical calculations or comparisons (ZIP < 30305), or other power fields (DECIDE("Include the toll-free number?")).

The IF power field uses the following syntax:

<If condition expression [ElseIf condition expression] [Else expression] EndIF>

Condition is a statement the power field must evaluate to determine if it is true.

Expression is the action the power field performs if the condition is true.

ElseIf is the second condition and resulting action.

Else is the action the power field performs if the condition is not true.

EndIF tells Ami that the If power field has ended.

Defined field The DEFINED field is designed to be used with the IF field to determine whether the bookmark, global variable, or merge field specified in the power field is defined. If the bookmark, global variable, or merge field, is defined, the IF statement performs one action; if the bookmark, global variable, or merge field is not defined, the IF statement performs a different action.

The DEFINED power field uses the following syntax:

Defined expression

Expression is a bookmark, global variable, or merge field.

Merge power fields

Ami lets you use Merge power fields to customize the merge process of combining standard and data documents. The Merge power fields can help you to create form letters, telephone lists, rosters, address labels, and many other types of documents. The Merge power fields are useful only for merging two documents. If you try to use them for other purposes, they do not work.

Merge Record field The MERGEREC field returns the number of the current merge record. MERGEREC does not count any records skipped during a merge because they did not meet conditions in the Merge Conditions dialog box or because of the SKIP power field. You can combine the MERGEREC power field with decision-making power fields to perform actions when the MERGEREC value reaches a certain amount.

The MERGEREC power field is useful for determining which records were printed, for identifying records that don't print properly, or if you need the record number for particular records on the standard document. For example, if you were creating a marketing mailing and you had a response code on the letter, the code could be a standard document filename and the addressee's record number in that file. A sample response code could be: GA0992.SAM-2. The "GA0992.SAM" is the standard document filename (including the state and date of the mailing), and the number two is the result of the MERGEREC power field. Figures 15-3 and 15-4 show a standard document containing the MERGEREC power field and one of the merged documents containing the MERGEREC result.

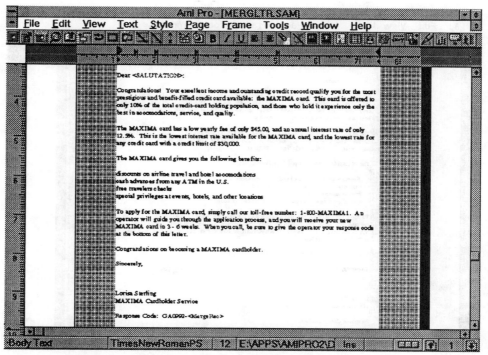

15-3 The MERGEREC power field in a standard document.

The MERGEREC power field uses the following syntax:

<MergeRec>

Next Record field Normally Ami places only one record on a page when it prints merged records. Using the NEXTREC power field, you can place multiple records on one page of the standard document. Technically, the NEXTREC advances to the next field during a merge. The result, however, is that you can print more than one record on a page.

To create a standard document using the NEXTREC power field, insert the merge fields on the second line of the document, adding the NEXTREC power field at the end of the line. Copy the line and paste it as many times as it takes to fill the page, or stop pasting when you reach the number of records you want to appear on the page. When you perform the merge, Ami places the records on the page.

The NEXTREC would be useful if you had a data document containing a list of conference speakers to which you were sending confirmation letters, but you also needed to create a list of speakers by their session time. You need all the records to appear on one page, rather than one record per page. Figure 15-5 shows a standard document containing the NEXTREC power field. The power field appears at the end of each line except for the last.

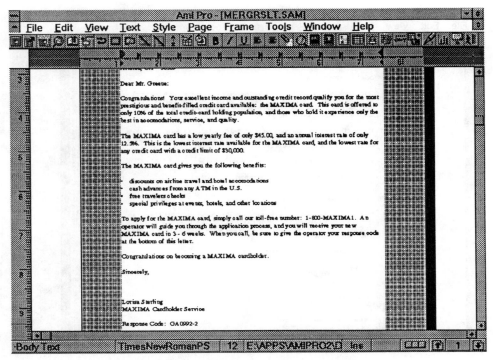

15-4 The result of the MERGEREC power field in the merged document.

The NEXTREC power field uses the following syntax:

<NextRec>

Skip Record field The SKIP power field skips the record you specify and continues to the next record. The SKIP power field is really the equivalent of specifying conditions in the Merge Conditions dialog box. You can combine SKIP with IF to create conditions even more powerful than those you can create using the Merge Conditions dialog box. Using SKIP and IF, you can create conditions based on the current record number identified by the MERGEREC field. Such conditions cannot be created using the Merge Conditions dialog box, because you are limited to conditions based on the values in the merge fields.

The SKIP power field uses the following syntax:

<Skip>

The SKIP and IF power fields also let you create target mailings that you can save in a standard document. Each time you want to send a mailing to a specific target group, merge the standard document with the data document containing the target audience you need. For example, if your company is offering a new credit card for people with incomes over $25,000, you could use the IF and

15-5 Insert the NEXTREC power field at the end of each record in the data document.

SKIP power fields to send the mailings to those people only. The power field you would create would look like this:

```
<If Income<25000 Skip Else NextRec EndIF>
```

Figure 15-6 shows a standard document that uses the SKIP and IF power fields.

Tip 15-9: Using the INCLUDE power field during a merge   One of the most powerful ways to create a standard document is to use the INCLUDE and IF power fields. The IF power field evaluates the contents of each merge record, and the INCLUDE power field decides what contents to insert into the standard document depending on the merge record's contents. For example, let's say your company is offering two new credit cards: one card is for those whose incomes are below $25,000; the other card is for those whose incomes are over $25,000. You can use the IF and INCLUDE power fields to insert the appropriate credit card offer depending on each merge record's income level.

Document Information power fields

Ami keeps track of document statistics such as the number of words, pages, edits, and other information in the Doc Info box. You can insert these statistics into a document using the Insert Doc Info Field command from the Edit menu, but you also can insert document statistics using power fields. Using document information power fields, you can insert the document's description, the date it was lasted edited, the file size in kilobytes, the number of characters, the number of edits, the number of pages, and the number of words in the current document.

Creation Date field   The CREATEDATE field inserts the date or time the document was created. You choose whether to display the date or time by adding a switch to the power field. The date and time the document was created appears in the Doc Info dialog box.

The CREATEDATE field uses the following syntax:

<Create Date [% date/time option]>

Description power field   The DESCRIPTION power field inserts the document description you entered in the Doc Info dialog box. The DESCRIPTION power field produces the same result as if you chose to insert the Document Description from the Insert Doc Info Field dialog box.

The DESCRIPTION power field uses the following syntax:

<Description>

Edit Date field   The EDITDATE field inserts the date or time the document was last edited. You choose whether to display the date or time by adding a switch to the power field. The date and time the document was created appears in the Doc Info dialog box.

The EditDate field uses the following syntax:

<EditDate [% date/time option]>

File size power field   The FILESIZE power field inserts the size of the current file, in kilobytes. The value FILESIZE returns reflect the document on the screen, not the document on disk. To update the FILESIZE field, you must select Update All from the Edit menu, print the document with the Update fields option selected, or generate a table of contents or index.

The FILESIZE power field uses the following syntax:

<FileSize>

Number of Characters power field   The NUMCHARS power field returns the number of characters in the current document, as of the last update in the Doc Info dialog box, or as of the last update of the power fields in the document. To update the NUMCHARS field, you must select Update All from the Edit menu, print the document with the Update fields option selected, or generate a table of contents or index.

The NUMCHARS power field uses the following syntax:

<NumChar>

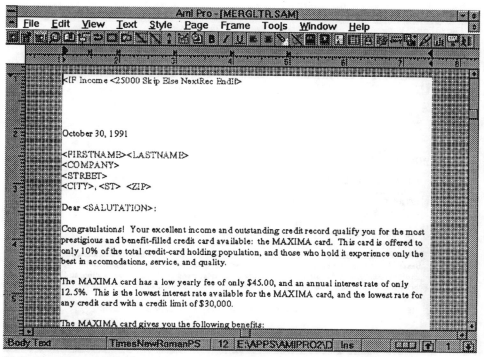

15-6 The SKIP and IF field used to created merged conditions in a standard document.

Number of Edits power field The NUMEDIT power field returns the number of times the document has been opened, changed, and saved. If you insert the Version number of the documentation in your document, it probably is not the same as the NUMEDIT field. The document has gone through numerous edits before it is ready to be published, and the number of times it has been edited isn't directly correlated with a document's Version number. You have either two choices if you need to insert the Version number in the document: you can type it manually, which is probably the easiest, or you can save the document using Save As from the File menu. If you use Save As, you must save the document, using Save from the File menu, as many times as needed to match the NUMEDITS value with the Version number.

The NUMEDITS power field uses the following syntax:

    \<NumEdits>

Number of Pages power field The NUMPAGES power field returns the document's page count. The NUMPAGES field is useful for creating page numbers that read "Page 1 of 35." You can create the page number and leading text using the Page Numbering command on the Page menu. To create the "of 35" portion, insert the cursor after the page number in the footer, type "of," and insert the NUMPAGES power field.

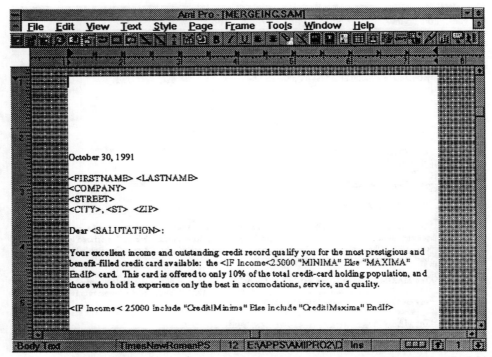

15-7 The INCLUDE field, along with the IF field, used to create a condition in a standard document.

To update the NUMPAGES field, you must select Update All from the Edit menu, print the document with the Update fields option selected, or generate a table of contents or index.

The NUMPAGES power field uses the following syntax:

<NumPages>

The Number of Words power field The NUMWORDS field returns the document's word count as of the last update of the Doc Info dialog box, or as of the last update of the power fields in the document.

To update the NUMWORDS field, you must select Update All from the Edit menu, print the document with the Update fields option selected, or generate a table of contents or index.

The NUMWORDS power field uses the following syntax:

<NumWords>

Total Editing Time field The EDITTIME field inserts the total number of minutes the document has been open, as of the last update of the Doc Info dialog box or as of the last update of the power fields in the document. The Total Editing Time information appears in the Doc Info dialog box.

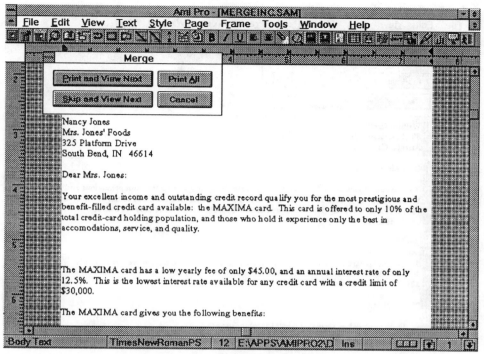

15-8 One result of the INCLUDE power field in a merged document.

To update the EDITTIME field, you must select Update All from the Edit menu, print the document with the Update fields option selected, or generate a table of contents or index.

The EDITTIME field uses the following syntax:

```
<EditTime>
```

Execution power fields   Execution power fiels execute another application or a macro within the current document. Ami has three execution power fields. The CALL power field executes a macro at the power field's position in the document. The EXEC power field executes an application from the current document. The VOID power field carries out an action, but does not return a result in the document.

CALL power field   The CALL power field executes a macro at the power field's position in the document. The macro runs when you update the field. The macro acts exactly as if you had pressed it's shortcut keys or selected Macros Playback from the Tools menu.

The CALL power field uses the following syntax:

```
<Call "filename[!function](p1,..)">
```

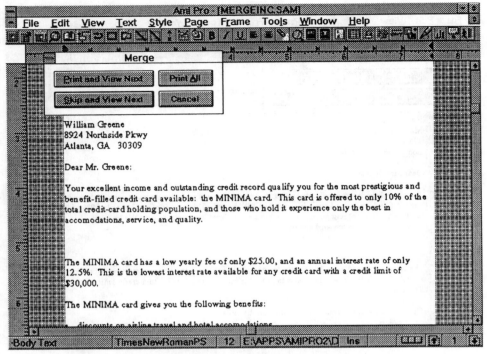

15-9 Another result of the INCLUDE power field in a merged document.

Filename is the name of the macro file, including its extension of .SMM, you want the power field to execute. Function is the macro function on which you want the macro to execute. P1 is the parameter for the macro function.

EXEC power field The EXEC power field starts another application from the current document. Using the EXEC power field, you can start another application, retrieve a file automatically, and display the application on the screen, all from the current document.

The EXEC power field uses the following syntax:

```
<Exec ("program[, parameters]" [,show])>
```

Program is the name of the application file you want to execute. Parameters are any DOS command line options you want to include for the application, such a filename to retrieve. Show maximizes the application you specified.

VOID power field The VOID power field neither executes a macro nor an application. However, you can use it with both the CALL and EXEC power fields to do so, but without inserting a value into the document. The VOID power field is useful for executing a macro or another application without affecting the current document. You could use the VOID power field, along with the EXEC power field, to display Window's calculator inside the current document. You can figure some quick calculations without creating a table or affecting your document's content. However, you are not limited to using VOID with only EXEC or CALC. You can use it with any other power field or macro function that performs a task for which you do not want to insert a value in the document.

The VOID power field uses the following syntax:

<Void expression>

Expression is the action you want the power field to perform.

Printer power field   The PRINTESCAPE power fields sends escape codes to your printer. The printer formats the document according to the codes you include in the power field, but Ami does not format the document's appearance to match the printed page. The codes you send to your printer differ according to the printer type you use. When you use the PRINTESCAPE power field, you must precede printer codes with the escape character, either in ASCII or hex format. The ASCII escape characters are [027], and the Hex escape characters are [Ox1b].

The PRINTESCAPE power field uses the following syntax:

<PrintEscape "[escape code]text">

Escape code is the ASCII or Hex code that represents an escape code. Text is the printer codes you send to your printer.

Formatting and manipulating power fields

Ami has a full range of power fields that format and manipulate text and numbers. These power fields are designed to work with the values that other power fields return. The FORMATNUM$ power field formats numbers, the LCASE and UCASE power fields change the capitalization of text, the LEFT$, RIGHT$, MID$ power fields retrieve a specified number of characters from a block of text or numbers, the LEN power field displays a specified number of characters in a block of text, and the STRCAT$ power field positions multiple blocks of text next to each other.

Format Number power field   The FORMATNUM$ power field changes the appearance of a number using the format you specify. You can specify a prefix, a suffix, and the number of decimals to display in the number.

The FORMATNUM$ power field uses the following syntax:

<FormatNum$(prefix, suffix, decimals, expression)>

Prefix is the text or symbol you want to display before the number. Enclose the prefix in quotation marks. Suffix is the text or symbol you want to display after the number. Enclose the suffix in quotation marks. Decimals is the number of decimal places you want to display in the number. Expression is the number you want to format.

Lowercase power field   The LCASE$ power field changes the string you specify to lowercase.

The LCASE$ power field uses the following syntax:

`<LCase$(expression)>`

Expression is the string you want to change to lowercase.

Left power field   The LEFT$ power field retrieves a specified number of characters from the left side of a string.

The LEFT$ power field uses the following syntax:

`<Left$(expression, count)>`

Expression is the text from which the power field retrieves characters. Count is the number of characters the power field retrieves.

Length power field   The LEN power field displays the number of characters in a string.

The LEN power field uses the following syntax:

`<Len(expression)>`

Expression is the string for which the power field counts its characters.

Middle power field   The MID$ power field retrieves a specified number of characters, starting with the character you specify, from a string or number.

The MID$ power field uses the following syntax:

`<Mid$expression, start, count)>`

Expression is the string from which the power field retrieves characters.

Start is the character in the string with which the power field begins retrieving.

Count is the number of characters the power field retrieves.

Right power field   The RIGHT$ power field retrieves a specified number of characters from the right side of a string.

The RIGHT$ power field uses the following syntax:

`<Right$(expression, count)>`

Expression is the string from which the power field retrieves characters.

Count is the number of characters the power field retrieves.

String Concatenate power field   The STRCAT$ power field joins blocks of text together and inserts the new block in the current document at the power field's location.

The STRCAT$ power field uses the following syntax:

`<StrCat$(expression, expression[,expression])>`

Expression is the string you want to join with the others.

String Field power field   The STRFIELD$ power field retrieves a field from a delimited string.

The STRFIELD$ power field uses the following syntax:

<StrField$(expression, fieldnum, separator)>

Expression is the string from which the power field retrieves a field.
Fieldnum is the number of the field the power field retrieves.
Separator is the delimiter the string uses to separate its fields.

Uppercase power field   The UCASE$ power field changes the string you specify to lowercase.

The UCASE$ power field uses the following syntax:

UCase$(expression)

Expression is the string the power field changes to uppercase.

Questions & Answers

Q: How are power fields different from macros?

A: Power fields and macros are similar, in that they both automate a process. Power fields, however, are codes that you insert into a document, while macros are programming statements or keystrokes you save in a file. Power fields are usually limited to the document in which they are located, while macros are not limited to playing back or recording in any file. Generally, power fields automate the document creation process by inserting text and graphics at power field's locations. Power fields also can call other macros, execute other applications, and use macro functions in their syntax. Macros capture keystrokes and use the Macro Command Language, but they cannot use power fields.

Summary

Power fields automate many of the tasks you already do everyday. Power fields are similar to macros, in that they both automate tasks; however, a power field's result appears at the location of the power field in the document. You also can control when a power field updates its results, instead of requiring you to execute the power field each time as you would with a macro. You insert a power field using the Edit Power Fieldcommand. If you have power fields that you use frequently, you can create a custom power field to automatically insert the power field and its instructions. You also can choose to view power fields' results or their syntax in the document.

16
CHAPTER

Importing and exporting files

Ami is a relatively new entry into the word processing market, so you probably chose it after using another word processor. If you created a large number of documents using your old word processor, you certainly don't want to recreate those same documents in Ami. Instead, you can import your old word processing files into Ami and continue working on them just as you would on Ami documents.

Ami also lets you export its own documents to other popular word processing file formats. Ami's import and export features are invaluable to companies that don't standardize their employees' word processors: accounting might use one application, personnel uses another, and legal uses yet another. If people among these departments need to share files, it could be a nightmare. Importing and exporting files is also valuable for team projects involving different companies that use various products. Sharing different word processing files is only a minor inconvenience using Ami.

Importing text files

You will need to tweak your file once you import it into Ami, even if both word processors support the same features (columns, tables, styles, etc.). Rarely does an imported file appear magically in its original format, with all tables, columns, and graphics in place. For example, if you import a WordPerfect document containing columns, Ami converts column breaks into page breaks. If you export an Ami document containing a table to WordPerfect, it doesn't recognize any connected cells in your table. So, you must do some formatting to your imported files, but it is usually a better solution than recreating them altogether.

Ami can import files using the following formats:

- Advance Write
- Ami Pro documents and macros
- ASCII (8 and 7 bit files)
- DCA/FFT
- DCA/RFT
- DIF
- DisplayWrite 4 and 5
- E-Mail
- Executive MemoMaker
- Lotus Manuscript 2 and 2.1
- Microsoft Word 4, 5, and 5.5
- Microsoft Word for Windows
- MultiMate 3.3 and MultiMate Advantage II
- Navy DIF
- PeachText 2.11
- Rich Text Format
- Samna Word
- SmartWare 1
- SuperCalc 3 and 4
- Windows Write
- WordPerfect 4.1 through 5.1
- WordStar 3.3 through 5.24
- WordStar 2000 1 and 3.

To import a file into Ami, follow these steps:

1. If you need to import the file into an Ami Pro document, place your cursor at the position where you need to place the imported document.
2. Select Open from the File menu.
3. Select the file format you need to import from the File Type list box.
4. Specify the correct drive and directory Ami should use to search for the file using the Directory and Drive list boxes.
5. Select the filename from the Filename list box.

6. Select Open to place the imported file into its own window. Select Insert to place the file into the current Ami document.

7. If Ami displays an Import Options dialog box, select the options you need and select OK.

Tip 24-1: Ami remembers the last directory you searched When you import a text file, Ami remembers the last directory in which you searched for that file type. The first time you open a file from another application, Ami remembers the directory you pointed to, so you don't have to specify it each time you open a file from that application.

Tip 24-2: Importing a file without specifying the file type Ami can recognize many popular file formats without requiring you to select a file type. You simply select the filename and select Open or Insert, and Ami automatically imports the file correctly. You can perform this "quick import" for DCA/RFT, DIF, DisplayWrite, Manuscript, Microsoft Word and Word for Windows, Rich Text Format, Samna Word, SmartWare, Windows Write, and WordPerfect 5.x files.

Tip 24-3: Ami does not list imported text files in Document Description dialog box Ami lists the imported graphics files and DDE links in the document description box, but it does not keep track of any imported text files. You can do so yourself, however, by creating a user-defined field in the Document Description dialog box. You also could list the text files you imported using a note.

Tip 24-4: Converting several word processing files to Ami Pro format If you used another word processor before changing to Ami Pro 2.24, you probably have an entire library of documents you need to import into Ami. Each time, you would need to specify the file format, the filename, the file's drive and path, and any import options, such as Ignoring Styles or Keeping Styles. An easier way is to use the CONVERT macro that lets you specify multiple files to convert to Ami Pro format.

Attributes Ami imports

Ami recognizes the major formatting attributes you included in your document. To what degree Ami can convert those attributes into its own depends on the file format you are importing. In some cases, your document might look the same, but you will not able to format it in the same way. Attributes you saved in paragraph styles in your old word processor might import into Ami as text attributes. The following list includes the attributes Ami can recognize in your imported file:

- paragraph alignment
- capitalization
- date codes

- fonts
- footnotes
- frames containing text
- headers and footers
- international characters
- line spacing
- page layout attributes
- page numbers
- paragraph styles
- hard spaces and hyphens
- text attributes.

The items in this list that Ami includes in its own styles, such as alignment, fonts, and line spacing, are converted to text attributes in imported files. Ami can recognize more or less attributes, depending on the file format you are importing. Refer to the following tips for information on the file format you use.

Importing ASCII Files

When you select the ASCII file type from the File Open dialog box, Ami displays an ASCII button. Select that button to display the following ASCII file import options:

CR/LF at lines   When you save a file to ASCII format, some word processors insert a paragraph return at the end of each line, and two paragraph returns at the end of each paragraph. The extra paragraph returns are not necessary, so select CR/LF at lines to insert paragraph returns at the end of a paragraph only.

CR/LF at paragraph ends only   Select CR/LF at paragraph end only if your file contains a paragraph return at the end of each paragraph. If you plan to edit the WIN.INI or AMIPRO.INI files, use this option.

Keep Style Names   The advantage to importing an ASCII file is that you can use the Keep Style Names option to assign styles to paragraphs as your import the file. The style names must use the same capitalization and spacing as they do in the Styles Box, they must appear as the first text in the paragraph, and they must be surrounded by brackets. If you have been using PageMaker or Ventura Publisher, the files already have style names in front of them. Change @Chapter Title = to Chapter Title and your files import into Ami.

Convert levels into styles   Select Convert levels into styles to change all levels in a structured document, or all the global settings from an unstructured document into paragraph styles. Ami imports fonts, text attributes, alignment, indention, tabs, outlines, leading text, and line spacing as paragraph styles.

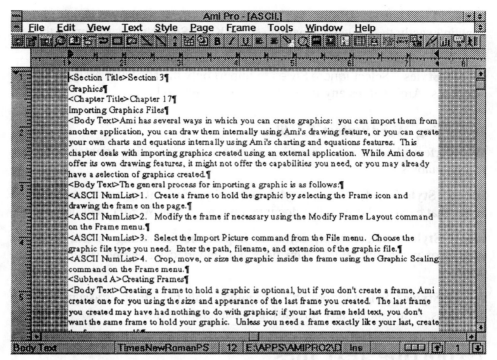

16-1 An ASCII file using style names before each paragraph. Ami Pro reads the style names and assigns the styles accordingly.

Apply levels Select Apply levels to import the formatting as a text attributes instead of paragraph styles.

Importing Microsoft Word, Word for Windows, or Rich Text format files

Ami can import page layout attributes, graphics, and tables in the document. Ami does not import annotations, bookmarks, fields, formulas, indexes, left and right lines, line numbers, side-by-side text, tables of contents, and vertical tabs.

You can select from the following options Ami displays in the Import Options dialog box:

Convert Styles If you are importing into an Ami document and it does not contain the same style names as the file you are importing, select Convert Styles to create those styles. Ami does not import lines around boxes, shading, or colors. If your Footnote style is named something else, Ami does not import footnote numbers.

Apply Styles Select Apply Styles to import the formatting as text attributes instead of paragraph styles. Ami does not import paragraph spacing or line settings.

Keep Style Names   If your current document and the file you are importing contain exactly the same style names, select Keep Style Names to import the text and assign the attributes in the Ami styles.

Ignore Styles   Select Ignore Styles to import only the attributes assigned as text attributes. Ami ignores any formatting in paragraph styles.

Importing WordPerfect 5.1 files

WordPerfect files keep their page layout formatting, including orientation, graphics, and tables.

Import Style Sheet   Creates styles and assigns formatting attributes for those styles that exist in the Ami Pro document but not in the WordPerfect document.

Apply Styles   Select Apply Styles to import the formatting as text attributes instead of paragraph styles. Ami does not imported paragraph spacing or line settings.

Ignore Styles   Select Ignore Styles to import only the attributes assigned as text attributes. Ami ignores any formatting in paragraph styles.

Exporting text files

Ami can export its own documents to the following file formats:

- Advance Write
- ASCII (8 and 7 bit files)
- DCA/FFT
- DCA/RFT
- DisplayWrite 4 and 5
- E-Mail
- Enable 1.5 - 2.5
- Executive MemoMaker
- Microsoft Word 4, 5, 5.1, and 5.5
- Microsoft Word for Windows
- MultiMate 3.3 and MultiMate Advantage II
- Navy DIF
- PeachText (up to 2.11)
- Rich Text Format
- Samna Word
- Windows Write

- WordPerfect 4.1 through 5.1
- WordStar 3.3 through 5.24
- WordStar 2000 1 and 3.

To export a text file, use these steps:

1. Open the document you need to export and make sure it is in the active window.
2. Select Save As from the File menu.
3. Select the file format you need to export from the File Type list box.
4. Specify the correct drive and directory Ami should use to search for the file using the Directory and Drive list boxes.
5. Enter a filename from the Filename list box.
6. Select OK.
7. If Ami displays an Export Options dialog box, select the options you need and select OK.

Attributes Ami exports

To what degree Ami can export formatting attributes in your document depends on the file format to which you are exporting. In some cases, your document might look the same, but you will not able to format it in the same way. Attributes you saved in paragraph styles in Ami might export to the new format as text attributes. The following list includes the attributes Ami can recognize in your imported file:

- paragraph alignment
- capitalization
- date codes
- fonts
- footnotes
- frames containing text
- normal headers and footers
- international characters
- line spacing
- page layout attributes
- page numbers
- paragraph styles
- hard spaces and hyphens
- text attributes.

Exporting ASCII files

When you select the ASCII file type from the File Save As dialog box, Ami displays an ASCII button. Select that button to display the following ASCII file export options:

CR/LF at lines   Select CR/LF at lines to insert a paragraph return at the end of each line and two paragraph returns at the end of each paragraph.

CR/LF at paragraph ends only   Select CR/LF at paragraph end to insert a paragraph return at the end of each paragraph.

Keep Style Names   Select Keep Style Names to insert the name of the style, surrounded by angle brackets, in front of each paragraph. If you import this file to an application that recognizes the style names, and the style sheet contains the same style names, the application can format the text in your document as you import it.

7 bit ASCII   Seven bit ASCII exports only the characters available on your keyboard. It does not import any international characters or ANSI characters.

8 bit ASCII   Eight bit ASCII exports most international characters, and Greek and math symbols. However, Ami converts these special characters to ANSI equivalents. If an ANSI equivalent does not exist, Ami usually replaces the character with an underscore or plus sign.

8 bit ANSI   Eight bit ANSI exports all ANSI characters you created within another Windows application.

Exporting DCA/RFT or DisplayWrite 4 files

The following export options are available when you export to DCA/RFT or DisplayWrite 4 files:

Apply Styles   Select Apply Styles to export all formatting as text attributes instead of paragraph styles.

Ignore Styles   Select Ignore Styles to export only those attributes assigned as text attributes. Ami ignores any formatting in paragraph styles.

Exporting E-Mail files

E-Mail files can use only the fixed-pitch Courier font, so Ami exports its documents using a line 79 characters wide. Before you export your document, change its font to Courier or another font that uses as close to a 79-character line as possible. Otherwise, the lines in your document will not wrap properly. Also, Ami changes all tabs, indentions, and alignment to spaces, based on a fixed pitch 10 characters per inch font.

When you select the E-Mail format, Ami exports to the 8-bit ASCII file format, inserting paragraph returns at the end of each line and paragraph.

Exporting Microsoft Word files

The following export options are available when you export to Microsoft Word files (this format is different than the Microsoft Word for Windows format):

Convert Styles   Select Convert Styles to export paragraph style names and formatting exported to the Microsoft Word file. Ami cannot export initial caps, first line bold, hanging indents, indents from both sides, add-in spacing, text tightness, line spacing, line length, line color, left page layout settings, page size and orientation, or line settings.

Keep Style Names   If your Ami document and the style sheet you are exporting to contain exactly the same style names, select Keep Style Names to export the text and assign the styles to the text.

Ignore Styles   Select Ignore Styles to export only the attributes assigned as text attributes. Ami ignores any formatting in paragraph styles.

Exporting MultiMate files

Ami adds a page break following each 64,000 characters in files you export to the MultiMate format.

Exporting Navy DIF files

Headers and footers exported to a Navy DIF file contain up to 150 characters of regular text. Ami cannot export special characters to Navy DIF files.

Exporting Microsoft Word for Windows or Rich Text Format files

Ami exports the document and its associated style sheet, so that all styles appear in the Word for Windows style sheet or the style sheet in a Windows application supporting Rich Text Format. The paragraphs automatically use the correct style in the exported document.

Ami cannot export initial caps, first line bold, handing indents, add-in spacing, line spacing, line length, line color, page break after, keep with previous paragraph, bullets, leading numbers, line above and line below, left page layout settings, page size and orientation, page numbering starting on a page other than the first, or line settings.

Ami does export some table attributes, but it does not export formulas, connected cells, line styles, line colors, or absolute table height/absolute cell width.

Exporting Windows Write files

Ami exports line spacing to single, line and a half, or double spacing, whichever is closest to your setting.

Exporting WordPerfect files

The following export options are available when you export to WordPerfect files:

Convert Styles   Select Convert Styles to export paragraph style names and formatting exported to the WordPerfect file. Ami cannot export add-in spacing, or keep with paragraph settings. The spacing for options under Special effects changes to a single space.

Apply Styles   Select Apply Styles to export all formatting as text attributes instead of paragraph styles.

Ignore Styles   Select Ignore Styles to export only the attributes assigned as text attributes. Ami ignores any formatting in paragraph styles.

You can export tables to both WordPerfect 5.24 and 5.1. Tables exported to 5.24 format convert to text, with columns separated by tabs, rows separated by returns, and returns within cells change to spaces. Tables exported to 5.1 format retain some attributes, but do not retain formulas, connected cells, protected cells, line styles, line colors, absolute table height, or absolute cell width.

Tip 24-5: Exporting tables   When you export an Ami Pro table, it loses much of its formatting, requiring you to change the table extensively inside the other application. A better way to export a table is to copy the table text using Edit Copy and save the text in an Ami Pro file using Save As from the File menu. Select File Save As to export the text file. Select the file format you need and select OK. When you load the exported file into your other application, create a table then cut and paste the text into the table. This process requires several steps, but it is much less confusing than trying to correct your exported table with some attributes but without others.

Importing worksheet and database files

Ami can import the following worksheet and database file formats:

- dBASE III, III +, IV
- DIF
- Enable 1.5 through 2.5 (exported to 1-2-3 format)
- Excel 3.24 and below
- Lotus 1-2-3 1, 1A, 2, 2.01, 3.24, 3.1
- Lotus Symphony 1, 1.01, 1.1

- Paradox 3.5 and below
- SuperCalc 3,4.

Importing files from your spreadsheet or database application requires a few extra steps than loading a text file. First, you must decide how you want the spreadsheet/database information to appear in your file. Do you need the information to be part of the text or separated from the body of the document in a table? Do you need to import the entire file or specific ranges or fields?

Ami offers several options for importing a spreadsheet/database file. Ami offers three locations in your document into which you import your file: at the cursor's location in the document, in an empty frame, or in an empty table.

If you import data into a frame, Ami creates a table containing the correct number of rows and columns for your file. Because a frame cannot span more than one page, however, your data can't either. If you import data into a table, Ami does not create additional rows or columns. Ami imports only as much of the file as will fit into the table. Also, when Ami imports data into a table, it has a habit of displaying the "Internal Error" message and kicking you out.

Tip 24-6: Importing all of your data into a table   The best way to import data into a table is more reliable than the direct methods; although it is complicated. Place your cursor inside your document, but not in a frame or a table. Use the File Open command to import the data into the document. Cut the text using the Edit Cut command. Create a table using the Tools Table command that approximates the file's size. You don't have to be exact about the number of rows and columns you need, because Ami will add them if you need them. Place your cursor in the first cell of the table and select Edit Paste. Ami inserts the data into table without losing any of it.

To import a spreadsheet or database file, follow these steps:

1. To place the file at the cursor's location, insert the cursor in the document at the position where you need the spreadsheet/database file. To place the file in an empty frame, select the Frame icon and draw a frame. Double-click on the frame to place the text cursor inside the frame. To place the file in an empty table, place the cursor inside the first cell into which you want to import data.

2. Select Open from the File menu.

3. Select the file format you need to import from the File Type list box.

4. Specify the correct drive and directory Ami should use to search for the file using the Directory and Drive list boxes.

5. Select the filename from the Filename list box and select the Insert button. Ami lets you choose to import the entire file, a selected range (worksheet files), or selected fields (database files). If you select a spreadsheet range, you can specify the range name or the cell address as you would in that

particular spreadsheet. For example, in 1-2-3 a range is specified with two dots (A1.H20), but in Excel a range is specified using a colon (A1:H20). If you need only certain fields of your database file, type those field names separated by a space or a comma. For example, if you needed only three fields from your file, specify them in one of the following formats:

- L_Name,F_Name, Company
- L_Name F_Name Company.

Tip 2-47: Ami does not list imported data files in Document Description dialog box   Ami lists the imported graphics files and DDE links in the Document Description dialog box, but it does not keep track of any imported data files. You can do so yourself, however, by creating a user-defined field in the Document Description dialog box. You also could list the data files you imported using a note.

Attributes Ami recognizes

When you import a worksheet, Ami imports the formulas' results, not the formulas. Ami recognizes different attributes depending on the file format you are importing. Ami recognizes alignment and numeric formatting in some formats, but only numeric formatting in others.

Importing DIF files

Ami imports DIF files using row formats and changes exponential numbers to normal numbers. Because DIF does not support international characters, they do not import into Ami.

Importing Excel files

Ami recognizes alignments, text attributes, and numeric formats. Ami does not import Excel fonts. Ami recognizes the same attributes whether you import an Excel file or paste it into the document.

You can select from the following options Ami displays in the Import Options dialog box:

Convert styles   If your Excel file contains paragraph styles that your Ami document doesn't, you can select Convert styles. Ami creates those styles and automatically assigns them to the data.

Apply styles   If you want to import all formatting as text attributes instead of paragraph styles. Ami does not assign those style to paragraphs. You must assign the styles to paragraphs once Ami imports the data.

Keep style names   If your current document and the file you are importing contain exactly the same style names, select Keep style names to import the data and assign the attributes in the Ami styles.

Ignore styles   Select Ignore Styles to import only the attributes assigned as text attributes. Ami ignores any formatting in paragraph styles.

Importing Lotus 1-2-3 3.24 and 3.1 files

When you import 1-2-3 release 3.24 and 3.1 files, Ami displays additional options for importing your data:

Entire file   Select Entire file to import all the worksheets in the file. Ami places the worksheets in alphabetical order.

Active worksheet   Select Active worksheet to import only the worksheet containing the cursor.

Range   You can specify a range address with or without a worksheet identifier (A1.F20 or A:A1.A:F20), the worksheet identifier to import the entire worksheet, or a range name.

   If your worksheet uses an .FM3 file, Ami displays additional options for importing your data:

Convert styles   If your Excel file contains paragraph styles that your Ami document doesn't, you can select Convert styles. Ami creates those styles and automatically assigns them to the data.

Apply styles   If you want to import all formatting as text attributes instead of paragraph styles. Ami does not assign those style to paragraphs. You must assign the styles to paragraphs once Ami imports the data.

Keep style names   If your current document and the file you are importing contain exactly the same style names, select Keep style names to import the data and assign the attributes in the Ami styles.

Ignore styles   Select Ignore styles. to import only the attributes assigned as text attributes. Ami ignores any formatting in paragraph styles.

Importing SuperCalc files

Ami recognizes all numeric formats, user-defined date formats, alignment, and international characters. Ami does not recognize repeating text preceded by a quote, control text, or the Formula Display option. Ami changes large and small numbers to scientific format, and parentheses around negative numbers to regular parentheses.

Questions & Answers

Q: I tried to import a spreadsheet into a table in my document, but Ami opened a new window instead.

A: Make sure you select Insert instead of Open from the File Open dialog box. To insert a file into the current document, you must use the Insert button.

Summary

Ami lets you import and export files using a wide variety of formats. In some cases, Ami does not require you to specify a file type; you can simply highlight the filename and select OK, and Ami recognizes the file type automatically. The ability to import and export files is essential if you are working on a team project in which the players do not use the same word processor, if your company does not have a standardized word processor, or if you have a large number of files in another format that you do not want to recreate.

Part 3
Graphics

17
CHAPTER

Importing graphics files

Ami has several ways in which you can create graphics: you can import them from another application, you can draw them internally using Ami's drawing feature, or you can create your own charts and equations internally using Ami's charting and equations features. This chapter deals with importing graphics created with an external application. Ami offers its own drawing features, but it might not offer the capabilities you need, or you might already have a selection of graphics created.

The general process for importing a graphic is as follows:

1. Create a frame to hold the graphic by selecting theFrame icon and drawing the frame on the page.

2. Modify the frame if necessary using the Modify Frame Layout command on the Frame menu.

3. Select the Import Picture command from the File menu. Choose the graphic file type you need. Enter the path, filename, and extension of the graphic file.

4. Crop, move, or size the graphic inside the frame using the Graphic Scaling command on the Frame menu.

Creating frames

Creating a frame to hold a graphic is optional, but if you don't create a frame, Ami creates one for you using the size and appearance of the last frame you created. The last frame you created might have had nothing to do with graphics;

if your last frame held text, you don't want the same frame to hold your graphic. Unless you need a frame exactly like your last one, create the frame yourself.

Tip 17-1: Create a frame manually with the icon You can create a frame using the Create Frame command from the Frame menu, but you must choose between creating the frame manually and creating it by specifying its size and position. When you select the Frame icon, Ami automatically lets you create the frame manually, which is much easier and you can see your results immediately. However, if your frame must be an exact dimension, such as .25″ × .25″, use the command from the Frame menu.

Tip 17-2: Position frames using the Styles Box You can align frames by enlarging the Styles Box and using it as a guide. Display the Styles Box and enlarge it so that it spans either horizontally or vertically on the page. Create the frames and place them against the Styles Box.

Modifying a frame

The first frame you create is rarely the exact one you need to hold your graphic. Ami's default frame has the following attributes:

- an inside margin of .10″ on all sides
- text wraps around the frame
- stays in same position even if surrounding text moves
- transparent
- round corners
- thin border between the margin and outside of frame
- drop shadow.

You can change these attributes using the Modify Frame Layout command on the Frame menu. Once you select the command, Ami displays the Modify Frame Layout dialog box, displayed in Figure 17-1.

The Modify Frame Layout dialog box is similar to the Modify Page Layout and Modify Style dialog boxes; Ami divides them into right and left sections. The left section of the Modify Frame Layout dialog box lists the attributes you can modify. The right section displays the options available for the frame layout attribute you chose in the left section. So, if you select the Type option button in the left section of the dialog box, the right section displays Type options.

The style attributes discussed in this chapter are: type, size & position, and lines & shadows. Columns and tabs are the same as the attributes discussed in chapter 7.

Tip 17-3: Work from top to bottom Each frame layout attribute's dialog box contains a rich assortment of options, but it can be confusing to know where to

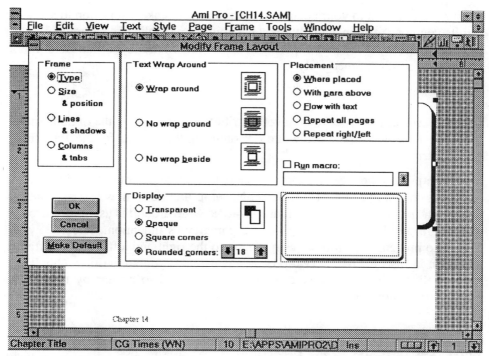

17-1 The Modify Frame Layout dialog box controls the frame's size, placement, and appearance.

start. One method is to start from the top of the dialog box and work your way down. Begin by selecting the Type style attribute and making all the selections you need in the dialog box, then select the Size & position style attribute and do the same. Continue until you have selected all the style attributes. You probably don't need to use all the attributes, but working from top to bottom is an efficient method.

Tip 17-4: Use the unit of measurement appropriate for your document In all dialog boxes except those for fonts, breaks, and table formats, you need to specify options in a unit of measurement. Ami uses inches as its default unit of measurement, but for many documents, inches is too large of a unit for practical use. Using fractions of inches to specify a frame size and margin would be frustrating and time-consuming to calculate. You can change the unit of measurement for each attribute by clicking on the inches button. Each time you select the button, a different unit of measurement appears. You can choose from inches, centimeters, picas, or points.

Tip 17-5: Use the dialog box examples as a guide Ami displays an example in each dialog box of the effect your frame layout attribute selections will have on your frame. These examples save you an incredible amount of time, because you don't need to return to your document each time you make a selection to see what results you got. You can actually see what your frame looks like before you return to your document. You can experiment with each frame layout attribute option and see the results immediately.

Type

Once you select the Type frame layout attribute, Ami displays the options shown in Figure 17-2. Discussed below are tips on using the options for the Type frame layout attributes:

Text Wrap Around   Select Wrap around to flow text around all sides of the frame, as shown in Figure 17-3. Select No wrap around to flow text normally as if no frame exists, as shown in Figure 17-4. No wrap around is useful if you place a frame in the document's margins or a paragraph's indention. Select No wrap beside to prevent text from appearing next to the right and left sides of a frame, as shown in Figure 17-5. No wrap beside is useful if you are writing a book or a training manual containing screen captures that need to appear by themselves between two paragraphs.

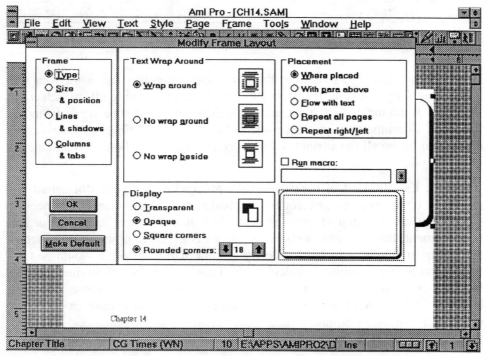

17-2 Type in the Modify Frame Layout dialog box controls the frame's placement, transparency, corners, and text flow.

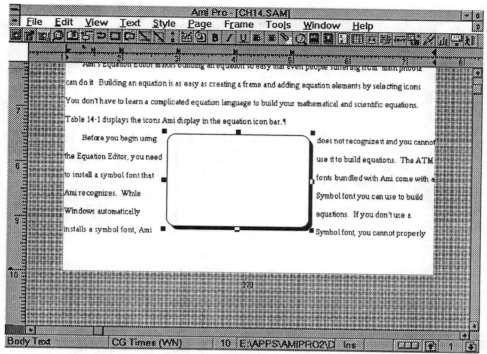

17-3 A frame using the Wrap around option.

Placement Frame placement is also known as frame anchoring, which controls the movement of frames when their surrounding text moves. Select Where placed to keep the frame on the page exactly at the position where you placed it. When the text moves, the frame stays put. Ami uses this frame anchor as the default. Select With para above to keep the frame with the paragraph above it. Ami attaches the frame to the last character of the preceding paragraph. As the text moves, Ami moves the frame, keeping it below the paragraph at all times. When you select With para above in the Modify Frame Layout dialog box, you cannot flow text around the frame—only beside it, or you can turn off text wrap. Select Flow With Text to keep the frame between the text in which you placed it. Ami attaches the frame to the character preceding it. Text anchors are useful for frames that contain graphics that need to remain next to or inside a block of text, not below it. When you select Flow With Text, Ami automatically selects Wrap Around as the text flow type. No other text wrap selection is available.

Choose Repeat all pages to display the frame in the same location on every page. Choose Repeat Right/Left to display the frame on only right pages or only left pages. If you create the frame on a left page and you choose this option, the frame appears only on left pages. To display a frame on all right pages, you must create the frame on a right page and select this option.

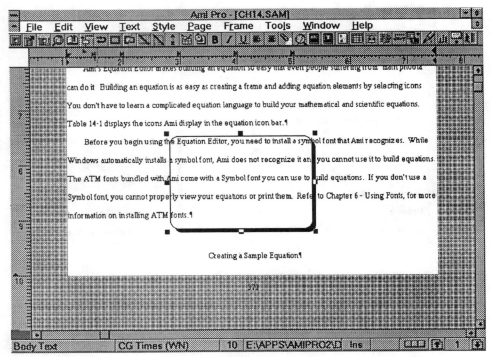

17-4 A Frame using the No wrap around option.

Display Select Transparent to see through the frame. Ami uses Transparent as the default. Select Opaque to hide whatever is behind the frame. Select Square corners to create a frame that is a rectangle or square. Ami uses Round corners as the default.

Run macro Select this check box to attach a macro to the frame. Type the macro filename in the text box. You must also turn on the Run frame macros option in the Doc Info dialog box to activate any frame macros. Refer to chapter 13 for more information on creating and running frame macros.

Tip 17-6: Repeating and anchor placement options are not exclusive You can select both an anchor option and a repeating frame option. For example, if you need a frame to appear on every page of the document and its surrounding text to act as if no frame exists, you would select Repeat all pages and No wrap around. The three anchor options, Where placed, With para above, and Flow with text are exclusive; you cannot select more than one, because they are the two repeating frame options.

Tip 17-7: Creating frames with Flow With Text anchors If you try to create a frame within an existing paragraph using a Flow With Text anchor, Ami moves the frame to the end of the paragraph. Don't wait until you type the entire paragraph

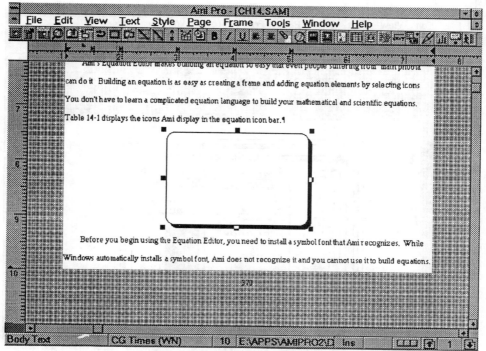

17-5 A frame using the No wrap beside option.

to place a frame inside it. Type the next to appear in front of the frame, create it, place the cursor after the frame and continue typing.

Tip 17-8: Moving frames using Flow With Text anchors Technically you cannot move a frame using a Flow With Text anchor. However, you can use a technique that achieves the same result, by moving the text instead. For example, say you have a frame at the beginning of a paragraph that needs to be in the middle of the first line instead. Highlight the text that should appear in front of the frame and cut it. Place the cursor in front of the frame and paste the text. Although you didn't move the frame, you achieved the same result moving the text instead.

Tip 17-9: Using With Para Above anchors in a multiple column page layout If you are using a page <figure> layout with multiple columns, such as a newsletter layout, and you need to use the With para above frame placement option, you cannot create the frame wider than the current column. If you need a frame to span several columns, you must use the Where placed anchor.

Tip 17-10: Hiding portions of a frame If you use more than one frame for your graphic, you can place frames on top of each other and use the Bring to Front and Send to Back commands to hide a portion of a graphic. Figure 17-6 shows two frames: the bottom frame contains the monitor graphic, and the top frame

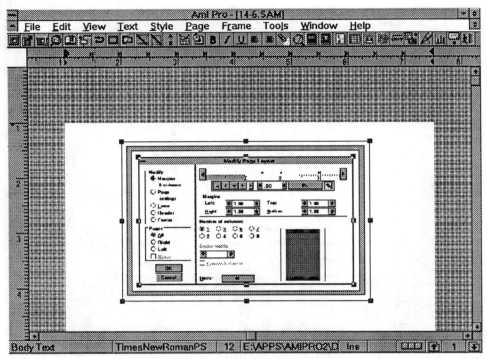

17-6 The monitor graphic is in two frames: the monitor graphic is in one frame and the screen files is in another frame.

holds a screen capture. While you are creating a graphic using multiple frames, use the commands on the Frame menu to rearrange frames' order and hide portions of their graphics.

Tip 17-11: Limitations for layering frames You can place one frame over another to create special effects with your graphics. However, to do so, each frame must use the Where Placed placement option. Ami does not let you layer frames using the Flow With Text or With Para Above options. Subsequently, if you have graphics in layered frames, you cannot make both frames flow with their surrounding text.

Tip 17-12: Selecting multiple or layered frames If you have several frames or frames on top of each other that you need to select, you need to use special key combinations to do so. To select multiple frames, hold down the Shift key while you select each frame. Ami selects all of the frames you select. To select a frame underneath another, hold down the Ctrl key while you select the frame. To select multiple layered frames, hold down both the Ctrl and the Shift keys while you select the frames.

Tip 17-13: Adding captions to a frame If you create frames to hold illustrations or screen captures for a book or a training manual, you probably need to create accompanying captions to explain the frame's content. Ami doesn't offer a caption feature, but you can create your own. Create a frame directly underneath the one holding the graphic. Then double-select the frame and add the text that makes up the caption. Click outside the frame and select both frames by holding down the Shift key and selecting each frame. Group the frames using the Group command from the Frame menu.

Ami keeps both frames together, so if one moves, so does the other. To make this process even easier, create a macro to repeat this procedure and assign it to a custom icon. For more information on macros and custom icons, refer to chapter 13.

Tip 17-17: Sequentially numbering figure or table text outside of a frame   If you need to number the figures or illustrations in your document, you can do so using the Seq power field. Create a custom Seq power field for each type of illustration you need to number. For example, if you have tables and figures and you number them separately, you would create one power field for tables and another for figures. To add figure or table numbers to text outside of a frame, you can use the Seq power field. To do so, follow these steps:

1. Place your cursor at the position in the text where you need to insert the number.

2. Select Power Fields from the Edit menu. Select Insert.

3. Select the Seq Power Field from the list box. Place your cursor in the text box, press the spacebar, and type a word that represents your figures or tables. You will use this same word each time you need to number figures or tables in this document. Figure 17-7 displays a sample Seq power field used to sequentially number figures. Select OK to return to the document. Ami inserts the number one at the cursor position.

4. Repeat steps one through three for each figure appearing in the document. Ami sequentially numbers each power field.

5. If you move, delete, or add frames, select the Update All command from Edit Power Fields to update the numbering scheme you created.

To further automate this process, you could create a macro that inserts a style with preceding text, such as "Figure 2-," and then inserts the power field. Assigning the macro to a custom icon would enable you to insert figure text and number figures with one click of the mouse.

Tip 17-15: Sequentially numbering figure or table text inside a frame   If your figure or table numbers are part of a caption inside a frame, you can sequentially number your illustrations using a different procedure than the one in Tip 17-14. You created one power field and inserted it at each illustration. Here you need to create three power fields for the first frame holding a graphic in a document, and two power fields for subsequent frames holding graphics. Figure 17-8

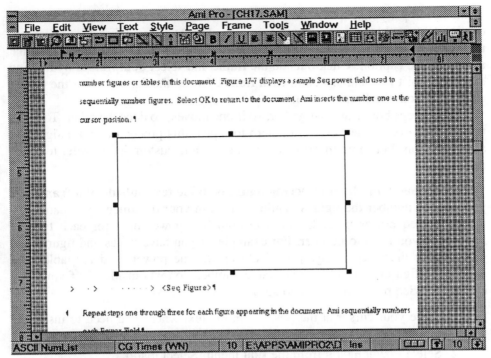

17-7 The Seq power field used to sequentially number a frame.

shows the final power fields for the first and second frames in a document. Creating a numbering scheme inside a frame is more detailed than doing so for regular text in a document, because power fields restart numbering for each frame. You can override that limitation by creating a variable that counts the number of illustrations you have and inserts that number in a frame. To add figure or table numbers to text inside a frame, you can use the Set Power Field. To do so, follow these steps:

1. Place your cursor in the first frame in which you need to insert a number.

2. Select Power Fields from the Edit menu. Select Insert. The first power field you create defines the variable that counts your illustrations.

3. Select the Set Power Field from the list box. Place your cursor in the text box, press the spacebar, and type a word that represents your figures or tables. This word is a variable that represents your figures or tables; you will use this same word each time you need to number them in this document. Press the spacebar and type zero. Select OK to return to the document. You don't see anything yet because you haven't told Ami to display a number. Press the End key to move behind the power field.

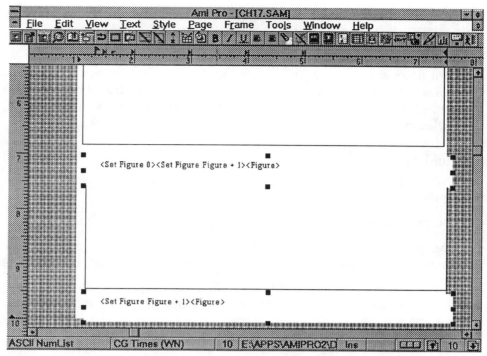

17-8 The Set power field used to sequentially number frames using captions inside another frame.

4. Repeat steps 2 and 3, but this time you need to create a count for your figure or tables. After you choose Set, press the spacebar, type your variable, and press the spacebar again. Then type your variable again, press the spacebar, type a plus sign, press the spacebar, and type the number one (Seq Figure Figure + 1). Select OK to return to the document. Again, Ami doesn't display a number yet. Step five displays the figure or table number. Press the End key to move behind the power field.

5. Display the Power Field dialog box, place your cursor in the text box, and type the variable you defined in step 3 (such as Figure). This tells Ami to display the number in the frame. Select OK. Ami inserts the number in the frame.

6. Move to the next frame and repeat steps one through five, omitting step three. Set the variable equal to zero in the first frame only.

7. If you move, delete, or add frames, select the Update All command from Edit Power Fields to update the numbering scheme you created.

To further automate this process, you could create a macro that inserts a style with preceding text such as "Table 7-," and then inserts the power field.

Assigning the macro to a custom icon would let you insert figure text and number figures with one click of the mouse.

Tip 17-16: Making text flow on at an angle   You can force text to appear as though it flows at an angle by placing frames in a stair pattern next to the text. Create a stair pattern of frames, each the same height as one line of text, starting at the margin or column edge. Text flows around the frames forming an angle pattern, as shown in Figure 17-9.

Size and position

Once you select the Size & position frame layout attribute, Ami displays the options shown in Figure 17-10:

Size   Change the original size of the frame by modifying its width and height.

Position on Page   Change the frame's original location on the page by specifying a new placement down from the top margin and in from the left margin.

Margins   Ami automatically assigns a .10″ inside margin for all sides of the frame, but you can change each margin by specifying a new one in the appropriate text box.

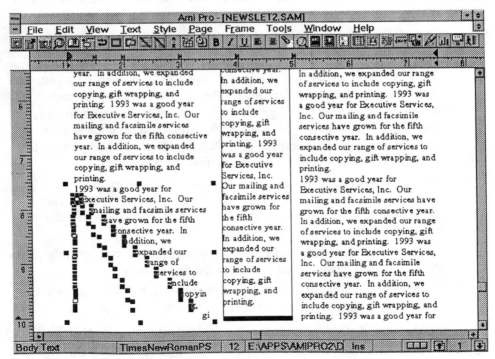

17-9   Text wrapping at an angle using frames placed in a stair-step pattern.

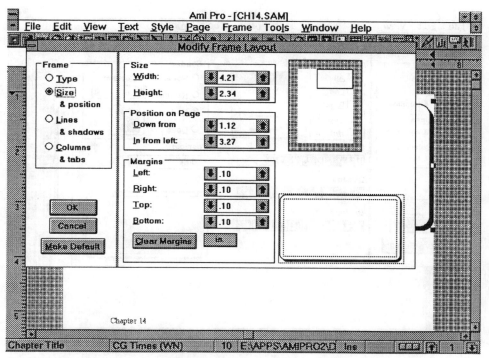

17-10 Size & position in the Modify Frame Layout dialog box controls the frame's size and placement on the page.

Clear Margins   Select this button to remove all inside margins from the frame.

Tip 17-17: Ami displays two example boxes in the Size & Position dialog box   The top example box represents the frame's size and position, and the bottom example box represents the frame's inside margins. Use the appropriate example box to preview your frame's appearance.

Lines and shadows

Once you select the Lines & shadows frame layout attribute, Ami displays the options shown in Figure 17-11. Discussed below are tips on using the options for the Lines & shadows frame layout attributes:

Lines   You can choose to display a line on all sides of the frame, on the left, right, top, or bottom side, or a combination of any sides. To remove a line, unselect that option.

Style   Select the line style to display around the frame by choosing a line from the Style list box.

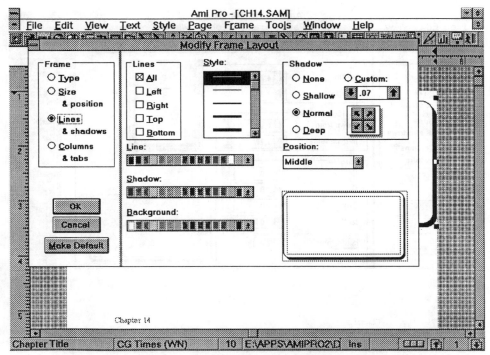

17-11 Lines & shadows in the Modify Frame Layout dialog box controls the frames borders, drop shadow, and background.

Position   Control the placement of the line relative to the frame's edge and its margins. Select from Inside, Close to Inside, Middle, Close to Outside, and Outside.

Shadow   Shadow boxes have become quite popular since DTP made them so easy to create, but use them sparingly. Select the direction in which to display the shadow by choosing the appropriate arrow button. Choose the size of the shadow by selecting from Shallow, Normal, Deep and Custom. If you choose Custom, enter a shadow amount in the text box.

Colors   You can display the frame's lines, shadow, and background in color. Select the color from the appropriate list box. If the color you need isn't displayed, select the down arrow, and Ami displays additional colors. If you need to create a custom color, double-select the color closest to the one you need, and Ami lets you create a custom color.

Tip 17-18: Making a new default frame   Ami's default frame might not be appropriate for your purposes. If you place screens in the frame, and you need square corners rather than rounded ones, you would need to change the frame each time you create one. An easier way is to create a frame, make the modifications you need, and make that frame the default. To do so, select the Make

Default button in the left section of the Modify Frame Layout dialog box. Ami remembers the frame's modifications and creates an identical frame the next time you create one.

Tip 17-19: Placing frames in the margin Ami lets you place a frame in the margin just as you can place one in the usable portion of the page. You could place a frame in the margin to serve as a tab for locating a specific chapter. If you use the frame in all of your documents, save the style sheet using the With contents option. Make sure the frame does not appear in the unprintable zone for your printer. Few printers can print to the very edge of the page, so refer to your printer manual to make sure your frame doesn't appear in the unprintable zone.

Tip 17-20: Using frames as bullets Ami has a limited selection of bullets, but you can create your own bullets using frames. Simply draw or import a graphic you would like as a bullet into a frame and place the frame in front of the paragraph. Attach the frame using a text anchor by selecting the Flow with text option in the Modify Frame Layout dialog box. Indent the entire paragraph so that it appears to the left of the frame.

Loading graphics into frames

Once you create a frame and modify it to your satisfaction, you can load a graphic into the frame. You can load a graphic using one of several methods:

- importing a graphic from an external application
- pasting a graphic from another Window's application
- linking or embedding a graphic from another Window's application supporting DDE or OLE.

Importing graphics

Importing graphics gives you the most control and stability in loading graphics into a frame. Once you import a graphic, Ami doesn't save the graphic as part of the document, but it does remember where the graphic is in your hard disk. The next time you open the document, Ami looks to the same graphics file and displays the result in the frame. If the file changed, Ami displays the updated version in the frame.

To import a graphic, however, the external application must be able to save the graphic in a file format Ami Pro can read. Such formats include:

- Ami Draw (SDW)
- Ami Equations (TeX)
- Computer Graphics Metafiles (CGM)
- DrawPerfect (WPG)

- Encapsulated Postscript (EPS)
- Freelance (DRW)
- Hewlett-Packard Graphics Language (PLT)
- Lotus Graphs (PIC)
- PC Paintbrush (PCX)
- Scanned Images (TIF)
- Windows Bitmap (BMP)
- Windows Metafile (WMF).

To load a graphic from an external application into a frame, use the following steps:

1. Create a frame to hold the graphic. Make any modification necessary using the Modify Frame Layout command on the Frame menu.

2. Select Import Picture from the File menu. Ami displays the Import Picture dialog box as shown in Figure 17-12.

3. Select the graphic file type from the File type list box.

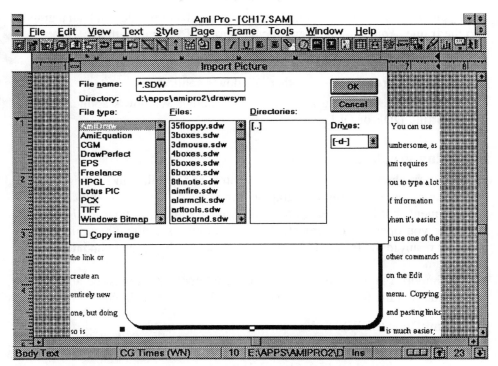

17-12 Importing a picture into a frame using the Import Picture command.

4. To save the graphic as part of the document, select Copy Image. Ami loses all references to the original graphics file but keeps the graphic in the document. If the external graphics file undergoes any changes, Ami will not update a graphic imported using Copy Image.

5. Specify the filename, path and directory. Select OK to return to the document.

Ami displays the graphic in the frame. If the graphic is not the size or position in the frame you need, you can change it.

Tip 17-21: Removing a graphic you loaded by mistake   If you load the wrong graphic by mistake, delete the entire frame. If you delete only the graphic inside the frame, Ami will not let you import another graphic. When you try to select Import Picture from the File menu, it is not available. Simply delete the entire frame, graphic and all. You can then select Import Picture, and Ami creates a frame exactly like the one you just deleted and imports the graphic you choose.

Tip 17-22: Selecting a graphic   How do you select a graphic inside a frame? Double-click on the frame. If you click on the frame, Ami selects the frame. If you click twice on the frame, Ami selects the graphic inside the frame.

Pasting graphics from another windows application

If you use a graphics application running under Windows, you can copy the graphic to the Windows clipboard and paste it into the frame in the Ami document. The only advantage to pasting a graphic rather than importing it is if you do not plan to save the graphic to a file, you can still paste it into the document.

To paste a graphic into a frame, start the Windows graphics application and draw the graphic or retrieve the file containing the graphic. Select the graphic and copy it to the clipboard. Then close the graphics application and start Ami. Select the frame into which you need to paste the graphic and select Paste from the Edit menu. Ami pastes the graphic into the frame.

Linking graphics from another application supporting DDE or OLE

A third way to paste a graphic into a frame is to create a link between the frame in your document and the external Windows application. The application must support Dynamic Data Exchange (DDE) or Object Linking and Embedding (OLE). You can use DDE or OLE to paste a graphic created in an external Windows application into your Ami document. The advantage of using DDE or OLE to create a graphic is if it changes in the external Windows application, Ami updates the graphic in your document automatically. The disadvantage of using DDE and OLE is that few applications support them.

DDE and OLE are essentially the same, because they both update a graphic in your document as the graphic changes in the external Windows application. DDE and OLE do have three major differences:

- DDE asks your permission to start the application from which you created the original graphic. If you answer no, Ami does not update the graphic in your document to reflect the changes you made in the Windows application.

- OLE starts the Windows application on its own, without your permission, and automatically updates the graphics in your document.

- OLE can link or embed information into an Ami document: a link pastes a graphic from a saved file, while an embed can paste a graphic from an unsaved file. DDE can link a graphic only from a saved file.

Whenever you link or embed data into Ami Pro, whether the graphic comes into Ami as a link or an embed depends on the application from which you are taking the graphic. Ami Pro accepts the graphic in the highest format available. The hierarchy for data formats is as follows: OLE embed, OLE link, DDE link, then Paste.

For example, if you are taking information from an application that supports the OLE embed format, Ami Pro accepts the graphic in that format. However, if the application does not support OLE embeds or OLE links, Ami Pro accepts the graphic as a DDE link. When an application does not support OLE or DDE, Ami Pro accepts the graphic as a regular paste operation.

The general procedure for linking or embedding a graphic to an Ami document is as follows:

1. Open the Windows application and create the graphic.
2. Copy the graphics or graphics data to the Clipboard using Edit Copy.
3. Minimize the application and start Ami.
4. Open the document into which you need to link the graphic.
5. If you are linking a graphic, create a frame to hold the graphic.
6. Link or embed the graphic using one of the following commands:

Paste   Select Paste to accept the graphic in the highest data format available from the external application.

Paste Link   Select Paste Link to link the graphic using the highest link format available: either OLE or DDE link.

Paste Special   Select Paste Special to accept the graphic using the format you specify. You can choose from the following formats:

Picture. Picture pastes the data using the Windows Metafile format. Use this format to paste graphics.

Bitmap and DIB. Bitmap and DIB paste the data using the Windows Bitmap format. Use these formats to paste graphics.

Rich Text Format. Select Rich Text Format to paste text and keep its formatting.

Link. Select Link to create a DDE link.

ObjectLink. Select ObjectLink to create an OLE link.

Native. Select Native to create an OLE embed.

Link Options   Select Link Options to create a link or change existing links.

Using link options

Ami automatically creates a hot DDE or OLE link, meaning that each time you open a document containing a link, Ami will attempt to update it. A warm link updates the information only when you tell it to. Updating a link can be a slow process, so if your document contains more than one, you might want to use a warm links to control when they update. You can use Link Options to change a hot link to a warm link, and vice versa. You also can change the link or create an entirely new one, but doing so is cumbersome, because Ami requires you to type a lot of information when it's easier to use one of the other commands on the Edit menu. Copying and pasting links is much easier; however, if you don't have enough memory to run both applications concurrently, using Link Options is an alternative.

Once you select Link Options, Ami displays the Link Options dialog box. The Links box displays the links in the current document. Each line displays the link number, type, status, application name, path name, and item description for one link.

Update   Select Update to update any outdated or warm links in your document.

Unlink   Select Unlink to delete an old link from your document.

Deactivate   Select Deactivate to convert a hot link to a warm link.

Change Link   Select Change Link to choose a new application, path (topic), and item (graphics or cell range) in a link.

Create Link   Select Create Link to create a new link in the document. Ami displays the Create Link dialog box. Specify the application name, path (Topic), and description (graphics or cell range).

Graphic file types

Ami can import most of the standard graphic file formats, giving you access to graphics created in an external application or in clip art libraries. How well the graphics import into Ami is another matter. Some graphics file formats import perfectly, but others are imported with portions of lines missing, garbled text, and other problems. Graphic file formats come in one of two varieties: object graphics or bitmap graphics.

Bitmap graphics

Bitmap graphics contain a collection of dots that compose a graphic. Bitmap graphics are also known as pixel-based graphics, images, or paint graphics. Bitmap graphics have one advantage over object graphics: they refresh the screen more quickly. However, Ami cannot rotate any bitmap graphics; it can rotate only certain object graphics. The bitmap graphic file formats Ami can import are PCX, TIFF, and BMP.

PC Paintbrush (PCX)   An abundance of clip art is available in PCX format, and most graphic applications can export and import PCX files. The PCX format was developed by ZSoft Corporation for its PC Paintbrush product. The PCX format is a bitmap format, so if you plan to scale the image to a larger size, it will appear to have jagged edges.

Scanned Images (TIFF)   TIFF (Tagged Image File Format) was developed to support scanned images (including gray-scaled images). Similar to PCX files, TIF is a bitmap format, so if you plan to scale your image to a larger size, it will appear to have jagged edges.

Windows bitmap (BMP)   Windows Bitmap files are the bitmap standard format for Windows applications. You can import BMP files to create your own icons, and you can use BMP files to create your own wallpaper in Windows.

Object graphics

Object graphics, also known as vector graphics or line art, contain lines and shapes. Object graphics require less disk space than do bitmap graphics because their lines and shapes do not require as much space as the individual dots of a bitmap. Object graphics have two major advantages over bitmap graphics:

- If you print to a high resolution device, such as a typesetter, diagonal lines in object graphics are smooth, whereas the same lines in bitmap graphics appear jagged.
- If you scale an object to a larger size, the quality is equal to the smaller version, while bitmap graphics' quality deteriorates when you increase the size.

The object graphic file formats Ami can import are Ami Draw, CGM, EPS, HPGL, Lotus PIC, and WMF.

Ami Draw (SDW)   Obviously, this format is the most compatible with Ami because it uses the format when saving its own graphics. You can't use Ami Draw files with most other applications, but all the clip art files supplied with Ami use this file format.

Ami Equations (TeX)   Ami can save any equations you create using the TeX format. Ami also can import any equations created externally and exported using this format.

Computer Graphics Metafiles (CGM)   Normally, the CGM format is one of the most reliable, depending on the application from which you import it. Free-lance, Harvard Graphics, and Arts & Letters all have their own versions of the standard metafile. However, when Ami imports a CGM file, it converts the file to Windows Metafile format, one of the most unreliable file formats available. Ami does have the ability to rotate many imported graphics, but it cannot rotate CGM files. If you have imported CGM files using other word processing or DTP appli-cations, you will not see the same results when you import CGM files into Ami.

When you import a CGM file, Ami displays the dialog box shown in Figure 17-13. You can choose from four options that will affect the appearance of your file.

Ignore Background. Ami ignores any background shading or fill patterns, making the graphic transparent. Ami import any shading or fill patterns in the graphic itself though.

Force Vector Fonts. Converts raster fonts that cannot be scaled, to vector fonts, which can be scaled. Using vector fonts, you have more flexibility as to the font style and size.

Dot Lines. Recognizes dotted lines in your graphic file. Unselect Dot Lines to convert dotted lines to solid lines.

Default Color Table. Maintains the proper colors when you import a Harvard Graphics metafile.

DrawPerfect (WPG)   Ami imports both DrawPerfect files and graphics sup-plied with WordPerfect. Both graphic file types work well with Ami, because their fill patterns, shapes, lines, and colors import satisfactorily.

Encapsulated Postscript (EPS)   EPS is a standardized object graphics format that stores shades and patterns well. However, you can take advantage of this format only if you have a PostScript printer. Otherwise, you cannot print the image or rotate EPS graphics.

Freelance (DRW)   Ami imports files from its sister Lotus application, Free-lance. Because Ami and Freelance are part of the Lotus family, Ami can import Freelance graphics files easily. Fill patterns, shapes, lines, and colors import sat-isfactorily.

Hewlett-Packard Graphics Language (PLT)   The HPGL format was devel-oped for plotters, and therefore does not store any shades or patterns, only out-

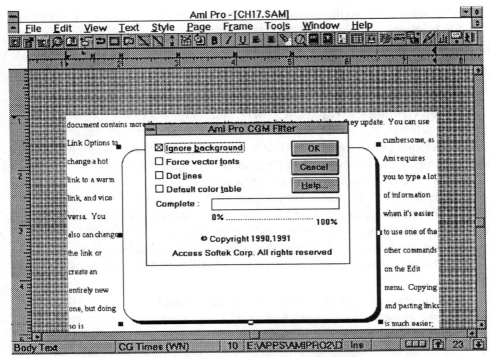

17-13 The CGM filter lets you control the appearance of imported CGM files.

lines. The outlines it stores, however, import well into Ami documents. Ami also converts HPGL files to the Windows Metafile format. HPGL page orientations (portrait and landscape) are opposite those of most laserjet and dot-matrix printers. So, if you need to import an image so that it prints a portrait on the page, create it using landscape orientation in your external application. Ami has the ability to rotate many imported graphics, but it cannot rotate HPGL files.

When you import a HPGL file, Ami displays the dialog box shown in Figure 17-14. You can choose from the three options listed that affect the appearance of your file. Most of the options affect plotters only, but even if you use another type of printer you can use the options to change your graphic.

Paper Size. Select the paper size your printer or plotter uses.

Orientation. The orientation for plotters is opposite that of most other printers: portrait prints horizontally, while landscape prints vertically. Even if you aren't using a plotter, your graphic will import sideways, unless you select landscape. The only other way around importing the graphic sideways is to change the printer orientation of the graphics application you used to create the graphic or rotate the graphic before exporting it.

Pen Colors. If you are not using a plotter, ignore Pen Colors, because your

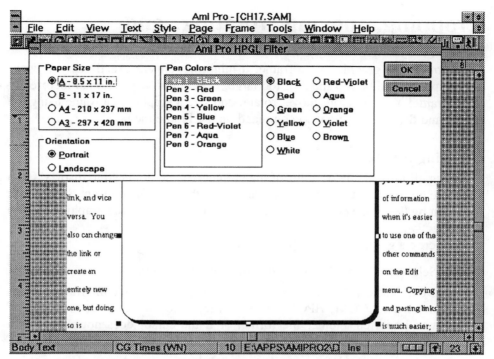

17-14 The HPGL filter lets you control the appearance of imported HPGL files.

printer does not use pens. If you do use a plotter, select the different color pens you plan to use.

Lotus graphs (PIC)   Ami converts Lotus PIC graphs into its own graphic file format of .SDW, so you must have the Draw feature installed to import PIC files. The chart labels and titles on Lotus graphs are somewhat small, but you can hide them by creating your own labels and titles in individual frames, selecting an opaque white background, and placing them over the old labels.

Windows Metafile (WMF)   Windows Metafiles are the object graphic standard format for Windows applications. Ami converts many other object graphic formats to this format when you import them (CGM and HPGL). However, WMF performance is unstable at best; portions of the image might be missing when you import it into Ami. The stability depends on the graphic—some import fine, while others are unacceptable. The files are overbearingly large and difficult to handle and store. Ami has the ability to rotate many imported graphics, but it cannot rotate Windows Metafiles.

Cropping, moving, rotating, and sizing graphics

Once you load a graphic into a frame, it might not appear exactly as you wish. The graphic could be too small or too large, or it might be positioned incorrectly in the frame. You can crop, move, rotate, and size a graphic in a frame using the mouse and the Graphic Scaling command on the Frame menu.

Cropping a graphic

Cropping eliminates any portions of the graphic you do not need to display. Crop a graphic by moving it around in the frame until the portion you want to eliminate is hidden by the frame edge. Usually, you also need to make the graphic larger to crop effectively.

To crop a graphic, follow these steps:

1. Select the frame that holds the graphic you need to crop.
2. Double-select the frame. Ami selects the graphic inside the frame. If you imported a CGM, HPGL, or WMF file, the cursor changes to a hand. If you imported another file format or if the cursor does not change to a hand, select Drawing from the Tools menu and select the Hand tool.
3. Hold down the left mouse button and drag the graphic until the portion you need to hide is eliminated.
4. Click outside the frame. If you imported an Ami Draw graphic, Ami asks if you want to save the changes to the file. If you need to save the changes, save them to a different filename so you can reuse the original Ami Draw graphic.

Tip 17-23: Making an eraser You can erase a small section of a graphic, frame, or text in your document by creating opaque white frames. Select the Frame icon and draw a frame the size you need. Select Modify Frame Layout from the Frame menu or the Modify Frame Layout icon and set Display to Opaque. Select Lines & shadows and unselect any lines around the frame.

Moving the graphic inside the frame

The process for moving a graphic is the same as cropping a graphic, except you do not hide a section of it. Simply double-select the frame holding the graphic and drag it to its new position in the frame. When you double-select an Ami Draw, Lotus PIC, or DrawPerfect graphic, Ami displays the Draw icon bar. Select the Hand tool from the icon bar and use it to move the graphic inside the frame. If you try to move these graphic types using the arrow, Ami resizes the graphic instead of moving it.

Tip 17-24: Moving a graphic between documents   You can cut or copy a frame and its contents from one document to another. Open both files and tile their windows so that you can see both on the screen. Select the frame you need to cut or copy. Cut or copy the frame and move the cursor to the next window. Insert the cursor at the position you need and paste the frame.

Tip 17-25: Cutting and pasting graphics   What happens when you cut or copy an imported graphic into another frame? Your results depend on the type of imported graphic, whether you selected the entire graphic or just a portion of it, and if you display the Draw icon bar. The results of cutting and pasting imported graphics are shown in Table 17-1. Although you cannot select portions of an .EPS, .PCX, .TIF, or .BMP file, you can paste them into a frame when the Draw menu is displayed, and you'll be able to draw over the imported images.

Rotating the graphic

You can rotate any graphic, except for CGM, HPGL, or WMF files. Ami provides two methods of rotating a graphic. You can double-click twice on the frame and drag the graphic to the position you need it. Your other option is to specify a degree of rotation in the Graphics Scaling dialog box.

Rotating the graphic using the first method gives you greater control, because you also can change the graphic's center of rotation.

To rotate a graphic using the mouse, follow these steps:

1. Double select the frame holding the graphic. Double click again to display the center of rotation and rotation arrows at the four corners of the graphic, as shown in Figure 17-15.

2. To rotate the graphic, position the mouse on one of the rotation arrows and drag the graphic until it's in the position where you need it.

3. To change the graphic's center of rotation, drag the black circle until it appears at the location you need. Now when you move the graphic, it rotates around the new center.

Table 17-1.   Pasting Imported Graphics

Cut from Original Frame	Pasted in New Frame	Pasted in New Frame When Draw Menu is Displayed
Entire graphic selected	Can't edit graphic, but can draw over it	Can edit graphic
A portion of the graphic selected	Can't paste into frame	Can edit graphic
Frame selected	Adds another frame	Can't paste into frame

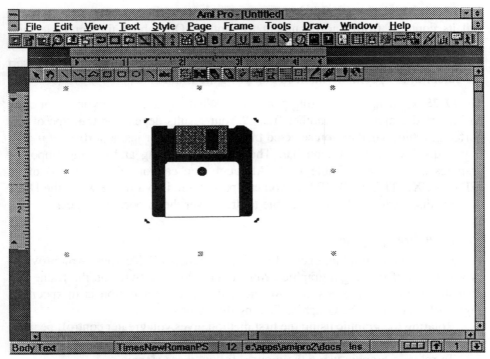

17-15 The arrows let you rotate a graphic; the circle in the center lets you move the graphic's center of rotation to achieve special effects.

4. Click outside the frame.

To rotate a graphic using the Graphic Scaling command, follow these steps:

1. Select the frame holding the graphic you need to rotate.

2. Select Graphic Scaling from the Frame menu.

3. In the Rotate box, enter the degree of rotation you need for the graphic. Select OK to return to the document. Ami rotates the graphic counterclockwise using the degree of rotation you specified.

Sizing the graphic

The mouse is used to crop and move the graphic, but to size the graphic use the Graphic Scaling command on the Frame menu. Ami automatically sizes all graphics so that they fit into the frame. However, that size might not be appropriate for your needs. Also, depending on the file format you used, the graphic might still be too large or too small for the frame.

To size a graphic, select the Graphic Scaling command from the Frame menu. Ami displays the Graphic Scaling dialog box as shown in Figure 17-16.

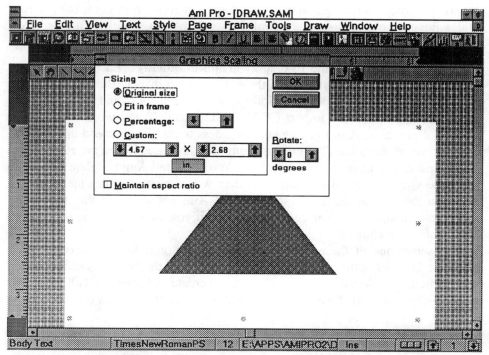

17-16 The Graphics Scaling dialog box lets you change the size of the graphic inside a frame.

Original Size   Select Original Size to convert the graphic to the same size that was specified in its original graphics application. Usually the size of the graphic in its original application has nothing to do with the size you need in your document.

Fit in Frame   Ami scales all graphics to fit inside the frame. If the graphic still appears too large or too small, it could be because Ami maintains the graphic's original height and width proportions, also called the aspect ratio.

Percentage   Enter a percentage in the text box to size the graphic to a percentage of its original size.

Custom   You can enter a customized height and width for a graphic in the appropriate text boxes. You also can change the unit of measurement Ami uses by selecting the inches button until it displays the unit you need.

Maintain Aspect Ratio   Ami automatically keeps the graphic's original proportion so that it doesn't appear distorted. You can turn off the aspect ratio by unselecting the check box.

Rotate   To rotate an image, specify the degree of rotation in the text box. Ami rotates images counterclockwise. Ami does not rotate CGM, HPGL, or WMF files.

Tip 17-26: Create .G00 files to display graphics quickly   Each time you load a graphic into a frame, Ami creates the file it uses to display the graphic on the screen. Ami assigns a .G00 extension to these screen files, and increases it by one for each graphic you import (.G01, .G02, etc.). If you work with a large number of graphics, Ami must be able to access these files to speed up perform-ance. However, each file Ami creates requires disk space. If you are running out of disk space, you have two other options. You could tell Ami to delete the screen files once you close the document. Ami then will recreate the files the next time you open the document. You also could tell Ami not to create the .G00 files. Ami's performance will slow considerably, but if you do not have the disk space, this is your only choice.

   To select one of these options, choose User Setup from the Tools menu. Select the Options button, and then the down arrow on the Graphic Display Speed Options button. Select Save for Fast Display to create and save the .G00 files (this is the quickest option). Select Save While Open to delete the files once you close

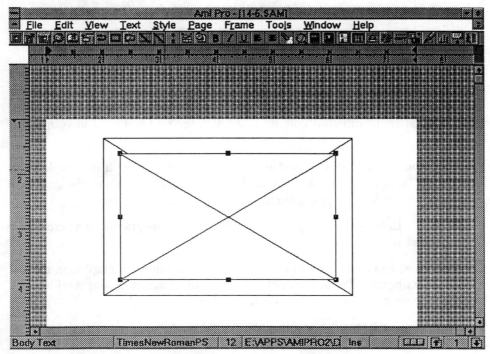

17-17   Ami Pro displays an "X" inside frames with hidden graphics.

the document, or select Conserve Disk Space to prevent Ami from creating .G00 files.

Tip 17-27: Speed up Ami by hiding graphics   Hiding graphics lets Ami perform more quickly, which is crucial if you are working on a long document or if you are using an 286 machine. After you load graphics into your document, hide graphics by deactivating the Pictures option in the View Preferences dialog box. Ami hides all graphics at one time; you do not have the option of hiding individual graphics. Instead of displaying the graphic in the frame, Ami displays an "X" in the frame. Figure 17-17 displays a frame with a hidden graphic. You can continue to hide the pictures while you add captions or draw arrows to the graphic.

Tip 17-28: Temporarily displaying a hidden graphic   Even if you hide the graphics in your document, there are times when you need to see a frame's content. You can temporarily display a hidden graphic by double-clicking on its frame. As long as the cursor is inside the frame, Ami displays its content. Once you place the cursor outside the frame, Ami hides the graphic again.

Questions & Answers

Q: I created a Flow with text frame, but it moved to the end of my paragraph. Now I can't move the frame to its correct position.

A: You can't move a Flow with text frame, but you can achieve the same results by moving the text around it. Cut the text in front of the frame that should appear behind it, and paste the text after the frame.

Summary

Ami's versatile graphics capabilities let you use a wide variety of graphic file formats. Once you create and modify a frame to your liking, you can paste, link, or import a graphics file into the document. You can choose whether to save the graphic as part of the document, or to create a pointer to the graphic, so when the original graphics file changes, the graphic in the Ami Pro document also changes. After you place the graphic in the document, you can crop it, move it inside the frame, rotate it (depending upon the type of the file you imported), and size the graphic inside the frame. These tools are quite useful for people who have a large number of graphics files they created using an external application.

18
CHAPTER

Ami Pro's drawing tools

The Windows interface makes moving among applications easier than doing so with DOS, but Ami makes life even easier by supplying its own Draw application. Once you use the Draw feature, you will never want go back to your external drawing package. The Draw feature truly sets Ami apart from other word processors in its field. No other word processor has such a full-featured drawing ability, and Ami's is so advanced it contains rotating, grouping, and shaping objects—features you expect find in commercial drawing programs.

With version 2.0, Ami has made creating a drawing more accessible. You no longer need to select a frame before you can use the drawing feature. Also, you can select Drawing from the Tools menu no matter what mode you are using. Ami creates a frame using the same size and attributes as the last frame you created, and places the frame at the cursor's position. Once you select the Drawing command, Ami displays the Draw menu and the Draw icon bar at the top of the screen, as shown in Figure 18-1.

Ami has two methods you can use to create a drawing: select Drawing from the Tools menu or double click on an imported object graphic inside a frame. After using either method, Ami displays the Draw menu and the Draw icon bar at the top of the screen. Select one of the eight drawing tool icons from the icon bar. After creating the drawing, select one of the 13 drawing manipulation icons, such as group, snap to, line style, or fill pattern, from the icon bar to edit your drawing.

Tip 18-1: Displaying the Draw menu   Ami displays the Draw menu as long as you have a frame selected. Once you click the mouse outside of the frame, Ami

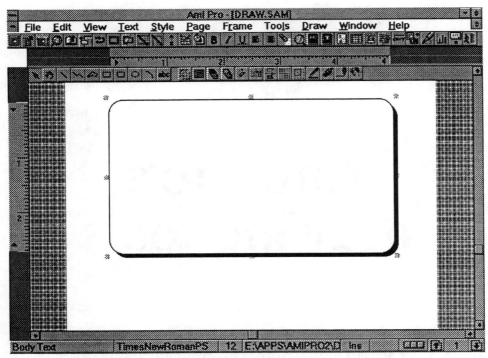

18-1 The Draw icon bar appears only after you select Drawing from the Tools menu.

removes the Draw menu from the menu bar. You can redisplay the menu by double-clicking on any frame containing a drawing.

Tip 18-2: Creating a drawing inside a table   You can create a drawing inside a table's cell, such as your company logo or a drawing to graphically represent steps in a sign or form. Ami does not require you to draw a frame to hold the drawing; instead Ami uses the cell as the boundary for the drawing. To create a drawing inside a table cell, position the cursor inside the cell and select Drawing from the Tools menu. You can display a grid and use all the other drawing commands available when you create a drawing inside a cell.

The Drawing icon bar

Ami's Draw icon bar has two sections: the left section displays the drawing tools available, and the right sections displays the manipulation and editing tasks available. To select a drawing tool or editing feature, select the icon. Table 18-1 lists the icons available in the Draw icon bar and the features they represent. You can hold down the Shift key while using certain drawing tools to create perfectly proportional objects. Table 18-2 lists the drawing tools affected by the Shift key.

Table 18-1.   Draw Icons

Icon	Drawing Tool	Icon	Drawing Tool
	Selection Arrow		Bring to Front
	Hand		Send to Back
	Line		Rotate
	Polyline		Flip Horizontally
	Polygon		Flip Vertically
	Square		Show/Hide Grid
	Rounded Square		Snap To
	Circle/Elipse		Extract Line & Fill
	Arc		Apply Line & Fill
	Text		Line Style
	Select All		Fill Pattern
	Group/Ungroup		

Table 18-2.   Icons Affected by the Shift Key

Icon	Result When Icon Is Used with Shift Key	Icon	Result When Icon Is Used with Shift Key
	Selects multiple objects.		Draws a perfect square.
	Draws a perfectly straight line.		Draws a perfect rounded square.
	Draws a curved polyline.		Draws a perfect circle.
	Draws a curved polygon.		

Using the Draw Object icons

Draw Object icons let you draw individual objects that make up a drawing. To use the icons, you must have a mouse. Ami does not have a keyboard equivalent or menu commands as an alternative to the Draw Object icons.

Selection Arrow   Use the Selection Arrow to pick, size, move, and delete objects in a drawing. To select an object, click on the Selection Arrow and click on the object. To select more than one object, hold down the Shift key while you select each object. To select an object underneath another, hold down the Ctrl key while you click on the object. To select both the object underneath and the object on top, hold down Ctrl and Shift as you click on the objects. To size objects, drag one of the black handles on the edge of the object. To move an object, place the cursor on the center of the object and drag it to its new location. To delete an object, select it and press the Del key.

Hand   Use the Hand tool to move all the objects in a frame or table cell, regardless of whether you have one, all, or no objects selected.

Line   Use the Line tool to draw a straight line. If you hold down the Shift key while you use the Line tool, Ami draws a perfectly straight line. Once you draw the line, you can select different line endings, line colors, and line styles using the Line Style icon or command on the Draw menu.

Polyline   Use the Polyline to draw an object made of several connecting lines, such as a highway on a road map or a triangle. If you hold down the Shift key while you draw a polyline, Ami draws a curved polyline. You also can use the polyline tool to draw a single curved line, which you cannot do using the Line tool. Once you draw the polyline, you can select different line endings, line colors, and line styles using the Line Style icon or command on the Draw menu.

Polygon   Use the Polygon tool to draw an object, made up of several connecting lines, that contains a fill pattern, such as a triangle or an octagon. The Polygon tool is similar to the Polyline tool; however, a polygon is a closed object to which you can add a fill pattern. Polylines cannot use a fill pattern. If you hold down the Shift key while you draw a polygon, Ami draws curved lines to make up the object.

Square   Use the Square tool to draw a rectangle with square corners. If you hold down the Shift key as you use the Square tool, Ami draws a perfect square with four equal sides. After you draw a rectangle or square, you can use the Line Style and Fill Pattern icons or commands from the Draw menu to customize your square.

Rounded Square   Use the Rounded Square tool to draw a rectangle with rounded corners. If you hold down the Shift key as you draw a rounded square, Ami draws a perfect square with four equal sides. After you draw a rectangle or square, you can use the Line Style and Fill Pattern icons or commands from the Draw menu to customize your rounded square.

Circle   Use the Circle tool to draw a circle or an oval. If you hold down the Shift key while you draw a circle, Ami draws a perfectly round circle. After you use the Circle tool, you can use the Line Style and Fill Pattern options to modify the circle.

Arc   Use the Arc tool to draw a curved line with equal amount of curvature on each side (also known as a parabola). Once you draw an arc, you can use the Line Style icon or command from the Draw menu to modify the line. The Arc tool is handy for drawing curved arrows that point to an object or an imported graphic.

Text   Use the Text tool to add text to a drawing. Text you create using the Draw icon or menu is considered to be graphic text, and you can move and size it just as you would any other object in a drawing. However, if you need to change the text's font, color, or specify a specific point size, use the Text menu.

Tip 18-3: Selecting and unselecting a frame and its contents   You can use the mouse and the keyboard to select or unselect a frame and its contents. By clicking the mouse a certain number of times, you can change a frame's selection status. Select the frame once to select the frame. Double-click once on the frame to select the drawing inside the frame. Double-click twice on the frame to rotate the drawing inside the frame. Press Esc to back up the frame's selection status.

Tip 18-4: Adding margins around a drawing   If you chose to wrap text around the frame holding your drawing, Ami might place the text too close to the frame. You always can add more room around the drawing by increasing the margins inside the frame using the Modify Frame Layout command on the Frame menu. Select Size & Position and increase the margins. You also can draw another frame around the one holding your graphic. Select Modify Frame Layout and choose Transparent in the Display box. Eliminate any borders around the frame by selecting Lines & Shadows and unselecting any lines that display around the frame. Select both frames by holding down the Ctrl and Shift keys as you click on the frames, and select Group from the Frame menu.

Tip 18-5: Should you use graphic text or normal text?   If your frame holds only text, which should you use: graphic text or normal text? You have more flexibility positioning text inside the frame when you use graphic text. Because it is an object, you can move it anywhere inside the frame. You also can rotate graphic text but not normal text.

Tip 18-6: Labeling drawings and imported graphics   Illustrations in technical manuals usually need some sort of labeling to identify different parts of a product or tool. You can label drawings or imported graphics by using the Text icon. Draw a frame large enough to hold the text and any lines or arrows you plan to draw to connect the label to the drawing. Select the Line tool and draw a line to point to the part of the illustration the text identifies. Select Line Style and choose the line endings to create an arrow, if needed. Select the Text icon and create the label next to the arrow in the frame. Modify the text face, color, and size using the Text menu. If you need to modify the label's position, press Esc to select the frame and move it to its new location.

Tip 18-7: Creating reverse text   Reverse text (white text on a black background) is useful for drawing attention to an area on a page. To create reverse text, select the Frame icon and draw a frame. Select Modify Frame Layout from the Frame menu and select Lines and Shadows. Select Black for the background color. Double-click inside the frame. Select Font from the Text menu and select White as the font color. Type the text inside the frame. Ami displays white text inside a black frame.

Tip 18-8: Creating a drop cap   The most effective way of creating a drop cap in Ami is to draw a frame and include graphic text inside it. Because you can position graphic text freely inside a frame, you can place text against the top right edge of the frame, which you cannot do using normal text. To create a drop cap, select the Frame icon and draw a frame. Select Modify Frame Layout from the Frame menu. Select Type and choose Wrap Around as the Text Flow Around option and Where Placed as the Placement option (Flow With Text frames wrap only the first line of text around the frame. Subsequent lines appear below the frame). Select Size & position and select the Clear Margins button. Select Lines & shadows and turn off any lines and shadows around the frame. Select Drawing from the Tools menu and select the Text tool. Click inside the frame and type the letter you need to appear as a drop cap. Modify the graphic text's font and point size using the Text menu or the status bar. Choose the Selection Arrow from the Draw icon bar and position the text inside the frame.

Tip 18-9: Creating objects not available from the Draw Tools icons   You cannot create some objects by simply drawing a circle and a square. You will need to create many drawings that are more complex and do not have the simple shapes of the tools on the Draw icons. However, you can still create more complex drawings by changing the shape of objects you draw using the Draw Tools icon. Double-click on an object and Ami displays black handles around the object that represent points. You can alter the object's shape by dragging one of the handles. As you drag the handle, Ami reshapes the object in the direction in which you are dragging. You can change curves to points or points to curves. Figure 18-2 shows complex objects created by modifying the shape of simpler objects.

Tip 18-10: Adding or removing points from a polyline or polygon   You can modify an object's shape, but you might not be able to create the shape you need, because the object has too few or too many points. You can add points to an

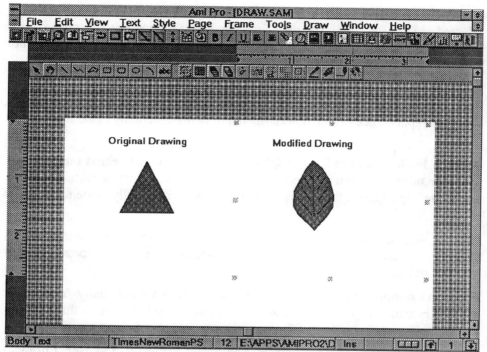

18-2 You can create objects not available on the icon bar by modifying points of a polygon and a polyline.

polyline or polygon by holding down the mouse button and dragging it toward the position where you need a new point. Release the mouse button and Ami adds the point. Now you can reshape the object by dragging the new point. You can remove a point from an object by double-clicking on the point or by clicking on the point with the right mouse button.

Using the Draw Command icons

Draw Command icons let you modify a drawing. The icons represent tasks similar to those available on the Draw menu; however, the icons are usually limited in that you cannot specify the detail available with the menu commands. Using the Draw Command icons, you simply apply the change, such as rotating the drawing or displaying the grid. You cannot specify a degree of rotation or grid spacing like you can using the menu commands.

Select All Select All is a toggle; the first time you select the icon, it selects all the objects in a frame or table cell. The next time you select it, Ami unselects all the objects. Select All differs from the Hand tool in that you can use Select All to select one or more objects and modify them using the Draw Command icons. The Hand tool is good only for moving an entire drawing.

Group   Group also is a toggle; the first time you select it, Ami combines the selected objects into one. The next time you select the icon, it separates the selected object into multiple ones. Group cannot separate an object that was not joined with the Group command.

Bring to Front   Bring to Front displays the selected object in front of others in the frame or table cell. You can use Bring to Front to hide objects partially and to create the appearance of one object when a drawing is actually made up of many objects.

Send to Back   Send to Back displays the selected object behind others in the frame or table cell. You can use Send to Back to hide objects partially and to create the appearance of one object when a drawing is actually made up of many objects.

Rotate   Rotate turns a selected object ten degree clockwise. If you need to rotate an object more than ten degrees, continue clicking on the Draw Command icon until the object is in the correct position.

Flip Horizontally   Flip Horizontally reverses an object horizontally. You cannot use Flip Horizontally on text, because Ami always displays text so that you can read it.

Flip Vertically   Flip Vertically reverses an object vertically. You cannot use Flip Vertically on text, because Ami always displays text so that you can read it.

Show Grid   Show Grid is a toggle; the first time you select the icon it displays a grid in the frame or table cell background. You can align objects manually by placing them against the grid, or you can force objects to align with the grid by selecting the Snap To icon. The next time you select Show Grid, it hides the grid.

Snap To   Snap To is a toggle; the first time you select the icon, it forces the object you draw or move to align along the grid. The next time you select the icon, it lets you place objects freely within the frame or table cell. The grid does not have to be displayed to use Snap To; you can turn on Snap To while the grid is hidden.

Extract Line & Fill   Extract Line & Fill lets you select a line style, a line color, line endings, and a fill pattern style and color in one step. It takes the line style and the fill pattern of a selected object and makes them the current line style and fill pattern. Use Extract Line & Fill to select a line style and fill pattern without having to select each option from the Line Style and Fill Pattern dialog boxes.

Apply Line & Fill   Apply Line & Fill lets you apply the current line style, line color, line endings, and fill pattern style and color to an object in one step. Use Apply Line & Fill to apply a line style and fill pattern without having to select each option from the Line Style and Fill Pattern dialog boxes.

Line Style   Line Style displays the Line Style dialog box, so you can choose a line style, line color, and line endings.

Fill Pattern   Fill Pattern displays the Fill Pattern dialog box so you can choose a fill pattern style and color.

Tip 18-11: Copying and pasting selected objects in a drawing   Duplicating an entire drawing is the same process as copying and pasting a frame: simply select the frame, choose Copy from the Edit menu, and then Paste from the Edit menu. However, duplicating selected objects within a drawing is more complicated because how you paste the objects determines whether Ami lets you edit them. Select the objects inside the frame and choose Copy from the Edit menu. Choose Drawing from the Tools menu and Paste from the Edit menu. Ami creates a new frame and places the objects inside. If you choose Paste without selecting Drawing first, Ami pastes the objects into a frame, but you cannot edit them.

Tip 18-12: Moving drawings between documents   The process of moving drawings between documents is the same as moving frames or text. Follow the instructions in Tip 18-24 to move a drawing between files. If you are moving only selected objects in the drawing, however, be sure to select Drawing from the Tools menu before you paste the objects in the document.

Tip 18-13: Drawing over imported images   Ami lets you edit Ami Draw, Lotus PIC, and DrawPerfect files directly. You can select these graphics and modify them using the Draw icons or menu. You also can draw over Windows Bitmap and Windows Metafiles when you use the Import Drawing command from the File menu. Import Drawing is similar to Import Picture, but you can import only Ami Draw, Windows Bitmap, and Windows Metafiles with Import Drawing. Import Drawing also displays the contents of the files in the example dialog box as you choose a filename from the dialog box. Import Drawing is available when you select Draw from the Tools menu. Ami normally does not let you draw over other imported file types; however, you can do using the following procedure:

1. Import the graphic into a frame.
2. Select the graphic inside the frame.
3. Select Copy from the Edit menu.
4. Delete the frame and draw a new one.
5. Select Draw from the Tools menu.
6. Paste the graphic into the new frame. Ami now lets you use the Draw Objects icons to draw over the graphic or inside the same frame.

Tip 18-14: Hiding portions of a drawing   If you need to prevent a portion of a drawing from appearing on the screen or page, you can hide it by drawing a white square that acts as an eraser. Select the Square icon and create a square the size you need. Select Line Style and choose white as the color. Select Fill Pattern, and choose the solid fill pattern and white for the color. Drag the object over the area of your drawing you need to hide. Select Send to Front so the white object is in front.

Tip 18-18: Creating a custom color for line styles and fill patterns   Ami provides a palette of 18 colors for line style colors and a palette of 120 colors for fill pattern colors. If the color you need isn't displayed, double-click on the color closest to the one you need and Ami displays the Custom Color dialog box as shown in Figure 18-3. The dialog box contains two boxes from which you can customize a color. The large box affects the amount of red, blue, and green in the color, and the hue and saturation. The small box affects the amount of red, blue, and green in the color, and the luminosity. Drag the cursor in each box until Ami displays the color you need in the example box. You also can specify a setting for each element by typing a number in the appropriate text box; however, dragging the cursor is more visual. Select OK to activate that color.

Rotating a drawing

Ami provides several ways for you to rotate a drawing: the Rotate icon, the Rotate command on the Draw menu, or by double-clicking on the drawing. Each method

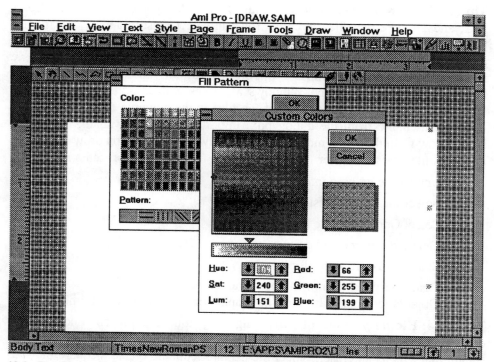

18-3   The Custom Colors dialog box lets you create colors not available from the default color palette.

provides a different level of control over the rotation direction and the degree of rotation. Each time you select the Rotate icon, Ami rotates the drawing ten degrees clockwise. If you need to rotate the object more than ten degrees, continue clicking on the icon until the drawing is rotated properly. When you select the Rotate command from the Draw menu, you can specify how many degrees to rotate the drawing and in what direction: clockwise or counterclockwise. You can achieve the same result by double-clicking on the drawing and dragging one of the rotation arrows in the direction and to the degree of rotation you need. Double-clicking on the drawing also lets you change the center of rotation. Ami normally places the center of rotation in the middle of the drawing, but you can achieve special effects by moving the center and rotating the object with the mouse, as shown in Figure 18-4.

Ami also can rotate Lotus PIC files and DrawPerfect graphics that you import into a frame or table cell. To do so, select the graphic inside the frame, display the Draw menu, and select the Rotate icon or command.

Aligning objects in a drawing

You can use Ami's grid to align existing objects or those you are creating. You can display a grid inside the frame or the table cell and change the grid spacing

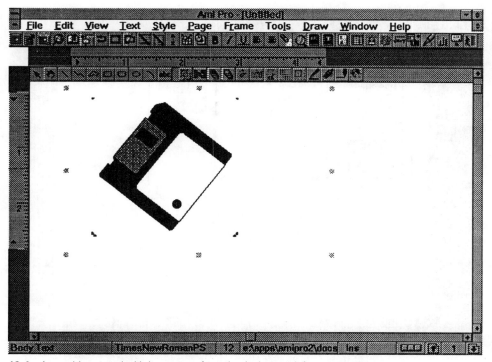

18-4 A graphic rotated with its center of rotation its bottom left corner.

and appearance. To display the grid, select the Show Grid icon, or select Show Grid from the Draw menu. Once you display the grid, you can use it as a guide for placing objects. You also can force Ami to align objects on the grid by clicking on the Snap To icon, or selecting Snap To from the Draw menu. If you find placing objects awkward while Snap To is turned on, turn it off to align objects more freely.

To change the grid spacing and appearance, select Grid Settings from the Draw menu. Ami displays the Grid Settings dialog box as shown in Figure 18-5.

Grid Spacing　Select from Fine, Medium or Coarse for the amount of space between each point on the grid. You also can redefine the measurement Ami uses for each setting by entering a new amount in the text box.

Grid Line　Select Dots at intersect to display dots at each point on the grid. Select Dotted lines to display intersecting lines between each point on the grid.

Make Default　If you want all future frames and table cells containing drawings to use the grid settings you chose, select Make Default. Frames or table cells containing drawings you created previously are not affected.

Tip 18-16: Using lines to align objects　If you find using the grid to be awkward, you can use another method to line up the objects in your drawing. Draw a

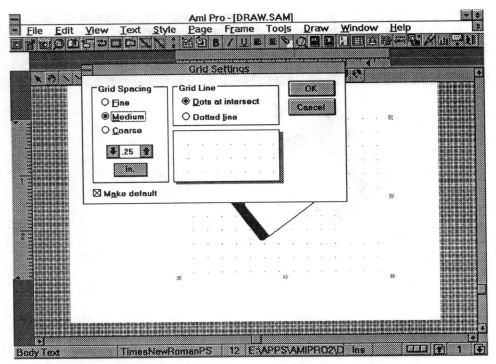

18-5　The Grid Settings dialog box lets you control the grid spacing and appearance.

straight line either horizontally or vertically, depending on the direction in which you need to align objects. As you draw objects, position them in the frame or table cell along the line. Once you position all the objects, delete the line. Your objects line up with each other, and the line you drew no longer exists in the frame or table cell, so it won't print.

Saving a drawing

Ami lets you save any drawings you create so that you can import them later using the Import Drawing or Import Picture commands. You have the option of saving the entire drawing or only selected objects within the drawing. To do either, follow these steps:

1. Select the frame containing the drawing.
2. Select Drawing from the Tools menu.
3. If you are saving only selected objects in the drawing, select those objects.
4. Select Save As Drawing from the File menu. Ami displays the Save As Drawing dialog box, as shown in Figure 18-6.

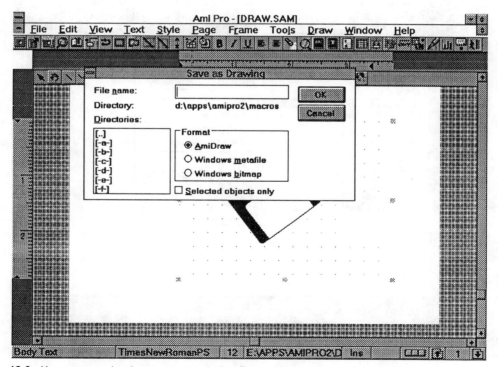

18-6 You can save drawings you create in Ami Pro to a file to reuse later.

5. Type the filename for the drawing in the text box.

6. Select the format in which you need to save the file: Ami Draw, Windows Metafile, or Windows Bitmap.

7. If you are saving only selected objects in the drawing, choose the Select Objects Only check box.

8. Select OK.

Ami clip art

Ami comes with over 100 clip art graphics that you can import into your document. Clip art is a graphic that is not copyrighted, so you can include it in your document and duplicate it without restrictions. You can view the contents of each clip art file by selecting the Import Drawing command (you must have a frame selected and have the Draw menu displayed). Once you highlight a filename in the dialog box, Ami displays the file's contents in the example box, as shown in Figure 18-7. To import the file, select OK. Some of the clip art is appropriate for business, and others are cartoon-like. If the images are not appropriate for your

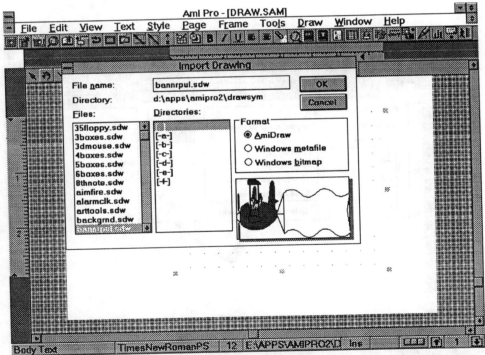

18-7 You can import Ami Pro clip art or drawings you saved to a file using the Import Drawing command.

use, you can import files from another clip art source as long as they come in one of the file formats supported by Ami.

Questions & Answers

Q: I created reverse text, but it isn't printing on my page.

A: If you use a 256-color display driver, Ami cannot print reverse text. Change to a display driver with a lower number of colors using Windows Setup. If you don't use a 256-color display driver, then your printer driver or your printer doesn't support reverse text. Call your printer manufacturer to ask if they can provide an updated printer driver.

Q: I created some drawings in my document, but they aren't appearing when I print.

A: First, check the Print Options dialog box to make sure you don't have the Without pictures option selected. If the option isn't selected, your printer driver might not support printing graphics in Ami. Call your printer manufacturer to ask if they have a newer version of the printer driver. You can check the version of your printer driver by selecting the About button from the Printer Setup dialog box.

Q: I created a drawing to use for a custom icon, but the drawing didn't appear in the Custom Icon box in the Customized SmartIcons dialog box.

A: Any .BMP files you create for use in a custom icon must be in the \AMIPRO directory, not the \DRAWSYM or any other directory. Move your files to the \AMIPRO directory; the next time you display the Customized SmartIcons dialog box, they will appear in the Custom Icon section.

Q: I created a drawing to use for a custom icon, but it appears too small in the Custom Icon box. I thought Ami scaled the .BMP files?

A: Ami does scale any drawings you create using it own Draw feature and save as .BMP files. If you create a drawing using an external application, however, you must scale it to the appropriate size for an icon, which is usually about .24 × .24 inches. If you use a SuperVGA display, scale the drawing to .33 × .33 inches.

Summary

Ami's drawing tools let you create drawings without needing to use an external graphics application. Ami lets you create lines, circles, squares, polylines, polygons, arcs, and graphic text. You can manipulate those objects by selecting and unselecting them, grouping them, rearranging multiple objects, rotating them, flipping objects, displaying and aligning objects along a grid, and adding color and fill patterns to the drawing. You can create special effects, such as reverse text and drop caps, using the Draw icons; however, you must have a mouse to use the Drawing feature. Without a mouse, the Drawing feature is not accessible.

19
CHAPTER

Ami Pro's charting tools

Ami provides all the tools you need to create effective, graphically-oriented documents and other communications. You can communicate graphically with charts, and with Ami, you never need to use an external charting application.

Ami can create the following 12 chart types:

- Column chart
- Stacked column chart
- Bar chart
- Stacked bar chart
- Line chart
- Area chart
- Line and picture chart (each data set on the same line)
- Line and picture chart (each data set uses same picture)
- Pie chart
- Expanded pie chart
- Picture chart
- Stacked picture chart.

Tip 19-1: Bar charts vs Column charts One of the idiosyncrasies of the software industry is terminology. Ami uses terminology for its Column and Bar charts that differs from just about every other charting application. What Am calls a

Column chart (a chart that displays bars vertically) other applications call a Bar chart. What Ami calls a Bar chart (a chart that displays bars horizontally) other applications call a Horizontal Bar chart. An easy way to differentiate them is to remember that in Ami, a Column chart displays bars vertically, while a Bar chart displays bars horizontally.

Creating a chart

The general process for creating a chart is as follows:

1. Copy data for the chart to the Clipboard (either from your Ami document or from a Windows application).
2. Select Charting from the Tools menu.
3. Select the chart type and any available charts options you want.
4. Use the Drawing feature to add pictures, arrows, or other enhancements to the chart.

Copying data to the Clipboard

Ami creates a chart using data that it finds in the Clipboard. If no data exists in the Clipboard, Ami displays a message saying so and asks you if you want to enter the data. If you answer yes, Ami displays a Chart Data dialog box in which you can enter the data. Entering data in the Chart Data dialog box is cumbersome, however, because you must separate columns of data with spaces (the Tab key doesn't work here), and you must press the Down Arrow key to move to the next row. If you press Enter by mistake, Ami closes the dialog box and creates the chart with the partial data. It's much easier if you enter the data in the document or in a Windows application, and copy it to the clipboard using Edit Copy.

Follow these guidelines when entering chart data into an Ami document or Windows application:

• Separate each column with a tab or a space.
• Enter x-axis labels in the first row.
• Enter legend labels in the first column.
• Enter one data set per row, because Ami reads each row as one data set.

Figure 19-1 displays an Ami document with chart data and the chart Ami created using that data.

Tip 19-2: Entering a label that has more than one word Because Ami reads a space between words as a column separator, Ami would mistakenly read *New York* as two separate labels. You can enter two words as one label by using an underscore instead of a space between the words. Ami reads the label correctly and does not display the underscore in the chart.

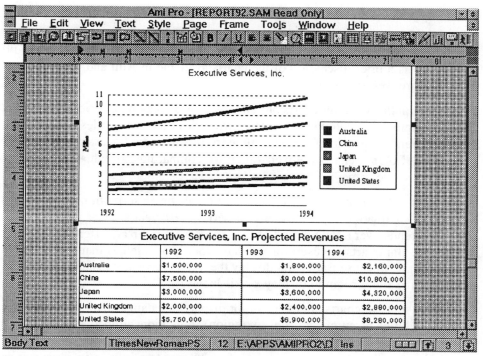

19-1 A chart and the data from which it was created.

Tip 19-3: Forcing Ami to recognize a number as a label Let's say you are entering x-axis labels in the first row of your data, but the labels are years: 1991, 1992, 1993. How can you make Ami read those numbers as labels instead of using them as the first data set? Type an underscore in front of each number and Ami will automatically recognize any number in the data as a label. Ami does not display the underscores in the chart.

Tip 19-4: Don't add text attributes or delimiters to chart data Ami accepts numbers and labels with text attributes (bold, font, or point size) and delimiters (commas, dollar signs), but it does not display them in chart. The only way to add text attributes and delimiters is by using the Drawing feature after Ami creates the chart. Select the text in the chart, select the Text tool, and modify the text.

Tip 19-5: Editing chart data Once you copy data to the Clipboard, how can you edit it? The easiest way is to edit the data in the document or the Windows application from which you copied the data, and copy it again to the Clipboard. Select Charting from the Tools menu. Select the Data button and paste the new data over the old in the Chart Data dialog box. You could display the Chart Data dialog box and make the changes manually, but Ami does not have a way of inserting a new line, and other editing operations are cumbersome.

Chart types

You can choose to display your data using one of 12 chart types. With so many charts to choose from, you might find it difficult to know what chart you should use. Below is a brief discussion of the charts available in Ami and what applications they are well suited for.

Column charts   Column charts are effective for displaying a series of numbers (sales by region), a relationship between two series (last year's sales vs this year's sales), or trends over a long period of time (profits up in first quarter over the past five years). Column charts are well suited for comparing individual items rather than changes over time.

Bar charts   Bar charts also are effective for displaying a series of numbers (sales by region), a relationship between two series (last year's sales vs this year's sales), or trends over a long period of time (profits up in first quarter over the past five years). Bar charts are useful if you have long x-axis labels that don't fit on a Column chart. Because Bar charts display the x-axis vertically instead of horizontally, Ami has more room to display x-axis labels.

Line charts   Line charts are effective for displaying changes over time (sales by quarter), a series of numbers (sales by region), a relationship between two series (last year's sales vs this year's sales), or statistical trends (interest rates for the past twelve months). Line charts are best for showing trends over time, especially if the change is dramatic.

Area charts   Area charts are Line charts that use a fill pattern or color between lines. Area charts are best for tracking a trend; they are not well suited for identifying individual values in a data set.

Line and picture charts   Line and picture charts are Line charts that display a symbol at each data point on the line. While Line charts are well suited for displaying trends, Line and picture charts are best for highlighting the actual values within the trend (interest rates over the past twelve months). Ami has two types of Line and picture charts: one displays each value in the data set using the same picture; the second displays each value in the data set using the same color or fill pattern.

Pie charts   Pie charts are useful for displaying values as percentages, displaying values as part of a whole, or displaying financial information. Pie charts differ from all other chart types in that they can display only one data set; all other charts can display more than one data set. To include a legend in the Pie chart, type the legend labels in the first column of data. Ami uses the second column of data as the data set and ignores any other columns.

Expanded pie charts   Expanded pie charts detach each slice from the pie. Refer to Tip 19-12 to learn how to create a Pie chart using only one detached slice.

Picture charts Picture charts display each value in a data set as a picture. The size of the picture depends on the value—the larger the value, the larger the picture. Picture charts are useful for communicating what the data in the chart represents. For example, a chart that displays housing starts for the first quarter could use a picture of a house for each value, and display each month's house using a different color or fill pattern. Picture charts are best for tracking a trend; they are not well suited for identifying individual values in a data set.

Stacked charts Ami has several varieties of stacked charts, including Stacked Column charts, Stacked Bar charts, and Stacked Picture charts. Stack charts display columns, bars, or pictures on top of each other, rather than next to each other. Stacked charts display data as a running total instead of individual values.

Choosing a chart type and chart options

Once you copy the chart data to the Clipboard, create the chart by selecting Charting from the Tools menu. Ami displays the Charting dialog box, as shown in Figure 19-2. The chart Ami displays in the example box uses the actual data in the clipboard, so you are viewing a true sample of your chart. Ami does not always use the contents of your document in other example boxes, but it does so here.

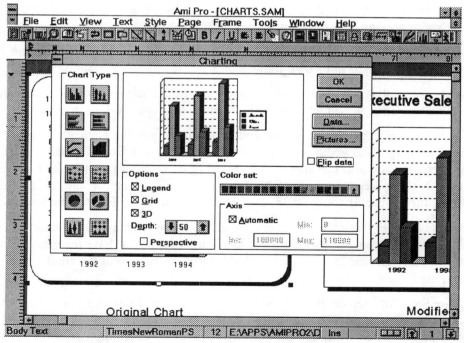

19-2 The Charting dialog lets you select the chart type, colors, and options.

Table 19-1. Chart Icons

Icon	Chart Type	Icon	Chart Type
	Column chart		Line and Picture chart (values in one data set use the same picture)
	Stacked Column chart		Line and Picture chart (values in one data appear on the same line)
	Bar chart		Pie chart
	Stacked Bar Chart		Expanded Pie chart
	Line chart		Picture chart
	Area chart		Stacked Picture chart

Chart Type Select from one of the twelve icons to choose the type of chart you need. The default is a Column chart. Table 19-1 displays each chart icon and the chart type each icon represents. Select a chart icon to display the different color, label, and picture options in the example box. The icon always displays the next option in the cycle. Not all icons have the same number of options: Picture charts have more options than Bar charts.

Legend To identify each data set, select Legend. Ami displays the Legend to the right of the chart in its own frame.

Grid To display horizontal dotted lines behind the chart's bars, lines, or symbols. select Grid. A grid lets you easily identify individual values in a data set.

3D To display the height, width, and depth of the graphic elements instead of the usual height and width select 3D. You can use 3D with Column, Bar, Pie, and Area charts. You also can specify how much of a 3D effect you need by typing a number in the Depth text box. The depth represents the percentage of the total width, for the bar. If you type 25, the 3D effect requires 25% of the bar's width.

Perspective Perspective increases the 3D effect by displaying the chart at an angle: graphic elements located at the left or top of the chart have the greatest 3D effect, while graphic elements located at the right or bottom of the chart have the smallest 3D effect.

Color Set Ami selects the colors in your chart from a row of colors called the color set. If your chart has three data sets, Ami uses the first three colors in the color set. You can rearrange the colors in the set by dragging a color to a new position. You also can choose new color sets by selecting the Down Arrow button and the color set you need. If you use a monochrome monitor, select the fill pattern color sets instead. You can create custom colors with text, lines, and fill patterns. See Tip 18-15 for more information on creating a custom color.

Axis Ami creates a y-axis according to the values in your chart. If you are not satisfied with the numbers on the axis, you can change them. Select the Automatic box to activate the Min, Max, and Inc boxes. Specify the minimum and maximum values for the y-axis, along with the increment you need Ami to use between the values.

Flip Data Ami considers one data set to be a row in your data. Ami plots each data set against the x-axis. You can force Ami to use the columns as data sets by selecting Flip Data. If you select a Pie chart and Ami displays only one color, select Flip Data to correct the Pie chart display.

Data Select the Data button to display the Chart Data dialog box, shown in Figure 19-3. You can edit the data in the dialog box or enter data if none exists in the Clipboard. Separate columns with a space, and move to the next row using Down Arrow. You cannot insert a new row, and if you press Enter, Ami closes the dialog box.

Pictures If you use any chart that uses pictures (Line and picture, Picture, or Stacked picture), you can include your own Ami Draw drawings in the chart,

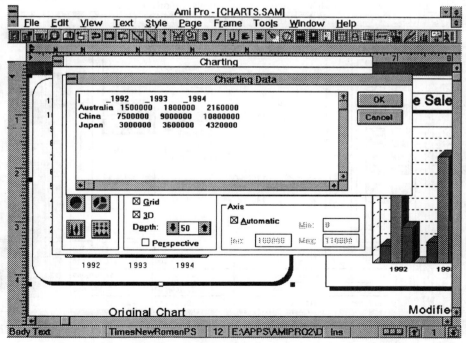

19-3 The Charting Data dialog box displays the data you copied to the clipboard.

rather than the symbols Ami uses as the default. Select the Pictures button and Ami displays the Pictures dialog box, as shown in Figure 19-4. Select the number of the data set you want to change and select the Drawings button. Select the filename of the drawing to use and click OK. Ami uses a separate set of pictures for Line and picture charts than for Picture charts, so if you want to use the same drawing for both charts, you must select the chart type and specify the picture for each type. To return to the original symbol Ami used as the default for that data set, select the data set number and choose the Defaults button.

Tip 19-6: Create a frame for your chart before selecting the Charting **command** You no longer need to create a frame to select the Charting command; however, you should unless you need a frame the same size as the last one created. Otherwise, you have to resize the frame after you create the chart, and then resize the chart inside the frame.

Tip 19-7: Resizing a chart If you change the size of a frame containing your chart, Ami doesn't increase the chart size automatically. If you choose Graphic Scaling from the Frame menu and select the Fit in Frame option, Ami updates the chart's size, but it might look awkward. An easier way to update your chart's size to fit the frame is to select the frame, select the Charting command from the Tools

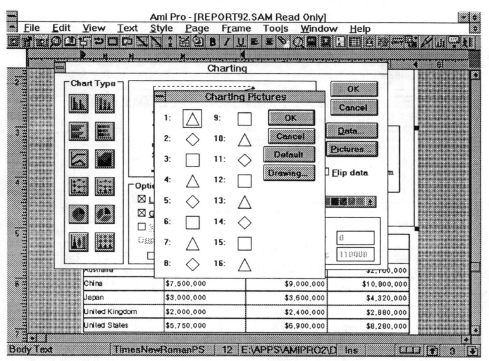

19-4 The Charting Pictures dialog box displays the symbols available for line and picture charts.

menu, and select OK. Ami automatically resizes the chart to fit the frame, and the fit is better than if you used Graphic Scaling.

Tip 19-8: Charting is for basics; drawing is for enhancements   The Charting command creates a basic chart from the data you copied to the Clipboard. The Charting command does not automatically add any chart titles, text delimiters, or other enhancements to the chart, nor does it have options to do so. Instead, Ami lets you enhance your charts or change just about everything in them with the Drawing command. So remember: the Charting command creates the basic chart; you add the bells and whistles using the Drawing command.

Creating a chart using DDE or OLE

You can use DDE or OLE to paste a spreadsheet or chart created in an external Windows application into your Ami document. If you paste a spreadsheet into the document, you can create an Ami chart from that data. The advantage to using DDE or OLE to create a chart is if the chart or data changes in the external Windows application, Ami updates the chart in your document automatically. The disadvantage to using DDE and OLE is that few applications support them.

DDE and OLE are essentially the same, because they both update a chart in your document as the chart or chart data changes in the external Windows application. DDE and OLE do have three major differences:

- DDE asks your permission to start the application from which you created the original chart. If you answer no, Ami does not update the chart in your document to reflect the changes you made in the Windows application.

- OLE starts the Windows application on its own, without your permission, and automatically updates the chart in your document.

- OLE can link or embed information into an Ami document: a link pastes data from a saved file, while an embed can paste data from an unsaved file. DDE can link data only from a saved file.

Whenever you link or embed data into Ami Pro, whether the data comes into Ami as a link or an embed depends on the application from which you are taking the data. Ami Pro accepts the data in the highest format available. The hierarchy for data formats is OLE embed, OLE link, DDE link, and Paste.

For example, if you are taking information from an application that supports the OLE embed format, Ami Pro accepts the data in that format. However, if the application does not support OLE embeds or OLE links, Ami Pro accepts the data as a DDE link. When an application does not support OLE or DDE, Ami Pro accepts the data as a regular paste operation.

The general procedure for linking or embedding a chart or chart data to an Ami document starts with opening the Windows application and create the chart or chart data. Copy the chart or chart data to the Clipboard using Edit Copy, then minimize the application and start Ami. Open the document into which you need to link the chart or chart data. If you are linking a chart, create a frame to hold the chart. If you are linking chart data into a table, create the table and insert your cursor in a cell. Link or embed the chart or chart data using one of the following commands:

Paste   Select Paste to accept the data in the highest data format available from the external application.

Paste Link   Select Paste Link to link the data using the highest link format available: either OLE or DDE link.

Paste Special   Select Paste Special to accept the data using the format you specify. You can choose from the following formats:

Picture. Picture *pastes the data using the Windows Metafile format. Use this format to paste graphics.*

Bitmap and DIB. Bitmap and DIB *paste the data using the Windows Bitmap format. Use these formats to paste graphics.*

Rich Text Format. Select Rich Text Format *to paste text and keep its formatting.*

Link. Select Link *to create a DDE link.*

ObjectLink. Select ObjectLink *to create an OLE link.*

Native. Select Native *to create an OLE embed.*

Link Options   Select Link Options to create a link or change existing links.

Using Link Options

Ami automatically creates a hot DDE or OLE link, meaning that each time you open a document containing a link, Ami will attempt to update it. A warm link updates the information only when you tell it to. Updating a link can be a slow process, so if your document contains more than one, you might want to use warm links to control when they update. You can use Link Options to change a hot link to a warm link, and vice versa. You also can change the link or create an entirely new one, but doing so is cumbersome, because Ami requires you to type a lot of information when it's easier to use one of the other commands on the Edit menu. Copying and pasting links is much easier; however, if you don't have enough memory to run both applications concurrently, using Link Options is an alternative.

Once you select Link Options, Ami displays the Link Options dialog box, as displayed in Figure 19-5. The Links box displays the links in the current document. Each line displays the link number, type, status, application name, path name, and item description for one link.

Update   Select Update to update any outdated or warm links in your document.

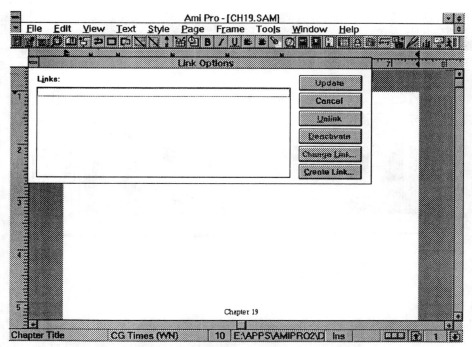

19-5 The Link Options dialog box lets you manage DDE and OLE links in your document.

Unlink Select Unlink to delete an old link from your document.

Deactivate Select Deactivate to convert a hot link to a warm link.

Change Link Select Change Link to choose a new application, path (topic), and item (chart or cell range) in a link.

Create Link Select Create Link to create a new link in the document. Ami displays the Create Link dialog box. Specify the application name, path (Topic), and description (chart or cell range).

Enhancing a chart using Ami's drawing feature

Ami considers any chart you create using its Charting feature to be a drawing. You can modify the chart by selecting the frame containing the chart and selecting the Drawing command on the Tools menu. You can change a bar's or pie slice's color, add delimiters to numbers, or change the font for text in the chart. All of the Drawing Tool and Command icons are available to modify a chart. Figure 19-6 displays an original chart created in Ami and the same chart modified using the Drawing command.

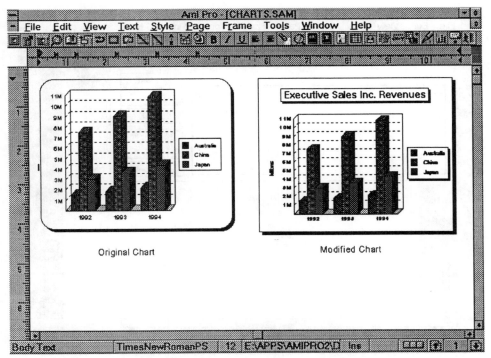

19-6 A chart before and after being modified using the Drawing feature.

Tip 19-9: Double-clicking on a chart frame When you double-click on a frame containing a chart, Ami displays the last menu you used with that frame selected: either the Drawing menu or the Charting menu. If you double-click on the frame expecting one menu and Ami displays another, simply select Cancel and choose the correct command from the menu bar.

Tip 19-10: Adding text delimiters To add delimiters to text in your chart, select the frame containing the chart and choose Drawing from the Tools menu. Select the Text tool and insert your cursor at the position in the text where you need a delimiter. Type the delimiter.

Tip 19-11: Adding titles to a chart Ami does not let you add descriptive titles to the chart or axes using the Charting command. You can, however, add titles using the Drawing command. Select the frame containing the chart and choose Drawing from the Tools menu. Select the Text tool and add the titles to the chart. To rotate a y-axis title, select the title using the Selection Arrow tool and choose Rotate from the Drawing menu. Enter 90 as the degree of rotation and counter-clockwise as the rotation direction. Position the title using the Selection Arrow tool.

Tip 19-12: Expanding one slice of a pie chart Ami's Expanded Pie chart can detach all the slices from a pie. Traditional Pie charts usually detach only one slice: either the largest or the smallest, depending on the effect you want to achieve. You cannot tell Ami to detach only one slice using the Charting command, but you can detach a single slice from a Pie chart with the Drawing command. Select the frame containing the chart and choose Drawing from the Tools menu. Choose the Selection Arrow tool and select the slice you need to detach. Drag the slice until it appears detached from the other slices.

Questions & Answers

Q: I added my own drawings to my Pictures chart, but I need to return to the original symbols Ami used. How can I return to the default symbol?

A: Picture charts and Line and Picture charts use different symbols, so make sure you have the correct chart icon selected in the Chart dialog box. Select the Picture button and the first data set number you need to change. Select the Default button. Continue selecting data set numbers and selecting Default for each symbol you need to restore. Click OK when you finish, and Ami should display your chart using its original symbols.

Q: I created a Pie chart, but it displays only one color. What did I do wrong?

A: Ami reads data sets differently for Pie charts than it does for other charts. Ami normally uses the first row as the first data set; for Pie charts it uses the first column (unless you have labels in the first column, and then Ami uses the second column). To correct the Pie chart, select Flip Data from the Chart dialog box. Ami should display the Pie chart correctly.

Q: I am trying to display labels for my Pie chart, but no matter how many times I select the Pie chart icon, Ami never displays them. Why not?

A: If you are displaying a legend, you cannot display labels too. Because a legend and slice labels display the same information, Ami does not let you display them both. To display labels for a Pie chart, make sure you do not have the Legend option selected.

Q: I am double-clicking on my chart's frame to display the Chart menu, but Ami displays the Draw menu instead. Why?

A: When you double-click on a chart, Ami displays the last menu you used when you selected the chart's frame. If you used the Draw menu last, you cannot display the Chart menu by double-clicking on the frame. You must select the Charting command from the Tools menu.

Summary

You can create charts within Ami using data from your document, data you import from another file, or data created by DDE or OLE. Once you copy the data to the Clipboard, you can select Charting from the Tools menu, and Ami displays the Charting dialog box. Inside that box is a sample chart using the data you copied to the Clipboard. You can select different chart types and options, and watch the chart change dynamically before you return to the document. You can make as many changes as you want without ever needing to return to the document. Once you create the chart, you can modify and embellish the chart using the Drawing feature.

Part 4
Special topics

20
CHAPTER

Printing tips

How can you get the most out of Ami Pro and your printer, whether you use a dot-matrix, deskjet, laserjet, or postscript printer? That is what this chapter is all about. You'll learn how to print your document as quickly and productively as possible. The general procedure for printing is to open the document you want to print, and make sure it is in the active window. Select Print from the File menu. Specify the number of pages to print from the document and select OK.

What if you need to print multiple copies? What if the document uses both portrait and landscape orientation? How do you print envelopes? What if printing is too slow? You can see how a seemingly simple process soon becomes complicated.

Printing with any program running under Windows often takes several tries to be successful. Unlike programs running directly under DOS, programs running under Windows also print through Windows. Thus, You must tell Windows what page orientation you plan to use, even if you already told your program.

Disabling Windows Print Manager

Ami Pro 2.0 comes with its own print manager, so you don't need to use Windows Print Manager, unless you are printing documents from several Windows applications at the same time. Disabling the Windows Print Manager speeds printing with Ami Pro, because it prints directly to the printer instead of first going through Print Manager and then to the printer. If you disable the Windows Print Manager and Ami has trouble communicating with the printer (printer is out of paper or off line), Ami continues to the display the Now Printing dialog box until it resolves the problem. Ami displays a dialog box with the printer port assignment displayed in the title bar asking you to retry or cancel.

Printing in the background

Normally Ami schedules printing as a foreground task, taking precedence over all other tasks. Ami assumes that printing a document is the most important task, so it sends the entire document to the printer before you can resume working. However, if you need to begin working on your document immediately after choosing Print from the File menu, you can print in the background. Ami still prints the document, but not as quickly as before. It waits for idle time when it is not doing any other processing (saving a file, repaginating, find and replacing), and prints the document during that time. Ami returns to the document more quickly than when it prints in the foreground, but Ami's performance slows while it prints in the background. If Ami has trouble printing the document, it will not display any message on the screen. Instead, you must minimize Ami, and open the AmiPrint window at the bottom of the screen. The AmiPrint dialog box will ask you to retry or cancel.

Stopping background printing

Even though the Now Printing dialog box displays and disappears in a flash, it isn't too late to stop printing. You can't stop printing from within Ami, but you can do so by displaying the AmiPrint window. Minimize Ami Pro and open the Ami Print window, as shown in Figure 20-1. Highlight the name of the file you need to stop printing and select Pause or Remove. To resume printing a document you paused, select Restart.

Printing nonconsecutive pages

When you select the Print command from the File menu, you can specify a range of pages to print, but that range must include consecutive pages, such as pages 5–11. What if you need to print pages 1–3, 5–9, 21, 43, and the last five pages of the document? Previously, you would have selected the Print command five different times, specifying a different page range each time. Now you can use the PRNPAGES macro to print nonconsecutive pages of a document.

Once you playback the PRNPAGES macro, Ami displays the Select Pages to Print dialog box, as shown in Figure 20-2. Using this dialog box, you can specify to print the first x pages, the last x pages, two page ranges, and individual page numbers. You can type the page numbers yourself, select them from the list box at the left.

Printing only selected text or graphics

The PRNSHADE macro lets you print only the text you have selected in the current document. This macro is handy for proofing a block of text or a graphic

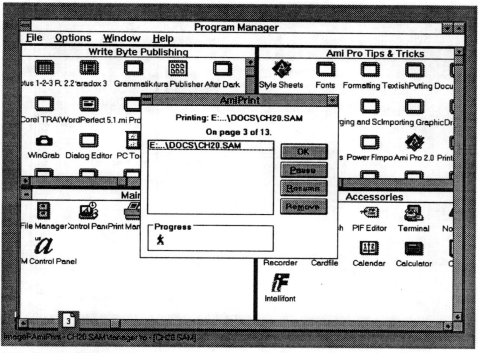

20-1 The Ami Print window.

without printing the entire document or page. Once you playback the PRNSHADE macro, it copies the text and graphics you selected, and pastes them into an untitled document. Ami displays the Print dialog box, letting you select any print options. Once you select OK, Ami prints the selected text and graphics and closes the untitled document without saving it.

Printing more than one document

Ami does not have an option in the Print dialog box to print multiple documents. Ami automatically prints the document in the active window. However, you can print more than one document by running a macro supplied with Ami named PRNBATCH.SMM. The macro lets you select the files to print from a list box, and prints them in the order you chose them. You also can print several documents by using a Master Document, but make sure you want page numbering updated across your files. If you need page numbers to remain the same as they are in the individual files, print using the PRNBATCH macro.

Tip 20-1: Generating and attaching files to a FAX cover sheet The FAX macro lets you generate a FAX cover sheet and attach Ami Pro files to it for printing. Once you run the FAX macro, Ami displays the FAX Cover Sheet Options dialog box. From this box, you can select a style sheet to use as the basis

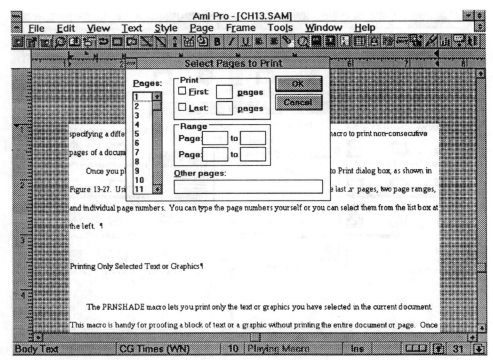

20-2 The PRNPAGES macro lets you print nonconsecutive pages, page ranges, and the first and last several pages of a file.

for the FAX cover sheet. Ami also adds a Compose FAX command to the File menu. The Compose FAX command lets you generate a cover sheet, and print the current file or other files along with the cover sheet.

Once you select Use Current Doc or New FAX Doc, Ami displays the FAX Cover Sheet Information dialog box, as shown in Figure 20-3. You can enter the recipient's company, a name, to whom a carbon copy goes, a FAX number, a telephone number, and any Special comments. If you want to print files other than the current document when you print the FAX cover sheet, select Files and choose the filenames.

Saving a document before printing

Always save a document before you print it. If an unrecoverable application error or a power outage occurs while Ami is printing a document, you could lose any unsaved work. Make a habit of always saving your documents before you print them.

20-3 Use the FAX macro to generate a FAX cover sheet and attach files to it for printing.

Printing multiple copies

You have several ways to print multiple copies of the same document: using Ami, using Windows, or using your printer. The easiest way is to use Ami, especially if your printer is down the hall. To print several copies of the same document using Ami, select Print from the File menu. Enter the number of times to print the document in the Number of copies text box. You also can print multiple copies using the Printer Setup dialog box in Windows. If your printer has the capability, you can use its control panel to specify multiple copies.

Collating several copies of a document

If you print multiple copies of a long document, Ami prints all of the first pages, then all of the second pages, and continues in the same manner until it completes printing. It doesn't automatically collate documents, unless you specify to do so in the Print Option dialog box. Select the Options button from the Print dialog box and select Collate.

Printing double-sided pages

You can print on both sides of the page, even if your laser printer doesn't have that capability. To print on both sides of the page, print only the even-numbered pages. Turn over the stack and place it back in the paper tray. Then print only the odd-numbered pages in reverse order.

To accomplish this task, follow these steps:

1. Open the document and make sure it is in the active window.

2. Select Print from the File menu.

3. Select All for the Page range, and Even for the Including option. Select OK.

4. Once Ami prints all the even-numbered pages, take the stack out of the top of the printer. Place the pages, printed-side down, in the paper tray. The last page Ami printed should be on top and it should be facing down.

5. Again, select Print from the File menu.

6. Select All for Page range, and Odd for the Including option. Select Options.

7. Select Reverse order. Ami prints odd-numbered pages in reverse order.

Printing crop marks

Do you need crop marks? If your page size is $8^1/2 \times 11$, you probably don't need them. If your page size is smaller, such as 7×10 or $5^1/2 \times 8^1/2$, you need crop marks. Crop marks tell your printer where to cut excess space on the page. If you created a custom page size using the Page Setting option in the Modify Page Layout dialog box, you need crop marks to tell the printer what size your final page should be. Ami does not display crop marks on the screen, but it will print them if you select the Crop Marks check box under Print Options. Ami prints crop marks a half-inch outside the margins. If for some reason you are using an $8^1/2 \times 11$ but you still need crop marks, you can draw them in a frame, and make the frame repeat so it appears on every page of your document.

Speed up printing by omitting graphics

Graphics print more slowly than text does, so you can print a quick draft of a document without all of its illustrations. To prevent graphics from printing, select Without pictures in the Print Options dialog box. Don't confuse hiding graphics with omitting them from your printed pages. Even if you turn off the graphics display by selecting Pictures in the View Preferences dialog box, Ami still prints them. You must turn off graphics printing in addition to hiding them on the screen.

Controlling print density on a laser printer

If you use a laserjet printer, you can change your printer's intensity to accommodate your document. Laserjets have a printer density dial inside the printer that you can adjust to increase or decrease the amount of toner the printer uses. To access the print density dial, press the button on the top of the printer to open the top. Lift the top and look at the left corner of the opening. You'll see a green dial with numbers on it. One is the darkest setting, five is medium, and nine is the lightest setting. The lower the number, the darker your print appears, and the more toner the laserjet uses. The laserjet ships using a setting of five. Using a density of nine makes type appear sharp and crisp, but any jagged edges might be exaggerated. Using a density of three or one puts extra toner on the page, making type look heavier. If your document is the final product, use a density setting of medium. Lighter density saves toner and makes the cartridge last longer, but fill patterns won't be as dark or solid. If your document is the original to be used for offset printing or photocopying, use a lighter setting, for lighter fill patterns and crisp type. The lighter fill patterns won't matter, because offset printing and photocopying will make them appear as solid black. Once you choose a new density setting, print about twenty pages to stabilize the new density before you print your final document.

Changing print orientation

One of the biggest frustrations to Windows' users is printing a document that uses both portrait and landscape orientation. Because you must tell both Windows and Ami the print orientation you use, inserting a new page layout in a document to use the new orientation isn't enough. You must print only the pages using the same orientation. When printing stops, you can change the orientation, and resume printing the pages using the other orientation.

Another frustration is forgetting that you changed to landscape orientation when you print a portrait document. Windows doesn't tell you that its orientation and Ami's don't match, so about half of what you needed to print ends up on the page.

Printing to a file

Eventually you will need to print a file. If the PC you are using doesn't have the correct printer or any printer at all, you can print to a file using the correct printer driver. Once you are at a PC that is hooked to the correct printer, you can print the file using the DOS Print command or using the Print command on the File Manager's File menu. To print to a file, select the Control Panel command from the System menu. The System menu is the white bar at the top left of your screen. Select the Printers icon from the Control Panel. Select the Configure button and

File from the Ports list box. Select OK until you return to the Ami document. Select Print from the File menu. Ami displays the Now Printing dialog box and then asks you for the name of the file. Enter a filename using any extension you wish (you are not limited to .PRN as you are with other programs). You must print the file from DOS using the Print command. Do not print the file using the File Manager.

When a document isn't printing correctly

Let's say you create a document that contains some impressive details: reverse text, rotated text, graphics, opaque white frames overlapping opaque black frames, along with several fonts. When you select Print from the File menu, your page prints, but it just doesn't print properly. Maybe the reverse text is missing, or the graphics disappeared, or the black bled through the white opaque frame. What happened?

First, check to make sure you created each element properly and you used all the appropriate settings. For example, make sure the white frame is opaque and not transparent. If you check all the details and you still can't figure it out, your printer driver is probably at fault. A printer driver is software that lets your printer talk to Ami. If a printer driver does not support a particular feature, such as reverse text, it will not work, even if the Ami documentation and the printer documentation say you can do it.

Before you call the technical support lines of your printer or Ami Pro, check to see what version of the printer driver you have. Select Printer Setup from the File menu. Write down the printer name that displays in the text box. Select Setup and then the About button. Windows displays the printer driver name and version. Write down the version number, because the technical support personnel will ask you for it. Usually if you call the printer manufacturer, they will send you the printer driver at no charge. If you have a modem, you also can access your printer manufacturer's bulletin board on CompuServe, and download the latest version of the printer driver. You can do the same on Lotus' bulletin board. Once on CompuServe, type GO LOTUSWP and follow the instructions to access the Ami Pro files.

Printing envelopes

Have you ever noticed how frustrating it is to print an envelope? Programs like Ami make creating complex documents relatively easy, but printing one measly envelope can make you want to write the address by hand. Ami comes with style sheets that prints envelopes on a Hewlett-Packard LaserJet II, IIP, IIP with a PostScript cartridge, III, and DeskJet printers. If you use another printer, you need to change the page size and margins in the Modify Page Layout dialog box. If you use a markedly different printer from the LaserJet II, such as a dot-matrix, you need to change the orientation, the page size, and the margins.

The best way to find out what page layout settings to use is to test printing an envelope using the ˜ENVELOP.STY style sheet. If the print is too low, high, or too far over on the envelope, adjust the page settings accordingly.

Creating a return address

If you use blank envelopes without any imprinted address, you can use a repeating frame on the envelope style sheet to create your return address. Select File New and choose the ˜ENVELOP.STY style sheet (or the appropriate style sheet for your printer). Select the Frame icon and draw a frame large enough to hold your address. Position the frame inside the printable area for your envelope. The most commonly used envelope size, COM 10, has a printable area of 3.6 × 9.1 inches. Place the cursor inside the frame and type your return address. Select Modify Frame Layout from the Frame menu. Select Lines & shadows and turn off any lines and shadows around the frame. Select Save as a Style Sheet and the With contents option. Save the style sheet under the same name and select OK.

Limiting one address per envelope

If you are printing several envelopes at once, you can ensure that only one address appears on each envelope. You can modify the Body Single style to use a page break after the paragraph and separate lines in the address with line breaks. Select Modify Style from the Style menu. Make sure the Body Single style appears in the text box. Select the Breaks attribute and select Page break after paragraph. When Ami returns to the envelope, type the address and press Ctrl-Enter at the end of a line instead of Enter. Once you enter the complete address, press Enter. Ami inserts a page break and moves to the next page automatically.

Tip 20-2: Starting a personal mailing list   You probably have a formal mailing list in a merge data document, but you can build a simple mailing list for your personal use without performing a merge. That old 80-20 rule applies to correspondence too: you send 80% of your mail to 20% of your clients. To create a file containing preaddressed envelopes, select File New and choose the envelope style sheet you use. Enter each address on a separate page. Add a bookmark to the beginning of each address by selecting Bookmarks from the Edit menu. Type the client's name and select Add. When you're ready to add a new address to the file, position the cursor at the front of the file and press Enter to move the current address to the next page. Type the address, add a new bookmark, and you've added a new client to your personal mailing list. To find the client you need, select the Bookmark icon, highlight the client's name and select Go To. Select Print from the File menu and print the current page.

Creating envelope letterhead

When you lay out a design to be used as camera-ready copy for your envelopes, create crop marks at the top left edge of the page, as shown in Figure 20-4.

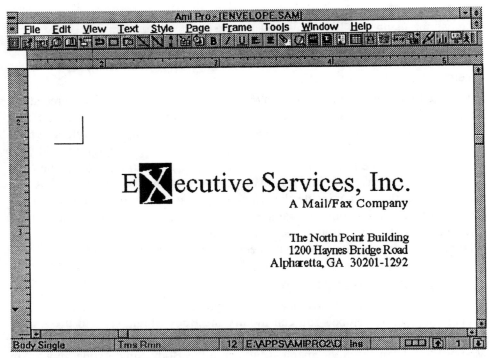

20-4 Crop marks on an envelope

Envelopes come in many different sizes, and you might not be sure what size is standard for your print shop. These crop marks ensure that your logo and address are placed the proper distance from the top and left side no matter what size envelope your print shop uses. To display only one set of crop marks, don't use the Crop mark option in the Print options dialog box. Instead, draw them using a frame. Select the Frame icon and draw a frame one half inch in size. Position the frame where the top left edge of the envelope should be. Select Modify Frame Layout and select Lines & shadows. Turn on the lines on the bottom and right sides of the frame and turn off the shadow. Ami displays a frame, but it appears as a crop mark.

Tip 20-3: Feeding envelopes into a Laser printer Laser printers are fussy when it comes to envelopes, so here are some types to avoid:

- those with ink that can't hold up to the heat of a laser printer
- those with pressure-sensitive adhesives
- those with an unusual texture or bulky sides
- those using metal clasps, strings, or windows
- those already fed through the printer
- damaged or crumpled envelopes.

Questions & Answers

Q: I created reverse text using a frame. It looks fine on the screen, but when I print it doesn't appear on the page.

A: If you use a display driver that displays 256 colors, Ami cannot print reverse text. If you are using that type of display driver, run Windows Setup from the Desktop and choose another display with fewer colors. Return to Ami and print the document and the reverse text should appear. If you are not using a display driver with 256 colors, your printer driver doesn't support reverse text. Call your printer manufacturer's support line to see if they have a newer version of the printer driver that supports reverse text.

Summary

To print your document, you can use the Print command from the File menu. However, you can print multiple documents, nonconsecutive pages, and all your documents more efficiently by using macros and Ami Pro's own print spooler. Most people use the Windows Print Manager, but it really isn't necessary unless you plan to print documents from several applications at the same time. Turning off the Print Manager is the most effective step you can take to speed up the printing process. All of these tasks are not available from the Print dialog box, but you can take advantage of them by using the tips included in this chapter.

21
CHAPTER

Speed tips

Running Ami on a 286 machine is like driving a Porsche in bumper-to-bumper traffic: you can't take full advantage of its power or its speed until you get it on the open road. Even if you are using a 386 or 486 PC, how efficiently you produce a document depends not only on your PC, but also on the choices you make about using Ami's interface, and how you achieve the results you need. This chapter is a road map of the shortcuts you can use to work more productively in Ami.

The basics

Surprisingly enough, you can speed up your performance by doing some relatively simple things. These are the basic tips that can help everyone, from the secretary using Merge to the writer using Document Compare.

Buy a mouse

As unbelievable as it seems, some people use Ami without a mouse. The best investment you can make after buying Ami Pro is a mouse. You can work more efficiently, select text more precisely, and just plain do things you can't do with the keyboard, like using the Draw feature. Save yourself the headache of trying to set tabs and draw frames with a keyboard, and buy a mouse.

Use keyboard shortcuts for menu commands

Ami Pro is definitely an icon-driven program, but you do have some keyboard shortcuts available. Appendix C includes a table listing Ami's keyboard shortcuts. Some of the most beneficial are:

- Saving with Ctrl-S
- Printing with Ctrl-P

- Cutting, copying, and pasting with Shift-Del, Ctrl-Ins, and Shift-Ins
- Undo by pressing Alt-Backspace
- Change display modes with Ctrl-M
- Modify a style with Ctrl-A.

Set Ami Pro defaults

Ami has a rich assortment of default settings you can customize to your own liking. The next time you save a file, draw a frame, or perform other operations, Ami uses the defaults you chose. Chapter 23 contains a table of all the Ami defaults available. Some of the biggest time-saving defaults are:

- directories for documents, styles, macros, and backups
- frames
- display mode
- display view
- fill patterns and line styles
- style sheet.

Reduce undo levels

You can undo up to four of your last actions, but the memory Ami requires to store those actions slows performance. If you are comfortable that you won't need to undo that many levels, select User Setup from the Tools menu. Select Undo levels and choose a lesser level.

Disable warning messages and on-line help

Ami warns you when you delete notes, page breaks, footnotes, tables, floating headers and footers, page layouts, anchored frames, links, and power fields. Once you are familiar with these items you don't need that reminder each time you delete, so you can turn off the warning messages by selecting User Setup from the Tools menu. Select Disable warning messages.

When you select a menu or a command, Ami displays a description of your selection in the title bar. If you are an experienced user and know Ami's menu and command structure like the back of your hand, you can turn off the description display. Select User Setup from the Tools menu and choose Disable on-line help.

Use the Status Bar

The Status Bar at the bottom of the screen provides several alternatives to menu commands and keyboard shortcuts. Use the status bar to:

- assign styles
- change fonts
- increase or decrease font point size
- display the current date and time
- display the cursor's line and column position
- switch between Insert and Typeover mode
- turn on Revision Marking
- display/hide the icon palette
- display the Go To dialog box
- move up or down one page.

Use icons rather than menu commands

You can select an icon with one click of the mouse to perform tasks that would otherwise require you to display several levels of menus or select options from a combination of dialog boxes. Display the icon bar where it is most comfortable to you: at the top, bottom, right, or left of the screen, or floating so that you can move it.

Specifying a different directory

To change a drive and directory in a dialog box, you can use the list boxes for each. However, typing the new drive and directory along with the filename in the text box is faster. Especially if you use a multilevel directory structure, choosing a different directory from the list box can be cumbersome.

Loading Ami Pro automatically

If you're comfortable editing the WIN.INI file, you can tell Windows to load Ami automatically every time you start your computer. In the WIN.INI file, change the RUN = line to include the Ami Pro executable file, like this:

```
RUN = C:\AMIPRO\AMIPRO
```

You don't need to include the .EXE extension, because Windows recognizes any .EXE file as a program file. Save the new WIN.INI file and the next time you load Windows, Ami starts automatically. If you don't load Windows automatically, you can do so by entering the WIN command to your AUTOEXEC.BAT file.

Increasing mouse double-click speed

You can speed up Windows' recognition of a double-click on the mouse. Any operation you select in Ami by double-clicking will automatically begin more quickly. To change the double-click speed, select the Control Panel from the System menu. Select the Mouse icon. Drag the Double Click Speed scroll box toward the fast side. To test your new setting, double-click on the Text box. If you are double-clicking fast enough, Windows inverts the test box. If not, drag the scroll box away from the fast side of the scroll bar.

Create custom icons

Ami comes with over 90 predefined icons that provide a mouse alternative to menu commands. You can create your own icons for the tasks you perform most often by creating a macro. Draw a picture to appear in the icon and assign the macro to the icon. To learn more about creating custom icons, refer to chapter 13.

Styles

Ami's styles are so versatile it can be difficult to know the best way to create, modify, and assign them. The following paragraphs wade through all the choices and present the best options.

Create styles from existing text

Instead of selecting style attributes from a dialog box, you can create a style by example. Highlight any paragraph containing the attributes you want in your style and select Create Style from the Style menu. Type the style name in the text box and select Based on existing text. You can then fine tune the style by selecting the Modify button.

Modify several styles at once

When you are creating a new style sheet or adapting a close relative, you usually modify the majority of the styles. Simplify this process by modifying all the styles when you display the Modify Style dialog box the first time. While you are in the Modify Style dialog box, change the current style and select Save. Select the next style you want to modify from the List box and change that style. You aren't forced to return to the document to see your results because you can use the Example box to see the effects. Repeat this process until you modify all styles in your style sheet.

Assign styles as you write

No matter what mode you use to compose your text, you can assign styles to your paragraphs by pressing a function key. Assign styles to your text as you write, rather than assigning styles once your text is complete. Paging through a long file to assign styles is too cumbersome when Ami gives you the power to do it as you create the text.

Moving around in the document

Funny how we become accustomed to doing things a certain way. The PgDn and PgUp keys work just about the same way in every application, so we use them without fail; however, there are better ways.

Use Go To for locating items

Some items in Ami are difficult to find using the keyboard or the cursor. Try positioning the cursor on a page layout or a field. The cursor might appear to be in the right spot, but when you try to remove that item or change it, the option in the menu is greyed. Instead, use Go To to move to the next page layout change, field, or other item. You might need to select Go To several times to select one of several page layouts, but it beats the hit and miss game of using the cursor. To make Go To perform more quickly, you can press Ctrl-H to move to the next item after you select it in the list box.

Use bookmarks to move to a specific topic

Bookmarks are one of the must-have features for writers. Place bookmarks throughout your file to mark the start of a new topic, facts needing verification, or client names in an envelope file (see Tip 20-2). Bookmarks expedite you to the correct place immediately, rather than selecting Go To several times to cycle through several occurrences of the same item.

Displaying documents

When it comes to changing a display, most people change their screen colors, and then don't give it much thought. You can increase Ami's performance and make creating documents easier by customizing your screen and display.

Lower your screen resolution

VGA monitors give you a sharp, colorful display, but displaying those details slows down your PC. If your system is really dragging, you can choose a lower resolution to speed up processing. VGA users can select an EGA display from Windows Setup. This tip is especially true if you have a SuperVGA card and you are displaying 1024 × 768 resolution. Select 800 × 680 or 640 × 480 and you'll notice a marked increase in your PC's speed. Also, don't select a display resolution that uses 256 colors, because all those colors slow down Ami's performance. Instead, choose a resolution using a lower number of colors. To select a lower resolution, select the Windows Setup icon from the Main group in Windows. Select Change System Settings from the Options menu and choose a lower display resolution.

Create screen files for faster display

Each time you display a page containing a graphic, Ami must redraw it on the screen. You can speed up your document's display by letting Ami store files containing the screen display of each graphic. The next time you move to a page with a graphic, Ami pulls the display from the file rather than recreating it in memory. To create graphic screen files, select User Setup from the Tools menu. Select the Options button. From the Graphic Display Speed Options list box, select Save for Fast Display to create and save the files, or select Save While Open to create the files and delete them once you close the file. Be aware, however, that each screen file Ami creates takes up disk space.

Hide graphics, charts, and drawings

Documents containing numerous graphics soon become sluggish. You can speed up the document's performance by hiding all graphics. Select View Preferences from the View menu and turn off Pictures. Ami hides all the graphics in every file you open until you activate the Pictures option. If you must see an individual graphic, double-click on its frame and Ami displays its content. Once you move the cursor outside the frame, Ami hides the graphic again.

Adjust the Working View Level

Moving back and forth from one end of the paragraph to the other isn't efficient editing. If you can't see an entire line of text in Working View, select View Preferences from the View menu and reduce the Working View Level percentage. If you use a SuperVGA display and you can see more of the line, increase the Working View Level to make the text bigger and easier to read.

Display rulers, icon palette, and Styles Box

All the screen elements Ami provides are designed to make creating documents easier. Use them. Display both the horizontal and vertical rulers, position the icon palette where you find it easiest to use, and if you aren't familiar with the style sheet, display the Styles Box.

Editing tools

Creating the elements that make up your publication requires the most effort, so this is where you can really save some time. These speed tips cover the gamut of document creation, including tab rulers, spell check, dates, text creation, frames, and pagination.

Create multiple tab rulers at one time

Inserted tab rulers affect only one paragraph or cell at a time. If several paragraphs or cells will use the same ruler, highlight them before you create the tab ruler.

Once you specify the tabs and their locations, Ami inserts the new ruler in each paragraph or cell you selected.

Spell Check in Draft mode

Change to Draft mode before you run Spell Check. Ami doesn't have to recreate the WYSIWYG display while checking words and operates more quickly. Do not run Spell Check in Outline mode, because Ami checks only displayed text. Ami ignores any hidden text during Spell Check.

Find and Replace in Draft mode

Ami also operates more efficiently during a Find and Replace if you switch to Draft mode before searching. You don't need to see fonts and pagination anyway, and Ami doesn't have to display the WYSIWYG details and search for text. Do not run Find and Replace in Outline mode, because Ami searches only displayed text. Ami ignores any hidden text during Find and Replace.

Use date codes instead of date text

If a document or style sheet you use frequently contains a date, insert a date code rather than typing the date. Date codes update to display the current date each time you open the file or style sheet. To insert a date code, select Insert from the Edit menu. Select Date/Time and choose the display format.

Compose documents in Draft or Outline mode

Ami operates too slowly in Layout mode when you need to enter large amounts of text. Also, Layout mode sluggishly refreshes the screen when you delete and insert individual characters—you can't always tell if you did so correctly. When you create a document, enter the text in Draft or Outline mode. Ami has improved Draft mode and new Outline mode displays the font, spacing, and indentions of paragraph styles, so you can be relatively confident that you are applying the correct styles to your paragraphs.

Create frames manually

Trying to enter a frame's size and position using the Create Frame dialog box is like trying to find your way through a maze blindfolded. If you make a wrong turn, you have to try again. Drawing a frame is so much easier using a mouse; you shouldn't do it any other way. To draw a frame manually, select the Frame icon. You don't have to choose the Manual button like you do when you select the Create Frame command.

Paginate in the background

When you cut and paste text, frames, or tables, Ami immediately flows text to its new position in the document. However, if you are editing a large document, it might take a few seconds for Ami to repaginate. You can start to work immediately after you cut and paste major blocks of text, frames containing complex graphics, or large tables by flowing text in the background. Select User Setup from the Tools menu. Select the Options button and choose Flow in background. Ami's performance might slow while it is repaginating, but you can return to work more quickly.

Printing

Printing long documents, or ones containing numerous fonts and complex graphics, can be time consuming. If your printer seems to be chugging along, try these tips to increase its performance.

Print without pictures

If you need to print a draft copy of your publication and you don't need graphics,you can omit them from printing. Ami prints faster without graphics, because it doesn't have to reproduce the detail in complex pictures. To omit graphics from printing, select Print from the File menu. Select the Options button and choose Without pictures.

Use Ami Pro's spooler

Have you ever wondered what the Windows' Print Manager does? You're not alone. Many people use the Print Manager without realizing its purpose, or if they need it. Print Manager schedules printing jobs from several Windows applications that are printing at the same time. So, unless you plan to print from several programs simultaneously, you don't need Print Manager. Ami Pro 2.0 comes with a new print spooler that reads the document and sends it to the Print Manager, who in turn sends it to the printer. If you turn off Print Manager, Ami sends the document directly to the printer, meaning faster printing. To turn off Windows' Print Manager, select the Control Panel command from the System menu. Select the Printers icon and turn off Print Manager.

Print in the background

Normally Ami schedules printing as a foreground task, taking precedence over all other tasks. However, if you need to begin working on your document immediately after choosing Print from the File menu, you should print in the background. Ami waits for idle time while it is not doing any other processing (saving a file, repaginating, finding and replacing), and prints the document then. Ami returns to the document more quickly when it prints in the background, but performance slows. If Ami has trouble printing the document, it will not display any message on the screen. Instead, you must minimize Ami and open the AmiPrint window at the bottom of the screen. The AmiPrint dialog box will ask you to retry or cancel.

Downloading fonts

If you added fonts to your printer, you can designate those you use the most as permanently resident. Downloading fonts permanently speeds up printing, because Ami doesn't have to wait for Windows to download fonts each time you print a document. Windows downloads temporary fonts only when you print a document that requests them. Windows removes the fonts once the document completes printing. To change the status of your fonts, select Printer Setup from the File menu and select Fonts. Highlight the font you want to change and select Permanent. Continue selecting fonts until you change the ones you use frequently. Be aware, however, that each font you download permanently requires printer memory, leaving less space for other fonts and your document.

Print using a parallel connection

If you print using a serial port, you are slowing your printer unnecessarily. A few years ago parallel ports were not as reliable as serial ports, but with improvements in parallel port technology, it behooves anyone printing long or complex documents to do so using a parallel connection.

File management

Any file that becomes too large is difficult to manage, so this section introduces a few tips for building and selecting documents with blazing speed.

Limit document size

Keep your documents under 40 pages, and editing will proceed much more quickly than if the document contained more pages. All the extra text and graphics in a large file slow down Ami. Keep your documents to a manageable size, and Ami will operate more efficiently.

Selecting a filename

When you select a file from a list, it is much quicker to double-click on the filename than to highlight the file and press Enter. To increase the speed of this process even more, refer to the tip about increasing your double-click speed on the mouse.

Open files from File menu list

Ami can display up to the last five files you opened, either documents or macros, at the bottom of the File menu. To open one of these files, simply select the filename. Displaying more than three filenames on the menu probably slows Ami somewhat, but the quickness with which Ami opens those files compensates for any sluggishness. To increase the number of the files Ami lists, select User Setup from the Tools menu. Enter a new number in the Recent files text box.

Loading a file automatically

You can load a file directly from the Windows Desktop by creating a document icon. When you select the icon, Windows starts Ami and loads that file automatically. To create a document icon, open the File Manager from the Main group in Windows. Resize the File Manager window so that you can see it and your document's destination window at the same time. Display the Ami document in the File Manager and drag the file into the destination window. Windows creates an icon for the document using the same picture as the Ami Pro icon uses. You can double-click on the document icon to start Ami and load the document.

Another method of creating a document icon is to select New from the File menu in the Windows Program Manager. Select Program Item from the New Program Object dialog box. Type a description of the file, and type the document's drive, directory, and filename in the Command line text box. To change the icon Windows associates with the document, select the Change Icon button.

Hardware

Changes you make in your hardware benefit not only Ami, but other programs you use as well. You might have some of these utilities and not even realize it. Windows comes with its own disk caching program, and some of the most popular *fix-it* utilities also have useful programs you can try for increased performance.

Configure your disk cache

When you setup Windows, it automatically installs a disk cache program called SmartDrive. Windows also sets up how much memory to use for the cache, which might or might not be appropriate for your needs. Exactly how much memory to allot to the cache is a tough call, because Ami Pro rarely tells you it's out of memory. Instead, it swaps program code to the hard disk, thereby slowing its performance.

A good rule to follow is to use no more than one-third of your memory for the cache. Always keep a minimum of 1.5 MB for Ami Pro. Table 21-1 lists sample lines in CONFIG.SYS that define a cache for PCs with different amounts of RAM. The first number in the line is the size of the cache, and the second line is the minimum size of the cache. If you use Ami's drawing and charting features extensively, decrease the first number to 384, 768, and 1024, respectively.

Many publications have been criticizing the cache for its lack of performance and flexibility; however, anytime you use another cache with programs running

Table 21-1. Disk Cache Sizes for 286 PCs

Amount of RAM	CONFIG.SYS Line
2MB	DEVICE = SMARTDRV.SYS 512 128
3MB	DEVICE = SMARTDRV.SYS 1024 512
4MB	DEVICE = SMARTDRV.SYS 1586 512

under Windows, you run the risk of losing data and hurting performance, rather than increasing it. SmartDrive was designed specifically to work with Windows, so it is your safest option.

Optimize your hard disk

Your mother would be appalled at the way DOS keeps house. It stores files wherever it finds room, so if DOS can't put the entire file in one place, it stores half the file in one location and the other half in another. When it comes time for Ami to load that file, it takes longer to retrieve if the file is scattered all over the hard disk.

How can you tell if you've got fragmented files? More than likely you do, especially if you have ever run out of room on your hard disk. To be sure, watch the hard disk light when you load a program or a file. Each time the light flashes, DOS is looking in another place on the hard disk. To clean up this mess, you need to use a disk optimizing utility. The program can tell you if files are scattered over your hard disk, show you a road map of your hard disk and those files located in several places, and let you reorganize the disk so that the files are located in one place. The disk optimizing utilities that are available are Optune, PC-Kwik Power Disk, and SpinRite. Other, more full-featured utility programs also offer optimizing utilities, including Norton Utilities, PC Tools, and Mace Utilities.

286 speed tips

Running Ami Pro on a 286 machine is slow—sometimes unbearably slow. Importing screen capture files, editing long documents, and other operations crawl at a snail's pace. The key is improving Ami Pro's performance through Windows; however, you can take some steps to increase your machines performance. Some tactics cost nothing, while others might cost a few hundred dollars, but all of your other programs under Windows will benefit also.

Add more memory

Even if Ami tells you that your machine has enough memory, add more. The free memory figure Ami displays when you select About Ami Pro from the Help menu is misleading. Ami places any program code it doesn't need immediately on your hard disk. If you notice a delay when you select a menu or perform other operations, Ami is probably looking to your hard disk for that part of the program. Adding memory to a 286 machine can make it run faster than a 386SX machine with less memory, so performance isn't entirely dependent on the processor.

Add extended memory

Adding memory is a step in the right direction, but you need to know what type of memory to add to get the best possible performance. Adding extended memory is the best option. Windows can use expanded memory only if you run in Real mode, which is much slower than Standard mode. Adding extended memory is usually less expensive, and provides better results than adding expanded memory.

Even if your PC doesn't have the capability to add memory to its motherboard, you can use memory cards, such as Intel's AboveBoard or AST Research's Rampage Plus/286 EMS memory card. These items usually provide expanded memory, but you can configure them to add extended memory.

Use a fast hard disk

When it comes time to buy a hard disk, most people look for size, but they don't consider speed. Until programs like Ami Pro, speed was a perk not a necessity. However, Ami Pro requires a good deal of disk space (6–8 megabytes), as do the other Windows programs you use.

The key to a fast hard disk is its seek time. The lower the average seek time, the faster the disk, and ultimately, Ami Pro runs.

Upgrade your video card

One of the biggest drains on your PC is its video card. Windows positively must have a quick VGA card to run at an optimum speed. If you use an EGA system, you can replace your card with a VGA adapter. Windows runs best at 640 × 480 VGA resolution, and VGA adapters are already faster than their EGA counterparts. Also, if you have an old or 8-bit VGA adapter, consider replacing it.

Once you have a VGA adapter installed in your 286 PC, run Windows in 640 × 480 in 16 colors only. Trying to run Windows in 256 colors or in SuperVGA mode is too much for your machine. There's no point in upgrading to a VGA board if your configuration is slowing the system down.

Don't use type managers

Type managers decrease Ami Pro's performance, because they require too many resources for a 286 machine. Instead, use other font sources such as ZSoft's SoftType, or Zenographics SuperPrint. These products still control the document's fonts, but they don't scale fonts. They do require a chunk of disk space, however, so make sure you have the available space necessary before investing in these items.

Another alternative to type manager is a font cartridge. You still get lots of fonts, but without the decreased performance or loss in disk space. Be prepared for a longer print time, however, and possibly no representative screen fonts for your display.

Select a simple wallpaper design

As simple as the concept of wallpaper seems, choosing a complex design can decrease Ami Pro's performance. Wallpaper is the design Windows uses to display in its desktop. However, Ami Pro also uses the wallpaper design as the shadows behind its example boxes in dialog boxes and as the dividing border in some dialog boxes. Such a simple decision has far-reaching effects. Select a single color wallpaper by selecting Control Panel from the Control menu. Double-click on the Desktop icon or select Desktop from the Settings menu. Select None from the Wallpaper files list box. Windows then uses the color assigned to the Desktop in the Color dialog box as the wallpaper color.

Summary

The whole idea around Windows' based programs is that they are easier to use and they let you be more productive, because they are intuitive and let you do multitasking. Major debates are raging about that point, but no user interface or program is perfect for everyone. Ami provides you with several means of performing the same task. The longer you use Ami, the more shortcuts you'll discover. Some speed tips don't include Ami itself, but require you to change Windows' settings or your hardware. With a little amount of effort, you can save yourself a lot of time.

22
CHAPTER

Safety tips

Nothing strikes fear into the hearts of users more than opening a file and knowing what you see on the screen isn't what you saved. Did someone else make changes? Did you accidentally delete the file? Was there a power outage while someone was working on the file? What happened?

I've seen people lose entire books, newsletters, and other major projects without having any backups. These were intelligent, successful people, but they never thought the unthinkable would happen to them. It does. Protect yourself and your company against the accidental loss of files.

How much extra time around the office do you have to spare? Few of us can afford to redo work lost in a fire, power failure, or loss or damage of disks. How much time would it take you to recreate your current project? How much time would it take you to recreate jus the work you've done today? The answer probably is "too long." My threshold for recreating lost work is about ten minutes, so I save my work that often. And it has saved me and my sanity countless times.

This chapter explains how to avoid the unexpected: unauthorized changes to a document, undoing disastrous editing, recovering missing files, and preventing unexpected delays and extra work in Ami.

Preventing changes to a document

With Ami's Lock for annotation feature, you can prevent others from making changes to a document. All the menu commands that let you modify the document and the style are greyed, and Ami will not let you edit the document. You can still view, open, and close the document, but Ami does not allow any changes. Lock for annotation is especially useful on a network where many people have access to the same files. To prevent changes to a document, you must perform two steps: enter your name in the User Setup dialog box, and turn on Lock for annotation. Select User Setup from the Tools menu. Type your name in the Name text box. Select Doc Info from the File menu and select Lock for annotation. Ami locks the document, letting you and others add only notes to it. The only person who can turn off lock for annotation is you.

You cannot lock a style sheet for annotation through Ami, but you can prevent others from changing it. More information is discussed on protecting style sheets later in this chapter.

Making style sheets read-only

If you work with a team of writers, you probably all use the same style sheet. To achieve a consistent appearance among all the documents your department produces, it is imperative that individual writers do not make changes to their copy of a style sheet. If one person modifies a style to use a smaller point size, while another person changes the style's paragraph alignment, their publications won't be consistent, giving a thrown-together appearance to your company's publications.

To prevent any tinkering to a style sheet, you can make it read-only. This still lets you use the style sheet and modify styles, converting them to document styles; however, Ami prevents you from saving those changes to the style sheet. If you attempt to do so, Ami displays an "Error writing to file" message. You can save the style sheet under another name and make changes to the newer one.

To make a style sheet read-only, select File Management from the File menu. Change the directory to the one containing style sheets by clicking on the directory, or by selecting Change Directory from the File menu. Type the directory where Ami can find your style sheets. Select Partial from the View menu and type *.sty in the text box. Once Ami displays the style sheet names, highlight the one you need make read-only. Select Attributes and choose Read-only.

Renaming style sheets

Before you begin using the style sheets supplied with Ami, rename them. If you make changes to the original and others want to use it, they'll be surprised to find that the style sheet doesn't match what is in the documentation. If you do make changes to an original style sheet, you can get another copy of the original from the Ami Pro disks. Run the Ami Pro setup and install only the style sheet files.

Devising a backup schedule

If you back up your files regularly, you are one of a rare breed. As important as backing up is, relatively few people do it. To prevent losing any of your work if a disaster would occur, you must back up your files on a regular basis and store one set of backup floppies in another location. After all, what good are backups if they're destroyed along with your other work?

You can use DOS to backup your files, or you can use a more full-featured backup utility package. Such applications include the Norton Backup, Central Point Backup, Fastback Plus, and others. The Norton Backup was rated as the best choice among backup utility programs in a recent *PC Magazine* (June 11, 1991) and *PC World* magazine (July 1991) survey. Whatever choice of backup software you make, research all of its features and experiment with them before you rely on it to safeguard your important data.

The best backup schedule is easy and one you should perform often. The following is a schedule that protects your data against accidental lost or mistakes:

1. Make a full backup of your work on Monday.
2. Make incremental backups (copying only those files that have changed) Tuesday through Friday.
3. Take the entire set of backup disks home with you on Friday. If you work at home, take the disks to another location where you can access them in a hurry if needed.
4. Continue steps 1 through 3 for two more weeks.
5. On the fourth week, bring the set of backup disks you made in Week 1 and start over.

Why make so many backups? The unthinkable can happen to your backup disks. If an error occurs when you are backing up to those floppies, and they are the only set you have, you're out of luck. Some backup utility software makes it too easy to accidentally choose Backup when you meant to choose Restore. Once you've realized your mistake, it's too late: your backup disk has been overwritten.

The following backup do's and don'ts will simplify and safeguard your backups:

- Do plan a backup schedule and follow it. You'll find yourself rummaging through disks trying to find the right file if you back up randomly.
- Do keep backups for at least one year.
- Do use 3.5″ floppy disks if your PC uses that size. The smaller disks are sturdier than the 5.25″ floppies.
- Don't use foreign or graphic characters in your filenames. Some backup software will treat these files as corrupted, and won't back them up.
- Don't store all of your backup disks in one place.
- Don't try to save a few pennies by purchasing generic floppies. Which is worth more: the few cents you'll save or your work?
- Don't rely on your backup program until you test it. Backup your work and restore it to a different directory on your hard disk. Use the DOS COMPARE command on both sets. If they match, your software is reliable.

Saving often

Ami makes saving so easy, you don't have any excuse not to do it regularly. Click that icon or press Ctrl-S every ten or fifteen minutes. The two most important times to save your document are before printing and multitasking. Printing can run into a glitch and freeze, as can switching to another program. So before you begin using those *power* features of Ami and Windows, save your document. If you can't remember to save your file regularly, Ami can do it for you. Select User Setup from the Tools menu. Select Auto-timed save and enter how often, in minutes, you want Ami to save the file in the active window. Ami can use the auto-timed feature only if you have saved the document previously; if it doesn't have a name, Ami won't save it.

Using revert to saved

Have you ever made seemingly simple changes that totally destroyed your document? Maybe you edited a perfect passage of writing, only to be horrified at the results, or maybe you tried to import data into a table that just didn't look right when it came in. Ami lets bygones be bygones and gives you the original file back. Using the Revert to saved command on the File menu, you can undo any changes, including those Ami can't revert using undo, by removing the file from the screen and retrieving the same file from disk. You can make Revert to saved even more effective by saving often. That way, you won't lose the changes you wanted to keep in addition to those embarrassing ones.

Creating separate directories

If you've created a work of major proportions, like a book or manual, and you store its files in the same directory as your letters, memos, and invoices, how do you know which files belong to your book? Are they easy to find and back up? Probably not. You can make life easier by making a subdirectory for each of your publications and storing all the related files for each in the appropriate directory. Then you won't be shocked when you return to that document months later and find out you are missing files you thought you backed up.

Limiting file size

Keep your documents under 40 pages and editing will proceed much more quickly than if the document contained more pages. All the extra text and graphics in a large file slow down Ami. Keep your documents to a manageable size and Ami will operate more efficiently.

Reviewing other's changes to a file

If several people contribute to the same file, review their changes before continuing with your own. Use Document Compare to check the newest version of the file with the last version you have. You can then use the Revision Marking options to review each revision before accepting or cancelling it, cancel all revisions, or accept all revisions. Document Compare can warn you of any deletions or insertions to the document you would otherwise be unaware of.

Summary

Accidents happen. But you can prepare for the unexpected so that it doesn't affect you or your work. Ami provides many protective features that let you safeguard your documents, your style sheets, and your reputation around the office. Lock for annotation, Document Compare, and Auto-timed save are all designed to help you keep your documents updated and protected. Sticking to a regular backup schedule is the single most important step you can take to prevent losing your work. Saving your document often also helps maintain your sanity during frequent power outages. Creating separate directories for your publications and limiting a file's size let you manage, find, and work with your files easily and efficiently.

23
CHAPTER

Customizing Ami Pro

No program or user interface is perfect for everyone unless you can change it. We all need help when we start using a program, but once we're familiar with its features, we don't need all the help messages and menus. Ami lets you work in the manner you are most comfortable with. You can use its menus, icons, keyboard shortcuts, and change a host of other features described in this chapter.

Customizing Ami's start up

You can choose to display the Styles Box, whether to maximize Ami in a window, and what display mode, view, and style sheet to use when you start Ami. To do so, follow these steps:

1. Select User Setup from the Tools menu. Select the Load button. Ami displays the Load Defaults dialog box, as shown in Figure 23-1.

2. Specify the mode, view, and style sheet to use when you start Ami.

3. Specify whether to display the Styles Box, and whether to maximize Ami in a window.

4. Select OK until you return to the document. Ami uses the defaults you chose the next time you load the program.

Customize Ami Pro and document windows

Ami Pro has its own window on the screen, as does every document you open. You can adjust properties for the windows that hold Ami Pro and your documents

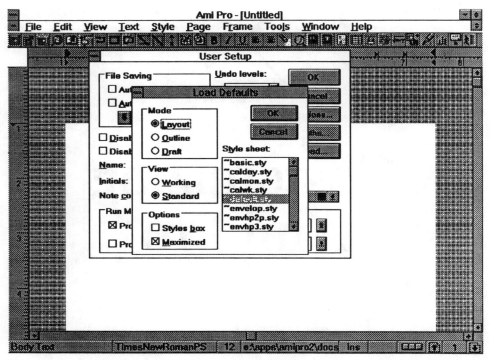

23-1   The Load Defaults dialog box lets you select a default mode, view, style sheet, and more. Ami Pro users your choices each time you load the program.

by changing the window border, size, and position. Changes you make to one window affect all other windows, be they for the document or for Ami Pro.

Changing window border width

Windows' default border width is five pixels, but you can make it as thin as one pixel or as wide as you need. To change the window border width by selecting Control Panel from the Control menu. Double click on the Desktop icon or select Desktop from the Settings menu. Type the new border width in the Border Width text box, and select OK. Select Close from the Control Panel Control menu. When you decide on a border width, choose a size that lets you select the border easily but lets you see as much of the screen as possible.

Changing a window's size

When you open a second document, Ami reduces the size of the current document and places the second document in a window of the same size. If you have only one document open, Ami displays the document window in its full size. However, you can change any document window in Ami, including the program window.

To modify the size of a document window or Ami's program window, follow these steps:

1. Select one of the sizing commands from the Control menu. If you want to resize the document window, select the command from the document's Control menu. If you want to resize the Ami Pro window, select the command from the Ami Pro Control menu (at the top left corner of the window). The commands available from the Control menu are as follows:

   Restore   Select Restore to return a window to its previous size.

   Size   Select Size to modify the window's width and height.

   Minimize   Select Minimize to reduce the window to an icon.

   Maximize   Select Maximize to restore the window to full size.

2. If you selected the Size command, a four-headed arrow appears. To resize height or width of the window, position the arrow on the edge and drag the mouse in the direction you need. To resize the height and width of the window, press an Up or Down Arrow key to move the four-headed arrow to one side of the window. Next, press the Right or Left Arrow key to change the four-headed arrow to an angled two-sided arrow. Now you can resize the window by changing its height and width at the same time.

Tip 23-1: Changing window size using a mouse   If you use a mouse, you don't have to select a command to resize a window. Just position the cursor on the edge of the window. When you see a two-sided arrow, drag the cursor in the direction you need. The window changes width, height, or both, depending upon the where you positioned the cursor.

Changing a window's position

When windows aren't full size, you can move them around on the screen. Changing windows' positions lets you compare documents by viewing their contents side by side or one on top of another. You can move a document window anywhere within Ami Pro's window.

If you use a mouse, simply place the cursor in the window's title bar and drag the window to its new position. If you use the keyboard, select the Move command from the Control menu and press an arrow key to begin moving the window in the direction you need. Continue pressing the arrow key until the window is in the correct position, and then press Enter.

Customizing the Icon Palette

Ami's improved icon palette is one of its most powerful features. If Ami doesn't supply an icon for your needs, you can create one using a macro and a .BMP graphics file. You also can choose the icons to display in the icon palette, and where to position the palette on the screen. To move the icon palette, select SmartIcons from the Tools menu and select its position from the dialog box: either floating, left, right, top, botton, or else hide it.

Selecting icons to display in the palette

To select the icons to display in the palette, select SmartIcons from the Tools menu and choose Customize. Ami displays the Customize SmartIcons dialog box, as shown in Figure 23-2. The icons Ami displays in the icon palette are listed in the Current Palette box. Your monitor might not be able to display all the icons listed, depending on the graphics card you have installed and resolution you selected in Windows Setup. Drag the icon you want to add from the Standard or Custom Icons box to the Current Palette box. Ami shifts the remaining icons over one position in the palette.

Creating custom icons

The steps for creating a custom icon are as follows:

1. Create the graphic to use in the icon using Ami's drawing tool or an external graphics application.

2. If you have an EGA display, make the picture 24 × 24 pixels. If you have a VGA display, make the picture 32 × 32 pixels. If you do not scale the picture according to your display, the icon will be too small to see in Ami. (In Windows Write, select the Image Attributes command under the Options menu. Select pels as the unit of measurement, and make the width and height the appropriate measurements.)

3. Save the graphic to a .BMP file format in the \AMIPRO directory.

4. Load Ami Pro.

5. Select Icon Palette from the Tools menu. Select Customize. Ami displays the Customize Icon Palette dialog box, and the icon you created appears in the Custom icons box.

6. Select the icon to which you need to assign a macro from the Custom icons box. If too many icons are displayed in the Custom Icons box, skip this step.

7. Select the Assign macro button. Ami displays the Assign Macro dialog box.

8. Select the macro you need to assign to the icon from the Macros list box. Click Save to save attach the macro to the icon.

9. To assign a macro to another icon, select the Next Icon button until the icon you need appears.

10. Repeat step seven to assign a macro to the icon.

11. Click OK to return to the Customize Icon Palette dialog box.

12. Drag your icon from the Custom icons box to the appropriate location in the Selected Icons box. Continue dragging icons until all the customized icons you need appear in the Selected Icons box.

13. Click OK to return to the document. Ami displays your customized icons in the icon palette.

Changing the number of files listed on the File menu

Ami already displays the last three files you opened, either macro or document files, on the File menu. If you frequently reuse more than three files, you can display up to five. Select User Setup from the Tools menu, and enter the number of files you want to display in the File menu in the Recent files text box.

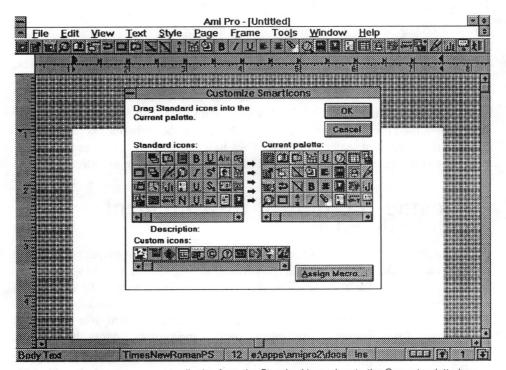

23-2 Move the icons you want to display from the Standard icons box to the Current palette box.

Increasing undo levels

Normally Ami can undo the last action you did in your document. However, if you really need some extra protection against yourself, you can increase the undo level so that Ami can revert your last four changes. To do so, select User Setup from the Tools menu and select a new setting from the Undo levels list box.

Specifying default paths

If you're like most of us, you save the majority of your files in the same place. You don't have to specify that drive and directory each time you use a document, style sheet, or macro, however. Instead, you can give Ami a default path to use for each of those file types. To specify default paths, select User Setup from the Tools menu. Select the Paths button and enter a default path for documents, style sheets, backup files, and macros. Ami gives backup files the same name as your original files, so you *must* specify a different path than the one you use for documents. Otherwise, Ami overwrites your document files with their older backup versions.

Customizing notes' display

You can change a note's background color, number them, and stamp them with your initials. Adding your initials to a note is especially useful if you work on a network and several people have access to the same files. To customize notes, select User Setup from the Tools menu. To add your initials to notes, type up to six characters in the Initials text box. To change the note's background color, select a color from the Note Color list box. Ami also displays the note marker using the same color. To display your initials next to the note marker and number them in the document, select Display initials in text. All these changes affect only the notes you create in the future; previously created notes are not affected.

Changing the unit of measurement on the tab ruler

Ami uses inches as the unit of measurement in the tab ruler it displays at the top of the window. Inches can be too large for positioning frames and drawing graphics in a document that uses smaller fonts and multiple columns. To change the unit of measurement Ami uses, click on the upper portion of the tab ruler. Select the inches button until it displays the unit of measurement you need. You can choose from inches, centimeters, picas, and points. Ami changes the ruler to display your new measurement. Click off of the ruler and Ami closes the tab bar.

Creating default frames

Ami's default frames uses the following attributes:

- an inside margin of .10″ on all sides
- text wraps around the frame
- stays in same position even if surrounding text moves
- transparent
- round corners
- drop shadow
- thin border between the margin and outside of frame.

If you create multiple frames that use different attributes, it's easier to modify a frame and make it the default than to modify every frame you place on the page. To create a new default frame, follow these steps:

1. Select the Frame icon or choose Create Frame from the Frame menu. Draw the frame on the page.
2. Select the Modify Frame Layout icon or select the command from the Frame menu.
3. Change the attributes you need to include in the default frame.
4. Select the Make Default button at the bottom left corner of the dialog box. Ami saves the current frame attributes as the defaults. The next time you create a frame, it uses the attributes you chose in the Modify Frame Layout dialog box.

Automatically backing up and saving documents

Remember the old saying, "an ounce of prevention is worth a pound of cure?" Well, Ami has its own ounce of prevention—two ounces to be exact, called Auto backup and Auto-timed save. Auto backup saves the previous version of the current file each time you save the document. Auto-timed save saves your document to disk at timed intervals you specify. Each option can save you from disaster (see chapter 23 for details). To turn on these features, select User Setup from the Tools menu. Select Auto backup and Auto-timed save and specify how often Ami should save your current file. Ami can save the document in the active window only if you have named it using File Save. Otherwise, Ami cannot save the file.

Turning off help messages

If you consider yourself to be a power user, you probably already know, without Ami telling you, that you are about to delete an important item from your document. You probably already know what each menu command does too.

Ami warns you when you delete notes, page breaks, footnotes, tables, floating headers and footers, page layouts, anchored frames, links, and power fields. Once you are familiar with these items, however, you don't need that reminder each time you delete. You can turn off the warning messages by selecting User Setup from the Tools menu and Disable warning messages.

When you select a menu or a command, Ami displays a description of your selection in the title bar. If you are an experienced user and know Ami's menu and command structure well, you can turn off the description display. Select User Setup from the Tools menu and choose Disable on-line help.

Running macros

You can execute a macro by pressing shortcut keys, selecting the macro filename, selecting a frame, loading a style sheet, opening and closing a document, or loading and exiting Ami. The last three options let you customize your style sheets, your documents, and Ami itself by running a macro at appropriate times. You can run a macro when you select a style with File New. You also can specify a macro to be run each time you load Ami. A useful application would be to load a style sheet with contents, a feature not available under User Setup.

To attach a macro to a style sheet, select Save as a Style Sheet and type the style name in the text box. Select Run macro and choose the macro name from the list box.

To run a macro when you load or exit Ami, select User Setup from the Tools menu. Select Program load or Program exit and specify the macro to run from the list box.

To run a macro when you open a file, open the file and make it the active window. Select Macros from the Tools menu and select Edit. Select Assign and either File Open or File Close. Type the macro filename in the text box.

For more information and additional options for running, creating, and attaching macros, refer to Chapter 13.

Customizing typographic controls

You can use the following typographic controls within Ami: hyphenation hot zone, widow/orphan control, and pair kerning.

The hyphenation hot zone is the area Ami uses at the end of each line to determine whether to hyphenate a word. If you increase the hot zone, Ami decreases the amount of hyphenation in your document. If you decrease the hot zone, Ami increases the hot zone. You can specify a hot zone between two and nine characters.

Widow/orphan control lets you tell Ami whether or not you want the first line of a paragraph to appear at the bottom of a page or the last line of a paragraph to appear at the top of the page. Normally, Ami does not let these lines appear by themselves on a page and turns on Widow/Orphan control.

Pair kerning reduces the amount of space between letters if you have a Post-script printer. If you use any other printer type, you should turn off pair kerning.

To change these typographic controls, select User Setup from the Tools menu. Select Options and choose the typographic controls you need.

Installing ATM fonts

Ami Pro comes with 13 ATM fonts. The installation process for ATM fonts is as follows:

1. Exit Ami Pro by selecting Exit from the File menu or by double clicking on the File menu.

2. Insert the ATM Fonts disk into drive A: and close the drive door.

3. Open the File Manager by selecting the icon and selecting Open from the File menu, or by double clicking on the icon.

4. Select the A: drive icon and display the files on the ATM Fonts disk.

5. Highlight the INSTALL.EXE and select Open from the File menu or double click on the filename.

6. Specify a separate target directory for outline fonts and font metric files.

7. Select the Install button.

8. If your printer has less than 512K of memory and you want to install PCL bitmap fonts, specify a directory. Choose Install to install the fonts. If you do not want to install bitmap fonts, select Skip.

9. Restart Windows to activate the fonts you just installed.

If you decide not to use the ATM fonts and you want to prevent them from displaying in Ami Pro font lists, open the ATM Control Panel in the Main group and select Off.

Customizing speed factors

The speed with which Ami works depends on several factors, including your PC's speed, how much memory your PC, printer, and display have, and how you work within Ami. You can increase Ami's speed by selecting two options from User Setup: Flow in background and Print in background

When you cut and paste text, frames, or tables, Ami immediately flows text to its new position in the document. However, if you are editing a large document, it could take a few seconds for Ami to repaginate. You can start to work immediately after you cut and paste major blocks of text, frames containing complex graphics, or large tables by flowing text in the background. Select User Setup from the Tools menu. Select the Options button and choose Flow in background. Ami's performance might slow while it is repaginating, but you can return to work more quickly.

Normally Ami schedules printing as a foreground task, taking precedence over all other tasks. However, if you need to begin working on your document immediately after choosing Print from the File menu, you can print in the background. Ami waits for idle time while it is not doing any other processing (saving a file, repaginating, finding and replacing), and prints the document then. Ami returns to the document more quickly when it prints in the background, but performance slows. If Ami has trouble printing the document, it will not display any message on the screen. Instead, you must minimize Ami and open the Ami-Print window at the bottom of the screen. The AmiPrint dialog box will ask you to retry or cancel. For more information on increasing Ami's speed, refer to Chapter 23.

Changing Ami Pro's colors

Windows controls the colors its applications use so that they display a consistent color scheme. When you change the colors for Ami Pro, you also affect any other Windows applications you use. You can change Ami Pro's color in one of two ways: by using the Control Panel, or by editing the WIN.INI file. Changing colors through the Control Panel is the easier of the two methods, but you cannot control as many settings as you can by editing the WIN.INI file.

Using the Control Panel to change colors

To change the colors by using the Control Panel, follow these steps:

1. Select Control Panel from the System menu (the grey box at the topmost left corner of the screen).

2. Select the Color icon. Windows displays the Color dialog box, as shown in Figure 23-3.

3. Select from one of the predefined color schemes in the Color Scheme list box. As you select a scheme, the sample screen uses the colors of the scheme you choose.

4. Select the Color Palette button to change individual elements of the screen.

5. Select the element you want to change by highlighting it from the Screen Element list box or by clicking on it in the sample screen. Figure 23-4

displays the screen elements you can change and their position in the Ami Pro window.

6. Select the color to use for that element by selecting a color from the Color Palette.

7. Continue steps five and six until the sample screen displays the colors you want.

8. Select the Save Scheme button to name the color scheme. Type a name, up to eight characters, and select OK. Windows changes its colors to reflect those you selected in the Colors dialog box.

Editing the WIN.INI File to change colors

Changing Ami Pro's screen colors is more difficult when you edit the WIN.INI file, but you can customize screen elements not available from the Control Panel. To specify a color in the WIN.INI file, you must know the red, green, and blue settings for the color you plan to use. The easiest way to determine these settings is to display the Control Panel, select the Color Palette, and select the color you want to use. Select Define Custom Colors and write down the red, green, and blue settings for the color you chose. Continue selecting colors until you have recorded all their settings.

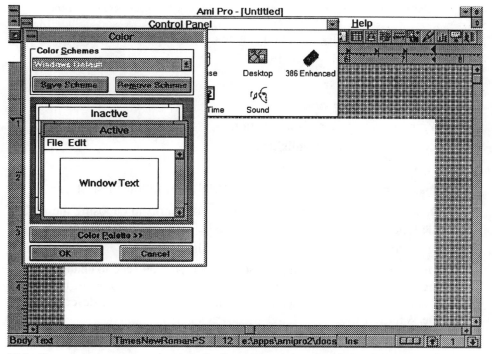

23-3 The color scheme you select from the Control Panel also controls Ami Pro's colors.

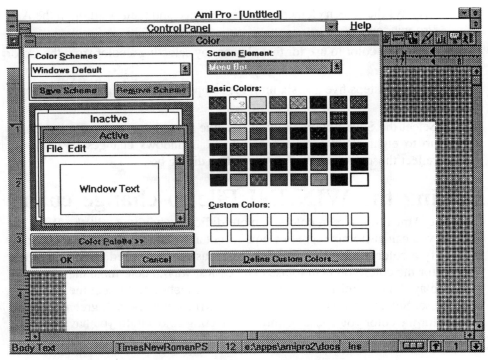

23-4 You can override the color scheme to assign individual colors to each screen element.

By editing the WIN.INI file, you can change the following screen elements:

- buttons
- button shadow
- button text
- dimmed menu commands and options
- background color for highlighted text
- text color of highlighted text.

To change the colors by editing the WIN.INI file, follow these steps:

1. Open the file in Ami Pro by selecting File Open and choosing the ASCII file type. Select ASCII Options, and CR/LF at paragraph ends only.

2. Move to the [colors] section heading in the file.

3. Modify the lines containing the screen element you need to change changing their red, green and blue settings. Separate each color setting with a space. Table 23-1 includes the screen elements and their descriptions in the WIN.INI file.

4. Save the file by selecting File Save. The next time you start Windows the new colors take effect.

Table 23-1. WIN.INI Color Command Lines

Command Line	Description
ButtonFace=	Color on buttons such as OK and Cancel.
ButtonShadow=	Shadow color around right edge of button.
ButtonText=	Text color appearing on button face.
GrayText=	Color of unavailable commands and option.
Hilight=	Background color of highlighted text.
HilightText=	Text color of highlighted text.

Editing the AMIPRO.INI file

In version 1.2, Ami saved its default paths, settings, and other options in the WIN.INI file in the Windows directory. In version 2.0, however, Ami creates its own .INI file, called AMIPRO.INI, and stores it in the Windows directory. This file takes the place of the old settings for 1.2 in the WIN.INI files. Ami ignores any old Ami settings that are stored in the WIN.INI, so you can remove them without affecting Ami's performance.

If you are comfortable editing .INI files, you can customize Ami's performance by modifying the file's settings. This is especially useful if you have two people using the same computer. You could have two AMIPRO.INI files, one for each person containing his or her favorite options.

Figure 23-5 displays a portion of the AMIPRO.INI file. The file contains two major sections: [AmiVISD] and [AmiPro]. You should modify only those settings that fall under [AmiPro]. You can edit the settings below the [AmiVISD] control the graphic file formats but you should never modify them.

Tip 23-2: Backup AMIPRO.INI before editing Always make an extra copy of the AMIPRO.INI before you make any modifications. If your changes produce disastrous results, you can overwrite the new file with the original AMIPRO.INI to restore Ami to its previous settings.

The following paragraphs explain the most useful lines in AMIPRO.INI and how you can change them to customize Ami Pro.

Application = <settings> The lines beginning with "Application" identify those file formats that Ami recognizes and can import. If you do not want to import a particular file format, you can remove the line identifying it in the AMI-PRO.INI file. Ami will not list that file format in the Type list box available in the File Open dialog box.

AutoMacroExit = <filename> AutoMacroExit is the macro Ami plays back everytime you leave Ami. Specify this macro by selecting User Setup from the Tools menu and entering a filename in the Program Exit text box.

23-5 The contents of the AMIPRO.INI file.

AutoMacroLoad − <**filename**> AutoMacroLoad is the macro Ami plays back everytime you start Ami. Specify this macro by selecting User Setup from the Tools menu and entering a filename in the Program Load text box.

Backup = <**path**> Backup is the default path for backup files Ami creates if you have the Auto backup feature selected in the User Setup dialog box. You must specify a path other than the one you use for documents, because Ami gives backup files the same name as their original files.

Defstyle = <**filename**> Defstyle is the default style sheet Ami loads when you start the program. Specify a default style sheet by selecting User Setup from the Tool menu. Select Load and choose a style sheet filename. Ami loads the default style sheet when you start the program and when you choose File New.

Dictionary = <**path**> Dictionary is the default directory for macro files. Specify a default directory for the dictionary by selecting the Language Options button from the Spell Check dialog box.

Docpath = <**path**> Docpath is the default directory for document files. Specify a default directory for documents by selecting the Paths button from the User Setup dialog box.

Glossary = **<filename>** Glossary names the Ami Pro file to use as the glossary file containing glossary entries.

Initview = **<integer>** Initview is the default view as specified in the Load Defaults dialog box when you choose Tools User Setup. A setting of three indicates Standard view, while a setting of two indicates Working view.

ISD = **&<Installed Option>** The lines beginning with *ISD* identify the installed options you chose during the Install procedure. The install options you can choose from include: drawing, charting, and equations.

LastOpen1 = **<filename>** LastOpen1 is the most recent file you edited. If the Recfiles line is set to one or more, this filename appears on the File menu. You can open this file by selecting it directly from the File menu rather than using File Open.

LastOpen2 = **<filename>** LastOpen2 is the second most recent file you edited. If the Recfiles line is set to two or more, this filename appears on the File menu. You can open this file by selecting it directly from the File menu rather than using File Open.

LastOpen3 = **<filename>** LastOpen3 is the third most recent file you edited. If the Recfiles line is set to three or more, this filename appears on the File menu. You can open this file by selecting it directly from the File menu rather than using File Open.

LastOpen4 = **<filename>** LastOpen4 is the fourth most recent file you edited. If the Recfiles line is set to four or more, this filename appears on the File menu. You can open this file by selecting it directly from the File menu rather than using File Open.

LastOpen5 = **<filename>** LastOpen5 is the fifth most recent file you edited. If the Recfiles line is set to five, this filename appears on the File menu. You can open this file by selecting it directly from the File menu rather than using File Open.

Macro − <key>,<key> = <filename> Any line beginning with the word *macro* specifies shortcut keys for a macro. The letters following the word *macro,* are the combination keys: S is Shift, C is Ctrl, A is Alt, and letter following the comma is the letter or number key. So, SC,D would be the shortcut key combination Shift-Control-D. The file after the identifying key letters is the macro assigned to the shortcut keys.

Macrodir = <path> Macrodir is the default directory for macro files. Specify a default directory for macros by selecting the Paths button from the User Setup dialog box.

PageNumStyle = <integer>   PageNumStyle is the page number style you specify from the Page Numbering dialog box. The settings are one for arabic number, two for uppercase roman, three for lowercase roman, four for uppercase alphabetical, and five for lowercase alphabetical.

QuickPlay = <key>,<key>   QuickPlay identifies the keystroke combination you assign to playing back a quick macro. Assign shortcut keys to a quick macro by selecting Options from the Record Macro dialog box. When Ami displays the Quick Macro Record options dialog box, you can specify shortcut keys for both playing and recording a quick macro.

QuickRec = <key>,<key>   QuickRec identifies the keystroke combination you assign to recording a quick macro. Assign shortcut keys to a quick macro by selecting Options from the Record Macro dialog box. When Ami displays the Quick Macro Record options dialog box, you can specify shortcut keys for both playing and recording a quick macro.

Recfiles = <integer>   Recfiles is the number of recent files you specified in the User Setup dialog box. These are the files you recently edited that appear at the bottom of the Files menu. If you list four files on the File menu, then your AMI-PRO.INI file would contain the line Recfiles = 4.

SideBarPlacement = <integer>   SideBar Placement controls the position of the icon palette on the screen. 1 is left, 2 is right, 3 is top, 4 is bottom, and 5 is floating.

Stypath = <path>   Stypath is the default directory for style sheet files. Specify a default directory for style sheets by selecting the Paths button from the User Setup dialog box.

TbUnits = <integer>   TbUnits controls the unit of measurement Ami displays in the horizontal and vertical rulers. 1 displays inches, 2 displays centimeters, 3 displays picas, and 4 displays points.

Thes4 = <filename>   Thes4 is the name of the thesaurus file you use.

UserInitials = <initials>   UserInitials are the initials you entered in the User Setup dialog box (up to 6). Ami displays your initials in any notes you insert into a document.

UserName = <name>   UserName is the name you entered in the User Setup dialog box. Ami uses this name for Lock for annotations. If you locked a document for annotations, you are the only person that can unlock the document.

Viewlevel = <integer>   Viewlevel is the percentage you specified as the Working view level in the View Preferences dialog box. The percentage is the percent of the page you see in Working view.

VISDSnapshotSave = <setting>   VISDSnapshotSave is the setting you specified for Graphic display speed options in the User Setup Options dialog box. Graphic display speed options specify whether you want Ami to create .G00 screen files for your graphics. The files help Ami to draw the graphics more quickly when you display them. The more .G00 files you have, the faster Ami operates, but the more disk space Ami requires. The available options are OnlyWhileOpen, ForFastDisplay, and Off.

Power fields and macros insert additional lines into the AMIPRO.INI file, so your file could include lines other than those listed in the previous paragraphs. Commonly inserted lines include the following:

[*Fields*] Fields precedes the section that includes any custom power fields you created. A sample line defining a power field could look like this:

Figure = Sequentially numbered figures in a document˜Seq Figure

Figure is the name of the custom power field. The phrase after the equals sign is the description of the power field. The tilde separates the power field description and the power field definition. Seq Figure is the custom power field.

Most lines inserted by macros include a section header, such as [Palette], which is followed by the settings for that macro. For example, the ICON-MAN.SMM macro, which lets you save and open different icon palettes, inserts the following lines into the AMIPRO.INI file:

```
[Palette]
LastPalette5 =
LastPalette4 =
LastPalette3 =
LastPalette2 =
LastPalette1 = 68210584.CP-maria
```

The first line, [Palette], is the section header. Each line following defines one of five icon palettes you can save and retrieve.

Summary

Your needs in a word processor depend upon your skills and the type of documents you create. Ami has the flexibility to adapt to your changing skills, so if you need on-line help and you use inches as your unit of measurement, you can use those options. If you later know Ami so well that on-line help is cumbersome, you would rather use picas, and you need a different default frame, you can change those options.

If you began writing correspondence and contracts, but you now also write newsletters and marketing materials, you can update Ami's settings to reflect your new documents' needs. Maybe you didn't need to display a horizontal or vertical ruler when you wrote contracts, but now that you product newsletters, rulers are important.

As your needs and your documents' requirements change, so can Ami. You can save different settings for different documents or users by creating several AMIPRO.INI files (AMIPRO.MAH, AMIPRO.DFP) and renaming the one you need before you start Windows.

24
CHAPTER

Building
a document

This chapter describes the entire process of building a document, from the basics, such as choosing a style sheet and entering the text, to more detailed procedures, such as adding tables and footers. You can create a report from start to finish with the steps outlined in this chapter. The final report is shown in Figure 24-1 Creating a report requires many of the same procedures you need to use to build a book, a newsletter, an advertisement, or a business card. You can apply these techniques to the other documents you create. Because a report is a document that people must read, even though they might not want to, you need to make its content easy to understand and comprehend. See chapter 10 for more details on strategies for designing documents.

The goal of this chapter is to take you step by step through building a report from start to finish. Later, after you create the document, you can review your actions and return to the chapters in this book that explain them in more detail.

The report you create will contain the following elements: text, a drawing, a table, a chart, and a footer. Although you could create the chart or drawing using an external application, the beauty of Ami Pro is that you don't have to. You can create all the elements for a successful document in Ami.

Preliminaries

Have you ever forgotten where you placed your files on the hard disk? Do you have several different versions of the same style sheet floating around? Have you ever lost your work due to a power outage or by accidentally deleting the wrong file? You can avoid these pitfalls by taking a few extra minutes to ensure yourself.

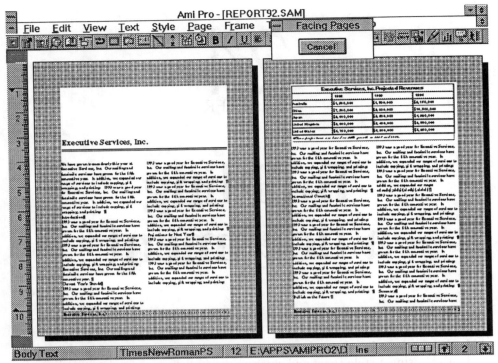

24-1 The first two pages of the final report you will create in the chapter.

Creating a document directory

Before you type the first word in Ami Pro, you should create a directory to hold your document's text and graphics files. Ami doesn't require you to do this, but though it remembers the location of your files, you might not. When it comes time to remove those files from your hard disk, you could accidentally delete too many or too few files, or forget where you put them. Also, copying graphics files to your publication's directory ensures that the original versions remain intact, even if you change the graphics in your document later. Once you have a directory for the document, you should start Ami Pro and specify the default document path as that directory. It uses the directory in which you placed the style sheets during installation as the default style sheet directory. You can change the default directory by selecting User Setup from the Tools menu and selecting Paths. If you copy a style sheet to a directory other than the default, you will not be able to access that style sheet.

You can create a directory in DOS or in Windows File Manger. To create a directory from DOS, type the following command:

    MD \REPORT

Type the following command to create the backup directory:

MD \REPORT\BACKUP

To create the directory in File Manager, use these steps:

1. From the DOS prompt, type WIN to start Windows.
2. Open the Main program group by double-clicking on it, or by selecting Open from the File menu.
3. Start File Manager by double-clicking on its icon or by selecting Run from the File menu.
4. Select the Create Directory from the File menu.
5. Type ANNUAL and select OK. Windows creates the ANNUAL directory. Before you create a backup directory under \ANNUAL, you need to select that directory's icon.
6. Highlight the ANNUAL directory. Select Create Directory again from the File menu.
7. Type BACKUP and select OK.
8. Select Exit from the File menu.

Specifying a default directory

Now that you have created a holding place for the report's files, you are ready to start working with Ami Pro. Because you will be storing your report and backup files in their own directories, you can tell Ami to use those locations automatically. To do so, use these steps:

1. Start Ami Pro by double-clicking on its icon from Windows or by typing WIN AMIPRO from the DOS prompt.
2. Select User Setup from the Tools menu. Select the Auto backup feature so that Ami saves the previous version of your report in the \BACKUP directory each time you save the report.
3. Select the Paths button. Specify the directories you created, \REPORT, and \REPORT\BACKUP, as the document and backup directories.
4. Select OK until you return to the document.

When you save the report, Ami automatically places the file in the \REPORT directory. Each time you save the file, Ami places the last version in the \REPORT\BACKUP directory. Maintaining backup files requires extra disk space, however. If your hard disk is cramped, you might not be able to use the Auto backup feature effectively.

Choosing a Style Sheet

One of the first decisions you must make regarding your document is what style sheet to use. You can select a style sheet in one of two ways: choose New from the File menu, or Use Another Style Sheet from the Style menu. The File New command lets you start a document from scratch and load the style sheet's contents, while Use Another Style Sheet lets you keep a document's original contents while applying new formatting.

You will use the REPORT1.STY style sheet for your report. The style sheet contains two columns and a frame to hold the report's title. Because the style sheet contains a frame, you should use File New to load the contents.

To select a style sheet, use these steps:

1. Select Close from the File menu to close the untitled document.

2. Select New from the File menu and choose the With contents option.

3. Select REPORT1.STY. You can load the style sheet using one of three methods: highlight the file and double click on the style sheet name; highlight the file and select OK; highlight the file and press Enter. Ami loads the style sheet. If you display the Styles Box, the style sheet name appears in the title bar.

Immediately after you tell Ami what style sheet to use to format your document, you should always save it under another name before you make any changes. Doing so lets you adapt the style sheet for the current document while preserving the original version for other documents.

To save the style sheet under another name, select Doc Info from the File menu. Insert the cursor in the Document Description box and type a description for the style sheet. The description appears when you select New from the File menu. Select OK or press Enter. Select Save as a Style Sheet from the Style menu, and type REPORT in the text box. Select the With contents option to save the frame in your new style sheet. Select OK or press Enter.

Saving the file

Before you begin modifying styles, page layouts, or typing text, name your document. Doing so lets you save periodically by simply pressing Ctrl-S. Ami cannot save a document when you select File Save or Ctrl-S, unless you have already named the document. To do so, follow these steps:

1. Select Save As from the File menu.

2. Type the following report name in the text box: REPORT92. You do not need to enter an extension, because Ami assigns an .SAM extension to all documents.

3. Turn off the Keep format with document option to maintain the document's association with the style sheet. If you save a file when Keep format with document is selected, Ami forgets what style sheet you used, but keeps its formatting. If you modify the style sheet the document originally used, Ami does not update the document's appearance. Similarly,

if you use another style sheet, Ami does not use the new formatting. The document's format becomes an island: the formatting you do in other style sheets doesn't affect your document, and formatting changes you make within the document don't affect other style sheets or documents.

4. Insert the cursor in the Document Description text box and type a description for the document. If the style sheet description appears, overwrite it. The description appears when you select File Open or File Management commands.

5. Select OK or press Enter.

Entering the text

After completing the preliminary steps of creating and assigning a document directory, choosing a style sheet, and saving the file, you can begin to enter the report's text. You can type the text shown in Figures 24-2 and 24-3 directly into Ami, use another document that contains over 600 words, or import another word processing file that Ami supports. The text of the document is not as important as understanding the overall process of entering text and formatting it according to your document's purpose. If you do use another document or word processing

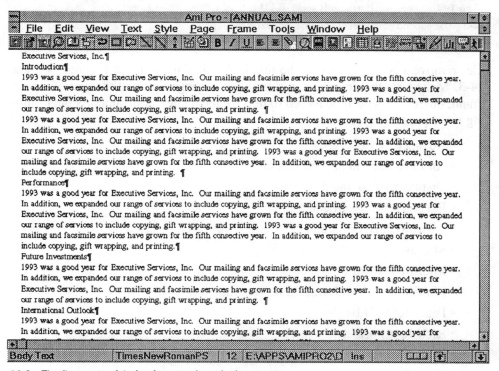

24-2 The first screenful of unformatted text in the report.

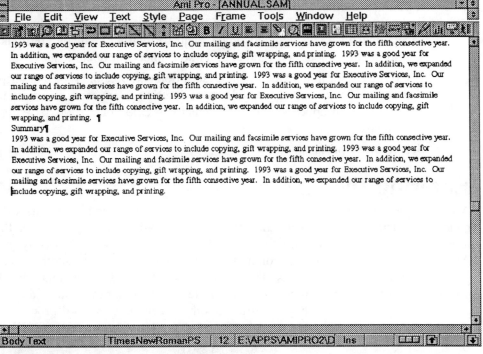

24-3 The second screenful of unformatted text in the report.

file, remove any formatting so the text looks similar to that in Figures 24-2 and 24-3. Make sure the document has only one carriage return at the end of a paragraph; otherwise, you'll be forced to remove them later. Ami supports the following word processing formats:

- Advance Write
- Ami Pro documents and macros
- DisplayWrite 4 and 5
- Executive MemoMaker
- Lotus Manuscript 2 and 2.1
- Microsoft Word 4, 5, and 5.5
- Microsoft Word for Windows
- MultiMate 3.3 and MultiMate Advantage II
- PeachText 2.11
- Rich Text Format
- Samna Word
- SmartWare 1

- Windows Write
- WordPerfect 4.1 through 5.1
- WordStar 3.3 through 5.0
- WordStar 2000 1 and 3.

You also can import word processing files not supported by Ami by importing them in ASCII or DCA format. To check whether your word processor has the capability of saving files to these formats, check under the File or Export commands or look in the documentation. To check if a file is in ASCII format, type the file's content at the DOS prompt using the Type command. If the contents display without any nonkeyboard characters, such as musical notes, the file is in ASCII form.

The general rule for importing files using other word processing formats is, if both programs support the formatting feature, such as alignment, spacing, and styles, then Ami can import those attributes. In practice, however, the process is not always as simple. To avoid extra work, keep formatting in your outside word processor to a minimum: bold, italics, and fonts. Leave other operations, such as aligning text, changing page layouts, and creating headers and footers, to Ami.

To enter the text by typing it directly in Ami, follow these steps:

1. Select Working from the View menu. Working view lets you see one line, from start to finish, across the page. Ami doesn't force you to scroll back and forth across the document to enter, edit, and view your text.

2. Select Draft mode from the View menu. You can enter text more quickly in Draft mode, and you don't need many of the extra screen elements available in Layout mode, such as rulers and column guides. When you change to Draft mode, Ami displays your document as using only one column. Not only does Ami not display column guides, but it also displays multicolumn documents as only one column in Draft mode. Not to worry, however. The change is for display purposes only. As soon as you return to Layout mode, you'll see that your columns are still intact.

3. Enter the text, pressing Enter only once after each paragraph.

4. Once you finish entering the text, move to the beginning of the document by pressing Ctrl-Home.

5. Cut the title by highlighting the text and selecting Cut from the Edit menu.

6. Change to Layout mode. Double click on the frame and highlight its existing text.

7. Paste the title in the frame at the top of the document by double-clicking inside the frame and selecting Paste from the Edit menu.

8. Increase the frame's length to three inches. Press Esc to unselect the frame's contents and select the frame instead. Drag the bottom center

black handle until the frame's border aligns at the four inch mark on the vertical ruler.

9. Save the chapter by pressing Ctrl-S. Save your file periodically as you progress through the chapter to prevent losing your work to UAE's or power outages.

Using styles to format paragraphs

The next logical step in building your report is to assign styles to the paragraphs. You won't need to do so for any paragraphs that use Body Text, because Ami defaults to that style automatically. Any text you type in Ami starts out using Body Text.

Styles contain a variety of formatting information including fonts, line and paragraph spacing, page and column breaks, bullets, lines above and below the paragraph, and even the numeric formatting they use in tables. Ami assigns a name to each style that describes its purpose. The styles contained in the REPORT.STY style sheet are:

- Body Text
- Body Single
- Bullet 1
- Bullet 2
- Heading 1
- Heading 2
- Number List
- Title
- Header
- Footer
- Assigning Styles.

Don't feel obligated to use all the styles in a style sheet just because they are there. If a style suits your purpose, use it. If the style is close to your needs, modify it before you begin using it. If a style is not what you need and never will be, remove it from the style sheet. Because you saved the style sheet under another name, none of the changes you make to it affect the original REPORT1.STY. You are free to experiment without fearing what effects your changes have on other documents.

To assign styles to the paragraphs in the report, follow these steps:

1. Make sure you are in Layout mode. Using Layout mode is not a requirement for assigning styles, but you can choose Full Page view only when you are in Layout mode. Assigning styles using Full Page view goes

quickly, because you can see all the paragraphs on the page at the same time.

2. Select Full Page from the View menu.

3. Insert the cursor in the paragraph to which you want to assign a style. Assign the Title style, and the Heading 1 style to the report subheadings.

4. Select the style. You can do so using one of three methods: press the function key representing that style; select the style name from the Styles Box; or selecting the style name from the status bar (click the mouse on the current style name and the style list appears; select the name from the list).

Assign the styles to the paragraphs using these procedures. The only paragraphs that need to use styles other than Body Text are headings and the title. Once you complete assign styles, save your report with Ctrl-S.

Modifying styles

The formatting Ami saves in each style might not be exactly what you have in mind. After you assign styles to the paragraphs in your report, you can modify the styles to suit your tastes or to reflect the document's purpose or audience. Look at the title inside the frame on the first page. The title looks lost inside such a large frame, doesn't it? Modify the title text and the frame containing the title. To do so, follow these steps:

1. Press Ctrl-Home to move to the first page.

2. Select Working from the View menu so that you can see the title more clearly.

3. Place your cursor inside the title.

4. Select Modify Style from the Style menu.

5. Turn off the italics by selecting the Italic check box, until the "X" inside disappears.

6. Select the Spacing attribute from the left side of the dialog box. Enter two inches as the Above paragraph spacing.

7. Select the Alignment attribute from the left side of the dialog box.

8. Turn off the indention by entering zero in the All text box.

9. Select the Lines attribute from the left side of the dialog box.

10. Select the Line below check box. Choose the eleventh line in the Line style box (it has a thick upper and thin lower line).

11. Select Margins as the line length.

12. Select OK or press Enter. Now you are ready to modify the frame.

13. Make sure the frame is selected or the cursor is inside the frame.

14. Select Modify Frame Layout from the Frame menu.

15. Select the Lines & shadows attribute from the left side of the dialog box.

16. Turn off any lines and shadows around the box.

17. Select OK or press Enter.

Inserting a table

Designing a table in Ami is really a three step process: create the table, enter the text, and format the text by modifying its style. You will do all three in building a table in the report. Ami separates its tables into two categories: page tables and frame tables. Although the tables themselves are the same, they differ in where you place them. Page tables are created directly on the page, but frame tables are placed inside a frame. Page tables can span across several pages, but you are limited to a left-aligned or centered table on the page. Also, page tables cannot span columns. You can position frame tables anywhere on the page by simply moving the frame. However, frame tables can be only one page long.

The table in the report will be a frame table, enabling you to create a table that spans two columns.

Creating the table

To create the table in your report, follow these steps:

1. While you are on the first page, insert a page break at the end of the last full paragraph on the page. To do so, place the cursor at the end of the paragraph. Select Breaks from the Page menu and select Insert page break. Ami inserts the break and moves the cursor to the next page.

2. Select the Frame icon or select the Create Frame command from the Frame menu. Select Manual if you chose the command.

3. Draw a frame by holding down the mouse button at the left corner of the document and dragging the frame down and to the right. Continue dragging until the frame is 2.5 inches long and extends the full width of the left and right margins.

4. Select Modify Frame Layout from the Frame menu.

5. Select Square corners as the frame's Display.

6. Select the Lines & shadows attribute from the left side of the dialog box.

7. Turn off any lines and shadows around the box.

8. Select OK or press Enter.

9. While the Frame is still selected, choose Tables from the Tools menu.

10. Specify four as the Number of columns and eight as the Number of rows.

11. Select OK or press Enter.

12. Highlight the cells in the first row and select Connect from the Table menu. Do the same for the cells in the last row.

Entering text into the table

To add the table's content, follow these steps:

1. Enter the text in the table, as shown in Figure 24-4. To identify the years as labels, press the spacebar before typing them.

2. Center the title by placing the cursor in the first row and pressing Ctrl-C. Highlight the title and press Ctrl-B to add the boldface attribute. While the text is still selected, increase the point size to 14 by selecting it from the Status Bar or selecting Font from the Text menu and selecting the correct point size.

3. Right-align the year labels by highlighting their cells and pressing Ctrl-R.

4. Italicize the last line in the table by highlighting the sentence in the last row and pressing Ctrl-I.

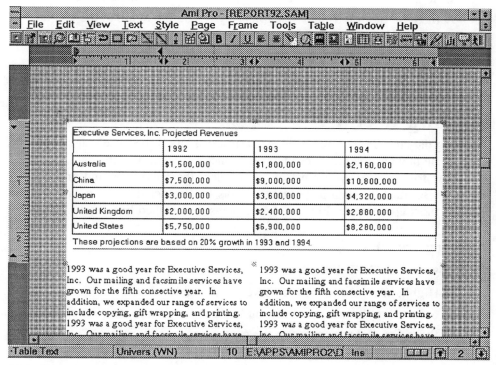

24-4 The unformatted contents of the report's table.

Modifying the table text style

The table in its current form is certainly more effective for displaying numbers than plain text, but you still can improve it. You can modify the Table Text style to display negative numbers in differing formats, add a currency symbol, and even change the thousands separator. You need to add a thousands separator, display a dollar sign, and change the table's fonts. To do so, follow these steps:

1. Place the cursor inside one of the table's cells. Look at the left side of the status bar and make sure it displays Table Text as the style. If it doesn't, assign the style to all text in the table.

2. Select Modify Style from the Style menu.

3. Select the Univers, Helvetica, or other nonserif font from the Face list box.

4. Select the Table format attribute from the left side of the dialog box.

5. Select Currency as the Cell format and enter zero as the Number of decimal places.

6. Turn on the Thousands separator by selecting its check box.

7. Select OK or press Enter.

8. Select the Modify Table Layout command from the Table menu.

9. Increase the row Gutter size to .11 by typing the figure in the text box.

10. Select OK or press Enter.

11. Highlight all rows in the table except for the last.

12. Select Lines/Shades from the Table menu and select All Sides.

Adding a chart

Creating the chart in your report is the easiest task of all, because you can use the data in the table as the basis for the chart. Once you give Ami the data, it creates the chart for you. All you have to do is select the chart type and any display options. Because the data in the table shows the predicted trend in sales, a line chart is most appropriate. Figure 24-5 displays the finished line chart.

Creating the chart

To create the line chart, follow these steps:

1. Highlight rows two through seven of the table.

2. Select Copy from the Edit menu to place the data in the clipboard.

3. Press Ctrl-PgDn to move to the next page.

4. Select the Frame icon or choose Create Frame from the Frame menu. Select Manual if you choose the command.

5. Draw a frame by holding down the mouse button at the left corner of the page and dragging the frame down and to the right. Continue dragging until the frame is 3 inches long and extends the full width of the left and right margins.

6. Select Charting from the Tools menu. Ami displays the Chart dialog box containing a sample chart it created from your data. However, Ami creates one line too many. It reads the year labels as numbers, and tried to chart them.

7. Select Data to change the years to a label format Ami can recognize.

8. Highlight the entire line containing the years and press Del.

9. Retype the years, inserting a space and an underscore in front of each label. Ami will use any number preceded by an underscore as a label. The underscore does not display in the chart. The space before the first label tells Ami that these are to be used as x-axis labels.

10. Select the Line chart icon.

11. Select the Legend and Grid options.

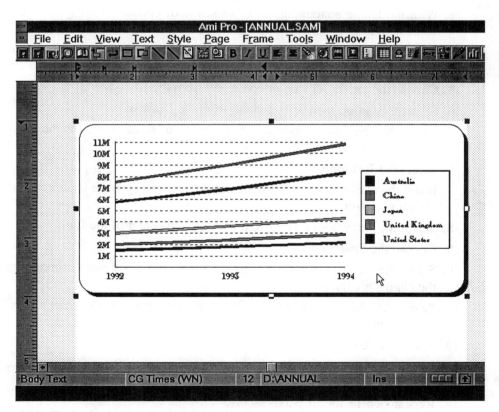

24-5 The basic chart created from the table data.

12. Select OK or press Enter.

13. Select Modify Frame Layout from the Frame menu.

14. Select Square corners as the frame's Display.

15. Select the Lines & shadows attribute from the left side of the dialog box.

16. Turn off any lines and shadows around the box.

17. Select OK or press Enter.

Modifying the chart using drawing

The chart is certainly presentable, but you still can make a few changes to make it easier to read. Remember, a report is usually documents people must read even though they don't really want to. Therefore, you need to make the report's content easy to understand and comprehend. Ami doesn't add any titles to its charts, but you can by using the Drawing feature. You also can edit labels and modify any other part of the chart using Drawing.

To modify the chart labels and add a title, use these steps:

1. With the frame containing the chart selected, choose Drawing from the Tools menu.

2. Increase the frame's length by dragging the bottom center black handle one inch down the page.

3. Choose the Select All icon or command from the Draw menu.

4. Select the Group icon or command from the Draw menu.

5. Move the chart to the bottom of the frame to make room for the chart title.

6. Select the Text tool.

7. Insert the cursor in the general area of the title and type the chart's title as shown in Figure 24-6.

8. Select the Arrow tool and move the title to the center of the frame.

9. Choose the Select All icon.

10. Select the Group icon or the command from the Draw menu to ungroup the chart's elements.

11. Select the chart and select the Group icon to ungroup the chart's bars, values, and text.

12. Select the Text tool.

13. Insert the cursor before the M in the top y-axis label. Press Del to remove the M.

14. Repeat step 13 for all y-axis labels.

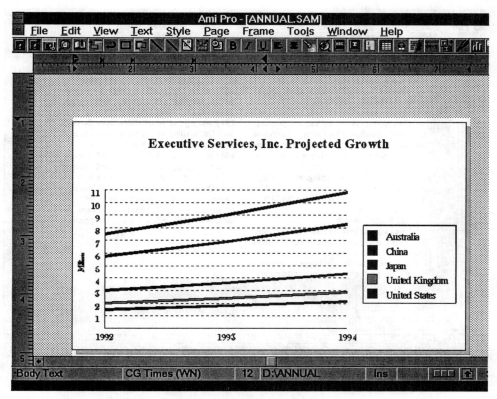

24-6 The line chart after being modified with the Drawing feature.

15. Select the Arrow tool and draw a box around the y-axis labels to select them.

16. Select the Group icon or the command from the Draw menu so that you can move all the labels at one time.

17. Select the Snap To icon or command from the Draw menu to keep the labels aligned with the grid in the chart.

18. Move the labels closer to the y-axis.

19. Select the Text tool and insert the cursor in a blank area. Type MIL-LIONS.

20. Select the Arrow tool and select the text.

21. Choose the Rotate command from the Draw menu. Do not choose the Rotate icon.

22. Select Counter clockwise as the Rotation direction and 90 as the Rotation degree.

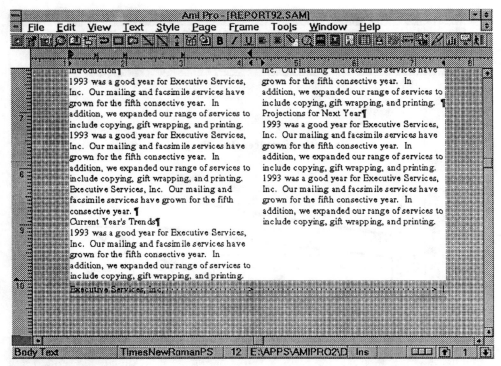

24-7 The report's footer.

23. Select OK or press Enter. The text rotates so that it appears sideways. The text might look awkward, but it will print fine.

24. Move the text to the y-axis to serve as the label for the axis.

25. Press Esc to unselect the chart and to select its frame.

26. Select Modify Frame Layout from the Frame menu.

27. Select the Lines & shadows attribute from the left side of the dialog box.

28. Select the Shadow box size as Normal. Select a grey shading color for the shadow.

29. Select OK or press Enter.

Adding a footer

Now you are ready for the last step: creating a footer. If you create a footer on one page, it will display on every page, all right pages, or all left pages. Because the report is a single-sided document, you don't need different footers for left and right pages. You can display the same footer on every page. Figure 24-7 displays the finished footer in the report.

To create the report's footer, follow these steps:

1. Press Ctrl-Home to move to the beginning of the document.
2. Place the cursor in the bottom margin.
3. Type the text of the footer and press Tab twice.
4. Select Page Numbering from the Page menu.
5. Select OK or press Enter.
6. Assign the Footer style to the text you typed in the bottom margin.
7. Select Modify Style from the Style menu.
8. Select Lines attribute from the left side of the dialog box.
9. Select Line below. Accept the default line style in the Line style list box.
10. Add .05 inches of spacing in the text box. This spacing inserts room between the footer and the line.
11. Specify the line length as Margins.
12. Select OK or press Enter.

Summary

Now that you created a sample business document, you can apply the methods you used to build your own documents. This chapter does not attempt to cover all the features you will use in creating your publications, but it does serve as a guide for the basic steps common to most documents. As you review the chapters in this book and you become more familiar with Ami's powerful features, you can use other, more advanced and specific, document creation and manipulation tools available in Ami.

A

APPENDIX

Ami Pro marks

Ami Pro inserts marks into your document whenever you insert a page or column break, an inserted tab ruler, a floating header or footer, or a note. These markers help you identify an item's location in the document. You can hide or display markers using the View Preferences command from the View menu. Select Marks from the View Preferences dialog box to turn on or off marks in the document. The marks still exist, but you can't see them in the document. Table A-1 lists the marks Ami Pro uses in its documents.

Table A-1. Ami Pro Marks

Mark	Element	Mark	Element
	Column Break		Floating Footer-All Pages
	Page Break		Floating Footer-Right Pages
	Inserted Tab Ruler		Floating Footer-Left Pages
	Floating Header-All Pages		Note
	Floating Header-Right Pages		Inserted Page Layout
	Floating Header-Left Pages		

B
APPENDIX

Resources

As a first generation Windows word processor, Ami Pro is designed to work with other software programs, including fonts, grammar checkers, and utility software. This is not a comprehensive list, but the programs mentioned in this book are listed below along with the vendor's mailing address and telephone number. Contact the vendor for more information about its product or for ordering information.

Adobe Type Manager
Adobe Systems
1585 Charleston Road
P.O. Box 7900
Mountain View, CA 94039-7900
800-833-6687
415-961-4400

Central Point Backup
Central Point Software
15220 North West Greenbrier Parkway
Suite 200
Beaverton, OR 97006
503-690-8090

Complete Font Library Cartridge
Pacific Data Products
9125 Rehco Road
San Diego, CA 92121
619-552-0880

Fastback Plus
Fifth Generation Systems, Inc.
10049 N. Reiger Road
Baton Rouge, LA 70809
800-873-4384
504-291-7221

Grammatik for Windows
Reference Software International
330 Townsend Street
Suite 123
San Francisco, CA 94107
4415-541-0226

Hewlett-Packard Font Cartridges
Hewlett-Packard Company
Boise Division
P.O. Box 15
Boise, ID 83707-0015
1-800-752-0900

Mace Utilities
Fifth Generation Systems, Inc.
10049 N. Reiger Road
Baton Rouge, LA 70809
800-873-4384
504-291-7221

Norton Utilties
Symantec Corporation
10201 Torre Avenue
Cupertino, CA 95014
408-253-9600

The Norton Backup
Symantec Corporation
10201 Torre Avenue
Cupertino, CA 95014
408-253-9600

Optune
Gazelle Systems
42 North University Avenue
#10
Provo, UT 84601
800-233-0383

PC-Kwik Power Disk
Multisoft Corporation
15100 S.W. Koll Parkway
Beaverton, OR 97006
800-274-5945
503-646-8267

PC Tools
Central Point Software
15220 North West Greenbrier Parkway
Suite 200
Beaverton, OR 97006
503-690-8090

Spinrite
Gibson Research Corporation
22991 La Cadena
Laguna Hills, CA 92653
800-736-0637

C
APPENDIX

Using Ami Pro without a mouse

Most of us can't fathom using a GUI program without a mouse. Programs using the Windows interface also must be accessible with a keyboard, but they are definitely and purposely designed for mouse users. Some handicapped persons are not able to use a mouse, while others want to begin using Ami Pro right away, before they have the chance to buy a mouse, and some people are still struggling to install their mouse, which isn't recognized by Windows. This section is for all of you, who for whatever reason, are winging it without a mouse.

Three major features of Ami Pro are not accessible unless you have a mouse. These features are Drawing, the Status Bar, and the Icon Palette. All other operations are available to the keyboard. Ami provides keyboard shortcuts for some of the more commonly used tasks, but not all menu commands have shortcuts. For some, the only way to select a command is to display the menu and select the command from it. Table C-1 lists the keyboard shortcuts available in Ami Pro.

Selecting a command from Ami Pro's menus

To access the menu bar, press F10. You also can press Alt and the letter underlined in the menu you want to display. Some menu choices are obvious, such as Alt-F for the File menu, but others are rather obscure, such as Alt-R for Frame or Alt-L for Tools. Once Ami displays the menu, you can select a command by pressing the underlined letter in the command or by moving the cursor up or down to highlight the command and pressing Enter. For example, to select Alignment from the Text menu, you would press Alt-T to display the menu, then press A to select Alignment.

Table C-1. Keyboard Shortcuts

Task	Keyboard Shortcut
Access Ami Pro's Control Panel Box	Alt-Spacebar
Access Greek keyboard	Ctrl-G while in Equation mode
Access Menu Bar	Alt or F10
Access Styles Box	Ctrl-Y
Access Symbol keyboard	Ctrl-Y while in Equation mode
Access the document's Control Panel Box	Alt-Hyphen
Add first line indent to tab ruler	1
Add indent from right to tab ruler	3
Add indent to tab ruler	0
Add rest indent to tab ruler	2
Add tab to ruler inside dialog box	Spacebar
Bold	Ctrl-B
Center Align	Ctrl-C
Copy	Ctrl-Ins
Create a frame	Spacebar-Arrow key
Cut	Shift-Del
Define left margin on tab ruler	Ctrl-[
Define right margin on tab ruler	Ctrl-]
Delete a tab on ruler inside dialog box	Del
Delete current row in table	Ctrl-Minus
Delete current word	Ctrl-Del
Delete previous word	Ctrl-Backspace
Demote a paragraph in outline mode	Alt-Right Arrow
Display a maximized document in a smaller window	Open another document
Display specific outline level	Alt-outline level number
Find and Replace	Ctrl-F
Glossary	Ctrl-K
Go To dialog box	Ctrl-G
Go To Next Item	Ctrl-H
Help	Shift-F1
Insert a fraction	Ctrl-1 while in Equation mode
Insert a radical	Ctrl-2 while in Equation mode
Insert a subscript	Ctrl-4, +, Ctrl-Down Arrow while in Equation mode
Insert a superscript	Ctrl-3, +, Ctrl-Up Arrow while in Equation mode
Insert row below current one in table	Ctrl-Plus
Insert text in Equation mode	Ctrl-T while in Equation mode
Italic	Ctrl-I
Justify	Ctrl-J
Left Align	Ctrl-L
Modify Style	Ctrl-A
Move a graphic within a frame	Arrow keys, Ctrl-Arrow keys

Table C-1. Continued

Task	Keyboard Shortcut
Move a paragraph down in outline mode	Alt-Down Arrow
Move a paragraph up in outline mode	Alt-Up Arrow
Move among multiple document windows	Ctrl-Tab or Ctrl-F6
Move cursor within tab ruler	Arrow keys, Ctrl-Arrow keys
Move paragraph and subordinate text down	Alt-outline level number, Alt-Down Arrow
Move paragraph and subordinate text up	Alt-outline level number, Alt-Up Arrow
Move tab on ruler inside dialog box	Spacebar-Right or Left Arrow
Move to header or footer	Edit Go To Header, Footer
Normal	Ctrl-N
Paste	Shift-Ins
Place cursor on current tab ruler	Edit Go To Ruler
Place cursor on tab ruler inside dialog box	Press Tab until cursor displays in ruler
Print	Ctrl-P
Promote a paragraph in outline mode	Alt-Left Arrow
Right Align	Ctrl-R
Save	Ctrl-S
Select a tab leader	Tab, Right or Left Arrow
Select Cancel in a menu	Esc
Select chart variations inside dialog box	Spacebar
Select OK in a menu	Enter
Select tab type inside a dialog box	Tab, Right or Left Arrow
Show/Hide SmartIcons Palette	Ctrl-Q
Show/Hide Styles Box	Ctrl-Z
Switch paragraph with one above	Alt-Up Arrow
Switch paragraph with one below	Alt-Down Arrow
Toggle Draft/Layout Mode	Ctrl-M
Toggle Full Page/Current View	Ctrl-V
Underline	Ctrl-U
Undo	Alt-Backspace
Word Underline	Ctrl-W

If you select the wrong menu by mistake, you can press the right or left arrow keys to display other menus. To leave the menu bar and return to the document, press Esc twice: once to leave the menu, and a second time to leave the menu bar.

To move among multiple document windows, press Ctrl-Tab or Ctrl-F6. To access Ami Pro's Control Panel, press Alt-Spacebar. To access the active document's Control Panel, press Alt-Hyphen. To display a document in a smaller window, you must open another document. The Size command does not work while the document window is maximized.

Drawing a frame

To draw a frame using the keyboard, you can either specify the frame's size and position in the Create Frame dialog box or you can draw the frame manually. To draw the frame manually, select Create Frame from the Frame menu. Select Manual. Using the arrow keys, move the cursor to the position in the document where you need the frame. To draw the frame, hold down the spacebar and press the arrow keys. To stop drawing the frame, release the spacebar. To move to an existing frame using the keyboard, use the Go To command from the Edit menu and select Next Frame.

Modifying the tab ruler

The only way to access the tab ruler is to select Go To (Ctrl-G or the Edit menu), select Next item, and choose ruler. Ami moves the cursor to the tab ruler and displays the tab bar above it. Use the arrow keys to move across the ruler, or use the Ctrl key along with the arrow keys to move in larger increments.

D
APPENDIX

Style sheets

Ami Pro comes with over 50 style sheets that are ready for you to use with your own documents. This appendix displays examples of documents using each style sheet. Some documents are shown with the contents they already contain, such as the calendar style sheets, while contents were added to other style sheets to show the format they use. Refer to Table 5-1 to learn which style sheets can use the **With contents** option and those that do not contain any contents. Lotus support staff continually develops new style sheets that you can find on CompuServe by typing GO LOTUSWP.

~BASIC.STY

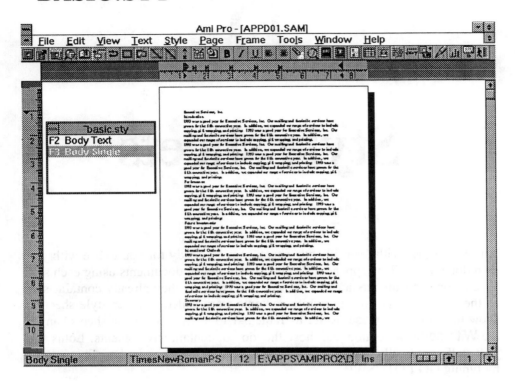

~CALDAY.STY

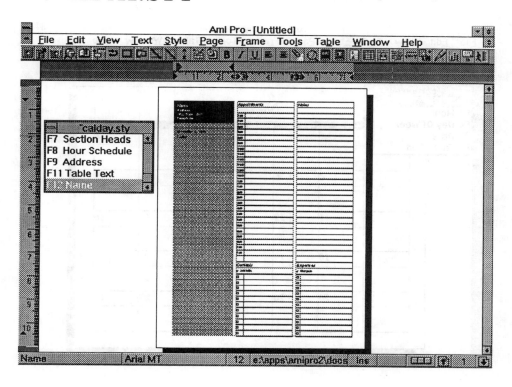

~CALMON.STY

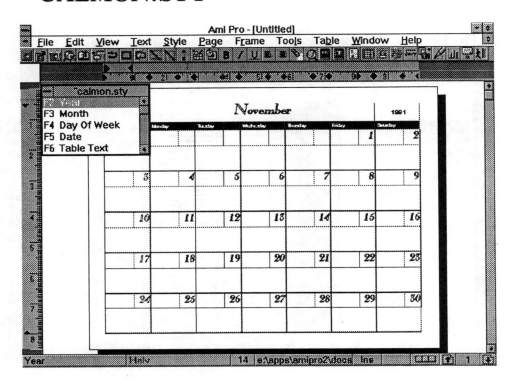

~CALWK.STY

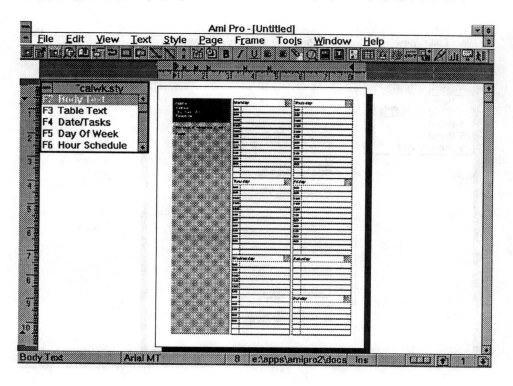

~DEFAULT.STY

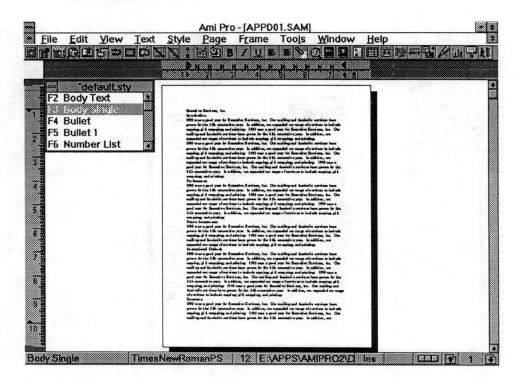

~ENVELOP.STY

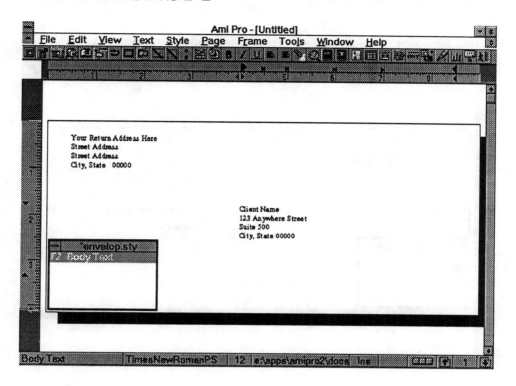

~ENVHP2P.STY

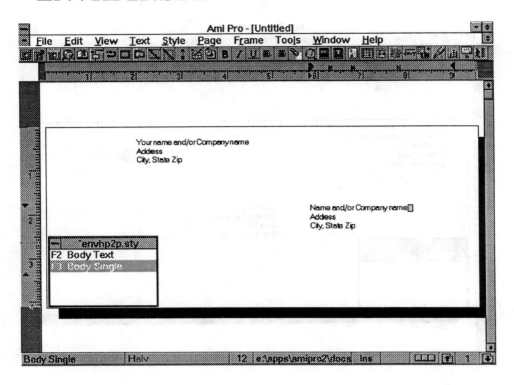

~ENVHP3.STY

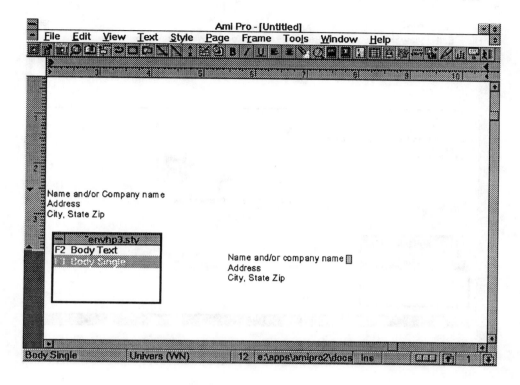

~ENVHPDJ.STY

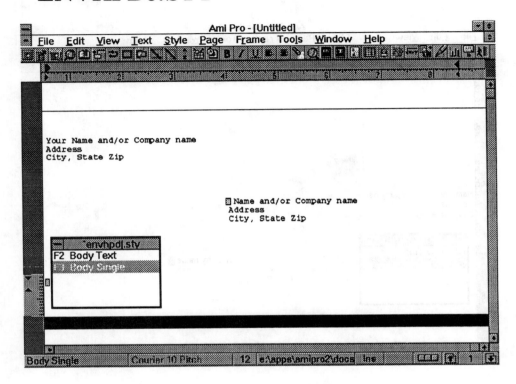

~ENVPSII.STY

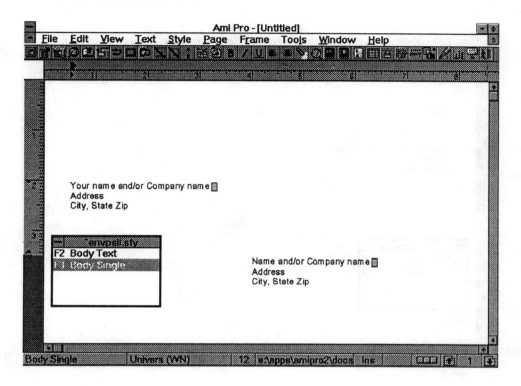

~ENVTIML.STY

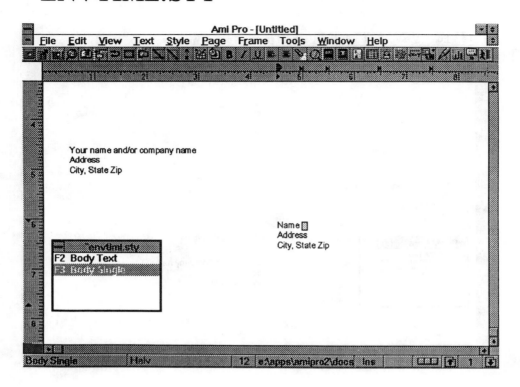

~EXPENSE.STY

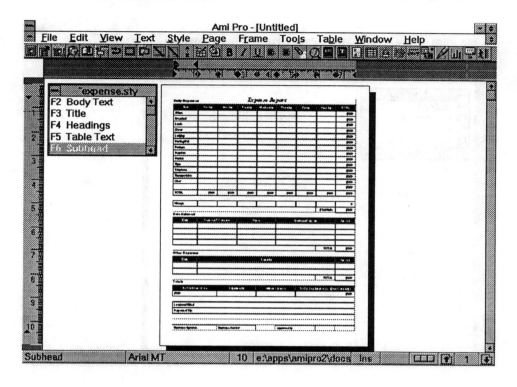

~FAX1.STY

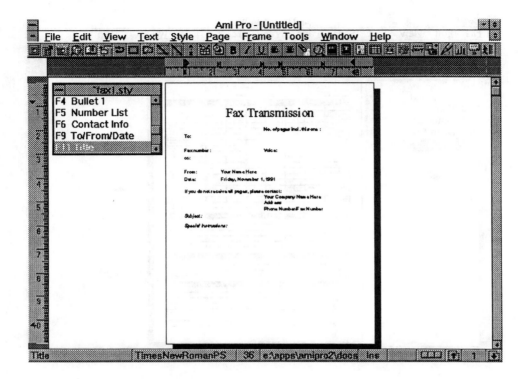

~FAX2.STY

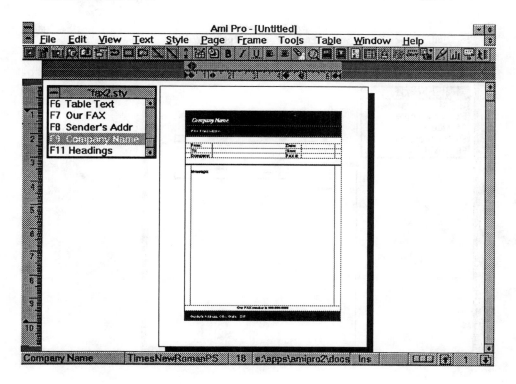

~FAX3.STY

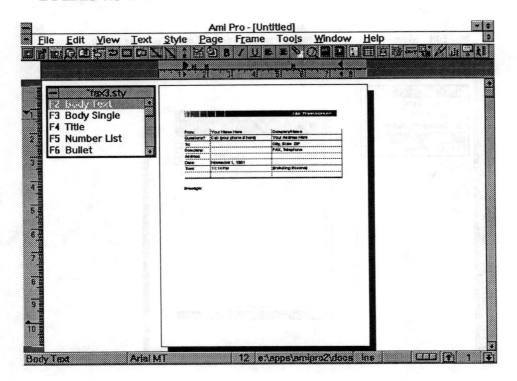

~INDEX.STY

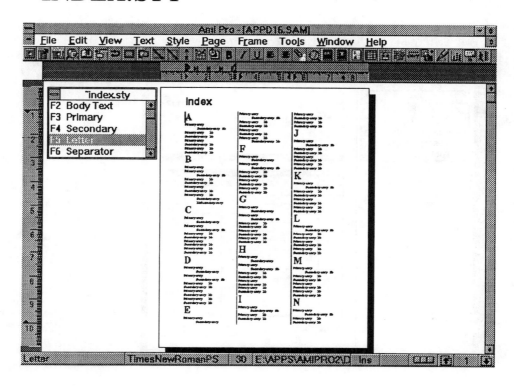

~INVOICE.STY

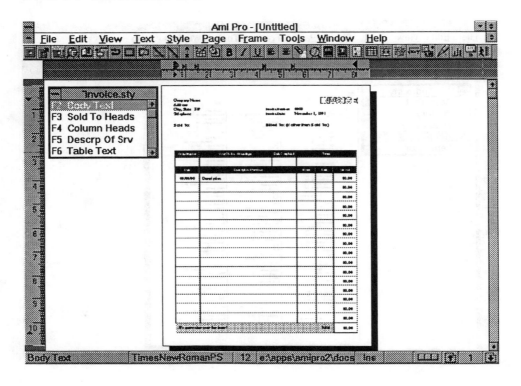

~LABEL.STY

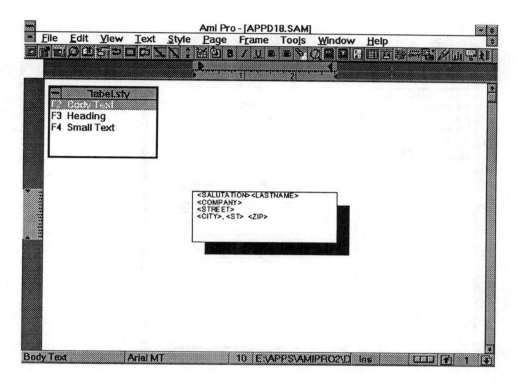

~LETTER1.STY

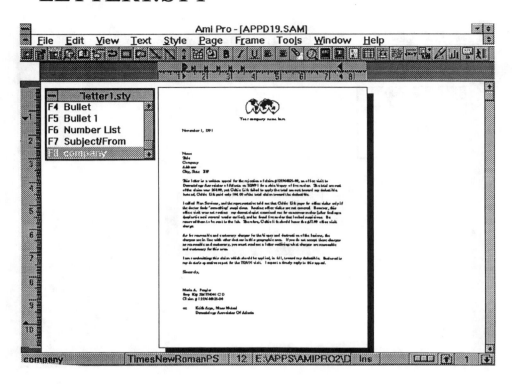

~LETTER2.STY

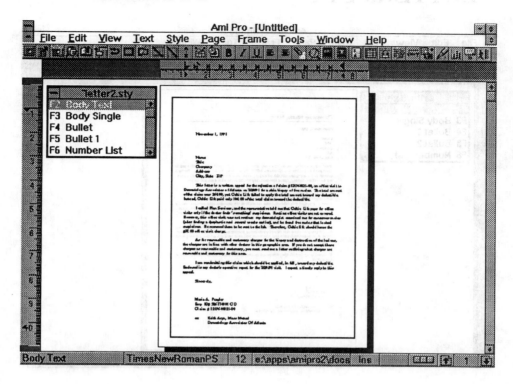

~LETTER3.STY

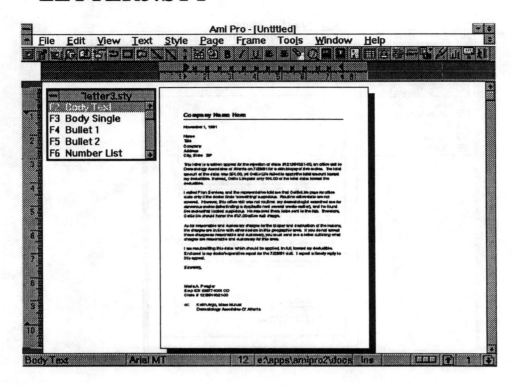

~LETTER4.STY

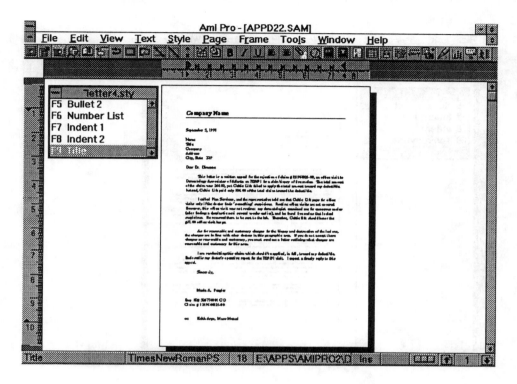

~MEMO1.STY

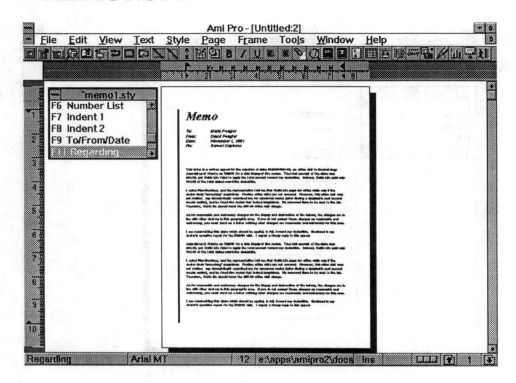

~MEMO2.STY

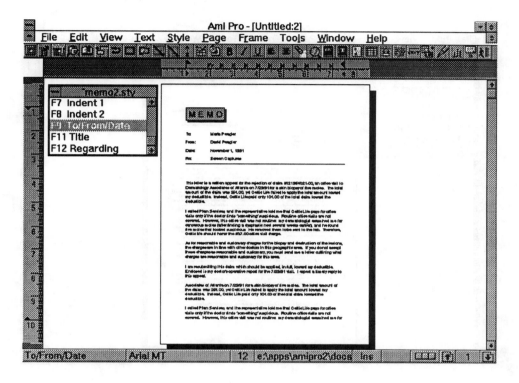

~MEMO3.STY

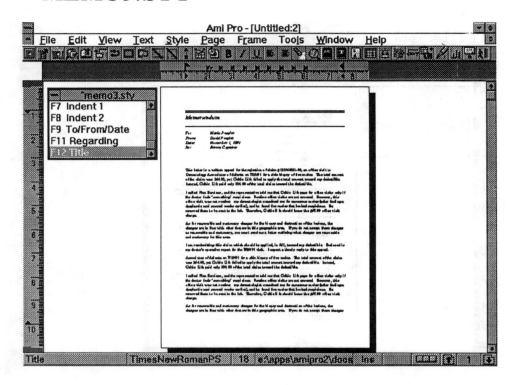

~MEMO4.STY

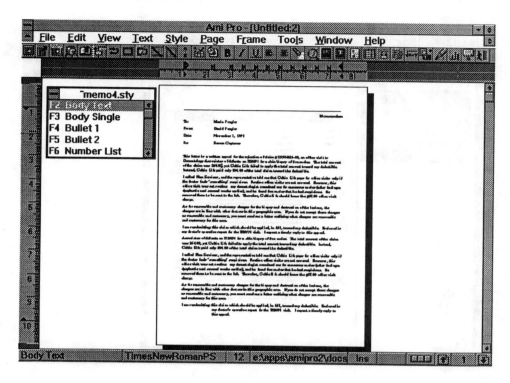

~MEMO5.STY

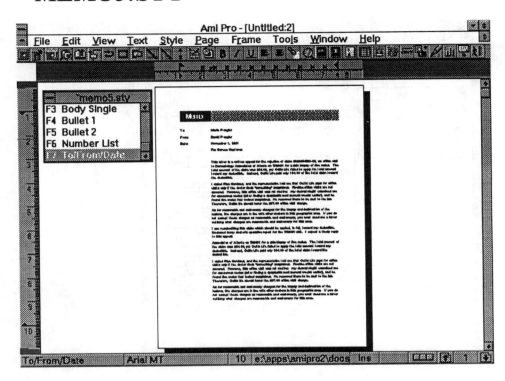

~MEMO6.STY

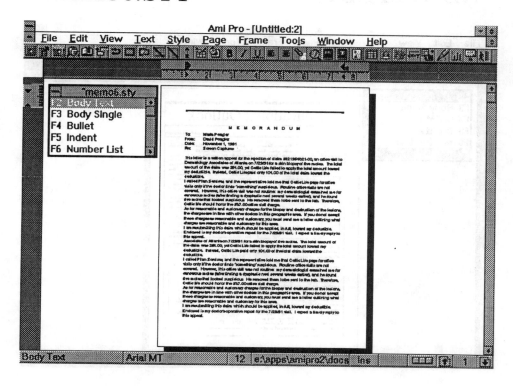

~NEWSLT1.STY

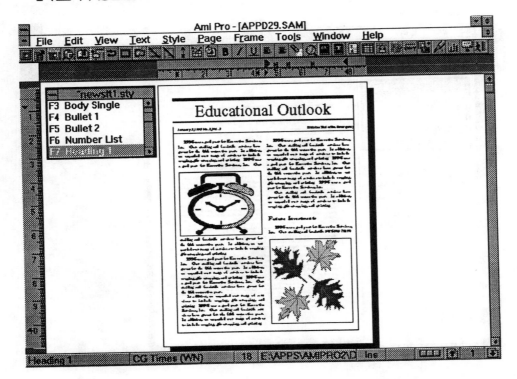

~NEWSLT2.STY

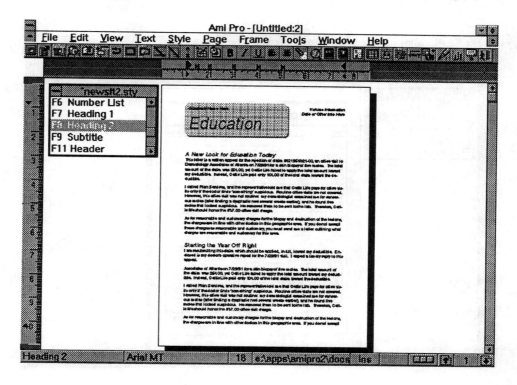

~NEWSLT3.STY

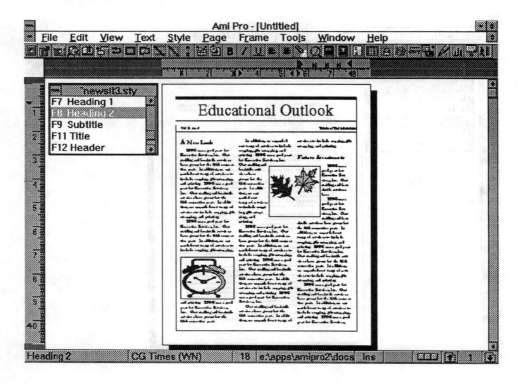

~NEWSLT4.STY

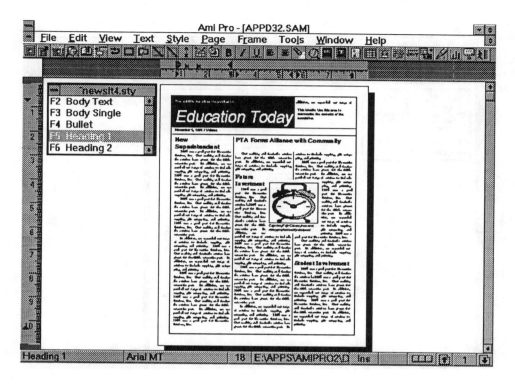

~NEWSLT5.STY

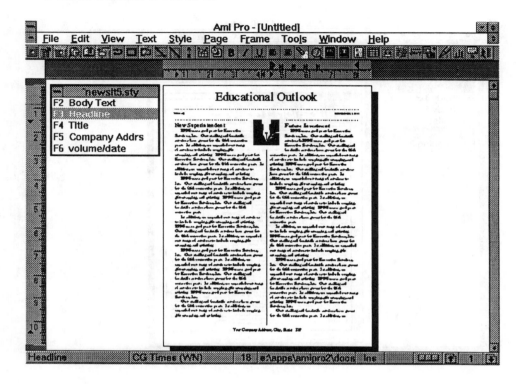

~OUTLIN1.STY

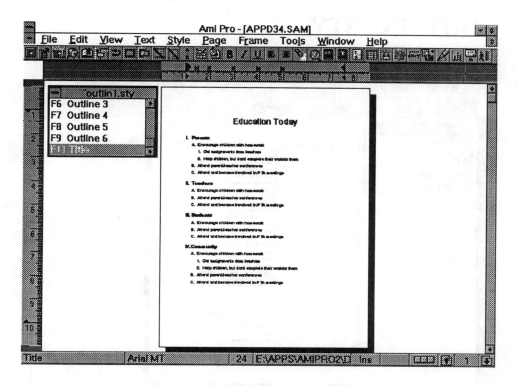

~OUTLIN2.STY

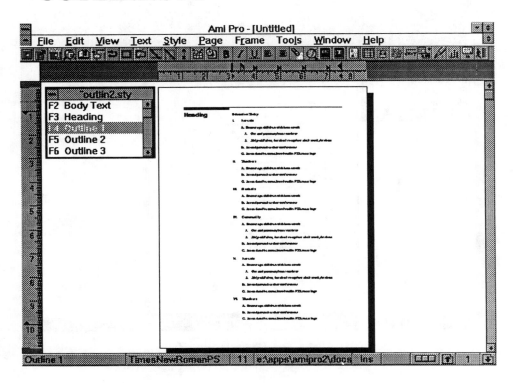

~OUTLIN3.STY

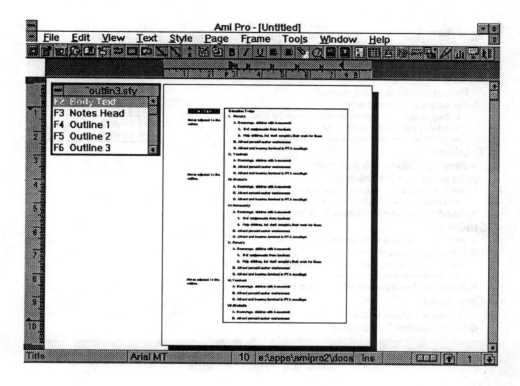

~OUTLINE.STY

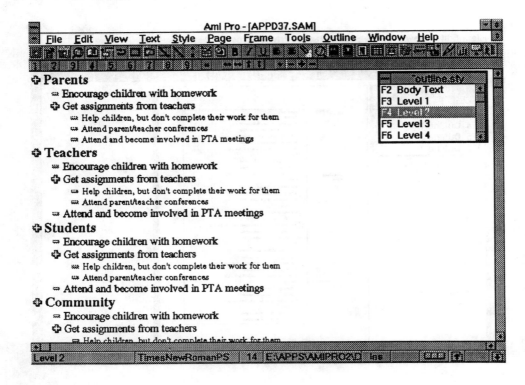

~OVERHD1.STY

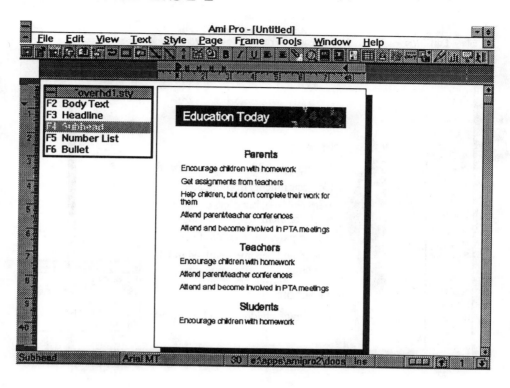

~OVERHD2.STY

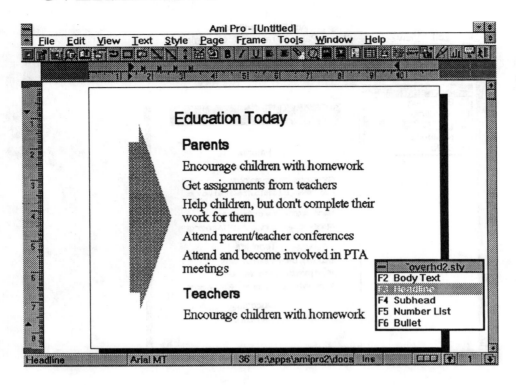

~OVERHD3.STY

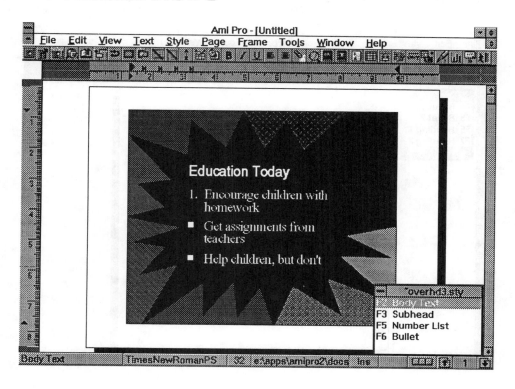

~OVERHD4.STY

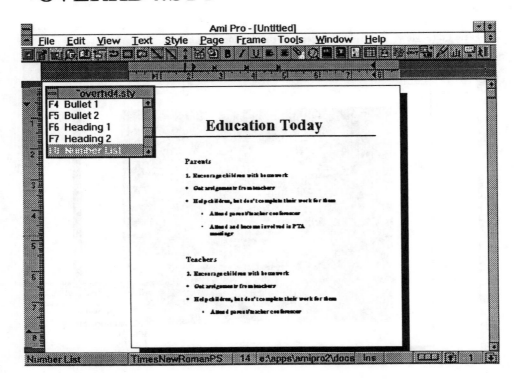

~OVERHD5.STY

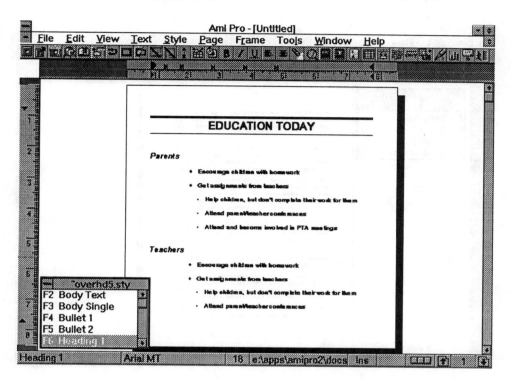

~PRESS1.STY

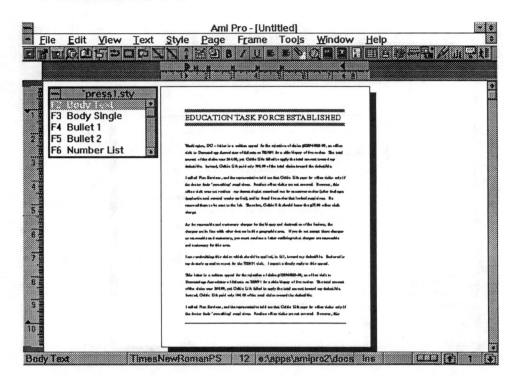

~PRESS2.STY

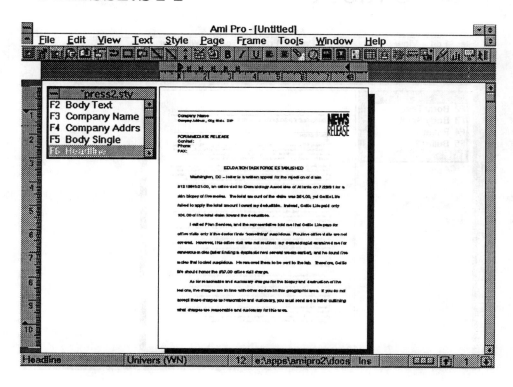

~PROPOS1.STY

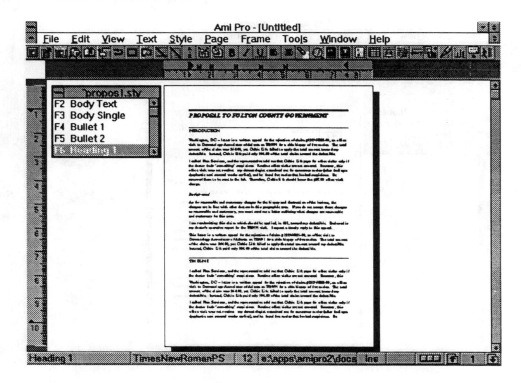

~PROPOS2.STY

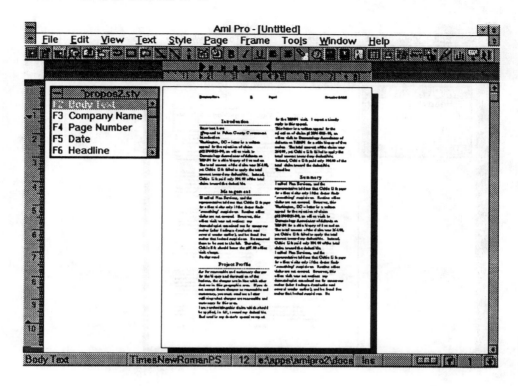

~REPORT1.STY

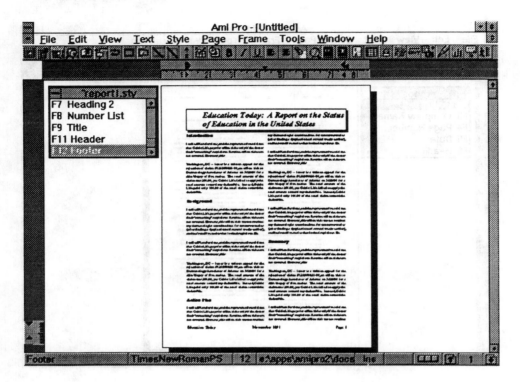

~REPORT2.STY

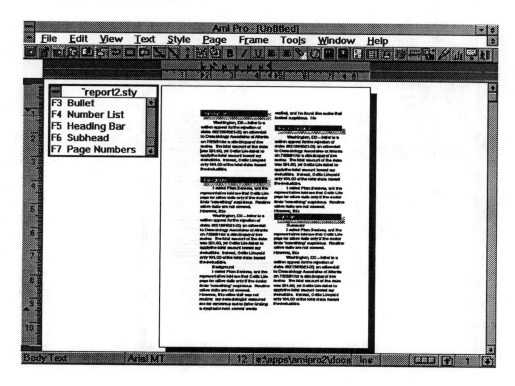

~REPORT3.STY

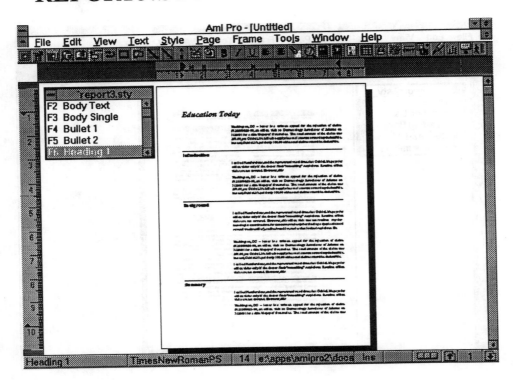

~REPORT4.STY

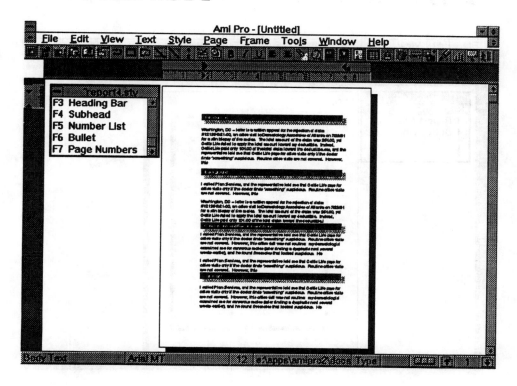

~TITLE1.STY

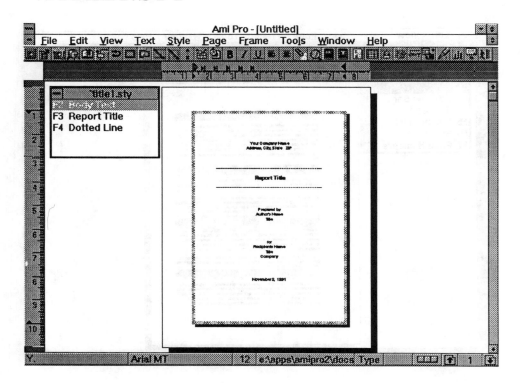

~TITLE2.STY

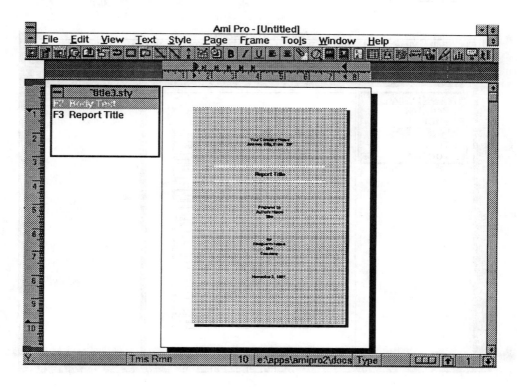

~TITLE3.STY

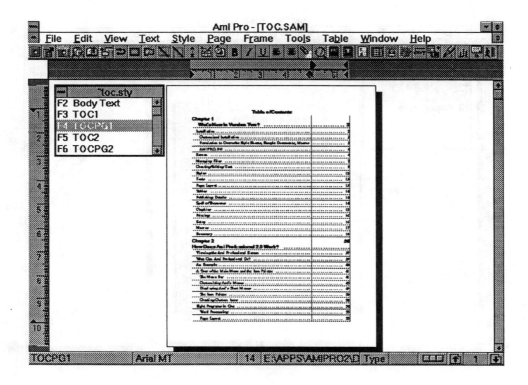

~TOC.STY

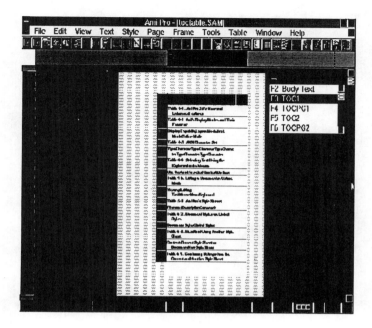

E

APPENDIX

Table E-1 Ami-Pro Icons

Icon	Macro	Icon	Macro	Icon	Macro	Icon	Macro
	Add a Frame		Copy		Edit Table Formula		FONTDN.SMM
	Bar chart		COPYRITE.SMM		Equations		FONTUP.SMM
	Bookmark		Customize Icons		Exit		Fraction Template
	Brackets		CUSTVIEW.SMM		Expanded Pie Chart		Full Page/Current View Toggle
	Brackets Template		Cut		Extract Line & Fill		Functions
	Bring Frame to Front		Define Style		FAX.SMM		GAME.SMM
	Bring Object to Front		Delete		Field Instructions/ Results Toggle		Go To Next
	Cascade Windows		Delete Column in Table		File Management		Go To Next Field
	CCMAIL.SMM		Delete Row in Table		Fill Pattern		Go To Previous Field
	Center Text		Delete Table Columns or Rows		Find and Replace		Graphic Scaling
	Charting		Delimiters		FINDTXT.SMM		Group/Ungroup Frames Toggle
	Circle		Document Compare		Flip Horizontally		Group/Ungroup Toggle
	Close		DOS.SMM		Flip Vertically		Hand
	CLOSEALL.SMM		Double Underline Text		Floating Header/ Footer		Import Picture
	Column Chart		Draft/Layout Mode Toggle		Floating SmartIcons		Initial Caps
	Column Guides On/ Off Toggle		Drawing		FLW.SMM		Insert Break

Icon	Macro	Icon	Macro	Icon	Macro	Icon	Macro
	Insert Column in Table		Mark Index Entry		Picture Chart		Select All
	Insert Date		Matrix		Pie Chart		Selection Arrow
	Insert Footnote		Merge		Polygon		Send Frame to Back
	Insert Glossary Record		Miscellaneous Characters		Polyline		Send Object to Back
	Insert Note		Modify Layout		Print		Set Frame and Add
	Insert Page Number		Modify Style		Printer Setup		Show Hide Input Boxes/Matrix Lines Toggle
	Insert Row in Table		Modify Frame Layout		PRNBATCH.SM		
	Integral		Modify Table Layout		PRNPAGES.SMM		Show/Hide Grid Toggle
	Italic Text		Modify Table Lines		PRNSHADE.SMM		Show/Hide Marks Toggle
	Justify		New		Quick Play		Show/Hide Notes Toggle
	KEYWORD.SMM		No Hyphenation		Quick Record/End Record Toggle		Show/Hide Pictures Toggle
	Label Position		Normal Text		Radical Template		Show/Hide Tab Ruler Toggle
	Left Align Text		NOTES.SMM		REGMARK.SMM		Show/Hide Tabs and Returns
	Line		Open		Revise Character		Show/Hide Vertical Ruler Toggle
	Line & Picture Chart 1		OPENBOOK.SMM		Revision Marking		Size Table Columns or Rows
	Line & Picture Chart 2		OPENDOCS.SMM		Right Align Text		SMARTYPE.SMM
	Line Chart		Operators		Rotate		Snap To Grid Toggle
	Line Style		Outline/Layout Mode Toggle		Rounded Square		Sort
	Lowercase Greek		Over/Under Template		Save		Spaces
	Macro Play		Parentheses Template		SAVEBOOK.SMM		Spelling
	Macro Record		Paste		SAVEINFO.SMM		Square
	Margins in Color Toggle		PHONBOOK.SMM		SAVSHADE.SMM		Stacked Bar Chart

Icon	Macro	Icon	Macro	Icon	Macro	Icon	Macro
	Stacked Column Chart		Superscript Template		Tile Windows		Uppercase Greek
	Stacked Picture Chart		Table of Contents, Index		TILEHORZ.SMM		View Preferences
	Start/End Macro Record		Tables		TM.SMM		WINFILE.SMM
	Subscript Template		Tables Connect Cells		Underline Text		Word Underline Text
	Subscript Text		Text		Undo		
	Superscript Text		Text/Math Mode		Update All Fields		
	Summation		Thesaurus		Update This Field		

Glossary

active window   The current window. The document in the current window is the one affected by your actions in Ami. The active window's title bar uses a different color than inactive windows to help you identify it.

alignment   The even placement of lines in a paragraph

ANSI   The 8-bit character set of the American National Standards Institute. The character set contains a total of 256 characters.

ASCII   The 8-bit character set for the American Standard Code for Information Interchange. The character set contains a total of 128 characters.

attribute   An enhancement to text such as boldface or italics.

bitmap   A graphic or a character stored as a series of digital bits.

body text   The default style Ami applies to all paragraphs.

bold   An attribute that darkens text.

break   A dividing point that begins a new column or page.

bullet   A small graphic element preceding a paragraph.

camera ready   A final document ready to be sent to the print shop.

cartridge font   A collection of one or more typefaces that you can insert into a laser printer or dot-matrix printer.

cascade   Overlapping windows that display the title bar of each and the content of the front window.

check box   A hollow box next to an option in a dialog box. The option is active if an "X" appears inside the check box.

click   To press and release a mouse button.

clip art   A collection of non-copyrighted illustrations. Clip art comes in books or on disk.

clipboard   A holding place for the last text, frame, or graphic you cut or copied. The clipboard can hold only one item at a time. If you try to store a second item, the first is erased from the clipboard.

Control menu A list of commands that appears on the menu bar, on the title bar of each document window, and in some dialog boxes. The Control menu lets you maximize, minimize, restore, move, size, and close the current window, application, or dialog box.

crop mark A small mark that indicates a document's edges. Printers use crop marks to trim excess paper from the page.

dialog box A rectangle that presents a message or lets you choose from available options. Ami uses dialog boxes to let you specify options, limitations, filenames, directories, and other information. Ami also uses dialog boxes to display error or warning messages.

dingbat Ornamental characters that are available in Post Script printers and soft fonts or font cartridges.

discretionary hyphen A hyphen you insert manually that overrides Ami's hyphenation process.

double-click Pressing and releasing the mouse button twice in succession.

drag Moving an item on the screen by holding down the mouse button and moving the mouse.

driver Software that lets Ami communicate with a printer, monitor, or other device. An old printer driver can limit how a printer interacts with Ami.

drop cap A large first character that begins a paragraph. A drop cap's ascender aligns with the first line's text, while its baseline extends below the line.

em A unit of measurement equal to the current font's point size. The em is used in measuring the width of dashes and spaces.

en A unit of measurement equal to half of an em. The en is used in measuring the width of dashes and spaces.

extension The three letters following the period in a filename. Usually the extension identifies the file's type or in what application the file was created.

flush left Text that aligns evenly against the left margin and unevenly against the right margin.

flush right Text that aligns evenly against the right margin and unevenly against the left margin.

font The characters and punctuation marks of one size and style of type.

footer Text and graphics that appear at the bottom of every page in a document. Often the footer holds a page number.

format A document's appearance. A document's format is determined by its page layout and its styles.

frame A storage area for text, drawings, charts, and tables.

gutter The space between columns or rows.

hanging indent A paragraph that extends its first line the entire width of the column or page, while the remaining lines are indented.

header Text and graphics that appear at the top of every page in a document. Headers often contain chapter names, publication names, and issue dates.

icon A graphic that represents an action, such as starting a program from Windows, loading a document, or selecting a command from a menu. Ami uses icons to represent tasks available within the program. You must have a mouse to use Ami's icons.

icon palette The collection of icons that display on the screen. The icon palette appears at the top, bottom, left, or right side of the window. It also can float within a window or be hidden.

indent One or more lines of a paragraph that are farther inward from the left or right margin than other lines in the paragraph or in the document.

italic A text attribute that slants characters. Italics are often used for emphasis or to identify the title of a book.

justified type Text that aligns evenly with the left and the right margins. Frequently, justified text has gaps between words to force the text to align evenly with both margins.

kerning Spacing two letters closer together. Ami calls kerning text tightness.

landscape Printing a page horizontally. Landscape orientation is useful for very wide tables or graphics.

leader characters Periods, dashes, or underlines that fill a gap between text. Leader characters are often used in price lists, tables of contents, and telephone directories.

leading The space between two lines. Leading is measured in points, so 10/12 leading specification would be 10 point text using 12 point leading.

line spacing Leading.

list box A box that presents multiple choices in a dialog box. A list box commonly displays filenames, line styles, fonts, point sizes, and other elements.

macro A set of keystrokes you record and playback later. A macro can also be a set of instructions you write using the Macro Command Language.

Maximize button The small up arrow box at the right end of the title bar. The Maximize button returns a window to its full size.

MDI Multiple Document Interface. A Windows technology that lets you open several documents at the same time.

menu bar The horizontal bar, below the title bar, containing the names of all the menus in Ami.

Minimize button The small up down arrow box at the right end of the title bar. The Minimize button reduces a window to an icon that you can maximize later.

mode A display option that controls how much detail you see on the screen. Layout is closest to true WYSIWYG, while Outline mode is the least representative.

object graphics Graphics that are stored as geometric instructions.

offset printing A printing process that transfers your document's image from a printing plate onto paper.

orphan The first line of a paragraph that appears as the last line on a page.

page layout The collection of margins, columns, tab settings, page size, orientation. and borders that give a page its appearance.

paragraph A block of text you end by pressing the Enter key. Ami assigns styles to paragraphs only. Blocks of text within a paragraph cannot use a different style.

paragraph spacing The amount of space between two paragraphs. Paragraph spacing is commonly used, in addition to line spacing, to make documents easier to read.

parallel interface A protocol for transferring information. Parallel is faster than the other protocol available: serial.

pica A unit of measurement often used in document composition. A pica is one-sixth of an inch.

pixel Picture elements. The smallest graphic unit on the screen.

point A unit of measurement often used in document composition. A point is one-twelfth of a pica. One inch contains 72 points.

portrait Printing text and graphics vertically on the page. Portrait is the most common print orientation.

PostScript A programming language from Adobe Systems that controls laser printers.

real mode A Window's processing environment that lacks memory management and multitasking features. The primary use of real mode is to run programs written for earlier versions of Windows.

Restore button The up and down arrow button on the right end of the title bar. The Restore button returns a maximized window to its previous, smaller size.

reverse text White text appearing on a black background. Reverse text in Ami consists of a frame with a blackground containing white text.

sans-serif A typeface that does not use serifs, such as Univers or Helvetica.

scaling Increasing or reducing a picture's size.

serial interface A protocol for transferring information. Serial is slower than the other protocol available: parallel.

serif A finishing stroke on the ends of the strokes of a character. Serifs make text easier to read as they help the reader identify different letters and characters. Most body text uses a serif typeface, such as Times Roman.

shortcut key One or more keys you can press to perform an action you normally would select from a menu.

standard mode The Window's processing environment that lets you run large applications, use large data files, and run Windows applications concurrently. Standard mode is the normal operating mode for Windows and is commonly the fastest operating mode also.

status bar An informational bar at the bottom of Ami's window that displays the current style, font, point size, path, date, time, line, column, cursor position, editing mode, and page.

style   A collection of formatting instructions Ami uses to control the appearance of a paragraph. Styles are stored in a style sheet.

style sheet   A collection of styles that you can use with a document. A document can use only one style sheet at a time, but a style sheet can be used with unlimited numbers of documents.

Styles Box   A dialog box that displays the current style sheet name and its collections of styles. You can assign styles to paragraphs by selecting the style name from the Styles Box.

System menu   The Control menu.

text box   A box into which you type information necessary to perform the action you are requesting. A text box appears inside a dialog box, and usually asks for a filename, number, description, or other information you provide.

tile   A method of displaying multiple windows so that you can view the content of each. Each window takes up an equal space on the screen.

title bar   A horizontal bar at the top of a window that contains a program or document names. The title bar also contains the Control menu, the Minimize, Maximize, and Restore buttons.

typeface   The entire family of a particular type design, such as Times Roman or Helvetica.

view   A way of displaying a document so that you see more or less of a page.

wallpaper   A design appearing on the Windows desktop.

widow   The last line of paragraph that appears as the first line of a page.

wildcard   A character, either ? or *, that represents one more characters when you search for text.

WYSIWYG   What You See Is What You Get. The theory that document's appearance on the screen is the same as its appearance on the printed page. You can choose to use a WYSIWYG display or not in Ami, as displaying such an accurate representation slows Ami.

Index

merging (*cont.*)

operators, select from list boxes, 239-240

power fields, 323, 340-344

power fields, INCLUDE, 244-245, 248-250, 336, 339, 343-344

power fields, MERGEREC, 240-241, 244, 245, 340-341

power fields, NEXTREC, 241-242, 246, 341-342

power fields, QUERY power field, 246, 336

power fields, SKIP and IF, 243-244, 247, 342-343

printing list of merged records, 252

selected-records only merge, 238-239

standard document creation, 236-237

table used as standard document, 237

tables used for merge, 178

MESSAGE power fields, 335

Microsoft Word, importing/exporting, 357-358, 361

MID$ power fields, 351

mouse use, 443, 445-446, 503-506

MultiMate, exporting, 361

multiple document interface (MDI), 7, 42

N

Navy DIF files, exporting, 361

negative numbers, 181

NEWSLET1.STY style sheet, 111, 536

NEWSLET2.STY style sheet, 111, 537

NEWSLET3.STY style sheet, 112, 538

NEWSLET4.STY style sheet, 112, 539

NEWSLET5.STY style sheet, 112, 540

NEWSLET6.STY style sheet, 541

newsletters, design guidelines, 215-216

NEXTREC power field, 241-242, 246, 341-342

non-Lotus application startup, 26, 266

non-mouse use of Ami Pro, 503-506

notes in document, 76-78

color-customization, 77

deleting notes, 77-78

initial-stamping feature, 76-77

printing notes within document, 77

NOTES.SMM macro, 26, 266

numbering paragraphs or lines, 152-153, 155-156, 166, 194-197

cumulative numbering, 196

custom line numbering schemes, 197

frame numbering, 199

legal-type numbering, 195-196

outline-type numbering, 195-196

restart after specified level, 196

restart after specified style, 196

simple list-numbering style, 195

NUMCHARS power fields, 345-346

NUMEDIT power fields, 346-347

NUMPAGES power fields, 347

NUMWORDS power fields, 347-348

O

object graphics, 388

OLE links, 67-69, 386-387, 423-425

OPENBOOK macro, 38-39, 286-287, 291

OPENDOCS macro, 287

operators, 299, 302-304, 314

optimizing hard disk, 453

orientation of pages, 161-162, 437

orphans, widows and orphans, 194, 471

OUTLIN1.STY style sheet, 112, 196

OUTLIN2.STY style sheet, 112, 196

OUTLIN3.STY style sheet, 112, 196

outline fonts, 131

Outline mode display, 57-58, 96-108, 449

editing in Outline mode, 102, 106

OUTLINE.STY style sheet, 105, 196, 545

OUTLINE1.STY style sheet, 105, 542

OUTLINE2.STY style sheet, 105, 543

OUTLINE3.STY style sheet, 105, 544

outlines, 8, 15, 57-58, 96-108

changing levels, 104

creation of outline, traditional style, 105

deleting levels, 104-105

editing documents in Outline mode, 102, 106

find-and-replace use, 102

hide/unhide sections of outlined document, 100-102

hierarchy for outline, levels, 98-100

moving sections of outline, 103-104

numbering lines, 100, 152-153, 155-156, 166, 194-197

Outline mode selection, 97-98

sorting, 102-103, 253, 256

spell checking, 102

style sheets, OUTLINE.STY through OUTLINE3.STY, 105, 196

views, outline buttons, 61

OVERHD1.STY style sheet, 112, 546

OVERHD2.STY style sheet, 112, 547

OVERHD3.STY style sheet, 112, 548

OVERHD4.STY style sheet, 112, 549

OVERHD5.STY style sheet, 112, 550

P

page breaks, 151-152, 166, 178

page layout, 10-11, 32, 158-164

all-, right-, left- or mirrored-pages, 158-159

attributes and formatting, 158

styles and style sheets (*cont.*)
   OVERHD4.STY, 112, 549
   OVERHD5.STY, 112, 550
   paragraph formatting, 488-490
   PRESS1.STY, 112, 551
   PRESS2.STY, 112, 552
   PROPOS1.STY, 112, 553
   PROPOS2.STY, 112, 554
   protecting style sheets from
     changes, 122
   read-only attribute to protect, 458
   renaming to protect, 458
   REPORT1.STY, 112, 555
   REPORT2.STY, 112, 556
   REPORT3.STY, 112, 557
   REPORT4.STY, 112, 558
   save changes, 164
   saving original style sheets,
     114-115, 125
   selecting alternative style
     sheets, 122-124
   selecting correct style sheets,
     110-117, 125-126, 483-484
   specifying style sheet to use,
     109-110
   style-by-example using attrib-
     utes, 10
   STYLES directory, 46, 53
   tab settings, 10
   TITLE1.STY, 112, 559
   TITLE2.STY, 112, 560
   TITLE3.STY, 112, 561
   TOC.STY style sheet, 203
   TULTR.STY, 112
   TUTOR.STY, 112
STYLES directory, 46, 53
style status indicator, 7
styles box, 7, 17, 370, 448
sub- and superscripts, 304
SuperCalc, importing/exporting,
   365
SuperVGA graphics, working
   views, 63
suppliers, vendors, resources,
   501-502
symbols and characters, 309, 311-
   313

T

tab ruler, 17, 468
   modifying tab ruler without a
     mouse, 506

tab settings (*see also* columns),
   10-11, 56, 60, 145-149, 159-
   161, 164-166, 178, 185, 448-
   449, 468
   find-and-replace use, 84
   headers and footers, 190-192
Table menu, 170
table of contents, 11, 202-204
tables, 11, 15, 169-185, 490-492
   absolute addressing, 180
   adding columns/rows, 180
   asterisks for too-long entries,
     184
   bullets, 173
   cell format, 181
   cell size changes, 174
   cells used as page or frame,
     172
   centering table on page, 171
   charts, 181
   column deletion, 172, 175
   column insertion, 175
   column width, 170, 175
   column/row heads, 169, 185
   connecting cells, 172, 184-185
   creating tables, 169-170, 490-
     491
   currency format, 181-182
   cursor movement within table,
     170-171
   cut, copy contents of cells, 174
   decimal format, 181
   delimiters: dollar signs, etc.,
     179-180
   fill patterns, 173-174
   formatting and layout, modify-
     ing table layout, 170-175
   formatting numbers, 179-182
   forms creation, 182-184
   formulas, 179, 184
   graphics inside tables, 400
   gridlines, 61, 169
   gutters between columns and
     rows, 170
   header creation, 173
   hide/unhide headings, 178
   importing data, 179, 363-364
   importing external records,
     merging, 248
   importing graphics, 174
   importing/exporting, 185
   leaders between cells, 178

leading zeroes, 180
lines around tables, 171-173
linking data, 179
logos, 183
margins around table, 173
merging, table used as standard
   document, 178, 237
negative format, 181
numeric table creation, 179-182
page break insertion, 178
pasting data, 179
position of table on page, 171,
   172
printing tables on forms, 183
protect/unprotect cells, 172,
   184, 185
resumes, 175-176
row deletion, 172-173, 175
row height, 170, 175
row insertion, 175
row/column heads, 61
rows spanning pages, 172
shading cells, 173
side-by-side text tables, 176-
   177
sorting text in table, 178-179
tab settings, 178, 185
Table menu displayed, 170
text table creation, 175-179
text within table, 170, 491-492
thousands-separator, 181
Undo use, 172
views, 61
warning messages, enable/
   disable, 173
task lists, menus, 26
telephone directory, PHONBOOK
   macro, 287-288
templates, equations, 299, 301, 318
TeX language, equations, 316-
   317, 389
text creation and editing (*see also*
   document creation; file management), 8-10, 15, 32, 55-
   108, 448-450, 485-488
   alignment/justification, 56
   ANSI character set, special
     characters, 72-76
   attributes, adding attributes to
     text, 79
   attributes, deleting attributes to
     text, 79